DYNAMIC GOVERNANCE

Embedding Culture, Capabilities and Change in Singapore

DYNAMIC GOVERNANCE

Embedding Culture, Capabilities and Change in Singapore

Boon Siong NEO
Geraldine CHEN
Nanyang Business School
Nanyang Technological University, Singapore

World Scientific

NEW JERSEY · LONDON · SINGAPORE · BEIJING · SHANGHAI · HONG KONG · TAIPEI · CHENNAI

Published by

World Scientific Publishing Co. Pte. Ltd.

5 Toh Tuck Link, Singapore 596224

USA office: 27 Warren Street, Suite 401-402, Hackensack, NJ 07601

UK office: 57 Shelton Street, Covent Garden, London WC2H 9HE

Library of Congress Cataloging-in-Publication Data
Neo, Boon Siong.
  Dynamic governance : embedding culture, capabilities and change in Singapore /
by Neo Boon Siong & Geraldine Chen.
     p. cm.
  Includes bibliographical references and index.
  ISBN 978-981-270-694-2 (alk. paper)
  1. Public administration--Singapore. 2. Political culture--Singapore. I. Chen, Geraldine.
II. Title.

 JQ1063.A58N46 2007
 351.5957--dc22

                             2007013740

British Library Cataloguing-in-Publication Data
A catalogue record for this book is available from the British Library.

First published 2007 (Hardcover)
Reprinted 2016 (in paperback edition)
ISBN 978-981-3203-42-6

Contents

Foreword

What makes government effective? This is among the most important questions facing any society, because the failure of government is all too common and often catastrophic. There are numerous examples of countries that have been saddled by bad government policies, poor implementation, ethical failures, and the inability of government to change when necessary. The victims are citizens, whose lives and livelihoods suffer.

In analyzing the effectiveness of government, the tendency is to focus on the many policy choices that any government has to make. Government sets policy in a multitude of areas, ranging from macroeconomics to education to health to personal security. Each of these areas has been extensively studied. In each area, there are best practices that have emerged from theory and comparisons across countries, about which there is often wide consensus. Since so many actual policy choices diverge from best practice, this provides a comfortable explanation for government success and failure.

There are several problems with this line of thinking. First, government faces too many policy priorities to realistically address, and too few resources to make progress against all of them simultaneously. Consider the area of economic policy, where there are hundreds of local circumstances that affect competitiveness and the rate of economic development ranging from the condition of the roads, to the quality of the universities, to the efficiency of permitting. No government can ever tackle everything that needs to be improved at once. Instead, the challenge is to set good priorities, tackle issues in a sensible sequence, and sustain implementation over time.

Second, the appropriate government policies and priorities shift as a country itself changes. In economic development, physical infrastructure and rule of law are key priorities in early stage development. Later on, many new challenges emerge in order to sustain a higher standard of living.

Third, the world outside the country changes. New opportunities emerge, neighboring countries improve or decline, international legal structures and institutions realign, and so on. These external changes mean that the appropriate government policy choices change, priorities shift, and standards for performance usually rise.

These complexities shatter any notion that good government is a static concept, and that government success depends on any individual decision. Instead, the essential challenges of government are dynamic, cut across many decisions, involve the need for continuous learning, and rest on effective and rapid implementation.

This book, *Dynamic Governance*, addresses these subtler and now decisive challenges of government. The book provides a revealing framework for thinking about how government *is able to make good decisions*, carry them out, and revise them without a crisis.

Singapore provides a marvelous case study with which to examine these questions. When it comes to government, Singapore often seems to defy the law of gravity. It has government organizations that are highly efficient. Decisions in Singapore usually get made on the merits, not because of corruption, ideology, or self aggrandizement. Government ministries are intensely self critical. Singapore changes its mind on highly charged questions, such as whether to legalize gambling.

How does this happen? All of it requires a set of government institutions that, to use Neo and Chen's framework, can think ahead, think again, and think across. This book offers a rich and interesting portrait of how this occurs, and the underlying causes. The lessons in *Dynamic Governance* apply to governments anywhere. Applying the ideas in this book gives us reason to be hopeful that governments in many countries can work, and that citizens' lives can get better.

Professor Michael E. Porter
Harvard Business School
7 May 2007

Preface

"Why do you want to write a book on the civil service?" We were asked this question at the start of practically every interview that we did for this book. Our curiosity was initially piqued by the typical response from business managers in the classroom to case studies that one of us had done on Singapore institutions such as TradeNet, the port, the national library, the national computerization effort and even the tax department — amazement that government agencies were capable of more than just being efficient — that innovation was possible and that organizational transformation actually took place in public agencies. There was a sense that the Singapore experience could have lessons for the business world. Its experience certainly appears to have learning value for other countries, if interest in Singapore-style industrial parks, housing estates and e-government systems is anything to go by.

But what exactly is this "Singapore model" that business managers and overseas officials seemed so keen to understand and apply? Many observers attribute Singapore's success to the strength of its political leadership. But there is an entire administrative body working quietly behind the scenes to create, develop, review and translate policies from perception to paper to practice. What is it about the way it manages its people and processes that others find interesting to understand and worthy to emulate? What are the principles behind the Singapore public sector system that made it work? Is the system good because it has perfected a set of "how-to's", or is there something more? Are these principles and practices unique to Singapore? How can the principles and practices be applied effectively beyond the public sector and beyond Singapore?

These ideas intrigued us but we did not seriously start developing them until 2005, after both of us completed our terms as Dean and Vice Dean in the Nanyang Business School at the Nanyang Technological

University. A chance conversation along the corridors as we were basking in our newfound peace and freedom reignited interest and focused thinking. An email to Peter Ho, the Head of the Singapore Civil Service and Lim Siong Guan, former Head of the Civil Service and then the Permanent Secretary of the Ministry of Finance with a go-ahead given two days later, set things in motion.

As we began sifting through the published material, it struck us that much of the work on Singapore focused either on its policies, or on its political landscape. Other than a handful of studies of specific institutions such as the Economic Development Board, the Port of Singapore and the National Library Board, remarkably little is known about an institution that has been the vanguard of Singapore's economic and social transformation. As we conducted our interviews and combed through internal data and documents, a picture slowly emerged of the civil service's role in governance and the workings of its underlying system of institutional culture and organizational capabilities.

We did not find simple explanations for the effectiveness of Singapore's public service. Its performance cannot be directly attributed to any single individual leader or any one particular cause or policy. Instead we found a working system with multiple interactions and interdependencies. Its unique historical and political contexts were important but so were the ambition and active efforts to create and secure its future. Leadership was crucial but so were the systems and processes that were institutionalized. There were deeply-held beliefs and assumptions but there were also openness to abandon past practices and experiment with new ideas. Social stability was desired but there were also strong commitments and capabilities to change. Agencies operate quite autonomously and yet there were some coherence in overall direction. There were many policy ideas that were learnt from others but there were also significant innovations. Policies were executed efficiently but were also adapted in the process of implementation. There were strong values and principles of governance that officials seemed to have internalized and yet these were mostly transmitted socially rather than formally. What we found is a remarkably resilient civil service that has been constantly learning, continually changing, quietly improving and innovating, a civil service that has grown and evolved in tandem with the demands and expectations of the society which it serves.

This is the story behind the Singapore story.

Acknowledgments

Much of the information for the study was culled from unpublished sources and from our interviews with ministers and public sector leaders, current and retired. The interviews were especially illuminating, injecting a richness and depth to the material that would not have been possible otherwise. We therefore wish to express our thanks to the following individuals for giving us their time and sharing their experiences, perspectives and insights with us.

- Lee Hsien Loong, Prime Minister of Singapore
- Teo Chee Hean, Minister of Defence and Minister in-charge of the Civil Service
- George Yeo, Minister of Foreign Affairs
- Andrew Chew, Chairman, Public Service Commission

- Peter Ho, Head, Civil Service and Permanent Secretary, Ministry of Foreign Affairs
- Lim Siong Guan, former Head, Civil Service and now Chairman, Economic Development Board,
- Chiang Chie Foo, Permanent Secretary, Ministry of Defence and Permanent Secretary, Prime Minister's Office
- Lim Soo Hoon, Permanent Secretary, Public Service Division, Prime Minister's Office
- Yong Ying-I, Permanent Secretary, Ministry of Health
- Peter Ong, Permanent Secretary, Ministry of Trade and Industry
- Ravi Menon, Second Permanent Secretary, Ministry of Trade and Industry

- Philip Yeo, Chairman, SPRING Singapore
- Lam Chuan Leong, Chairman, Infocomm Development Authority

- Ngiam Tong Dow, Chairman, Surbana Corporation
- JY Pillay, Chairman, Singapore Exchange Limited
- Sim Kee Boon, Director, Temasek Holdings
- Lee Ek Tieng, Group Managing Director, Government of Singapore Investment Corporation
- Eddie Teo, Singapore's High Commissioner to Australia
- Kishore Mahbubani, Dean, Lee Kuan Yew School of Public Policy, National University of Singapore
- Su Guaning, President, Nanyang Technological University
- Lim Hup Seng, Deputy Secretary, Ministry of Finance
- Rosa Daniel, Deputy Secretary, Ministry of the Environment and Water Resources
- Andrew Tan, Deputy Secretary, Ministry of Foreign Affairs
- Yeoh Chee Yan, Deputy Secretary (Policy), Ministry of Defence
- Lawrence Wong, Principal Private Secretary to the Prime Minister
- Lui Pao Chuen, Chief Defence Scientist, Ministry of Defence
- Jimmy Khoo, Future Systems Architect, Ministry of Defence
- Francis Chong, Director, National Youth Council, People's Association
- Tan Huck Gim, Deputy Special Representative of the Secretary General of the UN Integrated Mission in Timor Leste
- Jacqueline Poh, Director, Fiscal Policy, Ministry of Finance
- Ong Toon Hui, Director, Leadership Development, Public Service Division
- The late Tan Soo San, Senior Research Analyst, Civil Service College

Peter Ho, Lim Siong Guan and Lim Soo Hoon were especially generous with us, meeting us on several occasions to give us their perspectives on what we were observing and to clarify issues. We learnt much from them and appreciate the depth of their thinking and leadership.

Because of the dearth of information in the public domain, this book was possible only because of the access that the Civil Service gave us to internal data and documents and to various people of the organization. The Public Service Division was especially supportive, assigning June Gwee of the Civil Service College to assist us throughout the study and hiring back Ho Chui Kee, who came out of retirement to obtain and methodically collate tons of information for us. We want to thank June and Chui Kee for responding patiently to our countless requests for data and documents. June and various civil service staff also helped us verify the factual information on many portions of the final write-up.

Our research associates: Asif Iqbal Siddiqui who started the project with us, Lim Wee Kiat who provided support in the initial stages of the project, and Susan Chung who worked hard to help us wrap up the project and manage the publication process. Thanks to Angela Yeo for her tireless transcription of the interviews.

Our special thanks to our colleague and friend, Ang Soon, whose sharp insights and outsider's perspective challenged us to look more deeply, which helped us improve our study. Her interest and feedback on what we were observing were instrumental in helping us shape the conceptual underpinning of the study and also to decide (finally) on the title of this book!

Seah Chin Siong, Country Managing Director of Accenture Singapore was an enthusiastic supporter for our study and provided initial funding to get the project started. Dean Kishore Mahbubani believed that the study could contribute to a deeper understanding of governance in Singapore and provided support and resources to enable the first author to spend a sabbatical year at the Lee Kuan Yew School of Public Policy to work on the project. That opportunity led to a longer-term association as Boon Siong joined the school in August 2006 to become the founding Director of its newly formed Asia Competitiveness Institute.

About the Authors

Neo Boon Siong (E-mail: absneo@gmail.com) is a Professor and former Dean of the Nanyang Business School, Nanyang Technological University, Singapore. He taught for five years at the Lee Kuan Yew School of Public Policy and was the founder director of its Asia Competitiveness Institute. He received a Public Administration Medal (Silver) from the President of the Republic of Singapore in the 1999 National Day Honours Awards. He is a Certified Public Accountant (Singapore) and holds a Bachelor of Accountancy (Honours) from the National University of Singapore, and MBA and PhD degrees from the University of Pittsburgh, USA. He is a leading expert in strategy, process management and organizational change.

He has advised many major corporations, facilitated strategy workshops, and led management development programs for global enterprises. His clients include UBS Bank, Microsoft, Hewlett-Packard, British Petroleum, Siemens, BOC Gases, Dupont, Praxair Asia, DHL Air Express, Singapore Airlines, Shangri-la Hotels and Resorts, Singapore Press Holdings, Singapore Petroleum Company, Keppel Corporation, the Mauritius government, Monetary Authority of Singapore, National Healthcare Group, Infocomm Development Authority of Singapore, Trade Development Board, PSA Corp, Maritime and Port Authority, and other government agencies. He has also taught public sector officials of many countries, including Brunei, Cambodia, China, Dubai, Kazakhstan, Laos, Malaysia, Mauritius, Myanmar, and Vietnam.

He currently serves as Director on the Boards of OCBC Bank, Great Eastern Holdings Ltd, Great Eastern Life Ltd, Overseas Assurance Ltd, Keppel Offshore and Marine Ltd, J Lauritzen Singapore and English XChange Pte Ltd. He also serves as Member on the Boards of Securities Industry Council, Income Tax Review Board, and the Goods and Services Tax Review Board.

An economist by training, **Geraldine Chen** (E-mail: ayfchen@ntu.edu.sg) was all set to pursue the customary teaching-research career after obtaining her PhD from the University of London. But after a few years, she found something far more enjoyable — student work. For four years, she was Sub-Dean, Nanyang Business School's head undergraduate student counsellor, overseeing student academic matters. She then took a detour — a 5-year stint in corporate services work, during which she built up the school's professional services and during which time NBS attained both its AACSB and EQUIS accreditations. She is now back to working with students on a range of development activities as well as the undergraduate outreach program. After such a long spell in administration, Geraldine thought it was time to reacquaint herself with her academic roots and this book represented a novel opportunity for her to marry her economic policy training and her liking for writing and storytelling.

List of Cases

Framework for Dynamic Governance: Institutionalizing Culture, Capabilities and Change

In a world of uncertainty and change, current achievements are no guarantee for future survival. Even if the initial chosen set of principles, policies and practices are good, static efficiency and governance would eventually lead to stagnation and decay. No amount of careful planning can assure a government of continuous relevance and effectiveness if there is insufficient institutional capacity for learning, innovation and change in the face of ever new challenges in a volatile and unpredictable global environment.

But can government institutions be dynamic? The typical government institution is not usually regarded as a dynamic, entrepreneurial organization, but a slow, stodgy bureaucracy that consistently and, sometimes, mindlessly enforces outdated rules and sticks to procedures without any care or concern for individuals or businesses.

Can institutions ever be dynamic? Dynamism is characterized by new ideas, fresh perceptions, continual upgrading, quick actions, flexible adaptations and creative innovations. Dynamism implies continuous learning, fast and effective execution, and unending change. Dynamic institutions can enhance the development and prosperity of a country by constantly improving and adapting the socio-economic environment in which people, business and government interact. They influence economic development and social behavior through policies, rules and structures that create incentives or constraints for different activities.

Dynamic governance is the key to success in a world undergoing accelerating globalization and unrelenting technological advancement. If institutions can evolve and embed the cultures and capabilities that enable continuous learning and change, their contributions to a country's socio-economic progress and prosperity would be enormous. The lessons from their efforts in institutionalizing culture, capabilities and change would be useful for achieving similar outcomes in other types of organizations, such as business firms and volunteer groups. If bureaucratic public sector institutions can learn to be dynamic, the lessons from their efforts could provide meaningful and valuable insights for transforming organizations in other contexts. This is our primary motivation for writing this book.

This book explores how dynamism is created and sustained in public sector institutions that exercise the functions of governance. It explores how a supportive institutional culture and strong organizational capabilities result in continually improving rules, policies, incentives and institutional structures that enhance governance. It seeks to understand how such a supportive culture evolves and how enabling capabilities develop. It explains why and how policy choices are made and executed, and how policy improvements, innovations and adaptations become embedded into the Singapore governance system. It synthesizes major principles and lessons that may be applied in other contexts.

1.1 Need for Dynamism in Government

Government institutions have significant impacts on the economic competitiveness and social development of a country. They define the relationships between the government and people of a country. They set the tone for how society and business interact. They create the conditions that may facilitate or impede sustained development and growth. They influence the business environment and competitiveness of a country, and can make it more or less attractive to foreign investors. A nation's competitiveness is no longer primarily based on static factor advantages but in "providing an environment in which firms can operate productively and continuously innovate and upgrade their ways of competing to more sophisticated levels, thereby allowing rising productivity."[1] Although government cannot directly

---

[1] Michael Porter (1998). *On Competition*. MA: HBS Press, Chapter 6, "The Competitive Advantage of Nations," and Chapter 7, "Clusters and Competition: New Agendas for Companies, Governments, and Institutions."

create competitive industries, it can act as a catalyst and a challenger in shaping the context and institutional structure that stimulates businesses to gain competitive advantage.

But government institutions are not usually known for dynamism. Many government agencies function as monopolies and do not face the discipline of market competition in the delivery of their outputs and services. There are often no established market prices for their services, which may also be provided free-of-charge or at highly subsidized rates. They are funded through budget allocations that are often subjected to political influences. There are no objective measures of managerial performance and there are few incentives for improvement and change. They are not subjected to financial discipline from investors who demand an adequate financial return for the risks they take. Public managers tend to become highly conservative as they learn from experience that visible mistakes are often punished while personal achievements may not be rewarded. Is dynamic governance possible in this environment?

Our study of Singapore's government institutions highlights how a foundation of cultural values and beliefs can work synergistically with strong organizational capabilities to create a dynamic governance system that enables continuous change. Institutional culture can support or hinder, facilitate or impede dynamism in policy- making and implementation. Institutional culture involves how a nation perceives its position in the world, how it articulates its purpose, and how it evolves the values, beliefs and principles to guide its decision-making and policy choices. In addition, strong organizational capabilities are needed to consider thoroughly major policy issues and take effective action.

We conceptualize and discuss three critical governance capabilities: i) *thinking ahead* — the ability to perceive early signals of future developments that may affect a nation in order to remain relevant to the world; ii) *thinking again* — the ability and willingness to rethink and remake currently functioning policies so that they perform better; and iii) *thinking across* — the ability and openness to cross boundaries to learn from the experience of others so that new ideas and concepts may be introduced into an institution. The "Workfare" policy announced in the 2006 Singapore Budget and institutionalized in the 2007 Budget is an example of how these dynamic capabilities work in public policy making and implementation.

As Singapore's per capita income (and business costs) grew and even exceeded those of some developed countries, it had to *think ahead* to ensure that it maintained its competitiveness in the global economy. However as it restructured to compete in the new economy where knowledge and ideas had become the crucial factor inputs, it became clear that there were segments of the population that were lagging behind because they did not have the necessary education and skills to be employed in the new jobs that were being created in the new knowledge and high technology sectors. *Thinking ahead,* government officials realized that, going forward, economic growth per se would not be sufficient to lift all segments of the population; unlike the earlier years, structural unemployment was likely even when the economy grew strongly.

The government thus had to *think again* its approach to welfare. Historically, public assistance had been set at very low levels to induce unemployed persons to seek employment in the belief that their existing skills and experience was enough to make them employable. If they were not employed, it was probably because they lacked motivation or were irresponsible. But in the face of a permanent mismatch between the skills of the unemployed and the requirements of the jobs being created, a different approach was needed. At the same time, there developed a new strategic objective to strengthen the emotional ties of citizenship as more Singaporeans became globally mobile. This involved positioning Singapore as a land of opportunity and engaging citizens to actively participate in the country's development. The presence of a significant segment of society which did not have the skills to contribute substantively to the country's new developmental path or seize the new economic opportunities presented a challenge to Singapore's policy makers.

To obtain ideas on how to address this issue, public sector policy-makers had to *think across* boundaries and learn from the experiments and experience of a work-based welfare program called Wisconsin Works in the US. But the outcome was not a blind imitation of the

Wisconsin practice. The Wisconsin framework was thoughtfully adapted and adjusted to fit local circumstances and re-oriented to achieve the desired national goals for worker retraining, family responsibility and social mobility. The new approach involved providing financial support that was tied to work or efforts to find work, incentives for the unemployed to retrain for new jobs, and family support to ensure that their children's education was not compromised so that the next generation had the means to escape the poverty trap. These are multi-dimensional policy objectives appropriate to a more sophisticated and complex society.

"Workfare" was a fresh and innovative approach to the low-wage worker and structural unemployment issues. The unions' response to the implementation of the Workfare policy in 2006 was positive and in 2007 the government adopted it as a long-term feature of a new social policy that seeks to ensure social cohesion and industrial peace as Singapore transits to a more innovative economy to compete globally. Details of the Workfare program and the process of search, evaluation and adaptation are in Chapter 6.

The new Workfare policy is an example of the dynamism of governance in Singapore — the main theme for this book. Dynamism in governance is the result of new thinking and learning and is manifested in new paths, revised policies and restructured institutions. Even as we write this book, current policies continue to be reviewed and changed, and new ideas evolve into tentative policies to deal with emerging issues. Although we will refer to many examples of policy and institutional changes, this book is not intended to be a comprehensive examination of Singapore's social and economic policies. The policy and institutional changes are illustrations to help explore and explain why a dynamic governance system is important, how it works and how it may be developed.

This chapter provides an overview of the major themes of our study. We will discuss the concept of dynamic governance and why we choose a study of Singapore's government institutions. We then present our conceptual framework and discuss the flows and interactions of a dynamic governance system. The rest of the chapter discusses institutional culture and organizational capabilities — the two components of a dynamic governance system. We elaborate on the three elements of institutional culture and the three major constituents of organization capabilities that work together to generate dynamism in policy-making and implementation. We look at what dynamic governance capabilities are, why they are important, and how they were developed in the context of the Singapore public service. The rest of the book explains how culture and capabilities emerged, evolved, were energized and became embedded in the Singapore government institutions. We conclude by discussing the challenges and potential risks in the Singapore governance system, lessons that may be learnt from the Singapore experience, and how these principles and lessons may be applied in other contexts.

1.2 Concept and Importance of Dynamic Governance[2]

Governance plays an essential role in modern economies and societies by providing rules and institutions to facilitate exchange, and by offering opportunities to improve the outcomes of market failures arising from imperfect information, public goods, and externalities.[3] While market forces are widely accepted as the cornerstone of an efficient economy, a country's economic performance is determined largely by the quality and kind of institutions that support markets. As Nobel Laureate Douglass North said, "Institutions form the incentive structure of a society and the political and economic institutions, in consequence, are the underlying determinant of economic performance"[4], "if we are ever to construct a dynamic theory of change... it must be built on a model of institutional change."[5]

---

[2] This section gives an overview of the concept and importance of governance that is adequate for understanding the findings of our study and how they may be applied. A more detailed discussion of the concepts of governance, institutions and capabilities as they have been developed in the research literature is given in Chapter 2.

[3] Joseph Nye (2004). "Governments, Governance, and Accountability," *Ethos*. Civil Service College, April 2004

[4] Douglass C North (1993). "Economic Performance through Time," Nobel Prize Lecture, 9 December 1993.

[5] Douglass C North (1990). *Institutions, Institutional Change and Economic Performance*. NY: Cambridge University Press. p. 107.

Governance is "the relationship between governments and citizens that enable public policies and programs to be formulated, implemented and evaluated. In the broader context, it refers to the rules, institutions, and networks that determine how a country or an organization functions."[6] It is "the manner in which the government, working together with other stakeholders in society, exercises its authority and influence in promoting the collective welfare of society and the long-term interests of the nation."[7] Governance involves choices regarding rules, policies, institutions, and the resultant structures that collectively provide socio-economic incentives and constraints for different activities. Governance becomes dynamic when previous policy choices can be adapted to current developments in an uncertain and fast changing environment so that policies and institutions remain relevant and effective in achieving the long-term desired outcomes of a society. It is more than making a one-time change or recovering from a setback. It is about on-going sustained change for long-term survival and prosperity.

The importance of good governance and having honest and competent public sector institutions for a country's economic development and standard of living is widely accepted. The World Bank's director for global governance, Daniel Kaufmann, states that countries that improve their governance effectiveness raise their standard of living, as measured by per capita incomes, by about three times in the long run.[8] "Poorly functioning public sector institutions and weak governance are major constraints to growth and equitable development in many developing countries."[9]

Even so, sustained development and improving standards of living require more than the mere adoption of good practices. Governance structures adopted at a particular time, even if optimal,

---

[6] Gambhir Bhatta (2006). *International Dictionary of Public Management and Governance*. New York: ME Sharpe Inc.

[7] Andrew Tan *et al.* (2004). "Principles of Governance: Preserving our Fundamentals, Preparing for the Future." Special Study Report prepared by a group of Administrative Officers led by Andrew Tan.

[8] Quoted in *The Straits Times*, 17 September 2006. "Singapore Scores High on Governance." Singapore Press Holdings.

[9] World Bank Report (2000). *Governance Matters*.

may become dysfunctional as the environment changes. Past experience and beliefs may not be good guides for future decisions. Good governance that stays relevant and remains effective must therefore be dynamic. Continuous learning, dynamic adaptation and innovative change results in "adaptive efficiency"[10] — a country's effectiveness in creating institutions that are productive, stable, fair, broadly accepted and, importantly, flexible enough to be changed or replaced in the face of shocks to effectively deal with a changed reality.

Dynamism in governance requires continuous learning that enables a deep understanding of the future developments that may affect a country, a willingness to review rules and policies that may be out-dated as circumstances change, and an openness to adapt global knowledge to the unique contexts of the country. Dynamic governance is the ability of a government to continually adjust its public policies and programs, as well as change the way they are formulated and implemented, so that the long-term interests of the nation are achieved. Dynamism in governance is essential for sustained economic and social development in an uncertain and fast changing environment, and in an increasingly demanding and sophisticated society where citizens are more educated and more exposed to globalization.

1.3 Study of Public Sector Governance in Singapore

Our study[11] is based on Singapore's government institutions,[12] i.e., public sector agencies including government departments and ministries in the civil service and statutory boards[13] that together

---

[10] Douglass North (2005). *Understanding the Process of Economic Change*. NJ: Princeton University Press, p. 6.

[11] Data was collected through interviews with past and present public sector leaders. The authors were given access to data and documents in several government ministries and agencies as part of this study. In addition, over the years the first author has interviewed close to 200 public sector leaders and staff in relation to other studies and projects.

[12] We excluded political parties and government-owned for-profit corporate entities which are governed under the Companies Act legislation.

[13] Statutory Boards are public not-for-profit entities created by specific government legislation. They reported to a parent Ministry and performed specialized public roles and functions such as investment promotion, tourism development, and specific planning functions. They have their own governance structures such as Boards, and have more autonomy than their parent ministries in finance and human resource functions.

employed about 120,000 people in 2006. Good governance requires that both the political leadership and public sector work together to achieve important economic and social objectives. The political leadership sets the policy direction, agenda, tone and environment for the public sector. If the political leadership is corrupt and ineffective, the potential of the public sector, no matter how competent, would be severely hampered. Indeed, much of the published work on the Singapore governance system has focused on the political system and leadership,[14] including the popular two-volume memoirs[15] of its founding Prime Minister, Lee Kuan Yew, which have now been translated into many languages. Very little has been published on the public sector. Thus the focus of this book is on the dynamic governance capabilities developed by the public sector. However, we have included discussions of the political system and leadership where their choices and decisions have influenced dynamic governance in Singapore, and when they have had an impact on the development of the public service. The impact of the political leadership has been particularly evident in the values and principles of governance discussed in Chapter 4 and their strategic view of public sector leadership discussed in Chapter 7. These were the values and beliefs of the founding political leaders which have significantly influenced the paths taken by the Singapore public service.

Though Singapore's government expenditure is small relative to many other countries, accounting only for about 14–18 per cent of GDP in recent years, its public institutions consistently have been rated to be among the best in the world.[16] Singapore was ranked among the top ten nations in the world in governance in the 2006 World Bank's

---

[14] Some examples include:
Raj Vasil (1992). *Governing Singapore*. Singapore: Mandarin.
Michael Hill and KF Lian (1995). *The Politics of National Building and Citizenship in Singapore*. London: Routledge.
Diane Mauzy and RS Milne (2002). *Singapore Politics: Under The People's Action Party*. Singapore: Oxford University Press. Ho Khai Leong (2003). *Shared Responsibilities, Unshared Power*. Eastern Universities Press.

[15] Lee Kuan Yew (1998, 2000). *The Singapore Story*, and *From Third World to First*. Singapore: Times Edition.

[16] See the EDB website at www.edb.gov.sg for an updated and more comprehensive list of Singapore's international rankings.

"Governance Matters" Report.[17] Singapore's institutions were ranked
first in a sub-index of the 2006 Global Competitiveness Report,[18] in
which Singapore was ranked the overall fifth most competitive
nation in the world. It was rated highly for its speed, meritocracy
and incorruptibility. In a June 2006 study by the Hong Kong-based
Political and Economic Risk Consultancy (PERC), Singapore was rated
as having the lowest level of red tape and bureaucracy and the highest
standards of corporate governance in Asia. In 2006 PERC rated Hong
Kong and Singapore as the top two nations in Asia for the overall
quality and integrity of the judiciary system, including the consistency
in the application of laws. The World Competitiveness Yearbook 2006
ranked Singapore among the top three out of 61 countries in terms
of legal framework, and top 15 in terms of justice. Transparency
International ranked Singapore as the fifth least corrupt nation in the
world in their 2006 study of 163 countries and economies. In referring
to Singapore's economic culture, Professor Lester Thurow of MIT's
Sloan School commented that "the ability to adjust rapidly was more
important than economies of scale... no country comes closer to having
a corporate culture and to being run as a corporation where economic
growth replaces profits as the explicitly defined goal."[19]

The public sector's efficiency and effectiveness have contributed
significantly to the creation and sustenance of an environment that is
conducive for business and a good quality of life. In 2006, the World
Bank rated Singapore as the world's easiest place to do business.[20]
The Economist Intelligence Unit ranked Singapore as having the sixth
best business environment in the world for 2006–2010.[21] IMD rated
Singapore as having the second most attractive environment, after the
US, for highly-skilled foreigners.[22] A 2005–2006 study by Mercer HR

---

[17] The Straits Times, 17 September 2006. "Singapore Scores High on Governance." Singapore
Press Holdings.

[18] Published annually by the World Economics Forum.

[19] Lester Thurow (1996). "Forward." Strategic Pragmatism, by Edgar Schein. USA: MIT Press,
pp. vii and viii.

[20] Doing Business 2007: How to Reform. World Bank.

[21] Business Environment Ranking for 2006–2010. Economist Intelligence Unit.

[22] 2005 World Competitiveness Yearbook. Switzerland: IMD.

Consulting identified Singapore as the best place in Asia to live, work and play, and placed it 34th in the world.

Public sector agencies in Singapore stood out even when compared to private sector firms. For example, the majority of the winners in the competitive Singapore Quality Awards, the local equivalent of the Malcolm Baldridge Awards in the US, and the Singapore Innovation Awards have been public sector agencies. In a study of one of Singapore's best known public agencies, the Economic Development Board, MIT Professor Edgar Schein concluded that "the EDB runs as if it were a private company with all the concerns for efficiency, productivity, and service that one associates with a well-run organization."[23]

How have Singapore government institutions been able to achieve both administrative efficiency and policy innovation? What enabled them to change in response to environmental change, and often in anticipation of change? A dynamic governance model was not explicitly articulated or documented by the Singapore public service but rather was implicit in the minds of the leadership, and constantly refreshed with keen observations and thoughtful reflection. The process of learning was iterative and the management effort to adapt and change was sustained over an extended period, resulting in cumulative and cascading effects throughout the entire system. In our study, we looked for patterns in their actions, programs, and strategies and synthesized them into an overall conceptual framework that explain the manifestations and sources of dynamic governance in Singapore.

1.4 Framework for Dynamic Governance: Culture + Capabilities → Change

Dynamic governance does not happen by chance, but is the result of deliberate leadership intention and ambition to structure social and economic interactions to achieve desired national goals. It reflects the leaders' deliberate efforts to "shape their future... to try to structure human interaction — the alternative is anarchy and chaos. However

---

[23] Edgar Schein (1996). *Strategic Pragmatism*. MA, USA: MIT Press. p. 174.

imperfectly they are bound to do it... The issue is how they do it."[24] Sustained economic and social development takes place when there is leadership intention, cognition and learning which involves continual modification of perceptions, belief structures and mental models, particularly when confronted with global developments and technological change.[25] The two main impediments to dynamic governance are the inabilities to comprehend the changes in the environment and to make the institutional adjustments necessary to remain effective. The first is a function of culture since it acts as a filter to perceiving and interpreting evolving developments that may have future implications. The second is a function of capabilities, of the ability to identify current issues, to learn from the experience of others, and develop policy responses to deal effectively with the change.

Our framework of a dynamic governance system shown in Figure 1.1 depicts a supportive institutional culture interacting with proactive organizational capabilities to produce adaptive paths that incorporate continuous learning and change, which in turn result in the continual evolution of rules, policies, incentives, and structures to meet new challenges resulting from environmental uncertainties and technological developments. Dynamic governance is the outcome of the capacity to develop adaptive paths and policies, and their effective execution.

1.4.1 *The Elements of Dynamic Governance*

The desired outcome, *dynamic governance*, shown on the right is achieved when *adaptive policies* are executed. The foundation of dynamic governance is a country's institutional *culture*, shown at the base of Figure 1.1. The three dynamic capabilities of *thinking ahead, thinking again, and thinking across* that lead to *adaptive policies* are shown in the middle section. There are two main levers for developing dynamic governance capabilities, *able people and agile processes* and these are shown on the left of Figure 1.1. The external environment

---

[24] North (2005), p. 51.

[25] North (2005).

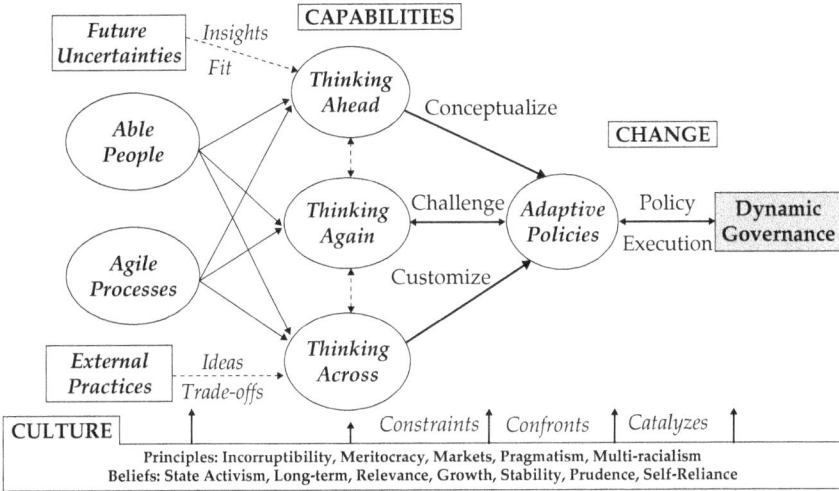

Figure 1.1. Framework for Dynamic Governance System

affects the governance system through *future uncertainties and external practices* that are shown as rectangles on the left.

Dynamic governance achieves current and future relevance and effectiveness through policies that continually adapt to changes in the environment. Policy adaptation is not merely a passive reaction to external pressure but a proactive approach to innovation, contextualization, and execution. Policy innovation means that new and fresh ideas are experimented with and incorporated into policies so better and different results may be achieved. These ideas are contextually designed into policies so that citizens will appreciate and respond favorably to them. Yet it is not just about new ideas and contextual designs but also policy execution that makes dynamic governance a reality.

Our cultural heritage — our shared values, beliefs, institutions, and customs — influences our behavior. While formal rules will reflect this heritage, it is the informal norms and conventions that are the most important carrier of cultural values. For example, in our interaction with others, we may choose not to engage in opportunistic behavior for our personal gain at the expense of others even when we can do so because we believe it to be wrong or socially unacceptable. Culture represents our collective learning in our adaptive attempts to solve frequently encountered problems of the past. The learning process is a function of the experiences we confront and how these experiences are perceived, filtered, categorized and interpreted by our mental models. A change in culture, beliefs and assumptions and mental models is necessary for institutional change, which in turn affects what public policies are reconsidered, redesigned, and renewed. For Singapore, the assumptions regarding the primacy of economic growth, the need for global relevance and the indispensable role of the state in creating the conditions for growth influence the thinking and approach to governance. The policy choices themselves are shaped by the cultural values of integrity, meritocracy, self reliance, pragmatism and financial prudence.

Leaders achieve the desired results not just by their own charisma and effort, but by developing capabilities in their organizations so that knowledge and other resources can be systematically deployed to solve problems. While an organization's culture may be enabling, on its own it does not generate the knowledge and skills needed for effective action. Dynamic governance requires new learning and thinking, the deliberate design of policy options, analytical decision-making, rational selection of policy choices and effective execution. "Good governance is not just a matter of quick action, but also of adequate comprehension... leaders of governance do have to look hard and think hard before they leap."[26]

The three cognitive capabilities of the learning process funda-mental to dynamic governance are *thinking ahead, thinking again and thinking across.* First, governments have to *think ahead* to understand how the future would affect the country and put in place policies to enable their people to cope with potential threats and to take advantage of the new opportunities available. Second, environmental turbulence and change can make past policies outdated and ineffective even if they had been carefully and thoughtfully chosen. Thus there is a need to *think again* existing policies and programs to assess whether

---

[26] Amartya Sen (2006). "Good Governance in the 21st Century," Keynote address at the Raffles Forum, organized by the Lee Kuan Yew School of Public Policy, 14 September 2006, Singapore.

they are still relevant to the national agenda and long-term needs of society. Policies and programs would then have to be revised so that they can continue to be effective in achieving important objectives. Third, in the new knowledge economy, survival requires constant learning and innovation to meet new challenges and exploit new opportunities. This means that governments need to *think across* traditional country and domain boundaries in their search for ideas and interesting practices that they can customize and contextualize to their domestic environments.

When governments develop the capabilities of thinking ahead, thinking again and thinking across, and embed these into the paths, policies, people and processes of public sector institutions, they create learning and innovations in governance that facilitate dynamism and change in an uncertain world. In essence, dynamic governance occurs when policy-makers constantly *think ahead* to perceive changes in the environment, *think again* to reflect on what they are currently doing, and *think across* to learn from others, and continually incorporate the new perceptions, reflections and knowledge into their beliefs, rules, policies and structures to enable them to adapt to environmental change. These dynamic capabilities represent the key elements of the Singapore governance system over its 42 years of development. In a recent interview, Prime Minister Lee Hsien Loong said that Singapore's success may be attributed to "a willingness to work hard, make changes and adapt to the world as it is and not as we wish it to be."[27]

Dynamic governance requires the embedding of the capabilities of thinking ahead, thinking again and thinking across into the strategies and policies of public sector institutions so that there is continuous learning, execution, innovation and change. The three thinking capabilities have to be embedded into the approach for policy choice, execution and evaluation for effective change to become a reality. Only then can chosen paths go beyond the imprint of the founders to create innovations in strategies and policies to meet the new requirements for success.

---

[27] Quoted by Kevin Hamlin in "Remade in Singapore," *Institutional Investor*, September 2006, NY.

Deliberate investments in institutional improvement and innovation for dynamic governance require choices made by people in positions of influence and leadership. Only humans can adapt and change within a context, and also consciously decide to reframe the context[28] that may lead to the reconfiguration of assets and capabilities in an institution. Making good decisions and choices requires that the organization's leaders possess the necessary motivation, attitude, values, intellect, knowledge and skills to envision the future, develop strategic options and select paths that give the institution the greatest scope for survival and success.

Processes are needed for getting things done in a coordinated and consistent manner, whether regular routine transactions, formulating and implementing policies, or inducing strategic renewal. Where there is no defined process, however broad or narrow, an organization would not be able to perform a required task even if the individuals in the organization have the knowledge and skills to do so. Even when there are defined processes, they need to be made agile through continual review and redesign to ensure that they are able to achieve their intended outcomes and not become outdated because of changing circumstances and changing technologies.

1.4.2 *The Systemic Interactions of a Dynamic Governance System*

If culture, capabilities and change operate independently of each other, there may be some individual effects but there would be no coherence and their overall impact on governance would be limited. They may even work at cross purposes and the impact of one may cancel out the efforts made in another. The creative power of culture, capabilities and change is maximized when they work interactively and synergistically as part of a dynamic system. The capabilities of thinking ahead, thinking again and thinking across also should not be merely stand-alone skills and should not operate as independent processes. The capabilities are inter-related and if they are linked and

---

[28] Stephan H Haeckel (1999). *Adaptive Enterprise*. MA: HBS Press.

work interdependently as a system, their potential effects could be reinforced and their overall impact amplified.

It is thus important to view governance not only in terms of their individual parts but as a system of interdependencies among different institutions in government, and to bear in mind their complex non-linear cause-and-effect linkages, and feedback flows. Only then can high leverage strategies and actions be identified and the energies of the creative elements released effectively. A systemic perspective of governance sensitizes leaders to the external forces impinging on the system and the internal forces emerging within, and how these may reinforce or counteract the effects of managerial actions. It also provides leaders with a greater appreciation of timing effects, that there are multiple inter-linked processes at work and inevitable delays in complex social systems before results become visible.

The two major elements of the governance system — culture and capabilities — when working systemically, interact and reinforce each other to generate the dynamics of continuous institutional learning and change. When a culture that supports learning and change is energized by the capabilities of thinking ahead, thinking again and thinking across, more options will surface to be experimented with and pursued. Some of the alternatives will work and some will not. The dynamism in governance comes from the capacity to consider and pursue different options, not just in identifying the winning formula. The increase in experimentation and pursuit of different kind of options enhance learning and increase the likelihood of a society's progress. Even when some options do not work, the lessons learnt serve to improve the quality of decision-making in the future. The capabilities of thinking ahead, thinking again, and thinking across interact with a culture that encourages learning to unleash the energies and creativity that are at the very heart of a dynamic governance system.

Conversely, if culture and capabilities work independently, the synergistic effects described above may not be realized, and while there may be some ad hoc results, their potential in energizing governance is limited. Worse, when culture and capabilities are not aligned, they may work at cross purposes and good governance ideas and intentions may not be executed effectively. For example, great cultural values and the beliefs of founders may be admired and respected but current leaders may not possess the vision or capabilities to build upon the cultural heritage to achieve significant progress; or good ideas and policies conceived through capable leaders and institutions cannot be implemented because they run counter to implicit cultural norms and assumptions. These non-alignments of culture and capabilities create discouragement and disillusionment in people and organizations, making current improvements impossible and future changes even more difficult to conceive and implement.

Thus, the development of dynamic governance cannot be achieved without understanding the interdependencies between culture and capabilities, between capabilities and the people and processes that are their sources, between capabilities and their interaction with the external environment, and between capabilities and their expression in adaptive paths and policies. These interactions and their cause-and-effect relationships unleash the reinforcing and balancing forces that either facilitate or impede dynamic change. Dynamic governance can be sustained only when there is long-term commitment to and investments in building each of the elements in the system and designing the necessary linkages for them to work as a whole. Understanding the interactions and flows in a dynamic governance system enables leaders to identify the areas of leverage in decision-making and the reinforcing and counteracting forces that would impact the timing and outcomes of specific policy decisions. The interdependent, interacting and reinforcing flows that are the heartbeat of dynamic governance are shown as connecting arrows in Figure 1.1.

The external environment affects the governance system through the uncertainties of future developments and the varied practices adopted in other countries. The external environment provides *ideas and insights* that stimulate thinking ahead and thinking across. Thinking ahead seeks a *dynamic fit* with the environment so that the policies remain relevant and their impacts desirable. Thinking across assesses the *trade-offs* that a society needs to make before new practices may be introduced. The internal environment, represented by the actual performance of existing paths, *induces* thinking again so that policies may be refined and renewed.

Able people and agile processes are the key drivers for the development of the three dynamic governance capacities of thinking ahead, thinking again and thinking across, which then are embedded in the paths of chosen strategies, policies and programs. Their approaches to the paths differ according to which dominant dynamic capability is being utilized. In thinking ahead, *new concepts* are developed from understanding the impacts of future uncertainties and from questioning implicit assumptions. In thinking again, the status quo of current performance is *challenged* in order to identify changes for improvements. In thinking across, innovations result from *customizing* the experience from other contexts to suit the local circumstances.

Long-term commitment and investments in developing able people and agile processes are required to sustain an unending cycle of thinking ahead, thinking again and thinking across. This will induce the constant *conceptualization, challenge and customizations* that are needed to enable people to learn, adapt chosen paths and policies, and change continually. This system of interdependent relationships among dynamic capabilities, people, processes, and paths enables guiding principles, formal rules, incentive structures, informal constraints, and the institutional structures to evolve with time to remain relevant and effective in the face of rapid technological change. This is the essence of a dynamic governance system.

1.4.3 *How Systemic Interactions Affect Change: The Example of Education Policy*

Education has always been a priority for Singapore. In the 1960s the main objective was to ensure that every child had a place in school. All students followed a similar education structure — drawn largely from the British education system and adapted for local conditions with the bilingual policy. It was only in 1979 that the system was overhauled following the recommendations of the Goh Keng Swee Report on Education, which sought to reduce wastage and premature attrition from the school system. Students were streamed in their third year (revised later to the fourth year) of primary school into classes that reflected their academic and language abilities as demonstrated in examination results. Top students with exceptional bilingual abilities from the national primary school leaving examinations were given options to study in specialized secondary schools to develop these capabilities further. On the whole, the education system was geared to train students to acquire the technical knowledge and skills that the economy needed. Schools were ranked according to the performance of their students in national examinations.

Though attrition rates declined and examination passes improved, there was much unhappiness. Parents put tremendous pressure on their children to study and do well in examinations to ensure that they were streamed into the best classes. Children streamed into classes intended for those with lower ability ("monolingual classes") were demoralized and their self-confidence suffered. Teachers assigned students heavy workloads to drill them for examinations and to get better results in school rankings. The range of subjects offered in schools narrowed as both teachers and students dropped qualitative subjects deemed difficult for students to do well in examinations. The management of schools and teachers was centralized in the Ministry of Education, which ensured that all policies and programs followed consistent standards and procedures. Schools were expected to follow strictly the ministry's directives. Teachers and principals felt powerless to improve the system. The education system was widely perceived as too examination-centered, too rigid, overly stressful on children, unforgiving, not catering to late bloomers, stifling to creativity, too narrow and de-motivating.

Though there was some fine-tuning to the system, the basic educational framework remained largely unchanged throughout the 1980s and much of the 1990s. This was due in large measure to the beliefs of the founding political leaders who had observed and learnt from the experiences of other newly independent countries. They had expanded their educational intakes post independence but many of the graduates produced had not been able to find jobs. This in turn had created large numbers of educated unemployed who were a potential source of political and social instability, a situation that Singapore's political leaders wished to avoid. Thus throughout the 1980s and much of the 1990s, educational expansion was undertaken within a manpower planning framework. Manpower requirements for the economy were forecast and educational intakes for each level adjusted accordingly. The recommendations of the Goh Report, in integrating the academic and vocational tracks, extended this thinking by trying to reduce wastage and seeking to ensure that all students left the school system with a skill that would help them secure employment.

In addition to these considerations, the system up to that point was aligned with many of Singapore's institutional values. There was continued improvement in examination passes; the approach was an efficient and pragmatic one which encouraged hard work and self-reliance. Students graduating from the system found employment and provided the manpower needed for economic growth. The rigor and objectivity of the examination system were highly regarded as benchmarks for meritocracy. Talent, based on academic performance, could be identified, nurtured and fast-tracked. The system was able to identify and produce talented individuals who became leaders in society regardless of their family background. A fundamental rethinking of the educational system was thus constrained by cultural values and beliefs which reflected the ethos at the time: efficiency, consistency, quantifiable improvements in examination results, and central control. While there was no educational crisis, voices of concern were nevertheless growing louder.

A confluence of factors led to a major review of the educational system in the latter half of the 1990s. Singapore's restructuring and transition to a knowledge-based economy required mental flexibility and creativity that the educational system had difficulty producing. The lack of entrepreneurship and innovation was starkly obvious when contrasted with beacons of the new economy such as Silicon Valley. Educational concerns were one of the main causes of emigration. The ministry also experienced difficulties in recruiting the qualified teachers needed and class sizes remained large by Western standards.

A shift in thinking occurred in the 1990s. The focus of education policy moved gradually from one that looked upon students solely as potential manpower for the economy to one that sought to nurture and help each student be the best that he or she could be. Subsequent reforms in the Singapore education system since 1997 were developed based on this new way of thinking and were led by highly regarded political and public sector leaders: Ministers Teo Chee Hean and Tharman Shanmugaratnam, and Permanent Secretaries Lim Siong Guan, Chiang Chie Foo, Lim Chuan Poh, and Tan Ching Yee.

They re-examined assumptions and fundamental educational policies which had been operating for many years and learnt from the experience of other countries. Implementation was carried out in phases and progress was cumulative. The objective to maximize the potential of every child based on Singapore's long-standing belief in developing its people remained unchanged. Teachers and principals were involved in a multitude of project teams that reviewed different aspects of how the educational system was actually working, and recommended changes for improvement. New ideas were introduced into educational paths and approaches to build upon existing strengths to maximize the potential of every child in a changed global environment and in a more sophisticated Singapore society and economy.

Comprehensive reforms in school management processes, systems and structures paved the way for subsequent substantive changes in educational policies regarding curriculum and pedagogy. Two slogans were used to convey the main themes and approach to reform: "Thinking Schools, Learning Nation," and "Teach Less, Learn More." There was a major change in direction towards thinking skills rather than mere content acquisition, and student-centered learning rather than teaching of textbook knowledge. Systemic changes in educational processes and structures included changes to:[29]

(i)   school management: giving more authority and autonomy to schools and organizing them in clusters, more structured development for school principals, flexible sabbaticals, more holistic assessment of schools including broader bases for school rankings;

(ii) school infrastructure: major investments in information technology and upgrading of school buildings;

---

[29] Speech by Minister Teo Chee Hean at the MOE WorkPlan Seminar on 18 September 2002.

(iii) career structures and development for teachers: developing their professional capabilities, external work attachments, more competitive salaries, enhanced recognition, faster promotions for high performing teachers, more support for teachers;

(iv) curriculum and assessment: broader and more integrated curricula, trimming curriculum requirements, more emphasis on thinking and creativity, reducing over-emphasis on examinations, second-language teaching pedagogy geared to developing interest with a focus on conversational skills, removing streaming in primary schools;

(v) educational structure: more diversity and flexibility to give students greater choice and more options, including integrated programs that bypassed the GCE "O" level examinations, new subjects, specialized schools in sports, arts, and mathematics and sciences, and private schools; setting up new polytechnics and universities.

Our purpose here is not to give a detailed account of the transformation of education policies. It is to illustrate how the systemic interactions worked to constrain and then drive education reforms in Singapore. It would be too shallow an analysis to attribute change to a single leader or a single cause. Both driving forces for change and counter-acting forces for stability build up in the system over time and need to reach a point when there is sufficient driving force to overcome the balancing forces before systemic change can be initiated. The educational system in the 1980s and 1990s reflected the cultural values and ethos then, and thus the major changes were difficult to achieve because the forces for stability were very strong, as illustrated by the cultural foundations at the base of Figure 1. 1.

We can also explain the driving forces and capabilities for change in education using the dynamic governance framework in Figure 1.1. External forces, in the form of the requirements for the new economy, created visible gaps in the educational system. Driven by strong beliefs in global relevance and people development, the educational system was reviewed to address new needs and plug the gaps to ensure continued success in the new economy. People and processes are the driving forces needed to move the change forward and in this case, the able and visionary leadership of new ministers and permanent secretaries re-defined the systemic long-term paths and policy changes required. They then created the structures and processes to initiate, execute and sustain the efforts. These processes involved harnessing, through teams and review committees, the energy, knowledge and interest of the major stakeholders — teachers, parents and external experts — to devise and recommend changes for improvement. New paths and policies were then articulated, contextualized and executed. This example clearly demonstrates that people, processes and policies are reinforcing forces that have to be actively managed as a system to achieve the desired outcomes over the long term. After ten years of sustained development, the transformation of education policy and management in Singapore is still an on-going effort. New energies have to be constantly infused into the system to prevent it from inevitable atrophy. That is the nature and challenge of dynamic governance.

The rest of the book explores and explains these dynamic flows and relationships and their applications in the governance system of the Singapore government institutions. The rest of this chapter discusses the two main parts of the dynamic governance system: why and how culture is the foundation for dynamic governance, and what the three major capabilities of dynamic governance are and how they work.

1.5 Culture as a Foundation for Dynamic Governance

Culture denotes certain group beliefs and values that are shared or held in common, so it can be thought of as the accumulated shared learning of a given community based on a history of shared experience. Governance rules and structures are choices made by a society and reflect the values and beliefs of its leaders. The beliefs of leaders shape the rules, informal norms and the enforcement mechanisms that are institutionalized. Douglass North calls cultural beliefs the "scaffolds human erect"[30] and they shape the nature of institutional choices and change, and "over time, the richer the cultural context in terms

---

[30] North (2005), pp. 48–64.

of providing multiple experimentation and creative competition, the more likely the successful survival of the society."[31] The values and beliefs may stay implicit and informal for a long time and may only subsequently be articulated after reflection and rationalization. Whether they are articulated or implicit, it is important to understand the cultural foundations of a society to appreciate why governance choices are made the way they are.

Culture affects governance in three ways. The first impact of culture is to *constrain* the agenda and policy making process. Issues that run counter to cultural values and principles are less likely to be accepted on the agenda, and even if they are accepted for consideration, the decision making process would be severely *constrained* by the implicit assumptions embedded in the culture. Second, cultural norms are often used to *confront* the consideration of innovative policy options that contradict them. The constraining and confrontational effects of culture mean that policy options that are contrary to existing values and norms would not be accepted. Sometimes these can become strategic blind spots that ultimately undermine a society's survival. Third, cultural values and norms *catalyze* decision-makers to actively look for alternatives and ideas that are aligned to and would further the implicit purposes of the group. The effects of these cultural values and beliefs are significant, though often implicit and informal, and are achieved mostly through the socialization of leaders. They affect the governance system through influencing the thinking and decision-making of leaders, and thus the choice of paths, policies, processes and practices that are adopted.

The culture of a society comes from an accumulation of experience derived from the adaptive, often partial solutions, to frequently encountered problems of the past. The perception of the value of these ideas in the progress of a society becomes deeply imprinted in the minds of the people. Over time, a common cultural heritage is formed, reducing the divergence of mental models, and creating a means for transferring these common social perceptions to future generations. This cultural heritage shapes how people think, evaluate, and decide

---

[31] North (2005), p. 36.

across a spectrum of choices, including governance. The cultural foundations of governance are derived from how founding leaders perceive the strengths and vulnerabilities of a society's position in its context, which then influence how they articulate the intended purposes of the governance systems and institutions. These belief and values determine the principles utilized to guide policy decision-making.

The leaders' perception of position, articulation of purpose and evolution of principles are the foundations for understanding why and how governance institutions and structures develop over time. At the same time, they provide a sense of center and stability for individuals in a society as it adapts to constant change. But a stable center can either facilitate or impede learning, help or hinder change. If there is no clarity of purpose and principles, institutional rules and structures can become ends in themselves, self-perpetuating and highly bureaucratic. When the environment changes, there is no basis to review and revise existing rules, systems and structures. Instead of seizing new opportunities, new developments may make incumbent leaders and organizations feel insecure and threatened because they may lack the competencies to function in the new context. These dysfunctional behaviors cannot be challenged without a shared sense of purpose and a strong commitment to principles that facilitate change. Responding adequately to change requires values and mental models that seek to perceive emerging patterns, understand them and adapt to a new reality. The Singapore's Public Service for the 21st Century (PS21) initiative was specifically aimed at inculcating the values of anticipating change, welcoming change and executing change so that the public sector can face the future more effectively. Details of the PS21 strategic initiative will be discussed in Chapter 8. The broad themes of the position, purpose and principles in the Singapore government institutions are shown as the foundations that are common across the three dynamic governance capabilities in Table 1.1.

Singapore's approach to governance is shaped by its leaders' view of its unique position, circumstances and history — its small size, lack of resources, geographical location and multicultural make-up.

Table 1.1. Cultural Foundations for Governance in Singapore

Capability / Culture	THINKING AHEAD	THINKING AGAIN	THINKING ACROSS
PRINCIPLES *Guidelines for Action Based on Values & Beliefs*	Integrity — Incorruptibility People are key — Meritocracy for best use of talent Results-oriented — Rationality with pragmatism Efficiency — Use of markets adjusted for social equity Stability — Multi-racial, multi-religious understanding		
PURPOSE *Strategic Imperatives of Governance*	Develop people as the key resource Inculcate self reliance through work, not welfare Financial prudence to build buffer for survival Domestic stability to attract FDI and talent Economic growth for survival Global relevance through connectivity and change Build long-term sustainability, not short-term political gains Government takes a proactive role in development		
POSITION *Unique Context & Constraints*	Small, resource-scarce, vulnerable to external trends Diverse cultures and ethnicity, threat to internal harmony Dominant single political party since 1959		

Since Singapore's founding by the British as a trading hub, it continues to depend on external connectivity, especially international trade and investments, for its survival. Its small market size led it to seek economic integration with Malaysia in 1963. Its separation from Malaysia in 1965 caused its leaders to look beyond its immediate region and "leapfrog" to the more developed nations for investments and trade to increase its chances for survival. Its historical experience shaped its deep sense of vulnerability, and the recognition of its dependency on developments in the global economic and security environment. Its lack of natural resources focused its leaders' minds on their people as the only strategic resource for the country, and the need to accumulate financial resources from economic growth in order to build buffers for survival during lean years. The perceived vulnerabilities of Singapore's position influenced the leadership's intent and purpose, its activist stance, and the adoption of several strategic imperatives for good governance: long-term thinking, global relevance, sustained economic growth, social stability, financial prudence, self reliance and people development.

A unique feature of the Singapore governance infrastructure is the dominance of a single political party. The political context is especially crucial because the public service leadership is accountable to the Cabinet, made up of ministers from the same political party that has ruled Singapore since 1959. The colonial heritage left by the British when Singapore obtained self rule in 1959 and the imprint and values of the founding fathers, especially its first Prime Minister Lee Kuan Yew and his trusted deputy, Goh Keng Swee, have influenced the developmental paths of and set the boundaries for governance in Singapore in the last 42 years. The political leadership's confidence in winning elections meant that they could adopt a decision-making approach that stressed long-term solutions and sustainable policies rather than short-term political popularity. Their confidence set the tone for rationality, systemic thinking and meritocracy in the development of the civil service, and the strength of the political leadership significantly influenced the values and principles of governance in the public sector.

Principles are guidelines for action based on the values and beliefs defined by leaders of institutions. Continuous change requires an ethical foundation that is stable and strong enough to withstand and support the constant re-examination and re-design of policies and programs. There are risks associated with constant change. Dynamic stability is achieved when there are clear principles founded on strong values and beliefs to guide the choice of what and how to change. Contrary to common perception, the Singapore civil service operates in a decentralized fashion with Permanent Secretaries being accountable to their respective Ministers. There are few formal coordinating structures at the civil service level. Though there are linkage mechanisms, most of the coordination structures are informal and social in nature, and founded on shared values and common principles. Socialization remains the main means of transferring values to younger members of the community.

Five principles set the tone for dynamic governance choices. First, the principle of anti-corruption is founded on a settled belief in the value of integrity and service to society. Second, the principle of meritocracy is founded on a strong belief that economic development depends on the value of people's knowledge and skills rather than family background and social status. Third, the principle of rationality with pragmatism rests on a strong value of performance and focus on results. Fourth, the principle of using market prices adjusted for social equity is based on a belief in market prices as the best means for ensuring efficiency in the allocation of resources, with government intervening to provide a social safety net only for those who genuinely cannot afford to pay. Fifth, the principle of multi-racialism is based on the belief that domestic stability can be achieved only when there are harmonious relationships among the people of various races and religions. These values and principles influence the choice of policies, how they are designed, implemented and evaluated. They provide the criteria for decision-making and thus a stable foundation for dynamic adaptations to environmental uncertainties and technological change. The historical context that influenced the leadership perception of position and purpose is discussed in Chapter 3 and the values and principles of governance are further elaborated in Chapter 4.

1.6 Dynamic Governance Capabilities: Thinking Ahead, Thinking Again, Thinking Across

Dynamic governance does not happen spontaneously. It is the outcome of leadership intention and ambition to ensure the survival of their societies. Dynamic leaders think differently, articulate their ideas so that peers and superiors appreciate and support them, and convert allocated resources into organizational capabilities that achieve desired results over a sustained period. Capabilities refer to an organization's attitude, knowledge, skills and resources deployed in conceiving and performing important coordinated tasks to achieve desired results. Capabilities are distinctive ways of doing things, and are developed over an extended period of time through processes of learning.

Dynamic leaders have the ability to govern with coherence in the midst of continuous change through clear strategic intent, astute management of their contexts, active learning and searching for adaptive paths that are relevant, and effective execution of policy decisions. They systematically build capabilities in their people and processes to ensure that good ideas are converted into realistic policies, projects and programs, and consistently coordinate action throughout the organization by articulating and reinforcing worthy goals and principles.

The characteristics of the three dynamic governance capabilities of thinking ahead, thinking again, and thinking across in the Singapore public service are summarized in Table 1.2.

Table 1.2 outlines the nature and objectives of each of these capabilities and how they are manifested in the paths for making policy choices and decisions. It also shows the organizational processes for embedding these capabilities in the public service and the attributes of the people in leadership who embody these skills. These dynamic governance capabilities are coordinated institutionally through a set of shared views of where Singapore is positioned in the world, the purposes of governance, and what principles, values and beliefs are essential for its survival and success. The shared view of position, purpose and principles that constitute the cultural foundations for the Singapore governance system and which provide coordinated guidance for the performance of the three dynamic capabilities are also set out in Table 1.2. It provides a useful framework and set of guidelines for our examination of the development of dynamic governance capabilities. We will discuss each capability in some detail, including the criteria for decision-making, the major activities in the organizational processes, the attributes and competencies of the people who are involved and brief examples of how these capabilities worked in the Singapore public service.

1.6.1 *Thinking Ahead*

Thinking ahead is the capability to identify future developments in the environment, understand their implications on important socio-economic goals, and identify the strategic investments and options required to enable a society to exploit new opportunities and deal with potential threats. The intent of thinking ahead is to gain foresight that

Table 1.2. Dynamic Governance Capabilities of the Singapore System

Capability / Driver	THINKING AHEAD	THINKING AGAIN	THINKING ACROSS
PATHS *Policy Choices, Execution, Adaptation & Innovation*	Future Uncertainties	Internal Issues	External Practices
	Foresight	Hindsight	Insight
	Refresh Goals	Better Quality	New Ideas
	Investments	Improvements	Innovations
	Beyond Present Circumstances	Beyond Past Legacies	Beyond Existing Boundaries
	Future to Current Implications	Current to Future Performance	Outside to Inside Programs
PROCESSES *Agile Structures & Systems*	Exploring and Anticipating	Understanding and Probing	Searching and Researching
	Perceiving and Testing	Reviewing and Analyzing	Discovering and Experimenting
	Strategizing	Redesigning	Evaluating
	Influencing	Implementing	Customizing
PEOPLE *Able Leadership Recruitment, Renewal & Retention*	Alert to Signals	Confront Reality	Learn from Others
	Scenario Builder	Problem-Solver	Knowledge-Broker
	Challenge Implicit Assumptions	Challenge Current Achievements	Challenge Accepted Models
	Credible	Candid	Contextual

PRINCIPLES: *Guidelines for Action based on Values & Beliefs*
PURPOSE: *Strategic Imperatives of Governance*
POSITION: *Unique Context & Constraints*

would prompt the institution to assess the risks of current strategies and policies, refresh goals, and conceptualize new policy initiatives to prepare for the future. The time frame of thinking is from the future back to the present, with an outside-in perspective of how the uncertainties in the external environment would affect the achievement of desired outcomes and objectives.

Future uncertainties, by nature and by definition, cannot be made totally intelligible nor can any organization be fully prepared for them. The purpose of thinking ahead is not to try to forecast an inherently unpredictable future. In an uncertain world, thinking ahead is about engaging people in strategic conversations[32] so that they can see the plausibility of future developments, which may be different from what they have assumed. It is a process of helping decision-makers to re-perceive the world, re-conceive the strategic responses needed, and reconsider existing policies and programs. People learn to appreciate how events fit into a pattern, and understand their impacts on the socio-economic goals of the community. Only then can they question their assumptions about the way the world works, develop fresh perspectives and recognize the limitations of the current policy framework when the world changes. Thinking ahead creates a culture of regularly questioning underlying beliefs and mental models, and asking how relevant they continue to be in a changing world. It creates the mental preparedness, flexibility and openness that enable quick response as events unfold.

Thinking ahead is more than just conducting a formal planning process, which often degenerates into a bureaucratic process of filling prescribed forms devoid of substantive thinking and dialog. Thinking ahead involves exploring and rehearsing the future before it arrives and sensitizing people in the organization to recognize early signals of its impending arrival. Strategies and policies may be tested for robustness under alternate futures, and contingencies may be planned. By thinking through the uncertainties ahead of their occurrence, people in the organization becomes less fearful when events do occur, and have more confidence to respond better, faster and with greater flexibility — in short, be better prepared to face the future.

Without the capability to think ahead, people are more likely to be caught by surprise and then react out of shock and fear. In such circumstances, when leaders are under the spotlight and under pressure to do something fast, there is less time for careful thought

---

[32] Kees vsn der Heijden (2005). *The Art of Strategic Conversations*, 2nd Edition. John Wiley & Sons Ltd.

and development of long-term strategic responses. They may engage in denial and redouble efforts at what is tried and tested, even when they know that these may no longer fit the new circumstances. They may choose a psychologically safe path by following the bandwagon in a wave of imitation of what others are doing, or go through a series of fire-fighting measures to alleviate short-term pain without finding long-term solutions. Thinking ahead recognizes that the best time to prepare for change is before the pressure or urgency to do so arises — because when they do, there is no time to think. That is why thinking ahead is a critical capability for dynamic governance.

The process for thinking ahead involves:

(i)   exploring and anticipating future trends and developments that may have significant impacts on policy goals,

(ii) perceiving how these developments would affect the achievement of current goals, and testing the effectiveness of existing strategies, policies and programs,

(iii) strategizing what options could be used to prepare for the emerging threats and exploit the new opportunities, and

(iv) influencing key decision-makers and stakeholders to consider the emerging issues seriously and engaging them in strategic conversations about possible responses.

The capacity to think ahead requires leaders who are alert to signals regarding emerging issues and evolving developments in the social, economic, technological and political environments. They need to understand how these trends may culminate into scenarios of plausible futures and articulate the cause-and-effect logic of how these scenarios, if they come about, would require different sets of strategies and policies. They need to be both perceptive thinkers and creative conceptualizers to challenge implicit assumptions and energize people to meet the new challenges. They must be credible in both their performance track record and be compelling in the logic of their analyses so that decision-makers would pay attention and be willing to re-examine their assumptions about the changing criteria for effectiveness. They need to tell compelling stories based on facts and plausible events that would influence policy-makers to rethink their beliefs and assumptions, and even to reconsider goals and objectives. Only then will they stimulate the openness and learning necessary to begin the process of change in mental models regarding goals, strategies, policies and programs.

Singapore's capability to think ahead is sometimes equated with its future-orientation and its capacity to think long-term, which have been widely admired. Its capacity to think ahead is not just a matter of plans and programs. It is a capacity that is deeply ingrained into its public sector leaders, embedded into its approach to policy-making, and entrenched into its institutional processes. It is an intangible skill and becomes clear only when one studies the pattern of thinking that characterized its approach to policy-making over the last 40 years.

Analyzing demographic changes provide the easiest approach to think ahead — for example, an aging population was not difficult to foresee since the baby-boomers born after World War 2 would be reaching retirement age within the next decade. In healthcare, it was foreseeable that an aging population would impose a greater burden of healthcare costs on the state. Thus policies were developed early for different levels of subsidies and for patient co-payments to ensure personal responsibility and choice, and to keep healthcare costs under control. At the same time limited competition was introduced into the healthcare delivery system to provide incentives for greater efficiency and achieve a higher standard of patient care and service.

The numerous master plans for priority policy areas are good examples of the public sector's capacity to think ahead, but by no means the only expressions of it. Over the years, much public sector effort has gone into developing master plans that took into account future trends and developments, and crafting strategies for ensuring success. In the early 1960s the planning process for economic development, as advised by Dr Albert Winsemius, identified the need for industrialization and a focused effort to promote foreign investment from leading multinational companies. Its success in creating jobs not only solved unemployment; it created a new policy issue in the 1970s: a shortage of labor. In the 1970s, Singapore invested in building a container port ahead of demand and ahead of other ports because of the strategic importance of trade to its economic development. It extended its role as an entrepot serving its immediate neighbors and became the world's largest transshipment hub, providing aggregation of volume, connectivity and frequency for major shipping lines to serve their customers throughout the Asia-Pacific region. In the 1990s a slew of "2000" (thinking ahead to the year 2000) and "21" (thinking ahead to the 21st century) planning efforts were conducted, including Army 2000, IT2000, Library 2000, Singapore 21, Manpower 21, Tourism 21 and others.

A recent example of a major effort to collectively think ahead was the Economic Review Committee chaired by then Deputy Prime Minister Lee Hsien Loong, with the participation of hundreds of business leaders, professionals and public officials. The committee's report was released in 2003 and it was aptly titled, "New Challenges, Fresh Goals."[33] The report discussed the global uncertainties caused by the social and political aftermath of the Asian financial crisis, the new security threats resulting from the 9/11 attack on the World Trade Center in New York, the emergence of China and India as major economic players, and the impact of globalization and rapid technological advances. It highlighted new external and domestic challenges for the Singapore economy. The committee outlined a new vision for Singapore as "a leading global city, a hub for talent, enterprise and innovation," and "the most open and cosmopolitan city in Asia and one of the best places to live and work." The report then discussed the policy changes needed to remake Singapore to realize this new vision, including expanding external ties, building a competitive and flexible business environment, nurturing entrepreneurship and welcoming global talent.

1.6.2 Thinking Again

Albert Einstein said, "The problem is not to think but to think again." *Thinking again* is the capability to confront the current realities regarding the performance of existing strategies, policies and programs, and then to redesign them to achieve better quality and results. The

---

[33] MTI (2003). "Report of the Economic Review Committee: New Challenges, Fresh Goals." Ministry of Trade and Industry, Singapore, February 2003.

timeframe for thinking is from the present situation to the future, with an inside-out perspective of how the performance of current policies and programs compares with the desired intent and outcomes. It involves utilizing actual data, information, measurements and feedback to surface issues and problems that impede better performance, and looks beyond the past legacy of a particular policy or program to seek ways to improve its performance.

If we have perfect feedback on the consequences of policy, the perfect mental model to correctly link the consequences to their true underlying causes, and the perfect knowledge to take corrective actions, the capacity to think again would be trivial. The reality is that there is so much noise in the system that it is difficult to have good and timely feedback, difficult to know what the feedback means, much less to be able to attribute them accurately. Even if we have the expertise to identify needed corrections, there may not be the political will or the resources to implement them.

Although thinking again is based on hindsight of what has already occurred, it uses the known facts and other feedback to ask questions, open up conversations and engage in dialog to facilitate learning about the underlying causes for the observed results. Thinking again is fact-based and creates an environment whereby people are constantly asking why they observe the results that they do and what they can do differently to obtain better or different outcomes. It removes the tendency to blame others or to take undue credit, both common responses whenever performance reviews are used for making judgments on people rather than for learning about the system. Thinking again leads to the reconsideration of the effectiveness and efficiency in the execution of policies and programs, as well as the appropriateness of their goals and strategies.

Thinking again may be triggered by success or failure — the key is how the results are perceived, interpreted and communicated to stimulate a rethink of the previous policy. Perhaps the most significant thinking again was done during the tumultuous two years between 1963 and 1965 when Singapore was part of Malaysia. The envisioned common market and bigger hinterland was not realized. Instead, the leaders from Singapore and Malaysia were embroiled in political struggles which led to disillusionment on both sides. When Singapore finally separated from Malaysia, it was obvious that its earlier belief and strategy of creating a bigger hinterland to ensure economic viability had to be re-examined. Partly out of desperation and partly because of external advice, it decided to "leapfrog" the region and seek investments and markets from faraway countries in the developed regions of North America, Europe and Japan.

The unintended consequences of success may also trigger a re-think of policies. Perhaps the most well known reversal of a successful policy was the population control policy. This was formulated in the 1960s to cope with the overwhelming demand for jobs, housing and other social needs of a rapidly growing population in a bleak economic environment. As the economy grew, the population became more educated and delayed marriages and child-bearing. The policy disincentives for bigger families exacerbated the situation such that fertility slowed to below replacement levels. The "stop-at-two" population policy over-achieved the intended results, created limits to economic growth and compounded issues related to an aging population. The policy was reversed and now generous incentives are provided for Singaporeans to have more children and at an earlier age.

The process for thinking again involves:

(i)   reviewing and analyzing actual performance data and understanding public feedback,
(ii)   probing into the underlying causes of feedback or observed facts, information and behavior, both for meeting or missing targets,
(iii) reviewing the strategies, policies and programs to identify features and activities that are working well and those that are not,
(iv)   redesigning the policies and programs, partially or completely, so that their performance may be improved and their objectives better met, and
(v)   implementing the new policies and systems so that citizens and customers are better served and enjoy a meaningful outcome.

The capacity to think again requires leaders who are willing to confront the realities of current performance and feedback, and to challenge the status quo. They need to be confident yet humble enough to be candid without being offensive and to engage people in open dialog and interaction so that they are energized to change and do better. They need analytical and problem-solving skills to drill into the details of how things are done and why the feedback or results occur as they do. They also need the skills to redesign the system so that better results may be achieved.

The purpose of thinking again is to identify changes needed for improvement. For leaders who have initiated earlier changes, thinking again becomes especially challenging. Although change is never easy, it takes extraordinary emotional fortitude and effort for a leader to "think again" what he has previously initiated or earlier changed, and to change again. The make-up of the organization that has grown with the current leader makes the capacity to think again a rare occurrence. A strong and successful leader tends to staff the organization with people who share his or her vision and values, and who have the competencies to execute and realize the current vision. Knowledge and competence can be double-edged — skill in doing something well can become the only way to do something. A core competence can become a core rigidity and a competency trap that blocks further learning. Over time, groupthink can develop in the leadership so that there is subtle denial of reality, and little diversity of views and perspectives. Although the team itself may view this as cohesion and teamwork, often the reality is that they have lost the capacity to re-look at their existing policies and programs with the objectivity and detachment needed to change again, especially if they had succeeded with their original changes.

That is why we often observe difficulties in renewing leadership perspectives and capabilities adequately for the same team to lead a second round of transformation necessary for an organization to continue to succeed. It also means that the regeneration of the leadership capacity to be able to *think again* requires deliberate strategies and effort to bring in new people with different backgrounds, skills and views, and to put in place mechanisms to ensure that the inevitable and ensuing political difficulties do not eventually hollow out the new leaders. There can be no dynamic governance without leadership renewal.

Singapore's policy for rotating its leaders, both political appointment holders and public sector leaders, every few years has created natural mechanisms for thinking again. Each change in leadership is invariably accompanied by a thorough review of past policies and performance. Although this can be disruptive to the organization and viewed skeptically as a new leader's egoistic desire to stamp his own mark on the organization, it has the effect of causing people in it to think again what has been done and how further improvements can be made. This has often led to strategic renewal in both policies and organization.

The transformation of Singapore's public libraries[34] from 3rd to 1st world in the 1990s was facilitated by changes in leadership and organizational forms. Although library membership and readership had been declining and facilities deteriorating for a number of years, the initiative to think again only started in 1991 when the new Ministry of Information and the Arts was set up and a new minister, George Yeo, appointed. The Library 2000 Committee comprising non-librarians was appointed officially to review (*think again*) the role and development of the public libraries. The chairman and deputy chairman came from the state IT agency, the National Computer Board, which in an earlier released IT2000 report had envisioned a digital library without walls. The new chief executive of the library appointed to lead the change was also a non-librarian.

The "think again" of the public library system led to a new mission: to enhance the learning capacity of residents, new concepts: lifestyle libraries, new facilities: bringing libraries to the people in shopping malls, new processes: self check-out, returns at other locations, faster availability of new books, better customer service, and new skills for librarians. The results have been revolutionary. Library facilities are now attractive places for people to visit and access information. Visitors and book loans have increased several fold. More and newer books, and other multimedia content are now readily available. Droves of overseas visitors have seen the changes

---

[34] Roger Hallowell, Carin Knoop and Boon Siong Neo (2001). "Transforming Singapore's Public Libraries." Harvard Business School Case Series.

first-hand to learn how the transformation was accomplished and managed without any staff lay-offs.

1.6.3 *Thinking Across*

Thinking across is the capability to cross traditional borders and boundaries in order to learn from the experience of others so that good ideas may be adopted and customized to enable new and innovative policies or programs to be experimented with and institutionalized. It goes beyond mere adoption or imitation of rules and practices that may have worked elsewhere. By learning from others, insight is gained and then adjusted to the unique needs of a country's cultural and historical context. Thinking across is a dynamic governance capability that introduces fresh ideas and innovation into a society. The timeframe and perspective for thinking adaptively is from the present-outside to the future-inside.

Thinking across seeks to find interesting practices beyond the traditional boundaries of a nation to understand why and how they have worked to achieve given policy objectives. It then creatively transfers that knowledge into tailored programs that may be tried within the local institutional and policy environment. Thinking across is learning from others to gain new ideas for innovation, for new and different ways of doing things. The intent of learning from the experience of others is not mere technical imitation of best practices, but a deep contextual understanding of why others adopted different approaches to similar issues, how their history and circumstances influenced the selection of different policies and design of different programs. It includes understanding the lessons they learnt in their implementation, and how they perceived what worked or did not work, and whether and how they would approach it differently if they could start over.

As a society's developmental issues become more complex, it cannot merely depend on the adoption of standard, generic policies and practices to solve its problems. It has to learn from the experience of others and the experiments that may have been conducted elsewhere to design solutions that are suitable for its own citizens. Thinking across recognizes that the traditional boundaries of functions, hierarchy, organizations, industries, sectors, geography, nations, culture, and knowledge domains are hurdles to learning. They create discrete mental categories that limit creativity in the search for holistic solutions to complex issues. A society that provides the incentives for people and organizations to explore alternative ways of solving problems, conduct trials to experiment with new ideas and learn from failures will progress faster, become more innovative, and increase their chances for continued success in a changing world.

Thinking across facilitates learning through exposure to different ideas and discovery of new insights and applications. It recognizes that breakthrough innovations happen often by a process of being exposed to interesting experiments in other communities, taking apart these ideas and re-assembling them in new combinations.[35] Thinking across overcomes the strategic myopia of a "not invented here" mindset. Instead of rejecting an idea or program because it came from elsewhere, thinking across makes "not invented here" a valued opportunity to tap the most creative ideas wherever they may be. It builds bridges to different cultures and backgrounds to open up new perspectives, and to find new approaches to governance and policy. Exposure to other domains allows people to see their own policies in a new light, question their own practices, and make new discoveries — how new connections may be made, and how different ideas may be recombined in new ways to create innovative approaches to emerging issues.

It recognizes that people who have grown up and lived in the same socio-economic and political environment often develop similar views and share similar blind spots. In being too familiar and too comfortable, they too easily reject ideas that do not fit into the local context in the first instance. It recognizes the need for people to step out of their familiar surroundings long enough to overcome their own blind spots and see what others are seeing.

The process of thinking across boundaries involves:

(i)   searching for novel and interesting practices adopted and implemented by others in approaching similar issues,

---

[35] Andrew Hargadon (2003). *How Breakthroughs Happen*. Cambridge, MA: HBS Press.

(ii)   reflecting on what they did, why and how they did it, and the lessons they learnt from the experience,

(iii) evaluating what may be applicable to the local context, taking into account the unique conditions and circumstances, and what would be acceptable to the local population,

(iv) discovering new connections between ideas and new combinations of different ideas that create innovative approaches to emerging issues, and

(v)   customizing the policy and programs to suit local policy requirements and citizens' needs.

Leaders need to think across and be open to learn from people and practices outside their own culture. They need to be confident to go beyond the boundaries of familiar domains and competencies to look for different ideas, and build intellectual and social linkages so that these new ideas are not rejected too early and too easily. The new ideas are not abstract; they have actually been tried and implemented elsewhere, albeit in a different country, domain or culture. Leaders become knowledge brokers who span boundaries, build linkages to distant communities, grow social networks for learning and interactions, and provide conduits for the flow of new knowledge for their institutions. The sharing of information and experiences in the leaders' social networks give them new knowledge with which they can challenge accepted approaches and solutions in their local environments.

Instead of playing the devil's advocate in criticizing new ideas, leaders need to take on new innovation roles[36], such as an anthropologist, an experimenter, a cross-pollinator, a set designer, and a storyteller. The role of leaders is to create an environment whereby people do not reject different ideas and solutions because of defensive 'they are not like us' attitudes that foreclose all learning. The uniqueness of one's context is not an acceptable excuse for not learning about other approaches. The uniqueness of context should focus the mind to learn even more in-depth so that the main principles and cause-and-

---

[36] See Tom Kelley (2005). *The Ten Faces of Innovation*. USA: Currency-Doubleday Publishers.

effect logics of a particular practice may be distilled and contextually applied to the local circumstances. Customizing a successful solution to fit the local context requires a deep understanding of the underlying trade-offs that are made and whether a different trade-off is needed to meet the needs of the local community. The adaptability comes from an internalization of a nation's position in the world, the purpose to be pursued for its governance and institutional framework, and the principles that guide its paths of development.

Thinking across boundaries to learn and adapt has been characteristic of Singapore's governance since its independence. Minister Mentor Lee Kuan Yew estimated that perhaps 70 per cent of the governance ideas implemented in Singapore were learnt and adapted from elsewhere[37]. He said that Singapore's decision to move the international airport from Paya Lebar to Changi and write off about S$750m of investments was motivated by his observation of aircraft landing and taking off at Boston's Logan airport that was located beside the sea. Building a new airport at Changi by the sea would solve the perennial noise problem created by aircraft landing and taking off over residential areas near the old airport at Paya Lebar.

When building its armed forces from scratch, the Ministry of Defence learnt from the military doctrines and training methodologies of the Israeli Defence Forces. The personnel appraisal system in the civil service and the public sector's approach to scenario planning were adapted from the Royal Dutch-Shell group. Growing Singapore as a garden city was motivated by what then-Prime Minister Lee saw in Phnom Penh. The National Parks Board (NParks) personnel had to experiment with plants from many countries to see what could grow well in Singapore's tropical climate. Thinking across brought new ideas to Singapore and with continual learning, led to new innovations. The Singapore Armed Forces evolved its own military doctrines, training methodologies and subsequently, new weapons and other military technologies. NParks later expanded the concept of a "garden city" to a "city within a garden" and developed a transformation of the

---

[37] Comment made in answer to questions in a dialog with student at the Lee Kuan Yew School of Public Policy on 3 November 2006.

entire island, including park connectors linking all parks on the island so that the city could be conceived as being in a garden.

1.6.4 *Example of How the Three Capabilities Work Interactively*

We have described the three capabilities that gave rise to the dynamism of the governance system in Singapore. While each of the three capabilities tends to lead to a different type of institutional change, major policy changes often require the exercise of all three sets of capabilities in an integrated, interdependent and systemic manner as shown in Figure 1.1. We conclude this section with a recent example of how the three capabilities worked synergistically to reverse a long-standing policy against the operation of casinos in Singapore.

In 2006, Singapore awarded tenders of more than S$5b of investments each for two integrated resorts with casinos, to be built in downtown Marina Bay and the resort island of Sentosa. In doing so, it *thought again* and reversed a long-standing policy against having casinos in Singapore. The policy change resulted from *thinking ahead* and setting a strategic goal to grow the tourism and hospitality cluster, especially meetings and conventions, into a major service sector of the new Singapore economy. The policy change was also the result of *thinking across* boundaries and discovering how such resorts transformed Las Vegas from a gambling city to a global entertainment and conventions hub. Describing the decision as the most difficult he had taken up to that point as Prime Minister, Lee Hsien Loong said:

> "Because if you're making a decision where the advantages are clear-cut and the opinions are not polarized, it's easy to do. But here the advantages were not so clear, and the dissenters had valid arguments, which we ourselves subscribed to for a very long time. But now the world is changing, and we're starting to think that we have to re-examine our position. Eventually, we decided to do it because, as we understood better how these resorts operate and the way Las Vegas was going and the way the

tourism scene was developing across Asia, it became clear that it was not just a plus which we were forgoing, but if we did not do this, we might be out of the game."[38]

However, it adapted the legalization of casinos with built-in social safeguards to discourage casino gambling among the locals. Guidelines were drawn up for the amount of space within the integrated resorts that could be used for casinos, charging an entrance fee for local residents at the casino, and allowing a person's immediate family to apply for him/her to be barred due to gambling addiction issues.

It adapted the process used for the procurement of complex military systems to the evaluation and award of the tenders (the IR tender evaluation process is described in Chapter 5). External consultants independently calculated the land price that the government would charge and this was announced beforehand to ensure fairness to all bidders. They also checked the bidders' financial projections and assessed the rigor of the financial estimates. A separate panel of experts assessed the architectural designs submitted. A committee of public sector leaders met the bidders and evaluated their bids independently of the political leaders, making their recommendations separately from the committee of ministers. Bidders who partnered with government-linked companies were not given special treatment: in the end no government-linked company won either of the two licenses. Throughout the tender process, Singapore maintained its trademark commitment to professionalism, transparency, objectivity, integrity and anti-corruption.

This is a clear example of how the three organizational capabilities built upon and reinforced one another systematically to bring about a major policy change, which nevertheless was implemented in a manner consistent with the values and principles that have guided policy decision-making and implementation in Singapore since its independence in 1965. It was a decision which resulted from dynamic capabilities with a stable center of values, i.e., dynamic stability at work.

---

[38] Interview with Prime Minister Lee Hsien Loong reported in "Remade in Singapore," *Institutional Investor*, September 2006.

The policy choice was different from those taken in the past but the underlying values of economic growth, pragmatism, market pricing, objectivity and honesty were maintained and reinforced. This is the essence of dynamic governance at work in Singapore. The rest of the book describes in detail how these dynamic capabilities are supported by a set of cultural values and principles, expressed through adaptable policies that are systemically executed, and developed through long-term investments in people and processes.

1.7 Synopsis of the Rest of the Chapters in the Book

The dynamic governance framework in Figure 1.1 provides the conceptual structure for the rest of the book. Singapore's history shapes its purpose for governance and provides the context for understanding the deliberate intent to build governance structures and systems that dynamically stay relevant. The principles that serve as guidelines for action are the core values and beliefs of its leaders and their early experiences in ensuring Singapore's survival. The systematic and practical development of paths, policies, people, and processes in the Singapore public service are drivers of the capacities to think ahead, think again and think across.

Chapter 2 provides a more detailed discussion of the major concepts — governance, institutions, and dynamic capabilities — that guided our research, data collection and analysis in this study, so that readers can understand their conceptualization. This chapter is optional for those who are primarily interested in the substantive findings of our study and how they may be applied in their own contexts. Those who seek to understand the development of these concepts in the literature and their references would find this chapter useful.

Chapter 3 describes the historical context for the development of the public sector. The major patterns of political, economic, security and social developments in Singapore over a 40-year period from independence in 1965 to 2006 are summarized and their impact on the public sector governance and development discussed. An understanding of the context for public sector development is important to be able to interpret many of the strategies and actions taken by the civil service in its transformation journey. The chapter will show how the transformation of the public sector is linked to changes in its context.

Chapter 4 describes the cultural foundations of governance in terms of the founding political leaders' perception of Singapore's position, their articulation of the purpose and the derived principles of governance in the public sector. The chapter describes the institutional culture of the Singapore public service and how it evolved from a set of shared values that emerged during the founding years of Singapore's independence.

Chapter 5 is the first of two chapters on how policies are adapted and executed. This chapter describes in detail the processes for making and executing policies, which affects policy choices and approaches. It provides a baseline for understanding the learning and adaptive capabilities that are embedded in the chosen paths and policies. Examples will show how these capabilities have enabled dynamism in the governance of the public sector.

Chapter 6 describes how the civil service, though constrained by path dependence, has been able to adapt policies to changing circumstances and improvise and innovate to meet new requirements. We describe the development of six policy areas — economic development, biomedical sciences, car ownership and road transportation, healthcare, the Central Provident Fund, and the working poor — over a number of years to illustrate the dynamism of these paths. From these, we draw lessons regarding policy adaptation and discuss the governance approaches that enabled the public sector to continue to learn and adapt to changing conditions and emerging issues.

Chapter 7 describes how fundamental governance capabilities are ultimately embodied in leaders through their recruitment, renewal, and retention in the public sector. We discuss the human resource philosophy and practices of the public service and explain why the development and socialization of people are so crucial to dynamic governance.

Chapter 8 describes how the public service sustains institutional renewal and reconfiguration through organizational processes for re-examining assumptions by anticipating the future, for renewing activities by allocating financial resources, and for redesigning structural linkages by applying systemic disciplines.

Chapter 9 integrates the material covered in Chapters 1 to 8 and draws lessons and principles that have served the public sector well in its continuous journey of learning and change. It discusses the continuing challenges and how the public sector is addressing them. It seeks to generalize the lessons and principles learnt from the study of the Singapore public sector to other contexts, whether public sectors in other developing countries in Asia or the private sector in Singapore or elsewhere.

2

Conceptual Foundations: Governance, Institutions and Capabilities

This chapter describes the fundamental concepts of governance, institutions, and dynamic capabilities that form the bases for our framework for the study. Our conceptual framework, as shown in Figure 1.1 of Chapter 1, attempts to integrate and apply these ideas to develop a meaningful model for understanding how a system of dynamic governance works and may be developed. These concepts are mostly drawn from the institutional economics and organizational theory literature. We also drew on the work of the World Bank and other development agencies as they sought to operationalize the concept of good governance in their objectives and programs. The review in this chapter contains the highlights of our literature research and the main theories that guided our thinking, data collection, interpretation and analysis. An understanding of these concepts provides a deeper appreciation of the findings of our study and their applications to other contexts beyond Singapore.

The definitions and descriptions of the concepts in this chapter are not required to understand the principles, paths, policies, practices, and perspectives of how dynamic governance is achieved in the Singapore public service and the lessons that may be learnt. Although this chapter may be deferred without disrupting the overall flow of the book, we would recommend that the reader return to this chapter as a reference for the concepts used in the book. We will discuss the following concepts in this chapter:

(i)   governance and governments — the main themes of the book,
(ii)   institutions and institutional culture — the foundations of governance, and
(iii) organizational capabilities and how they are developed — the drivers of dynamism in governance.

This chapter describes the development of these concepts in the literature and links them to the framework in Figure 1.1 of Chapter 1 that guided the study of the Singapore public service. Our framework explores how the creation of dynamic capabilities is expressed and executed over time through adaptive paths of response to emerging policy issues, and driven by able people who led the organization, and agile processes that stimulated renewal. These provide the platform for continuous institutional learning, change and improvement. It also explores how the constant reinforcement of several authentic values expressed as abiding principles of governance became the enabling cultural foundations for dynamic institutional adaptation.

2.1 Governance and Governments

Governance deals with the processes and systems by which a society makes decisions regarding its key policy issues and objectives. Government refers to "the structures and function of public institutions. Governance is the way government gets its work done."[1] It is the process of decision-making and how decisions are implemented.[2] Government acts by using institutions, structures of authority and collaboration to allocate resources, coordinate activities and enforce rules in society.

The World Bank defines governance as "the traditions and institutions by which authority in a country is exercised."[3] It includes the:

(i)   process by which governments are selected, monitored and replaced;
(ii) capacity of the government to effectively formulate and implement sound policies; and
(iii) respect of citizens and the state for the institutions that govern economic and social interactions among them.

---

[1] Donald F Kettle (2002). *The Transformation of Governance*. Baltimore, Maryland: Johns Hopkins University Press, p. x.

[2] United Nations Economics and Social Commission for Asia and the Pacific. See website: www.unescap.org

[3] Daniel Kaufmann, Aart Kraay and Pablo Zoido-Lobaton (1999). "Governance Matters," Policy Research Working Paper 2196, World Bank Institute, October.

Six dimensions of governance are defined by the World Bank[4]:

(i)   Voice and accountability — the extent to which a country's citizens are able to participate in selecting their government, as well as freedom of expression, freedom of association, and free media;

(ii) Political stability and absence of violence — perceptions of the likelihood that the government will be destabilized or overthrown by unconstitutional or violent means, including political violence and terrorism;

(iii) Government effectiveness — the quality of public services, the quality of the civil service and the degree of its independence from political pressures, the quality of policy formulation and implementation, and the credibility of the government's commitment to such policies;

(iv) Regulatory quality — the ability of the government to formulate and implement sound policies and regulations that permit and promote private sector development;

(v)   Rule of law — the extent to which agents have confidence in and abide by the rules of society, and in particular of contract enforcement, the police, and the courts, as well as the likelihood of crime and violence;

(vi) Control of corruption — the extent to which public power is exercised for private gain, including both petty and grand forms of corruption, as well as capture of the state by elites and private interests.

Governance is "the relationship between governments and citizens that enable public policies and programs to be formulated, implemented and evaluated. In the broader context, it refers to the rules, institutions, and networks that determine how a country or an organization functions."[5] Governance is about "government's

---

[4] Daniel Kaufmann, Aart Kraay and Massimo Mastruzzi (2004). "Governance Matters III: Governance Indicators for 1996, 1998, 2000 and 2002," *World Bank Economic Review*, Vol. 18, pp. 253–287.

[5] Gambhir Bhatta (2006). *International Dictionary of Public Management and Governance*. New York: ME Sharpe Inc.

changing role in society and its changing capacity to pursue collective interests under severe external and internal constraints."[6] A civil service project team led by Andrew Tan refers to public sector governance as:

> "the manner in which the government, working together with other stakeholders in society, exercises its authority and influence in promoting the collective welfare of society and the long-term interests of the nation."[7]

We use the term "governance" in this study to refer to the chosen paths, policies, institutions and the resultant structures that collectively provide the incentives and constraints to facilitate or impede interactions that lead to economic progress and social well-being. Dynamic governance thus refers to how these chosen paths, policies, institutions, and structures adapt to an uncertain and fast changing environment so that they remain relevant and effective in achieving the long-term desired outcomes of a society. Nobel laureate Professor Amartya Sen argued that:

> "the experience of successful capitalism has always been based not just on market mechanism...but also on the development of an institutional combination of which the market economy is only one part. The invisible hand has often relied heavily on the visible."[8]

Singapore's Prime Minister Lee Hsien Loong highlighted the role of good governance when he opened the IMF-World Bank Annual meetings in September 2006:

---

[6] Jon Pierre and B Guy Peters (2000). *Governance, Politics and the State.* New York: St. Martin's Press.

[7] Andrew Tan *et al.* (2004). "Principles of Governance: Preserving our Fundamentals, Preparing for the Future." Special Study Report prepared by a group of Administrative Officers led by Andrew Tan.

[8] Amartya Sen (2006). "Good Governance in the 21st Century," Keynote address at the Raffles Forum, organized by the Lee Kuan Yew School of Public Policy, 14 September 2006, Singapore.

"The paradox of globalization is that it limits the role of governments and yet make good governance more important than ever. Good governance is not just about opening up the economy and freeing up the dead hand of bureaucracy. It is also about creating the conditions for sustained development and actively pursuing policies to make life better for all segments of the population."[9]

Good governance accomplishes social goals in a manner that is free of abuse and corruption, and with due regard for property rights and the rule of law. Good governance defines an ideal that is difficult to achieve in its totality. However, to ensure sustainable human development, actions need to be taken to work towards this ideal. The United Nations Economic and Social Commission for Asia and the Pacific defined good governance as having eight characteristics:

"It is participatory, consensus-oriented, accountable, transparent, responsive, effective and efficient, equitable and inclusive and follows the rule of law. It assures that corruption is minimized, the views of minorities are taken into account and that the voices of the most vulnerable in society are heard in decision-making. It is also responsive to the present and future needs of society."[10]

Governance capacity refers to "the capability of actors (both public, i.e., government, and private, i.e., firms) to define and shape the various processes that are necessary to provide goods and services that are demanded in society. This capacity is said to be conditioned by many variables, including the regulatory structure in which production takes place, and the institutional context that is evident in a particular setting."[11] The uniqueness of the governance context includes its

---

[9] Speech by Prime Minister Lee Hsien Loong at the opening ceremony of the IMF-World Bank Annual Meetings, 19 September 2006.

[10] www.unescap.org.

[11] Bhatta (2006).

historical, cultural and political heritage. Understanding context is necessary to decide what governance principles and structures to adopt, and how they may be adapted to suit a particular society. Of particular importance are the informal and cultural norms that have significant influence on behavior and may limit or negate the workings of formal governance rules and processes.

In a fast changing environment, the key drivers affecting a country's development and survival shift rapidly. Past success does not guarantee future survival. Good governance that stays relevant and remains effective must be dynamic. Governments need to anticipate future developments, learn continuously and renew their mindset in their approach to social and economic issues. Policies and programs that worked well in the past have to be reviewed and re-thought. Dynamic governance is about thinking ahead so that a country is better prepared for the future, thinking again so that new ideas and innovations may be incorporated into existing programs, and thinking adaptively so that the best practices may be contextualized and adapted to the needs of a particular society.

Government relates to how a society organizes itself and how governance systems are set up to achieve national goals. Does government make a difference? A special issue of the Academy of Management Review on the perspectives of how governments matter puts it simply, "After September 11, no one wondered for long *whether governments mattered* (emphasis in the original). Those in the airline business *knew* that government mattered, as all planes were grounded in less than two hours... and it was clear that governments **really** (emphasis in the original) mattered in the heroic conduct of those men and women of New York City's police, fire, and emergency services."[12] And New York's Mayor Rudy Giuliani's public leadership of the rescue effort made him a management guru on the global stage.

Can governments continually change, improve and innovate? All large, complex organizations are governed by hierarchical structures, formal rules and detailed procedures to carry out stable routine tasks in

---

[12] Peter Ring, GA Bigley, T D'Aunno and T Khanna (2005). "Perspectives on How Governments Matter," *Academy of Management Review*, Vol. 30, No. 2, pp. 308–309.

order to achieve organizational efficiency.[13] Thus public bureaucracies are often viewed to be slow, inflexible, impersonal, stifling, energy-sapping, and unable to change. Conversely, dynamic organizations are often described as fast, flexible, responsive, creative, energetic and constantly changing. These entrepreneurial organizations operate in uncertain and fast changing environments where continuous adaptation is crucial for survival and success. Public institutions that perform governance functions can enable or impede the interactions and exchanges that the private sector needs to undertake to succeed in an increasingly complex economy and sophisticated society. How can governments adapt to the need for change, be more entrepreneurial, move more quickly, and become more competitive in attracting investments and talent — in short, how can public institutions develop dynamism in their governance structures and system?

The main actors in government are the political leadership and the public sector. Both groups are needed for effective policy-making and execution. In a democratic society, political leaders are elected and ultimately accountable to the citizens. The citizens entrust political leaders with the right to make public policy decisions and to exercise the power to implement them in order to achieve desired national goals. If they do not deliver economic and social outcomes that improve the lives of their people, they may lose the legitimacy to govern and may lose the right to do so in the next elections. The political leadership sets the national agenda, is ultimately responsible for the policy choices they select and accountable for the substance and impact of the policies. The political leadership sets the policy direction, tone and environment for the public sector.

The public sector runs the public institutions that are necessary to implement policy, provide service, ensure security, and enable human interactions and exchange. Public sector institutions such as the civil service are governance organizations created through legislation to make and implement public policies to achieve national goals. Officials in the public sector are not elected through the political process but

---

[13] Charles Perrow (1986). *Complex Organizations: A Critical Essay*, 3rd Edition. NY, NY: Random House, pp. 3, 4.

are appointed under employment contracts similar to those of large private sector organizations. Public sector officials are expected to be politically neutral and be able to work with whichever political party is elected by the people. But they have to be politically sensitive to social issues so that they can work synergistically with the political leadership in making and implementing public policies and programs. In this study, our focus is on the dynamic governance capabilities developed by the public sector and the interface and impact that the political leadership has on that development.

The public sector is often huge, employs large numbers of people, and accounts for a significant portion of GDP. They shape society through their role in developing and implementing public policies, and in providing the basic infrastructure needed for a country's development. They manage policies, systems and procedures that could either facilitate or impede economic growth, improve or reduce the citizens' quality of life, and enhance or destroy a country's reputation and standing in the international community. They may manage public systems with competence and integrity, and thus help build the social capital that would enable even higher national aspirations and achievements. Or they could allow corruption to creep in and corrode the social values and fabric that eventually destroy the foundations of education and work, and the pursuit of progress.

The fundamental roles of government have not changed: promoting economic growth, maintaining social stability and ensuring security. But governments have been under pressure to become more entrepreneurial and to use less of its regulatory and coercive power. Osborne and Gaebler identified ten patterns of public sector transformation in America in the 1990s:[14]

(i)   Catalytic government: Steering rather than rowing;
(ii) Community-owned government: Empowering rather than serving;
(iii) Competitive government: Injecting competition into service delivery;

---

[14] David Osborne and Ted Gaebler (1992). *Reinventing Government*. NY: Penguin Books.

(iv) Mission-driven government: Transforming rule-driven organizations;

(v)   Results-oriented government: Funding outcomes, not inputs;

(vi) Customer-driven government: Meeting the needs of the customer, not the bureaucracy;

(vii) Enterprising government: Earning rather than spending;

(viii)Anticipatory government: Prevention rather than cure;

(ix) Decentralized government: From hierarchy to participation and teamwork;

(x)   Market-oriented government: Leveraging change through the market.

Four types of governance systems have been identified:[15]

(i)   procedural governance — the traditional bureaucratic manner of doing things;

(ii) corporate governance — governance that is goal-driven and where plans are the primary form of control over managerial action;

(iii) market governance — governance that relies on competition, and where contracts are the controls; and

(iv) network governance — governance that relies on network and co-production.

Governance by network creates public value by organizing resources across public-private boundaries rather than owning and controlling resources within the public bureaucracy. It represents a confluence of four influential trends that are altering the shape of public sectors worldwide[16]:

(i)   Third-party government: the increase in using private firms and non-profit organizations — as opposed to government employees — to deliver services and fulfill policy goals;

---

[15] Bhatta (2006).

[16] Stephen Goldsmith and William D Eggers (2004). *Governing by Network*. Washington DC: Brookings Institution Press.

(ii) Joined-up government: the increasing tendency for multiple government agencies, sometimes even at multiple levels of government, to join together to provide integrated service;

(iii) The digital revolution: the technological advances that enable organizations to collaborate in real time with external partners;

(iv) Citizen demand: increased citizen demand for more control over their own lives and more choices and varieties in their government services, to match the customized service provision technology that has spawned in the private sector.

2.2 Institutions

Institutions refer both to the social rules and legal framework within which activities take place in society, and the organizations set up to coordinate the activities or enforce the rules.

> "Institutions are patterns of social activity that give shape to collective and individual experience. An institution is a complex whole that guides and sustains individual identity... Institutions form individuals by making possible or impossible certain ways of behaving and relating to others. They shape character by assigning responsibility, demanding accountability, and providing the standards in terms of which each person recognizes the excellence of his or her achievements."[17]

Institutions are the rules of the game in a society, the humanly devised constraints that structure incentives in human exchange and shape human interaction. Institutions form the incentive structure of a society and the political and economic institutions, in consequence, are the underlying determinant of economic performance.[18] By structuring the incentives in specific ways, they provide the inducements for

---

[17] RN Bellah, R Madsen, SM Tipton, WM Sullivan and A Swidler (1991). *The Good Society.* NY: Knopf, p. 40.

[18] Douglass C North (1993). "Economic Performance through Time," Nobel Prize Lecture, 9 December 1993.

people and organizations to invest in, expand, and apply their knowledge and assets to solve problems important to a particular society.

As a society develops, more of its economic and social transactions move from personal to impersonal exchange which exploits division of labor, specialization of knowledge and economies of scale. But the move to impersonal exchange increases the costs of transaction even as it decreases the costs of production. Though an effective price system is an essential prerequisite, it is not adequate for ensuring that the distributed knowledge resulting from specialization is linked effectively to produce desired social goods and services.

> "The essential public goods, asymmetric information, and ubiquitous externalities require that institutions and organizations be created to integrate the dispersed knowledge at low costs of transacting." [19]

Institutions and the technology employed determine the transaction and transformation costs that add up to the costs of production. They reduce uncertainty by providing a stable structure for exchange, reducing transaction costs, and enabling people to make substantive choices. Without institutional constraints, the information asymmetry among parties and their self-interested behavior would foreclose complex exchange because of the uncertainty that the other party will find it in his or her interest to live up to the agreement.[20] Institutions matter when it is costly to transact. They affect economic performance by their effect on the costs of exchange and production. As institutions evolve, they alter the choices available to market participants.

Institutions may be formally constituted rules, laws and constitutions or informal constraints such as social norms, conventions and self-imposed codes of behavior that dictate how interactions

---

[19] Douglass North (2005). *Understanding the Process of Economic Change*. Princeton University Press, p. 121.

[20] Douglass C North (1990). *Institutions, Institutional Change and Economic Performance*. NY: Cambridge University Press, p. 33.

take place among people and organizations. Informal constraints are socially transmitted information that forms the heritage and culture, and they arise to coordinate the repeated interactions among people. Informal constraints are:

(i)   extensions, elaborations and modifications of formal rules,
(ii)   socially sanctioned norms of behavior, and
(iii) internally enforced standards of conduct.[21]

Informal social norms sometimes exert a greater influence than formal rules by constraining the maximizing behavior of otherwise self-interested parties. They make complex exchange viable by reducing measurement and enforcement costs. However, as the increasing specialization and division of labor in economic transactions make societies more complex, more of the unwritten traditions and customs tend to be formalized and written into constitutions, legal rules and regulations, property rights, and contracts.

Changing formal rules and structures to conform to practices of good governance is only a start. The deeply ingrained informal norms and practices in the local governance and institutional context may limit the application of these rules or may require adaptation before they are accepted politically and socially. After this process is complete and the new governance rules are enacted, individual and organizations would begin to play by the new rules and eventually develop new rigidities that make them to continue reinforcing the chosen paths. This pattern of governance becomes risky when technology changes, competition intensifies and new global developments may make what was once "good governance", obsolete.

Institutions also are used to refer to a collection of organizations such as government agencies and banks, which are part of what is known as an institutional milieu in the public management system.[22] Using a metaphor of a competitive game, a distinction can be made between institutions as rules, both formal and informal, and institutions as players (organizations). Institutionalism refers to the notion that

---

[21] North (1990), p. 40.
[22] Bhatta (2006).

"institutions play a large role in the effect of public policies, and the belief in the primacy of institutions as a way to understand how public actions are done and how citizens' demands are aggregated."[23]

Institutional arrangements and functioning go beyond rules and include the cost and effectiveness of enforcement, such as ascertaining violations and the severity of punishment.[24] Even when the rules are the same, the outcomes may differ because of differences in enforcement mechanisms, the way enforcement occurs, the norms of behavior, and the subjective mental models of the players. Institutions assure cooperation among contracting parties by forming a communication mechanism that provides information to police deviations and ensuring a credible threat of coercive force of state-sanctioned authority for punishing violations. It is difficult to sustain complex exchanges without a third party to enforce transactions. That is why a fair and functioning legal system is such an important institution.

Enforcement is typically imperfect because of the costs of measuring performance and determining violations, and "the fact that enforcement is undertaken by agents whose own utility functions influence outcomes."[25] Institutions and organizations become inseparable when organizations are inevitably created to formulate, implement and enforce the rules. "An institutional environment that induces credible commitment entails the complex institutional framework of formal rules, informal constraints and enforcement that together make possible low-cost transacting."[26]

The overall stability of an institutional framework makes complex exchanges possible across time and space. They allow people to go about the everyday process of making exchanges without having to think out exactly the terms of an exchange at each point and in each instance.[27] Institutional stability is a necessary condition for human exchange but not a sufficient condition for efficiency.

---

[23] Bhatta (2006).

[24] North (1990), p. 4.

[25] Ibid, p. 54.

[26] Ibid, p. 58.

[27] Ibid, p. 83.

Policies and institutions are interlinked in several ways.[28] First, policy design should take institutional capacity into account. When institutions are weak or dysfunctional, simple policies that limit administrative demands and public discretion work best. Where institutions are stronger, more challenging public initiatives can be effective. Second, policies do not emerge from a vacuum but are shaped by the institutional and political rules of the game. Third, policy choice can significantly influence the way institutions develop.

2.3 Dynamic Governance and Institutional Culture

Dynamic governance implies a proactive approach to policy-making and implementation that constantly anticipates future developments, gathers feedback, evaluates performance and learns from others so that governance systems and institutions remain relevant and effective for economic and social development. The essence of dynamism in governance is continuous learning, new thinking and new ideas that lead to continuous modifications of institutions — rules, incentives, structures and enforcement mechanisms — as problems evolve and new issues emerge. Mantzavinos, North and Shariq state that:

> "The greatest challenge for the social sciences is to explain change — or more specifically, social, political, economic and organizational change. The starting point must be an account of human learning, which is the fundamental prerequisite for explaining such change. The ability to learn is the main reason for the observed plasticity of human behavior, and the interaction of learning individuals give rise to change in society, polity, economy and organizations."[29]

---

[28] This section is drawn from the World Bank Report (2000) on "Reforming Public Institutions and Strengthening Governance".

[29] C Mantzavinos, D North and S Shariq (2004). "Learning, Institutions, and Economic Performance," *Perspectives on Politics*, Vol. 2, No. 1, pp. 75–84.

Institutions tend to change incrementally and gradually through marginal adjustments when immediate issues require solutions that are determined by the relative bargaining power of organizations in the specific institutional context. Institutional change is characterized by path-dependency, where previously chosen paths narrow the choices that are feasible for the future. History matters when it comes to institutional change. Four self-reinforcing mechanisms that give rise to increasing returns and path-dependence in technological change apply equally to institutional change.[30] They are:

(i)   large set-up or fixed costs,
(ii) learning effects,
(iii) coordination effects, and
(iv) adaptive expectations.

Once institutions are set up and working at significant costs, people learn how to operate and coordinate their exchanges, and expect that the arrangements would persist. "The interdependent web of institutional matrix produces massive increasing returns."[31] Path-dependence comes from the increasing returns from mechanisms that reinforce the direction on a given path. The switching costs are high and people would be reluctant to abandon existing accepted practices.

The political framework provides the environment for evolutionary institutional change. When political leadership changes in response to societal changes in values and preferences, there would be pressure to re-examine the institutional framework prevalent under previous political regimes. Institutional change tends to be incremental and path-dependent because the process by which we arrive at today's institutions is relevant and constrains future choices. Even when formal rules change, informal constraints that are culturally derived and defined may not change immediately and can continue to exert significant influence on behavior.

---

[30] Brian Arthur (1988). "Self–Reinforcing Mechanisms in Economics," in *The Economy as an Evolving Complex System*, PW Anderson, KJ Arrows and D Pines (eds.). MA: Addison-Wesley.

[31] North (1990), p. 85.

Nobel laureate Douglass North explains five characteristics of institutional change:[32]

(i)   The continuous interaction between institutions and organizations in the economic setting of scarcity and hence competition is key to institutional change.
(ii)   Competition forces organizations continually to invest in new skills and knowledge to survive. The kind of skills and knowledge individuals and their organizations acquire will shape evolving perceptions about opportunities and hence choices that will incrementally alter institutions.
(iii) The institutional framework provides the incentive structure that dictates the kinds of skills and knowledge perceived to have the maximum payoff.
(iv)   Perceptions are derived from the mental constructs of the players.
(v)   The economies of scope, complementarities, and network externalities of an institutional matrix make institutional change overwhelmingly incremental and path-dependent.

He further elaborates that in an economic system determined by demographic features, the stock of knowledge and the institutional framework, the process of change is really the process of learning. Learning involves a cognitive structure of how we perceive and categorize events, and the mental models used to interpret and make sense of the environment. Learning takes place when we reflect on feedback, new information and experiences, other people's ideas and experiences, and allow them either to strengthen or modify our mental models.

Dynamic governance recognizes that governments and societies have to continually learn and adjust in order for their countries to survive and succeed in an era of intense competition, global connectivity and rapid technological change. Even though vigorous competition creates incentives for institutional learning and change, there is no guarantee that the cumulative past experience of a society,

---

[32] North (2005).

whether they were successes or failures, would adequately prepare it to face new challenges or exploit new opportunities. "The speed of economic change is a function of the rate of learning... Societies that get 'stuck' embody belief systems and institutions that fail to confront and solve new problems of society complexity."[33] The strengthening of our current thinking and the development of new thinking patterns are thus fundamental to learning and provides the foundation to institutional change and dynamic governance.

The culture of a society comes from an accumulation of experience and its collective learning in its adaptive attempts to solve frequently encountered problems of the past. The learning process is a function of the experiences we confront and how these experiences are perceived, filtered, categorized and interpreted by our mental models. The perception of the value of these ideas in the survival and success of a society becomes deeply imprinted in the minds of the people. Over time, a common cultural heritage is formed, reducing the divergence of mental models, and creating a means for transferring these common social perceptions to future generations. This cultural heritage shapes how people think, evaluate, and decide across a spectrum of choices, including governance. The cultural foundations of governance are derived from how leaders perceive the strengths and vulnerabilities of a country's position in the world, which then influence the intended purposes of the governance systems and institutions that are created. Principles are then derived to guide policy decision-making and implementation so that the purposes may be accomplished.

The dynamic process underlying institutional change depends on clear intentions of leaders to adapt to changing circumstances, and a fundamental change in their mental models, both of which emerge from social learning that then shapes the institutional framework, as Nobel Laureate North elaborates:

"There are three parts to the process of economic change: the 'reality' of an economy, the perceptions humans in a

---

[33] Douglass North (1994). "Economic Performance Through Time," *American Economic Review*, June, p. 364.

society possess about that reality, and, given the beliefs that they possess, the structure they impose to reduce uncertainty and control the economy. The process of change results from a continuous change in that reality which results in changing the perceptions, which in turn induce the players to modify or alter the structure, which in turn leads to changes in that reality — an ongoing process." [34]

If governance is not guided by clear purpose and principles derived from perceptions of position, then adopted rules and structures become self-perpetuating and bureaucracy grows. When the environment changes, there is no basis to review and revise existing governance systems and structures. In fact the changes may make incumbent leaders and organizations feel insecure and threatened because they may lack the abilities to function in the new context. These dysfunctional behaviors cannot be challenged without a shared sense of purpose and a strong commitment to principles that facilitate change. Comprehending the imperative to change requires values and mental models that want to understand the need to adapt and are able to perceive emerging patterns that show that need. A change in culture, beliefs and assumptions, and mental models is necessary for institutional change, which in turn affects what public policies would be reconsidered, redesigned, and renewed.

2.4 Organizational Capabilities: Knowledge and Skills to Perform Activities to Achieve Intended Results

An organizational capability [35] refers to an organization's deliberate use of its knowledge and resources to perform a coordinated task

---

[34] North (2005).

[35] David J Collis (1994). "How Valuable are Organizational Capabilities?" *Strategic Management Journal.*
G Dosi, RR Nelson and SG Winter (eds.) (2000). *The Nature and Dynamics of Organizational Capabilities.* NY: Oxford University Press.
CE Helfat (ed.) (2003). *The SMS Blackwell Handbook of Organizational Capabilities.* MA: Blackwell Publishing.

to achieve specific results. Capabilities are distinctive ways of doing things, and organizations often differ in how they accomplish functionally similar tasks. Knowledge is conceived as know-how embedded in the organization's activities, not as passive library stocks in the heads of participants.[36] Capability is understood in terms of the organizational structures and managerial processes that enable productive activity. The implication is that organizations with superior systems and structures are more capable and perform better.[37]

Capabilities are developed and deployed through conscious and deliberate decisions, choices, planning, organized activity and deployment of expertise. They are acquired over a protracted period of time through processes of organizational learning.[38] These systems of learning include incremental learning by doing and learning by using[39] and step-function learning that may result in fundamental change to core knowledge.[40] Managerial cognitive maps, especially their beliefs, problem representations and feedback interpretation, influence the direction of capability development.[41] Managers select and promote particular capabilities because of their perceived success in responding to the demands of markets and in enabling their organizations to enhance their reputations and reap financial rewards. However, organizations tend to satisfice rather than optimize in learning new capabilities as evidenced by empirical observations

---

[36] B Kogut and U Zander (1992). "Knowledge of the Firm, Combinative Capabilities and the Replication of Technology," *Organization Science*, Vol. 3, pp. 383–396.

[37] DJ Teece, G Pisano and A Shuen(1997). "Dynamic Capabilities and Strategic Management," *Strategic Management Journal*, Vol. 18, pp. 509–534.

[38] L Dietrickx and K Cool (1989). "Asset Stock Accumulation and Sustainability of Competitive Advantage," *Management Science*, Vol. 35, pp. 1504–1513.

[39] N Rosenberg (1982). *Inside the Black Box: Technology and Economics*. Cambridge, UK: Cambridge University Press.

[40] CE Helfat and RS Raubitschek (2003). "Product Sequencing: Co-evolution of Knowledge, Capabilities and Products," in CE Helfat (ed.) *The SMS Blackwell Handbook of Organizational Capabilities*. MA: Blackwell Publishing.

[41] G Gavetti (2005). "Cognition and Hierarchy: Rethinking the Microfoundations of Capabilities' Development," *Organization Science*, Vol. 16, No. 6, pp. 599–617.

of how learning tends to lose momentum when a threshold cost or achievement is reached.[42]

The bounded rationality of managers, the accumulated learning of organizations and the tendency to search for solutions to problems in proximate locations lead to path-dependence in the development of organizational capabilities.[43] Options for the development of capabilities are often constrained by past heritage and existing accumulated investments in physical, organizational and human capital. Further, organizational capabilities are contextually connected to a broader institutional and policy environment that may regulate or provide incentives for their development.[44]

Organizational capabilities are closely related to concepts of organizational routines[45] and organizational resources[46]. The literature suggests that organizational capabilities are developed from strategically combining and recombining[47] routines (basic functional and operational activities) and resources (knowledge, skills and their complementary assets). The concept of dynamic capabilities adds a second-order dimension to our understanding of the development of organizational capabilities. Dynamic capabilities are conceptualized as the capacity to change both routines and resources or core capabilities to adapt to technological and environmental change. These concepts will be discussed in more detail in the following sections. The conceptual differences among the various terms are subtle and researchers often use terms like "competencies", "capabilities" and "resources" synonymously.

---

[42] SG Winter (2000). "The Satisficing Principle in Capability Learning," *Strategic Management Journal*, Vol. 21, pp. 981–996.

[43] WM Cohen and DA Levinthal (1990). "Absorptive Capacity: A New Perspective on Learning and Innovation," *Administrative Science Quarterly*, Vol. 35, pp. 128–152.

[44] Winter (2000).

[45] RM Cyert and JG March (1963). *A Behavioral Theory of the Firm*. NJ: Prentice Hall. RR Nelson and SG Winter (1982). *An Evolutionary Theory of Economic Change*. Cambridge, MA: Harvard University Press.

[46] J Barney (1991). "Firm Resources and Sustained Competitive Advantage," *Journal of Management*, Vol. 17, pp. 99–120; RR Nelson (1991). "How Do Firms Differ, and How Does it Matter?" *Strategic Management Journal*, Vol. 12, pp. 61–74; B Wernerfelt (1984). "A Resource-based View of the Firm," *Strategic Management Journal*, Vol. 5, pp. 171–180.

[47] Kogut and Zander (1992).

2.4.1 *Routines: Standard Processes for Operational Activities*

Routines are regular ways of doing the repetitive tasks of voluminous daily business activities which are often executed semi-automatically in response to internal or external input flows. They involve recognizable patterns of interdependent actions involving multiple people and organizational units.[48] Routines are the basic processes and policies for performing normal, predictable administrative, functional and operational transactions in a coordinated manner to produce specific outputs. They are similar to standard operating procedures that bring stability to organizational activity.[49] They are predictable, rule-based, well specified and stable, with strong elements of continuity. Examples of organizational routines include technical procedures for producing things, processes for hiring people or ordering goods, policies for advertising, capital investments, and R&D.

Routines are identifiable behavioral patterns of organizational activities embodied in human and capital assets that both provide value and create constraints for organizational change.[50] They enable an organization to reduce complexity, promote cognitive efficiency and achieve operational results. Well-defined routines structure a large part of organizational activities at any particular time and they employ the individual skills and tacit knowledge of the organization.

Routines are like genes, encoding the essential coordinating information for efficient functioning of the organization and they are remembered through repetition. They are both the product of and the platform for organization learning.[51] Routines define desired behavior norms and are subject to normal management monitoring and control.

---

[48] MS Feldman and BT Pentland (2003). "Reconceptualizing Organizational Routines as a Source of Flexibility and Change," *Administrative Science Quarterly*, Vol. 48, pp. 94–118.

[49] Cyert and March (1963).

[50] Dosi, Nelson and Winter (2000); Nelson and Winter (1982); M Zollo and SG Winter (2002). "Deliberate Learning and the Evolution of Dynamic Capabilities," *Organization Science*, Vol. 13, pp. 339–351.

[51] B Levitt and JG March (1988). "Organizational Learning," *Annual Review of Sociology*, Vol. 14, pp. 314–340.

Prevailing routines define a truce, and attempts to change routines often provoke conflicts in the organization.[52]

Routines form the constituents of organizational capabilities, individually or collectively. An organizational capability can be defined as a "high-level routine (or collection of routines) that, together with its implementing input flows, confers upon an organization's management a set of decision options for producing significant outputs of a particular type."[53] Capabilities may be differentiated from routines in terms of scale — capabilities are larger; significance to the organization — capabilities have bigger impact; and the intentionality of design and management control — organizations have greater consciousness of capabilities.

The structure of routines evolves slowly over the long term with progressive change in an evolutionary manner following the economic analogue of biological processes of variation, selection, and retention. The evolution of routine structures through performance feedback and via trial and error experimentation can result in enhanced capabilities.[54]

However, actual performance of the routines by specific people at specific times in specific places may vary from the prescribed structure as they respond to prevailing circumstances and to their own perceptions and reflections.[55] Individuals can exercise such flexibility because formal structures typically specify a routine only for a typical situation, and even then cannot specify all the possible contextual details needed. These are not extraneous exceptions but an inherent part of the performance of a routine. Further, people continuously adapt and change the performance of a routine in response to whether the intended outcome is achieved and whether other unintended (may be desirable or undesirable) outcomes arise.[56] The process of

---

[52] Nelson and Winter (1982).

[53] Winter (2000).

[54] D Lavie (2006). "Capability Reconfiguration: An Analysis of Incumbent Responses to Technological Change," *Academy of Management Review*, Vol. 31, pp. 153–174.

[55] Feldman and Pentland (2003).

[56] MS Feldman (2000). "Organizational Routines as Sources of Continuous Change," *Organization Science*, Vol. 11, No. 6, pp. 611–629.

engaging in organizational routines through reflective thought and adaptive action is a form of organizational learning and can lead to new capabilities for the organization.

The intentional or unintentional variations in the routines that are repeated may become selectively retained to modify the original structure of the routines, resulting in adaptation and change. While routine performances may be flexible, the persistence of the routine structure depends on its embeddedness, which is the degree to which the use of the routine overlaps with other technological, coordinating, and cultural structures in the organization's context.[57]

2.4.2 Resources: Tangible and Intangible Assets for Executing Strategies

The resource-based perspective conceptualize organizations as bundles of resources to explain how organizations create and sustain superior performance over time.[58] Resources are tangible assets such as specialized equipment, and intangible assets such as knowledge, skills and expertise that enable an organization to conceive of and execute unique strategies to achieve its purposes and desired outcomes. Although this view of resources is similar to the concept of capabilities described earlier, the specific focus on differentiated strategies and superior outcomes is fairly unique. Otherwise, the terms "competencies", "capabilities" and "resources" are sometimes used synonymously.

Performance and growth are understood in terms of the possession, development and exploitation of a bundle of unique and idiosyncratic resources.[59] Resources are idiosyncratic because they are not easily separable from their organizational context and may not have a natural market price. Strategic input resources cannot simply

---

[57] JA Howard-Grenville (2005). "The Persistence of Flexible Organizational Routines: The Role of Agency and Organizational Context," *Organization Science*, Vol. 16, No. 6, pp. 618–636.

[58] CK Prahalad and G Hamel (1990). "The Core Competence of the Corporation," *Harvard Business Review*, June, pp. 79–91; Barney (1991); Nelson (1991); Wernerfelt (1984).

[59] ET Penrose (1959). *The Theory of the Growth of the Firm.* NY: Wiley.

be purchased because of non existent or imperfect strategic factor markets. Organizations in the same industry may possess different bundles of resources and these resource differences may persist over time.[60] The development of resources is often tacit and complex and the augmentation of resources takes time.

Value-creating organizational resources that are not easily replicated have four main attributes: valuable, rare, inimitable, and non-substitutable.[61] They should be valuable in enabling the organization to exploit opportunities or neutralize threats, rare in that the resources are not readily available to all players in abundance, costly to imitate, and not easily substituted with other resources. Imitation may be costly because of the need for a high level of initial resources, time compression diseconomies in building intangible assets, dependence of unique historical conditions that cannot be replicated, or socially complex and causally ambiguous linkages in the organization.[62]

Routines are predefined ways of performing standardized transactions that are fairly common across organizations, and while valuable, do not necessarily possess attributes of rareness, inimitability and non-substitutability. While routines are previously learned patterns of action, resources that have potential for strategic options require deliberate direction, definition, and decision. Resources may be derived from a major routine or a combination of routines[63] but their development requires clear strategic intent, managerial choice, and focused investments sustained over extended periods. Leveraging organizational routines and resources requires the managerial ability to perceive their strategic value, to amplify their contributions, to replicate them across settings, and to creatively combine them in

---

[60] J Barney and AM Arikan (2001). "The Resource-Based View: Origins and Implications," in MA Hitt, RE Freeman and JS Harrison (eds.). *The Blackwell Handbook of Strategic Management.* Oxford, UK: Blackwell Publishing.

[61] J Barney (1997). *Gaining and Sustaining Competitive Advantage.* MA: Addison Wesley.

[62] Dietrickx and Cool (1989).

[63] Samina Karim and Will Mitchell (2003) "Path-Dependent and Path-Breaking Change: Reconfiguring Business Resources following acquisitions in the US Medical Sector, 1979–1995," in CN Helfat (ed.). *The SMS Blackwell Handbook of Organizational Capabilities.* MA: Blackwell Publishing.

novel ways to establish new capabilities.[64] Organizations need to identify their critical resources and continue to nurture, maintain and renew them through appropriate long-term policies and investments. Organizations with resource disadvantages may seek to improve their performance by acquiring the needed resources or duplicating them through imitation or substitution.

2.4.3 *Dynamic Capabilities: Capacity to Change Routines and Resources*

In situations of rapid and unpredictable change, established routines and resources often cause organizations to continue existing ways of doing things that may no longer be relevant or competitive, which may lead to organizational failure. In periods of major technological change, incumbents are often slow in adjusting their capabilities and strategic leadership often passes to new players.[65]

New entrants are more dynamic because they are not constrained by path dependencies and the rigidities of existing organizational positions inherited by incumbents. Incumbents often find making path-breaking change to be very difficult because of the values and behavior imprinted into the organizational system by its founders, leading them to engage in only marginal changes in path-dependent ways.[66] The development of dynamic capabilities is shaped by an organization's asset position through its accumulated investments in its knowledge

---

[64] SG Winter (1995). "Four Rs of Profitability: Rents, Resources, Routines, and Replication," in CA Montgomery (ed.). *Resource-based and Evolutionary Theories of the Firm: Towards a Synthesis*, Chapter 7. London: Kluwer Academic Publishers, pp. 147–178.

[65] RM Henderson and KB Clark (1990). "Architectural Innovation: The Configuration of Existing Product Technologies and the Failure of Existing Firms," *Administrative Science Quarterly*, Vol. 35, pp. 9–30; M Tushman and P Anderson (1986). "Technological Discontinuities and Organizational Environments," *Administrative Science Quarterly*, Vol. 31, pp. 439–465.

[66] B Kogut (2003). "Imprinting or Emergence, Structure or Rules, or Why Dirty Dancing is Always Better When You Are More Than Two," in CE Helfat (ed.). *The SMS Blackwell Handbook of Organizational Capabilities*. MA: Blackwell Publishing; Daniel A Levinthal (2003). "Imprinting and the Evolution of Firm Capabilities," in CE Helfat (ed.). *The SMS Blackwell Handbook of Organizational Capabilities*. MA: Blackwell Publishing; A Stinchcombe (1965). "Social Structure and Organizations," in J March (ed.). *Handbook of Organizations*. Chicago: Rand McNally.

and other complementary assets. The evolutionary paths of dynamic capabilities are constrained by what an organization has adopted or inherited, which affect their trial, feedback and evaluation.[67]

Dynamic capabilities may be learned and systemic organizational processes can be designed, implemented and sustained to build, integrate, adapt and reconfigure operational routines and core capabilities in pursuit of improved effectiveness.[68] Dynamic capabilities rest on three organizational processes:

(i)   organizational coordination and integration through coherence in design and execution,
(ii) organizational learning through repetition, experimentation, social interaction and search, and
(iii) organizational transformation through the reconfiguration of capabilities.

Organizations with dynamic capabilities have the capacity to renew their competencies so as to achieve congruence with their changing environments.[69] Dynamic capabilities thus often take the form of search and learning routines. The concept of dynamic capabilities emphasizes the role of strategic leadership in appropriately adapting, integrating and reconfiguring internal and external organizational skills, resources and competencies to match the requirements of a changing environment. Examples of dynamic capabilities would include business model reinvention, process improvement, product development, organizational restructuring and post-acquisition integration.

Dynamic capabilities emerge from the co-evolution of the learning mechanisms of tacit experience accumulation with explicit knowledge articulation and codification activities. Experience accumulation builds skills based on repeated execution of similar tasks and thus is a central learning process for developing routines. Organizational capabilities improve as people become more aware

---

[67] Teece, Pisano and Shuen (1997).

[68] Zollo and Winter (2002).

[69] KM Eisendardt and JA Martin (2000). "Dynamic Capabilities: What Are They?" *Strategic Management Journal*, Vol. 21, pp. 1105–1121; Teece, Pisano and Shuen (1997).

of the performance implications of their actions, which is a direct consequence of knowledge articulation efforts aimed at understanding the causal links between action and results. Knowledge codification goes beyond knowledge articulation by capturing the knowledge in explicit documents and tools to facilitate replication of specific actions to obtain the desired results.

Capabilities may also be reconfigured through the acquisition, recombination, integration, and shedding of resources.[70] The mechanisms for reconfiguring capabilities include substitution in the overall capability portfolio, capability evolution involving continuous experimentation, and capability transformation through purposeful managerial action and organizational investments.[71] New capabilities are often developed by recombining existing capabilities with other knowledge, which is affected by the organizing principles guiding an organization's operations.[72]

The nature of dynamic capabilities depends on the rate of change in the market. In moderately dynamic markets where change occurs along roughly predictable and linear paths, stable routines and processes can become robust capabilities, relying on learning before doing and detailed execution with existing knowledge. In high velocity markets where market boundaries are blurred and successful business models unclear with players who are ambiguous and shifting, capabilities are more improvisational processes relying on a few simple rules that specify boundary conditions or priorities relying on learning by doing and iterative execution to gain new knowledge for adaptation.[73]

Dynamic capability development is a quest for strategic resilience. Resilience is not about responding to a one-time crisis or setback, but is about continuously anticipating and adjusting to deep secular trends that may impair the effectiveness of an organization.[74] Resilience is

---

[70] Eisenhardt and Martin (2000).

[71] Lavie (2006).

[72] Kogut and Zander (1992).

[73] Eisenhardt and Martin (2000).

[74] G Hamel and L Valikangas (2003). "The Quest for Resilience," *Harvard Business Review*, September, pp. 52–63.

about having the capacity to change before the case for change becomes desperately obvious. Resilience requires innovation with respect to those values, processes and behavior that systematically constrain organizations from the transformation needed to face new challenges and new realities.

2.4.4 Routines, Resources and Resilience: An Integrated Framework of Organizational Capabilities

The above descriptions of routines, resources and resilience reflect the development of organizational capabilities in the literature. There is overlap in the use of these terms and in understanding how these capabilities may be developed. We integrate the concepts of routines, resources and resilience as three forms of organizational capabilities into an overall framework as shown in Figure 2.1.

The framework shows the commonalities, differences and relationships among routines, resources and resilience. While routines, resources and resilience represent three forms of organizational capabilities in that they reflect an organization's deployment of tangible and intangible assets to perform tasks in a coordinated manner to

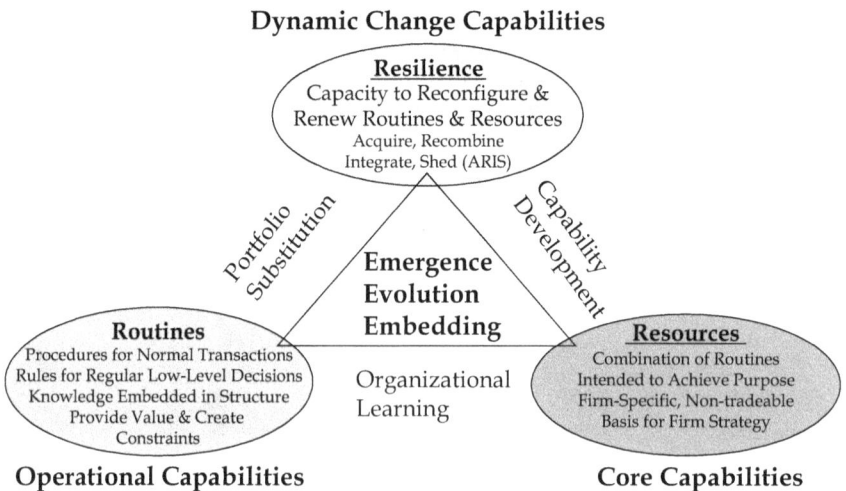

Figure 2.1. An Organizational Capabilities Framework

achieve specific outcomes, they differ in the nature of tasks for which they are most effective.

Routines are operational capabilities since they are well specified rules and procedures designed for the regular, predictable, repetitive and high volume transactions of an organization. *Resources* are core capabilities because they enable an organization to formulate and execute unique value-creating strategies to achieve its mission and purpose. Core capabilities have a strategic focus that go beyond the operational nature of routines although they may come from specific critical routines or be formed by combining routines. Dynamic capabilities reflect a second-order organizational capability to change and adapt internal resources that develop strategic *resilience* in a changing environment. Dynamic capabilities are transformational in nature because their focus is the reconfiguration and renewal of both routines and resources.

The mechanisms for capability reconfiguration[75] are mapped as sides of the triangle in the framework in Figure 2.1 to show the relationships among operational routines, core capabilities and dynamic capabilities. Operational routines can be evolved into core capabilities through *organizational learning* processes such as continuous experimentation, environmental scanning and knowledge codification.

The relationship between operational routines and dynamic capabilities takes the form of *portfolio substitution*. Since operational routines provide the capacity for performing basic organizational activities, organizations can adapt and change only when their portfolio of operating routines change. The process of portfolio substitution involves determining which existing routines to keep and discard and what new routines would need to be acquired or built.

The relationship between core capabilities and dynamic capabilities involve deliberate synchronized action and investment to transform existing capabilities and develop new ones so that new value creating strategies may be implemented in response to environmental

---

[75] Lavie (2006).

and technological change. The process of *capability development* may involve hiring people with different skills and perspectives, learning from alliance partners or newly acquired businesses, and integrating existing capabilities with new skills and know-how into new systems and structures.

An example of an academic institution would clarify the differences among operating routines, core capabilities and dynamic capabilities. The regular, predictable activities that form the operating routines of a university involve the rules and procedures for evaluating and accepting potential students, enrolling new students, registering for classes, recording grades, and graduating students. For faculty, there are operating routines for hiring faculty, assigning them to teach classes, assessing performance and administrating research fund allocations. These are operating routines common to all universities and involve the basic activities necessary to operate a university. However, these operating routines do not differentiate one university from another in terms of quality, strategy or academic reputation

The core capabilities of a particular university relate to what it is able to do differently or do particularly well in pursuit of its chosen strategy. For example, a university that seeks to excel in research may develop policies and processes to select and attract highly qualified faculty, to provide faculty with the time, support and resources they need for research, to assess research performance and potential, and to retain the professors who meet the required standards. The capabilities for implementing such a strategy would differ from the operating routines of another university that view faculty as mere teachers for mounting the required classes in the curriculum. Similarly, all universities have routines for recruiting and selecting students, and yet a particular university may go beyond a regular recruitment routine and build it into a branding capability that attracts highly qualified students as part of its strategy. The research or branding capabilities may be built from existing operating routines but they are imbued with higher levels of expertise, or executed with totally different policies and procedures. They may combine existing routines and integrate them so that they become self-reinforcing and attain qualitatively different and superior outcomes.

An example of dynamic change capabilities in a university could be how it deploys and exploits its resources to continuously adapt and renew its curriculum and pedagogy to meet the changing requirements of the graduate marketplace and the global economy. Another dynamic capability could be its capacity to attract new talent and expertise to reposition itself for emerging areas of scientific research.

For product manufacturers, routines comprise policies and procedures common to all manufacturers such as maintaining facilities, hiring workers, buying raw materials, making products and managing inventory. Manufacturers competing on the basis of product quality may develop capabilities in product design, quality management, marketing and branding, while other manufacturers competing on the basis of cost may develop capabilities for raw materials sourcing, just-in-time inventory systems and lean production, outsourcing and off-shoring management. Dynamic change capabilities for manufacturers include research and development, mergers and acquisition integration, and customer relationship management.

For financial institutions like banks, routines include the procedures for handling various financial transactions such as deposits, loans, cheque clearing and funds transfer. Depending on the strategy of banks, capabilities may include dynamic risk management, retail distribution network, superior customer service and corporate banking in specific sectors. Dynamic change capabilities may include technology development, product development, new market development and integration of new acquisitions.

The framework of organizational capabilities provides the conceptual basis for identifying the operating routines, core capabilities and dynamic capabilities in the Singapore public sector. These are shown as operations, policy and change capabilities in Figure 2.2.

Routines are the rules and procedures for managing operations in the public sector. Many operational activities may be listed depending on the specific public agency involved. Generally, operational routines in the public sector relate to what are common transactions for most government agencies, which include the delivery of public services, the monitoring, processing and approval of permits and licensing of regulated activities, managing and maintaining public infrastructure

Change

Dynamic Capabilities
Think Ahead
Think Again
Think Across

Emergence
Evolution
Embedding

Routine Capabilities
Deliver Public Services
Regulated Activities
Manage Infrastructure
Keep Law & Order

Core Capabilities
Identify Issues
Influence Choices
Implement Decisions

Operations   Policy

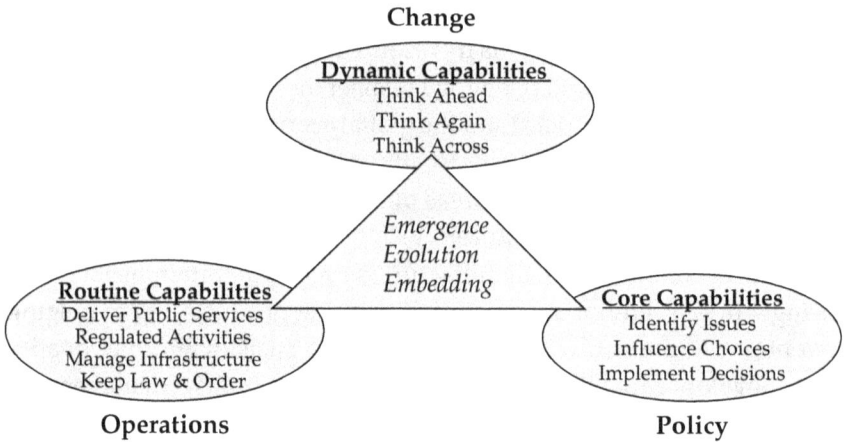

Figure 2.2. Three Levels of Public Sector Capabilities

such as roads, ports, utilities and the power grid, and the maintenance of law and order such as policing and administration of justice.

The leadership of the Singapore civil service views public policy as its main mission and thus the core capabilities relate to policy-making and implementation processes, which include identifying key issues for policy attention and review, influencing the choices of major decision-makers and stakeholders, and implementing the decisions made so that desired outcomes are achieved.

Dynamic change capabilities that enable the continuous transformation of the Singapore public sector are derived from a strong future orientation among the leaders, an ability to think systemically and long-term and a pragmatic approach to problem-solving that encourages learning and adaptations that work. These are expressed as the capabilities to think ahead, think again and think across. The cumulative result is continuous change in public policies that ensure more effective outcomes, redesign of operating routines that achieve better efficiencies, and development of new platforms for public service delivery.

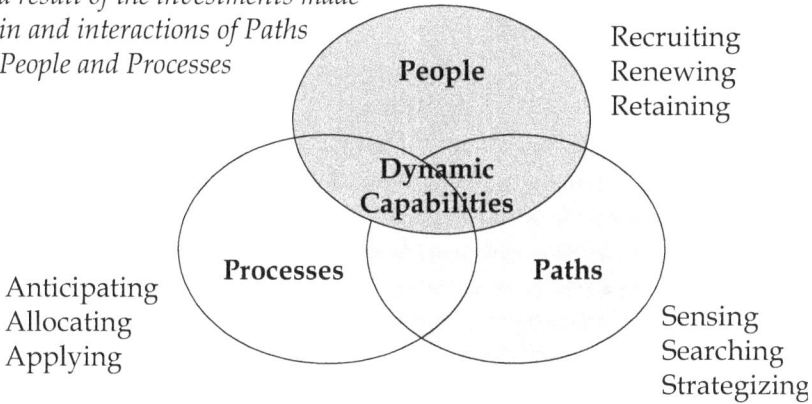

Capabilities become dynamic as a result of the investments made in and interactions of Paths People and Processes

People

Recruiting
Renewing
Retaining

Dynamic
Capabilities

Processes

Paths

Anticipating
Allocating
Applying

Sensing
Searching
Strategizing

Figure 2.3. Creating and Sustaining Dynamic Capabilities

2.4.5 *Creating and Sustaining Dynamic Capabilities*

The framework in Figure 2.2 shows that the possession of dynamic change capabilities enables operating routines and core capabilities to be renewed and reconfigured. But how do organizations create and sustain such dynamic capabilities? The literature suggests that dynamic change capabilities rest on an organization's accumulated asset positions, transformational processes and paths constrained by heritage and past choices.[76]

A conceptual framework for creating and sustaining dynamic change capabilities is shown in Figure 2.3. It shows that capabilities become dynamic as a result of the investments made in people, processes and paths, and the interactions among the three.

The people category is an adaptation of the concept of asset positions. Asset positions consist of both tangible assets (such as specialized equipment) and intangible assets (such as knowledge and skills). Tangible assets are necessary as part of the deployment of organizational capabilities but they are hardly dynamic. Once bought or deployed, these long-lasting capital equipment become legacy

---

[76] Teece, Pisano and Shuen (1997).

assets, which often constrain rather than enable change. The relative importance of intangible assets over tangible assets is assumed in the resource-based view. The dynamism of intangible assets may be embodied in human capital — the people dimension in the framework or embedded in organizational capital — the process dimension. The framework for creating dynamic change capabilities recognizes the critical role played by people in interaction with processes and paths in enabling transformational change.

People are the first and most important determinant of dynamic capabilities because deliberate investments in organizational improvement and innovation require choices made by people in positions of influence and leadership. Only humans can adapt and change within a context, and consciously decide to reframe the context[77] that may lead to the reconfiguration of assets and capabilities in an organization. Making good decisions and choices require organization leaders to possess the necessary motivation, attitude, intellect, knowledge, skills and values to envision the future, visualize strategic options and select paths that give the organization the greatest scope for survival and success.

Leadership decisions and choices affect the other two determinants of dynamic change capabilities — the paths taken by the organization and the design of organizational processes that would also affect the potential reconfiguration of resources. Dynamic capabilities in people are developed through how an organization recruits the needed talent from the marketplace, how it continuously renews the skills and knowledge of its people, and how it retains the crucial expertise for creating and implementing its strategies.

Organizational processes are needed for getting things done in a coordinated manner, whether they are for regular business transactions (operational routines) or for formulating and implementing strategies (core capabilities). Where there is no defined process, however broad or narrow, an organization cannot perform a required task even if the individuals in the organization have the knowledge and skills to do

---

[77] Stephan H Haeckel (1999). *Adaptive Enterprise*, MA: HBS Press.

so. Even when there are defined processes, organizations would still need to continuously review and redesign them to ensure that they are able to achieve their intended outcomes and not become outdated because of changing circumstances and changing technologies.

In the development of dynamic capabilities, the focus is on processes that enable the reconfiguration of both operational routines and core capabilities — the organizational capacity to reorganize existing functions and structures to enable new ways of working, to reallocate financial resources from existing uses for investments in new priorities, and to redesign existing infrastructures to enable new networks to be built and better services to be delivered.

An organization's capacity for change has been characterized as being path-dependent because of the imprint of its heritage and constraints imposed by past decisions. Therefore an organization's change capabilities are determined by what it does in adapting and improving its paths to meet the new requirements for survival and success, and innovating in path-breaking strategies and policies.

We have described the fundamental concepts of governance, institutions and capabilities and how they are used in the literature. From our study, we found three cognitive learning capabilities that define dynamic governance in Singapore: thinking ahead, thinking again and thinking across. These capabilities are grounded on a set of cultural values and beliefs that have to be continually reflected and refreshed to facilitate dynamic adaptation and change. We have described the major players and outlined the three dynamic governance capabilities in Chapter 1. The development of these dynamic governance capabilities through principles, paths, people and processes are the subject of subsequent chapters. What is not shown in the conceptual framework in Figure 1.1 of Chapter 1 are the historical, social and political contexts that have been critical influences on the development of governance ideas and principles in Singapore. These were briefly discussed in Chapter 1 and will be elaborated in Chapter 3.

3

Context for Development: Establishing Imperatives for Governance

An awareness of Singapore's political, social and economic context when it became independent in 1965 and the evolution of this context over time is necessary to understand why and how dynamic governance developed in Singapore. The historical context that shaped the economic and social development in Singapore provides the background as to how its founding leaders perceived the nation's position and articulated the purpose of governance. We operationalize the cultural foundations of governance in Figure 1.1 of Chapter 1 as the leadership perception of the position of a nation, which influences its statement of purpose, the conception of principles of governance and the adoption of specific practices deemed appropriate for the nation. Chapters 3 and 4 discuss these cultural foundations of governance in detail. This chapter outlines the historical, political, social and economic contexts and discusses the principles and values of governance that are derived from them.

Like many countries in Southeast Asia, Singapore lived through a long period of colonial rule under the British and suffered the atrocities of the Japanese occupation. The post-war years saw a push for self-government, a move complicated by expanding communist elements in Southeast Asia, arising from the ascendancy and entrenchment of the Chinese Communist Party. However, Singapore subsequently took policy paths that were not consistent with the general desire of former colonies to rid themselves of all semblance of their former rulers. This, together with the story of how its leaders managed to create and build a nation-state from scratch and ensure its continued viability over the past 40 years, is the context of the development of Singapore's governance system — how it was influenced by history and geography, the factors and values that guided its policy choices, and how it continually adapted to changing domestic and international requirements.

Singapore's development can be roughly divided into two broad periods, with 1985–86 as the watershed years. These years were much more than the years of Singapore's first economic recession; they marked a turning point in the direction of the Singapore economy and the start of shifts in the approach to governance, heralded by the first major post-independence political transition with the handover of power from Lee Kuan Yew to Goh Chok Tong. The period after 1990 was marked by greater economic volatility and greater security and social concerns in the wake of the September 11, 2001 terrorist attacks. The new environment after 1990 precipitated changes in the public sector's approach to governance.

3.1 Context and Constraints that Defined Governance in Singapore: 1965–1985

The cultural foundations of governance in Singapore grew out of the response of the political leadership to the situation facing Singapore at independence in 1965. The circumstances of its independence were less than auspicious, having been unceremoniously ejected from the Malaysian Federation. It became a sovereign nation of some two million immigrants who had lived through a tumultuous decade of racial and religious conflict, fueled by the flames of communism. Singapore's traditional economic lifeline — entrepot trade — was declining, a result of the efforts of Malaysia and Indonesia to compete economically and reduce their dependence on historical transport and trade links with Singapore. Singapore's vulnerability was stark: it had no viable security to speak of. Unlike many other developing countries, it had no natural resources such as rubber or oil. Nor did its immigrant population have any special skills, which could form the basis of economic development. The shock of separation and the subsequent scramble for economic survival in a new country that had no apparent means of supporting itself not only left an indelible mark on the psyche of its founding political and public sector leaders but also fostered a deep sense of vulnerability that shaped its entire philosophy and approach to governance.

At its independence, Singapore was an island of some 620 square kilometers with a population of just over two million, a predominantly Chinese community in a largely Muslim Southeast Asia. Openness to the rest of the world was not a choice; it was a necessity dictated by its almost total lack of natural resources. That this would make it highly exposed to external shocks and events was a factor that conditioned the thinking of its founding leaders and shaped the complexion of the economic and social policies that were subsequently enacted. Beyond geography, its multi-racial and multi-religious population created natural fault lines which were an ever-present source of potential social instability. The societal tension was heightened by high unemployment which hovered at 14 per cent at independence.

Even today, after more than 40 years of growth and development, its leaders' consciousness of Singapore's precarious situation has not diminished. As Foreign Minister George Yeo remarked, "Like it or not, we live in a state of perpetual insecurity. That is our *karma*... in our modest way, we must have our own sense of destiny."[1] The belief continues to be deeply held that Singapore's continued survival depends on its being able to play a useful and valuable role in the world. The severity of its circumstances explains the rational, pragmatic, non-ideological approach to policy making.

Singapore's survival as a nation was predicated on economic survival. The circumstances of its independence created two underlying strategic imperatives that remain until this day: economic development and domestic stability. Singapore the nation-state is, for all intents and purposes, Singapore the economy; economic considerations have been dominant in almost all aspects of policy making. The abiding belief has been that only when the economy is strong can a society have the opportunity to achieve all other desired objectives. Thus while social and security concerns have gained ascendancy since the 1990s, the economy continues to be the bedrock of Singapore society.

---

[1] George Yeo, Minister for Foreign Affairs as quoted from Alain Vandenborre (2003). *Proudly Singaporean: My Passport to a Challenging Future*. SNP Editions, p. 15.

All this formed the backdrop of Singapore's development and underpinned the foundations of governance — the openness, the emphasis on learning from and establishing links with the rest of the world, the push to stay relevant, its efforts to increase its international space and sphere of influence. Singapore exemplified the concept of "connectivity" long before the IT age made the word fashionable. The bottom line of Singapore policy-making was summed up by the first Prime Minister and current Minister Mentor, Lee Kuan Yew: Singapore is "man-made… contrived to fit the needs of the modern world and it has to be amended all the time as the needs change."[2] In the same vein, the transformation of the international economic environment over the last 40 years has demanded that Singapore continually change its modus operandi, which in turn has influenced its adaptability, its functioning and its decision-making.

Domestic political stability has been the key factor enabling Singapore to change and adapt with consistency and continuity. The People's Action Party (PAP) came to power in 1959 under Lee Kuan Yew when Singapore attained self-government from the British. Its longevity is premised on its ability to deliver the economic goods; the strength of the economy has been the source of its legitimacy. This long-standing one-party dominance and the pervasive reach of government policy into all spheres of life have earned the party and government numerous epithets, not all of which are complimentary. However, one significant result of PAP dominance has been a strong future orientation and long-term perspective in policy-making. It has also meant that the values and principles of the founding generation of leaders have left a large imprint and continue to shape the ethos of government.

The interventionist approach of the government was a stark contrast to the *laissez faire* approach of the pre-1959 era under the British. As surmised by Goh Keng Swee, acknowledged as Singapore's

---

[2] Interview with *New York Times* on 3 August 1995, quoted in Usher CV Haley, Linda Low and Mun-Heng Toh (1996). "Singapore Incorporated: Reinterpreting Singapore's Business Environments through a Corporate Metaphor," *Management Decision*, Vol. 34, No. 9, pp. 17–28.

economic architect, the *laissez-faire* policies of the colonial era "had led Singapore to a dead end, with little economic growth, massive unemployment, wretched housing, and inadequate education." Singapore thus "had to try a more activist and interventionist approach."[3] Given the circumstances at independence, there was little alternative but for the government to play a very large and key role in driving the Singapore economy. The story of how Singapore overcame its geographical constraints with its then novel industrialization approach has been extensively documented.[4] The objective here is not to re-describe the policies but to examine what these policy choices reflected of the values, beliefs and assumptions of the founding leaders which shaped the nature and approach to governance. To build a new society, the government took action on five broad fronts:

(i) building the economy,
(ii) managing population growth and the labor market,
(iii) building up physical infrastructure,
(iv) building social systems and practices, and
(v) building up security and defense.

3.1.1 *Building the Economy*

Singapore's industrialization strategy based on foreign investment and export orientation has been widely emulated and accepted as part of conventional wisdom. But it did not start out that way. The two economic pillars of postwar Singapore were entrepot trade and British military expenditure, each of which accounted for 18 per cent of total output in 1960. The British bases were directly and indirectly responsible for about 20 per cent of total employment. When Singapore attained self-government in 1959, unemployment was around 14 per cent and expected to rise with population growth of more than 3 per cent annually. Industrialization was recommended

---

[3] Devan Nair (1976). *Socialism that Works: The Singapore Way*, p. 84.

[4] For example, Peter SJ Chen (1983). *Singapore Development Policies and Trends*. Oxford University Press; Lim Chong Yah (ed.) (1996). *Economic Policy Management in Singapore*. Singapore: Addison-Wesley; Henri Ghesquiere (2007). *Singapore's Success: Engineering Economic Growth*. Thomson Learning Asia.

by the United Nations Industrial Survey Mission headed by Dr Albert Winsemius as the way to generate employment. More than 200,000 new jobs had to be created in the 1960s alone, with about half of these in manufacturing — a daunting task in view of the fact that the manufacturing sector accounted for only 27,000 jobs or about 7.5 per cent of total employment in 1960. As Singapore then lacked capital, technology and manufacturing expertise, foreign investment became the obvious solution. The Economic Development Board (EDB) was set up in August 1961 as Singapore's inward investment promotion arm based on the prospect of a common market with Malaya. All kinds of labor-intensive industries — food, textiles, toys, and wood and porcelain products — were welcomed to set up on specially designated land.

The loss of the potential common market at independence precipitated the switch to an export-oriented strategy: Singapore began positioning itself as an offshore production for MNCs. The success of this strategy has been widely attributed to the generous policy packages — tax incentives, especially pioneer status and export incentives, loan schemes and investment allowances — plus the favorable international economic conditions. It is undeniable that these two factors were critical to Singapore's early success. Shell was the first company to benefit from the fiscal incentives as a pioneer industry. Outlying islands became a petroleum refining hub as Singapore took advantage of its location along one of the world's busiest trade routes. Petroleum refining in turn created new opportunities in industries such as ship repair and other supporting engineering industries. At the same time, the rise of relatively low-cost Japanese manufacturing fueled demand by American and European manufacturers for low-cost offshore production facilities to meet the Japanese challenge.

Even though the international economic conditions were fortuitous, the road to securing investments was long and arduous. As a newly independent country with no track record in hosting foreign investors, the early results were dismal: annual investments were less than S$100 million in the first few years. The need to create jobs in the early days was so great that the EDB accepted any investments that came along. As Ngiam Tong Dow described it, "(T)he label 'high-tech, low-tech' never entered our vocabulary. Any 'tech', which can provide our young school-leavers with jobs, will do."[5] Industries such as garments, hair wigs and transistor radio assembly were the order of the day. The situation became even graver in 1967 when the British announced the withdrawal of all their military bases east of the Suez by 1971 and in Singapore, these bases accounted for about one-fifth of all employment.

Efforts only started to pay off in 1970. The breakthrough came when the EDB managed to persuade some key companies such as General Electric, National Semiconductor and Fairchild to set up production operations in Singapore. These investments were the result of the dogged determination of the EDB and its overriding mantra to do whatever was needed to impress and meet the needs of its investor clients. The way in which the EDB handled these investors generated goodwill and positive word of mouth, which helped put Singapore on the radar of similar organizations looking for offshore production bases. Net investment commitments surged almost nine-fold between 1972 and 1982 which generated the much-needed growth. In the 10 years following independence, GDP averaged 11 per cent growth per year and despite an increase in population, Singapore's per capita GDP increased about 10 per cent a year, reaching S$5,943 (US$2,506) in 1975 and S$14,696 (US$6,484) in 1984.[6] The impact on job creation was clear and positive: employment generated by pioneer manufacturing establishments rose from 50,000 in 1970 to 96,000 in 1973.[7] As a result, unemployment which stood at 10 per cent in 1970 was more than halved by 1972. By the mid-1970s, the unemployment problem was solved, and the rate stabilized at between 3.5 per cent and 4.5 per cent.[8]

Singapore's domestic policies supported and complemented its industrialization efforts. It gained the confidence of foreign

---

[5] Ngiam Tong Dow (2005). "Big Country, Small Country: Strength and Limitations," Seminar Series of the School of Humanities and Social Sciences, Nanyang Technological University, 18 June 2005.

[6] Figures provided by Singapore Department of Statistics, 2006.

[7] Singapore, *Economic and Social Statistics Singapore 1960–1982*, Department of Statistics.

[8] Singapore, Economic Survey of Singapore, various years.

investors with a prudent budgetary stance and fiscal and monetary policies that gave priority to long-term sustainability. The unique relationship between the government and the trade unions helped establish a climate of stability conducive to economic development. Policy makers opted to formally retain the currency board system in 1967 with the set up of the Board of Commissioners of Currency of Singapore (BCCS).[9] The Monetary Authority of Singapore (MAS) was set up in 1970 as the de facto central bank, with the aim of promoting monetary and exchange rate conditions conducive to the growth and stability of the economy. The banking and monetary system inherited from the colonial era was expanded and deepened with the setting up of the Asian Dollar Market in 1967 and later the Asian Bond Market, both of which grew rapidly. In the 1970s, further measures were taken to deepen the money market, the forward exchange and capital markets. The open banking system, favorable taxation system and full convertibility of the Singapore dollar on the capital account all contributed to fiscal and monetary systems that supported industrialization and helped fuel growth and development.

In addition to establishing the policy infrastructure and attracting foreign investors, the Singapore public sector was also instrumental in building up key business corporations. Civil servants played catalyst roles in pioneering industrial ventures. State-owned enterprises were established in areas where both foreign investors and local entrepreneurs did not have the resources nor the inclination to venture. Companies such as Singapore Airlines, Sembawang Shipyard, Neptune Orient Lines and Chartered Industries of Singapore were established during this period. The Development Bank of Singapore, now one of the largest banks in Singapore, was born as a spin-off from the EDB, to handle the financial requirements of investors. At its height, there were more than 600 state-owned companies and government-linked companies. However unlike state-owned companies in other countries, those in Singapore from the

---

[9] Under a Currency Board system, each unit of currency issued is backed 100 per cent by gold and foreign exchange.

outset were run along commercial principles; many were profitable and internationally competitive.

Beyond policies, Singapore's leaders established a mindset and a collection of systems, structures and institutions that created capacity and enabled Singapore to derive maximum benefits from industrialization and growth. The positive results from the foreign investment policies were due as much to the quality of the execution of the policies as the policies themselves. This was reflected in the way the EDB went about its work. Comprising predominantly scholars and civil servants, the EDB co-opted and borrowed expertise, learnt to interact with and understand what CEOs wanted, and accommodated their requirements. It established a network of overseas offices, made cold calls on companies and CEOs, and learnt to sell and hustle for Singapore. The EDB officers learnt on-the-job how to market, to understand what companies were looking for, to build relationships with CEOs, and, by thorough, consistent and timely execution which delivered results, built Singapore's reputation as a responsible and responsive host country. EDB organized and positioned itself as a one-stop shop for investors. Being a one-stop shop meant that the EDB had to work closely with and align the efforts of various agencies whose work and inputs were integral to the whole process. The set up of the National Semiconductor factory to be operating and shipping semiconductors two months from the date of the CEO's first visit to Singapore was a case in point.[10] These stories of successful start-ups raised Singapore's profile, attracted other investors and established Singapore's reputation as a country that delivered results.

3.1.2 *Managing Population Growth and the Labor Market*

(i) *Establishing industrial stability*

Financial incentives and a favorable international economic climate would have counted for nothing if investors had not been assured of a stable long-term industrial and political climate in which to reap

---

[10] Chan Chin Bock (2002). *Heart Work*, pp. 44–46.

returns on their investments. Singapore had inherited an adversarial style of labor management relations from the British, and prior to 1959, communist elements had instigated strikes and stoppages in their struggle for worker support and the control of the unions. For instance, in 1961, there were more than 100 industrial stoppages involving some 43,000 workers and 1,225 trade disputes.[11] Reducing the power of the unions required adroit handling, particularly as the unions had supported the PAP in their quest for self-government. By successfully rallying the unions behind the need for industrial stability, the government managed to align the interests of the trade unions and define a new working relationship between trade unions and employers, and between the unions and the government, to forge a tripartite approach to managing labor market issues.

Several key pieces of legislation were passed. The Trade Unions Amendment Ordinance of 1959 was designed to promote responsible trade unionism, and the Industrial Relations Ordinance of 1960 laid down efficient procedures for the resolution of industrial disputes and the setting up of the Industrial Arbitration Court (IAC). Under this Ordinance, a strike was deemed illegal once the IAC had taken cognizance of a dispute, with cognizance effected when both the employer and the union submitted a joint application for arbitration or when the Minister for Labour directed the case to be heard by the IAC. This meant that a strike was only possible with the tacit consent of the Minister.

The imminent withdrawal of the British troops prompted two more pieces of legislation in 1968 to tighten industrial discipline. The Employment Act consolidated earlier laws and made new provisions. Among other things, it stipulated the rights and duties of employees, the number of holidays, rest days, sick leave, annual leave, and rate of pay for work on holidays. The standard work-week was set at 44 hours and bonuses were limited to one month's wage. Workers were entitled to retrenchment and retirement benefits only after three and five years of service respectively. The Industrial Relations (Amendment) Act gave more managerial power to the employer by

---

[11] Singapore, *Economic and Social Statistics Singapore 1960–1982*, Department of Statistics.

excluding specific issues from collective agreements. Examples were promotion, transfers, retirement, retrenchment, dismissal and work assignment. To reduce the possible incidence of work stoppages, the duration of collective agreements was extended to a maximum of three years to reduce the frequency of negotiation between unions and management.[12]

Union leaders supported the government's stance that these laws were necessary to attract foreign investors and create jobs. The erosion of traditional trade union functions led to a redefinition of the role of the unions. The result of this is the unique tripartite framework among employers, unions and the government that exists today. This framework enabled the government and the country to take unusual policy measures to regulate the labor market and to respond in times of economic crisis.

This tripartite approach was reflected in the structure of the National Wages Council (NWC) which was formed in 1972. The labor market had tightened by the early 1970s and there were signs of upward wage pressures. The NWC was the attempt to manage this. The Council, consisting of representatives of employers, unions and the government and chaired by an academic, was charged with recommending "orderly wage increases" so as to maintain Singapore's competitiveness in labor-intensive industries which formed the bulk of its manufacturing sector.

(ii) *Curbing population growth*

Like many other post-war developing countries, Singapore's population growth after the war was high, averaging 4.4 per cent annually. The Singapore Family Planning and Population Board (SFPPB) Act 1965 was passed by Parliament in December 1965, with the establishment of the Singapore Family Planning and Population Board in January 1966. The quick passage of the Act through

---

[12] This section draws from Tan Chwee Huat (1984). "Towards Better Labour-Management Relations," in You Poh Seng and Lim Chong Yah (eds.), *Singapore: Twenty-Five Years of Development*. Nan Yang Xing Zhou Lianhe Zaobao, pp. 189–205.

Parliament and the equally quick set-up of the SFPPB was the result of a realization of the urgency to control population growth.

The impact of a high population growth on the economy was dire. As Ngiam Tong Dow reminisced,

> "Our first Minister for Finance, Dr Goh Keng Swee, one day told me that he felt depressed every time he passed by a school at the end of the school day at 1 pm, or 6 pm. Because of a shortage of classrooms, Singapore operated a two session school day, 7:30 am to 1 pm, and from 1:30 pm to 6 pm. … When I asked Dr Goh why he felt depressed, he asked me how we were going to find gainful employment for the 25,000 to 30,000 school-leavers each year."[13]

Singapore's approach to family planning had two major platforms: the Abortion Bill and the Voluntary Sterilization Act, both of which came into effect in early 1970. The first bill legalized abortion if the family and financial circumstances of the woman warranted it. In 1974, the Act was further liberalized, making possible abortion on demand, subject to certain safeguards. The number of legal abortions rose from 1,913 in 1970 to 7,175 in 1974, and then doubled to 14,855 in 1979.[14] The Voluntary Sterilization Act complemented the Abortion Act by allowing adults over the age of 21 to apply for sterilization if they had three children; this was later revised downwards to two. To further encourage this option, children of parents who had undergone voluntary sterilization were given priority in getting places in schools of their choice. In addition, corresponding changes to paid maternity leave benefits and accouchement fees in public hospitals were made to discourage large families. The effectiveness of these measures was reflected in the fall in the average number of children born to

[13] Ngiam Tong Dow (2005). "Big Country, Small Country: Strength and Limitations," Seminar Series of the School of Humanities and Social Sciences, Nanyang Technological University, 18 June 2005.

[14] Saw Swee Hock (1984). "Population Trends, Problems and Policies in Singapore," in You Poh Seng and Lim Chong Yah (eds.), *Singapore: Twenty-Five Years of Development*. Nan Yang Xing Zhou Lianhe Zaobao, pp. 141–159.

each resident female, from 5.76 in 1960 to 3.07 in 1970. By 1980, the average number of children had fallen to 1.82, well below replacement fertility.[15] This reversal would completely change the context of social policy after 1990.

(iii) *Boosting education and developing manpower*[16]

With people as its only resource, the heart of Singapore's push for economic growth was the education, training and upgrading of the skills of her people. Right from the beginning, Singapore's education philosophy was functional and content driven, with the focus on technical and vocational education to ensure a well-trained pool of labor. The period 1961 to 1967 saw phenomenal growth in technical and vocational education and a rapid increase in the number of vocational and technical schools.[17] In 1961, there were some 1,400 students in these schools but this figure more than doubled the following year and had increased by seven-fold by 1967. The vocational institutes focused on craft courses which included skills like electrical fitting and installation, radio servicing, motor vehicle mechanics, refrigeration and air-conditioning, sheet metal and welding. As Singapore's foreign investment efforts started paying off in the late 1960s, policy makers understood the need to prepare skilled and technically trained manpower in large numbers ahead of the factories being built.

The Technical Education Department was created within the Ministry of Education in 1968 to oversee all technical and vocational education and emphasis was given to higher-level technical skills. A new National Industrial Training Council and the Ministry of Science and Technology were set up in 1968, part of a concerted effort to develop technical education at all levels. Centralized workshops were

---

[15] Singapore, *Yearbook of Statistics*, various years.

[16] This section draws from Pang Eng Fong (1982). *Education, Manpower and Development in Singapore*. Singapore University Press, pp. 6–7.

[17] This section draws from Mickey Chiang (1998). *From Economic Debacle to Economic Miracle: The History and Development of Technical Education in Singapore*. Singapore: Ministry of Education, Times Editions.

set up to enable students in the traditional academic route to gain some exposure to technical education. This move helped to dispel the mindset common in many post-colonial developing countries that only an academic education was the passport to a good job. Technical education was consolidated in 1973 with the formation of the Industrial Training Board (ITB) which was renamed the Vocational and Industrial Training Board in 1979. A national skills certification system and a public trade test system were set up to help standardize quality. At the same time, the Singapore Polytechnic and Ngee Ann Polytechnic were expanded to produce more technicians and the number of places in professional courses in the university was increased.

The other main player in technical education was the EDB. Since the early days, EDB recognized that the new industries it was attracting to Singapore would require skilled personnel with specific skills to handle specific machines and equipment. As a result of its interaction with foreign investors, the EDB realized that the need for specialist training could not be met within the normal technical education framework. Thus the EDB helped large industrial companies set up facilities to train personnel for their own needs and to help meet the manpower needs of the industry. In 1972, the Tata-Government Training Centre was set up to meet the need for trained manpower in precision engineering in manufacturing trucks, excavators, locomotives and machine tools. The EDB provided land and buildings, some S$1.5 million in equipment and machinery and covered some 70 per cent of the operating costs of the training center. Following the system established by the ITB, the apprenticeship system was adopted. All trainees signed a bond to serve the EDB or any company directed by the Singapore government for a period of 5 years. Tata's yearly requirement was 50 so the annual intake was 100 to meet the manpower needs of the industry. This was the template adopted for the Rollei-Government Training Centre in 1973 and the Philips-Government Training Centre in 1975. These centers provided training that was relevant and contributed significantly to the establishment of the precision engineering industry.

In the late 1970s, this approach expanded to government-to-government technical institutes to facilitate the rapid transfer of new technology to Singapore. The institutes set up under this framework were the Japan-Singapore Training Centre, the German-Singapore Institute and the French-Singapore Institute. This arrangement enabled Singapore to tap into foreign expertise and teaching systems, and facilitated a "Teaching Factory Concept" which became the hallmark of the EDB teaching institutes. The Japan-Singapore Institute of Software Technology was set up in 1982 to produce the anticipated large numbers of personnel that would be needed by the computer software industry. The training in these institutes was later merged into the polytechnics, which had also been expanding their intakes rapidly during this time. To encourage employers to send their lower-skilled workers for skills upgrading, a Skills Development Fund was set up in the late 1970s. It was financed by a 2 per cent levy on the wages of workers who earned less than S$750 a month and grants were made available for approved training schemes.

At the same time, many primary and secondary schools were built to match the rapid increase in the number of school-going children. The training of teachers was accelerated with the establishment of the Teachers' Training College. To optimize resource allocation where labor was scarce, the output of vocational, technical and tertiary institutions were set according to indicative projections of manpower requirements carried out annually by the government in the late 1970s and 1980s. This was the period when the labor market was extremely tight and various measures were taken to try to ensure that every child reached his or her potential. This was the thinking that led to a major revamp of the education system in 1979. The Singapore system was based on the Cambridge model[18], modified for Singapore's multi-racial context and immigrant history. In addition to being taught English, which was the medium of instruction, every student also learned a second language, usually their mother tongue. Many children could

---

[18] A typical student went through six years of primary education, four years of secondary education and two years of pre-university education, with nation-wide exams at the end of the sixth year, the tenth year and the twelfth year. The latter two exams were the exams moderated by the University of Cambridge Examinations Syndicate but administered in Singapore.

not cope, resulting in high dropout rates. The 1979 Goh Report[19] proposed an education structure with the objective of minimizing wastage: new paths were to be created to cater to students with different abilities in the second language. A technical path was also devised to cater to those who were less academically inclined to ensure that they left the formal school system with technical, if not academic, qualifications. Students were thus "streamed" at predetermined stages according to their perceived ability to do well in the academic route as reflected in their performance in standard examinations and their ability to cope with two languages. The recommendations of the Goh report formed the backbone of the education system for many years.

An indication of this emphasis on developing manpower was the increase in the annual government expenditure devoted to education: between 1960 and 1982, the student population increased by about 30 per cent but annual expenditure on education increased by more than 20 times.[20] Complementing the stress on technical education, Singapore's education system has had an overwhelming slant towards mathematics, engineering and the hard sciences as these disciplines were perceived by policy makers to be the most functional and relevant to Singapore's development. A testament to this focus was Singapore's first placing, years later, in the Third International Mathematics and Science study testing the average scores of 13 year-olds from a group of 41 developed and developing countries.[21]

(iv) *Regulating the labor market*

Industrialization had mopped up most of the excess labor in the late 1960s, which prompted two major adjustments. The first was the relaxation of immigration rules to allow employers to bring in foreign workers. In 1970s, non-Singaporeans comprised 12 per cent of

[19] The review was headed by Dr Goh Keng Swee, Deputy Prime Minister, and the review team comprised a group of systems engineers from the Ministry of Defence.

[20] Peter SJ Chen (1984). "Social Change and Planning in Singapore," in You and Lim (eds.), pp. 315–338, Table 1.

[21] *The Economist* (1997). "Education and the Wealth of Nations," and "World Education League: Who's Top?" 29 March 1997, cited in Lam and Tan (eds.).

the labor force.[22] While efforts were boosted to increase the number of qualified professionals, technicians and specialists by channeling young people to various skill training programs, qualified technicians and professionals were granted work visas without the need for sponsorship by an employer. The NWC recommended relatively high wage increases in the early 1970s to encourage more efficient utilization of labor. This policy was reversed following the 1973–74 oil crisis when wage restraint was necessary to maintain export competitiveness. Nevertheless, policy makers realized that Singapore had to move up the skills and technology ladder for economic growth to be sustained. Thus while efforts were made to promote the upgrading of existing industries in the mid 1970s, the EDB also became more discerning in its investment promotion strategy, targeting middle and high technology firms to upgrade the industry. Such industries included the chemicals, transport equipment, precision equipment and machinery industries.

A high wage policy was enacted in 1979 for three years to push firms to reduce labor-intensive methods of production. Despite the push, Singapore's dependence on unskilled foreign labor did not diminish significantly. In 1980, non-Singaporeans comprised about half of the labor force while those earning less than S$600 made up 7 per cent of those employed. By 1985, the non-Singaporean component in the total labor force had shrunk to 31 per cent but those earning less than S$600 had increased to 10 per cent.[23] The aim to phase out foreign workers from the economy after 1990 except in specific sectors was not possible without compromising growth, and the policy was replaced in April 1987 by the foreign worker levy system. Under the levy system, the recruitment of foreign workers could continue in the manufacturing, hotel, construction and domestic services sectors but unskilled workers from non-traditional sources would be confined to construction, shipbuilding and domestic services.[24] The initial monthly

---

[22] Lim Chong Yah and Associates (1988). *Policy Options for the Singapore Economy*. Singapore: McGraw-Hill, p. 143.

[23] Calculated from Table 6.7 of Lim (1988).

[24] Only Malaysia is regarded as a traditional source. All other countries, e.g., India, Bangladesh, Philippines and Korea are regarded as non-traditional sources.

levy for a construction worker and a domestic maid was S$120, and S$150 for all other sectors.

3.1.3 *Building the Physical Infrastructure*

Singapore's development has been infrastructure-intensive. The approach has been to anticipate and build ahead of demand to facilitate growth and development. In the early years, the focus was on ports, industrial estates, finance and transportation networks, and this later evolved to communications and IT systems. Statutory bodies proliferated in the 1960s and early 1970s to provide infrastructure and essential services. Land was set aside for factories as well as housing, which meant that it had to be cleared, and sewage, drainage and power systems built and laid. The Jurong Town Corporation (JTC), set up in 1968, took over the factory development and building function from the EDB, overseeing the growth and planning for the Jurong Industrial Estate that had been set aside as factory space for foreign investors. The Urban Redevelopment Authority was likewise later spun off from the Housing and Development Board (HDB) to look after the renewal of the town center; the Public Utilities Board, to ensure the provision of water and electricity; the Telecommunication Authority of Singapore, for the provision of telephone and postal services.

Singapore also leveraged on its strategic location and established itself as a key node in international transportation networks. The Port of Singapore Authority (PSA) was formed in 1964 to expand and deepen Singapore's port services.[25] In view of the declining entrepot trade as a result of the increasing trade links between regional countries and their markets in developed nations, PSA invested in building container terminals and created for itself the role as the transshipment node for the region. A similar approach was taken to develop Singapore as an international air transport node, with the building of Changi International Airport which was completed in 1981.

Significant investments were made in building up the road and rail networks. Between 1965 and 1975, the length of roads increased by

---

[25] PSA took over what was previously Singapore Harbour Board.

almost 25 per cent but the motor vehicle population jumped by 45 per cent.[26] The problem of traffic congestion surfaced in the early 1970s. Singapore was the first country in the world to introduce congestion pricing with the Area Licensing Scheme (ALS) in 1975, under which drivers had to pay a toll to enter the city center during morning peak hours, later expanded also to the evenings. This early manual road pricing scheme was the manual forerunner to the electronic road pricing system launched in the mid-1990s. The construction of the backbone of Singapore's transport system, the Mass Rapid Transit (MRT), began in the early 1980s and was completed in 1987. Costing S$5 billion, it was Singapore's most expensive project.

3.1.4 *Building the Social Infrastructure*

(i)   *Housing, home ownership and community-building*

Both Lee Kuan Yew and Goh Keng Swee set out to create and build a new society and understood that development required a stable social-political environment. Singapore in the early 1960s was a patchwork of urban slums. Its immigrant population was still feeling the effects of a decade of religious and racial conflict. What bound them together was the severity of the economic situation; it was this that made them rally behind the government's efforts to kick-start growth. Giving each family a physical stake in the country was deemed necessary to build a stable society. This was how the housing and home ownership program became definitive elements of Singapore society.

The HDB was set up in 1960 to solve the severe housing crisis created by the rapid post-war population growth and the colonial government's dismal performance in housing.[27] The linchpin of the urban renewal and housing policy was the Land Acquisition Act of 1966 that allowed the state to acquire land for state purposes by compensating land owners. Direct land acquisition by the government guaranteed that land would be available for public purposes and

---

[26] Singapore, *Economic and Social Statistics Singapore 1960–1982*, Department of Statistics.

[27] Formed in 1932, the Singapore Improvement Trust built only 23,624 units of flats in its 32 years of existence. Quah (1987), p. 123.

enabled the execution of the housing, industrialization and urban renewal projects at an affordable cost.[28]

The HDB's immediate objective then was the construction and provision of low-cost public housing through a series of five-year plans. The number of flats built during the period of the first plan, 55,430, rose to 108,392 in the period 1971–1975, and further to 130,432 between 1976 and 1980.[29] At the building peak in the 1960s, the HDB was building one flat every 39 minutes.[30] The aim was to get the flats up so that families could move in; scant attention was given to aesthetics and design and uniform blocks of flats went up all over the island.[31] The housing program was effective. In the early 1960s, only about 10 per cent of the population was living in high-rise flats, the proportion of which rose to about 80 per cent in the mid-1980s.

Having achieved its objective, the HDB expanded its role to upgrading flats, to provide asset enhancement opportunities for the HDB flat-owning population. At the same time, community building and national integration objectives surfaced. High-rise living made for minimal interaction which resulted in highly impersonal relationships among neighbors. There was also the fear that racial enclaves would form again as families and friends tried to live close to one another. Pre-independence Singapore had seen the congregation of certain racial groups in certain quarters. Urban resettlement and renewal involved concerted action to disperse and integrate people of different races into different HDB estates. This was taken one step further when racial quotas were established for each HDB estate, right down to individual blocks of flats. At the same time, precincts and

---

[28] Land Acquisition Act 1966, Section 5(1) states, "Whenever any particular land is needed: (a) for any public purpose; (b) by any person, corporation or statutory board, for any work or an undertaking which, in the opinion of the Minister, is of public benefit or of public utility or in the public interest; or (c) for any residential, commercial or industrial purpose, the President may, by notification published in the Gazette, declare the land to be required for the purpose specified in the notification." Quoted from Lim *et al.* (1988). *Policy Options*, p. 78.

[29] HDB Annual Reports cited in Pugh and Cedric (1989), p. 848.

[30] Ngiam Tong Dow (2004). Speech given during closed door luncheon to the Economic Society of Singapore, 15 January 2004.

[31] Lee Kuan Yew (2000). *From Third World to First — The Singapore Story: 1965–2000*, p. 119.

townships, community centers, residents' committees and citizens' consultative committees were formed to give residents a voice and a stake in managing their neighborhoods.

(ii) *Financing home ownership and Singapore' economic development: the Central Provident Fund*

To most Singaporeans, the Central Provident Fund (CPF) is synonymous with home ownership. Indeed it was the Singapore government's adaptation of the British pension scheme that enabled Singaporeans over the years to own their own homes, pay for their medical expenses, plan for retirement and educate their children at local universities. It is a cornerstone of Singapore's economic and social policy. A system like the CPF was indicative of the values and beliefs of its founding fathers and the underlying principles of governance.

The CPF is a compulsory savings scheme set up initially to provide workers with retirement benefits. Monthly contributions are made by employers and employees into the employees' CPF accounts at government-stipulated rates. CPF accounts are personal to holder and account holders can withdraw the bulk of their CPF savings at the age of 55. The system began in 1955 with initial contribution rates of 5 per cent each by the employer and employee. When the home ownership drive began in the early 1970s, the rates of contribution to CPF were steadily increased to help Singaporeans finance the purchase of a new flat. Contribution rates were raised steadily throughout the 1970s, to 25 per cent each in 1984 and 1985 for a total of 50 per cent. In 1984, the CPF system was expanded to include a savings account — "Medisave" — to enable individuals to save to meet the cost of their medical expenses.

The number of active contributors increased from 465,000 in 1967 to 927,500 in 1982. Annual contributions rose by 70 times. In 1982, the amount contributed amounted to 13.5 per cent of GDP and one-third of total national saving in 1982. The CPF has been the key source of domestic savings that has enabled Singapore to finance its economic development without resorting to aid or foreign borrowing. Because of its structure, CPF contributions have not distorted resource allocation and the labor market. As the government mandated component of labor cost, the ability to vary the quantum of the employers' CPF contributions has been a critical tool to manage costs in response to economic shocks. Reductions in employers' CPF contributions were made in 1986 and again in 1997 in the wake of the Asian financial crisis. Structural changes were made in the changed economic environment in the aftermath of the Asian financial crisis. The employers' contribution rate was reduced to 13 per cent to reduce the overall cost burden. The employees' contribution rate remained at 20 per cent. More details of the evolution of the CPF over the years are provided in Chapter 6.

(iii) *Fostering "desirable" habits — building an economically viable society*

The government also used policies and systems to foster desirable habits, social change and integration. For example, the CPF system entrenched a culture of saving that was boosted by the establishment of the Post Office Savings Bank (POSB) in 1971. The POSB, as it is commonly known, was set up to encourage the savings habit particularly among children and young adults, and to mobilize these savings for national development. Its tax-free status for savings deposits and underwriting by the government did much to spur the savings habit at all levels of the population. The value of savings deposits increased 55 times, from S$91 million to S$5 billion, between 1971 and 1982.[32] The number of accounts increased from slightly more than half a million in 1971 to more than two million in 1982. Thus for the population at that time of 2.45 million, almost every family member had a POSB account. Most of the deposits were invested in government securities to finance public investments.

The education system was also harnessed to effect social change and integration, most significantly through the bilingual policy. With its history of racial conflict, language had been a particularly sensitive issue in the late 1950s and early 1960s. An early decision was taken

---

[32] Quoted from Li Sheng-Yi (1984). "Money, Banking and Finance in Singapore," in You and Lim (eds).

to promote the use of English as the medium of instruction and rational parents seeking to maximize economic opportunities for their children enrolled them *en masse* in English language schools. By 1984, more than 95 per cent of all primary one students were in English language schools. The bilingual policy was aimed at mitigating the weakened links to indigenous culture and roots. The preoccupation with integration also showed up in the promotion of Mandarin as the common language within the Chinese community.

Attempts were made to mold culture and behavior through national campaigns. Some of the earliest campaigns were the Operation Big Sweep (anti-litter campaign) first started in 1958, "Stop at Two" (to encourage family planning), and "Keep Singapore Clean and Pollution Free" from 1968–1972 (to build the image of a clean and green Singapore). From 1979, national campaigns were coordinated by the Prime Minister's Office and these included "Speak Mandarin," "Courtesy is Our Way of Life," (complete with a courtesy lion as a mascot) and a reversal of the family planning policy "Have Three or More if You Can Afford It." Campaigns were used liberally in the early years in an attempt to bud-graft first world habits but have been used much more sparingly since the late 1980s.

3.1.5 *Building up Security and Defense Capability*

Singapore's vulnerable position right after independence spurred the rapid build-up of her defense capability. At independence, Singapore had two battalions that were under the control of a Malaysian brigadier and there were elements in Malaysia that wished to reverse Singapore's separation. Thus building up the armed forces became a top priority. The build-up of Singapore's defense capability was carried out quietly so as not to unduly antagonize neighboring countries. The assistance of the Israelis to train the army was sought and given.

As a large standing army would have been costly given Singapore's finances at the time, the policy option selected was for a smaller standing army and a large reserve force that could be called upon at short notice. In 1967, the National Service Ordinance was passed. All able-bodied male Singaporeans have to enlist at age 18 for two or two-and-a-half years of National Service, and thereafter remain operationally ready as part of the reserves for the following 20 years.

The announcement in 1967 of the withdrawal of the British troops by 1971 made the build-up of the army more urgent. The pace and scale of the military build-up was significantly boosted by the strong economic growth in the late 1960s and early 1970s. By 1971, there were 17 National Service battalions (16,000 men) with 14 battalions (11,000 men) in the reserves, infantry and commando units, artillery and armor units and a full complement of field personnel. The Singapore Armed Forces Training Institute had been established for basic training and officer cadet training. Air defense capability build-up had also been started. Tremendous investments were made to boost defense, as reflected in the generous block budget that the Ministry of Defence is given every year, the largest of all the ministries.

The changes that took place in the first 20 years of independence are encapsulated in Table 3.1.

3.2 Impact on the Development of Public Sector Governance

The early development of public sector governance was shaped by the exigencies of nation building. Singapore's small size, lack of resources and tenuous security situation made it inevitable that the government would take the lead in developing the economy and the country. This period not only saw the expansion and transformation of the structure of the civil service, but also the establishment of the values and approach to governance.

One of the core but tacit beliefs of the Singapore public sector is that "implementation is policy."[33] This was reflected in the way the public sector developed. In the early years, the bulk of the expansion in the government machinery was in the statutory boards.[34] While they

---

[33] Lim Siong Guan. The approach to policy implementation is examined fully in Chapter 5.

[34] A statutory board is a quasi-government body established by an Act of Parliament, which specifies the reasons for its existence.

Table 3.1. Transformation from 1965–1985

	1960[a]	1970[a]	1984
Area (sq km)	581.5	586.4	620.2
Population at Mid-year ('000s)	1,646	2,074.5	2,529.1
Annual Change (%)	2.4	1.5	1.1
Number Employed ('000s)	448.6	644.2	1,174.8
Unemployment Rate	4.9	6.0	2.7
GDP (at 2000 market prices S$)[*]	6726.3	16090.7	52080.2
GDP Per Capita (S$)[*]	1306	2798	14696
GDP Per Capita (US$)[*]	427	914	6890
Gross Domestic Fixed Capital Formation at 1968 Prices	219.9	1712.0	7575.1
Gross Fixed Capital Formation as % of GDP	9.4	32.2	47.2
Gross National Saving (S$m)	-52.3	1129.7	17645.2
As % of GNP		19.3	44.3
As % of GDFCF		59.8	93.9
Total Trade (S$m)	7554.8	12289.6	112473.6
Exports (S$m)	3477.1	4755.8	51340.0
Domestic Exports (S$m)	217.1	1832.2	33051.2
% Employment in Manufacturing	na	22	27
Transport and Communications			
Vessels Cleared (Million NRT)	34.4	73.0	169.6
Seaborne Cargo Handled (Million FT)	11.9	43.6	104.2
Aircraft Landings ('000s)	6.2	17.1	35.3
Tourist Arrivals ('000s)	90.0	521.7	2991.4
Balance of Payments (Overall) S$m	140.1	564.8	3230.6
Official Foreign Reserves S$m	na	3097.9	22748.0
Public Debt S$m	na	2016.6	28077.3
Domestic	na	1842.8	27435.9
External	na	173.8	641.4
Infant Mortality (per 1000 live births)[b]	34.9	20.5	7.3
Life Expectancy[b]	62.9	65.8	73.3
Literacy[b]		72.2	85.0
Female Labor Force Participation[c]		29.5	45.8

Source: Singapore, Economic Survey of Singapore 1985, Ministry of Trade and Industry.
[a] These figures refer to averages for the decade.
[b] These figures provided by Ministry of Trade and Industry.
[c] Yearbook of Statistics 1986.
[*] These figures came from Singapore, Department of Statistics.

report to parent ministries, statutory boards have greater flexibility than government departments in day-to-day operations. Singapore's policy options and directions after independence were clear: getting things done in the most efficient way was the primary focus — execution was paramount. Statutory boards became the main vehicles for the implementation of economic and social policies. In 1984, there were a total of 83 statutory boards — with 18 under the Social Affairs Ministry, 11 under the National Development Ministry, nine under Trade and Industry, eight in Education and six in Finance.[35] This early period saw the formation and expansion of economic and social institutions that became synonymous with key aspects of Singapore's development: the EDB, the HDB, the Ministry of Defence, the MAS and others. Goh Keng Swee recognized the fundamental importance of people and institutions in economic development:

> "What holds them (developing countries) back is not inadequate aid or trade, but their failure to establish competent organs of public administration and their failure to develop durable and enlightened social and political institutions."[36]

In the same vein, this emphasis on institutions saw the development of a public sector modeled on the British colonial administration, an elite bureaucracy where "the top echelon civil servants constitute an important section of the intellectual elite of the country."[37]

The fact that statutory boards, institutional legacies of Singapore's colonial history, were used as vehicles to drive economic growth says

---

[35] Quoted from Jon ST Quah (1984). "The Public Bureaucracy in Singapore," in You and Lim (eds), pp. 288–314.

[36] Goh Keng Swee (1983). "Public Administration and Economic Development in LDCs," Fourth Harry G Johnson Memorial Lecture delivered at the Royal Society, London on 28 July 1983.

[37] Ian Patrick Austin (2004). *Goh Keng Swee and Southeast Asian Governance*. Singapore: Marshall Cavendish Academic, p. 24.

much about the values of the political leadership. Singapore retained the British Currency Board system, which imposed discipline on macro-economic management. It retained and expanded the CPF system, crafting and adapting it to suit Singapore's development objectives. To ensure the integrity of the education system, Singapore adopted the Cambridge system of certification as the benchmark which is in existence until today. The government thus had no reservations with adopting and adapting structures inherited from the colonial government if these were perceived to be in Singapore's long-term interest. This highly rational, non-ideological, pragmatic approach is a hallmark of the Singapore style of governance. The workability of solutions was the primary criterion for assessing policy alternatives: if they were thought to work and fitted into the strategic long term framework, they were implemented, even though they may not have been fashionable at the time or politically correct.

In the face of clear objectives, well-defined solutions and a lack of other viable institutions, the public sector became the main institutional force for Singapore. It assumed the roles of director, controller, regulator and pace-setter. The gravity of the situation produced a congruence between the political party and the public sector leaders as they worked together to create the right conditions for economic development. Against the backdrop of a small economy with no natural resources, Singapore's development "options" were stark — export or perish. With foreign investment as the critical node in this strategy, creating an investment-friendly environment with social stability and the rule of law was paramount. The late 1960s saw policies made, and construction and infrastructure development proceeding at a frantic pace. Land was cleared, electricity, water and sewage systems were laid, factories were built, labor was trained in preparation for the jobs that it was hoped foreign investors would bring. And when the jobs finally came, everyone understood that success rested on Singapore's ability to be efficient and effective, and to deliver results. In the absence of other viable institutions, the public sector drove practically all aspects of the development of the Singapore economy and society. It developed task-oriented structures and processes to support the achievement of objectives.

The public sector also worked hand-in-hand with the political leadership to mold and shape the values and ethos of the new Singapore society. In some ways, the suddenness of its separation from Malaya and the severity of the immediate post-independence predicament gave the political leadership a relatively clean slate on which it could design and mold a new Singapore society. After more than a decade of racial and religious strife and political tensions with neighboring countries, the population was ready to accept the new government's views on what had to be done to ensure Singapore's survival. The environment enabled the political leadership to imbue the public sector and the new society with values, tacit tenets of governance and ways of looking at the world that would go a long way in enabling the public sector to develop capabilities that would explain its continued effectiveness across significantly different social and economic contexts.

The clean slate meant that the values and views of the founding political leaders were translated into the new society that was being created. For example, the values of self reliance, personal responsibility and a strong work ethic were shaped by the views and experiences of Lee Kuan Yew and Goh Keng Swee who had seen, first hand, the impact on incentives of a welfare-type philosophy during their years of study in Britain. For a developing country that needed to retain its cutting edge drive, Lee and Goh believed that a welfare society type approach would not be appropriate. The impact of this philosophy is reflected in the absence of social safety nets such as unemployment benefits, and the promotion of personal responsibility through a fully-funded pension scheme where the benefits one enjoys during retirement are tied to what each individual has been able to put aside during his working life. The family is deemed to be the basic unit of society and children are encouraged to look after their parents. Children could draw on their own medical savings to pay for their parents' hospitalization expenses. These values, assumptions and beliefs and their impact on governance will be examined in greater detail in Chapter 4.

The relationship between the political leaders and the population was also shaped during this period. The people were told that if they worked hard, avoided activities that could endanger social stability, kept wage demands to a minimum and planned their families, government policy would produce jobs, a roof over their heads and education opportunities for their children. An understanding arose between the government and the population: whatever Singapore wanted, Singaporeans would have to create for themselves — "no one owes us a living." If they worked and managed their lives in accordance with the "ground rules" stipulated by the government, economic growth would follow. The government, i.e., the political and public sector leadership, was judged by the delivery and results of its policies. Economic growth became the source of legitimacy for the ruling party and the pursuit of this growth, the driving force and life-blood of Singapore.

3.3 Reinventing Singapore: 1986–2006

The late 1980s were watershed years for Singapore. The first 25 years of growth and prosperity created a viable nation-state with economic opportunities sufficient for an increasingly well-housed, well-educated population. However the relentless drive for economic growth, coupled with rapidly changing international conditions, the coming of age of the post-independence generation of Singaporeans with new expectations and unparalleled levels of mobility and access to information, generated new demands on policy and increased tensions in Singapore society. These new pressures and conflicts demanded changes in the Singapore government's mental models, the approach and tenets of governance and new processes and approaches to policy-making and problem-solving.

3.3.1 *Changes in Economic Context: 1986–1997*

The 1985–86 recession brought into sharp relief the vulnerability of the Singapore economy and the weaknesses of the early development model. A lack of diversification of sources of growth, an over-reliance on manufacturing, especially electronics and construction, poor labor productivity gains relative to wage costs — all worked to amplify a downturn in demand in the main export markets of the US and Japan brought about by a collapse in world commodity prices including oil. The Economic Committee chaired by Lee Hsien Loong, then Minister of Trade and Industry, brought together public and private sector and union leaders to craft immediate remedial action. The Committee also examined the longer term problems and prospects of the Singapore economy, identified new growth areas and defined new strategies for promoting growth. The Economic Committee review was significant because it marked the first of many continual refinements of economic strategy that were adopted in response to the changing regional and international environments.

The year 1986 marked a significant shift in economic strategy. Economic policy was broadened to include services as a pillar of growth to complement manufacturing, and the objective of maintaining competitiveness entered the policy-making lexicon. After the immediate wage freeze and cuts in CPF contributions rates to restore competitiveness, broader long-term measures were taken to develop a more flexible and cost-effective work force. Steps were taken to benchmark wages to those in developed nations and to those of developing country competitors. As a small open economy, Singapore has always had to take a supply-side approach, ensuring that the costs of doing business here compared well to the rest of the region. The 1985–86 recession taught policy-makers an important lesson: that wage levels could not be dictated centrally and arbitrarily and in an environment of increasing economic volatility; flexibility and speed of adjustment were critical elements. From the early 1990s, effort was expended on promoting flexibility in wage systems. The recession clearly brought home to policy makers that Singapore had to develop a new value proposition to diversify its economic structure. The key new ideas to move the economy forward were consolidated and elaborated in the 1991 Strategic Economic Plan: Towards a Developed Nation.

Greater use of information and communications technologies (ICT) was encouraged as a means to raise efficiency and to allow Singapore to remain competitive vis-à-vis other developing countries despite higher wage costs. In 1981 the Civil Service Computerization Program was launched with the establishment of the National

Computer Board. The push to IT and communications systems was also critical to Singapore's effort to establish the services sector as a leading growth sector. With good transport and communications links plus a well-educated English-speaking workforce, Singapore had unwittingly developed a comparative advantage in the export of services.

As part of this move, Singapore was repositioned as a "Total Business Centre" to encourage growth of services and service-related activities. Activities such as transportation and logistics that were directly complementary to manufacturing were identified and actively promoted. In this vein, manufacturing-based Multi-National Corporations (MNCs) were encouraged to expand their operations and establish their Operational HQs (OHQs) in Singapore. The Singapore OHQ would undertake the whole spectrum of an MNC's manufacturing operations support not only for Singapore but also for the region. This included purchasing and all other manufacturing support, logistics and supply chain management, finance and later, R&D. In the first year of this initiative, about a dozen MNCs established their OHQs in Singapore, including companies like Caltex and Matsushita. Singapore thus set out to build and develop the new infrastructure to propel and support this new growth strategy. Singapore also boosted its profile as a convention city — BTMICE (business travel, meetings, incentive travel, conventions and exhibitions) became a new growth area.

While services were being actively promoted, manufacturing still remained the key pillar of growth. While Singapore had become too expensive in terms of land and labor costs to continue to support low-cost manufacturing, it still lacked the critical enabling technology that would propel it to close its gap with developed countries. Initiatives were put in place to upgrade the technological profile of Singapore's manufacturing base. To encourage MNCs to undertake higher value-added, more technology-intensive activities, steps were taken to encourage the growth of supporting industries that would be able to undertake the production of parts and components needed by more high technology-intensive MNCs.

The importance of MNCs as the driver of labor-intensive industrialization had focused the attention of policy makers, to the detriment of the development of local enterprise. For a long time, local small and medium enterprises (SMEs) had been viewed as key supporting players in economic strategy, but the recession had highlighted the weakness of a development strategy that relied only on government-linked companies and MNCs. Steps were taken from the second half of the 1980s to help develop SMEs in their own right, rather than merely as components in the supply chain of MNCs. The National Productivity Board and the Small Business Bureau were put in charge of helping small local firms upgrade their operations to raise efficiency and improve their access to capital.

To complement measures to boost the SMEs, the government put in place plans to privatize state-owned firms. In 1986, a Public Sector Divestment Committee was formed "to identify government-linked companies (GLCs) [and statutory boards] for divestment, put together a divestment program, and make recommendations on the implementation of the program." The aim was for the government to withdraw from areas not vital to Singapore's interests — to give private sector firms scope to take over — while remaining a catalyst for new ventures deemed essential to the progress of the economy. Over the course of a 10-year privatization program, the Committee recommended the "maximum privatization" of 41 GLCs, the winding up of nine and a further review of 43, many in the defense-related industries. Previously publicly provided services were contracted out; rules and regulations were relaxed to make it easier to form new companies and for existing ones to compete with new ones for contracts. Several key GLCs were listed. Many were partially or fully divested. Singapore Telecom, the national telecommunication authority, was the first statutory board to be converted to a private company. Its shares were offered for sale to the public in 1993. Other statutory boards were subsequently privatized or corporatized — the Public Utilities Board, the Port of Singapore Authority, and the National Computer Board.

In addition to encouraging MNCs to upgrade the skill and technology profile of their activities in Singapore, policy makers sought to create new opportunities for MNCs to retain their low-cost production activities close by to foster a network of linkages that would help to anchor MNCs in the ASEAN (Association of Southeast Asian

Nations) region. The fall in commodity prices had adversely affected the growth prospects of the ASEAN economies, which together also accounted for a significant share of Singapore's exports. However this meant that the costs in these countries were appropriate for low-cost manufacturing industries that were seeking new production bases. The early 1990s saw the launch of Singapore's regionalization efforts and the concept of a Growth Triangle among Singapore, the Malaysian state of Johor and the Indonesian Riau Islands. Firms were encouraged to take their operations to neighboring Malaysia and Indonesia. As wages and other business costs in Southeast Asia were still significantly lower than in Singapore, companies could locate their more labor-intensive operations in Malaysia and Indonesia whilst retaining the higher-wage, higher value-added functions in servicing, distribution, financing and logistics in Singapore. To this end, Singapore worked with Indonesia to build industrial parks in the Indonesian islands of Batam and Bintan. While the results of this initiative were mixed, this marked the start of the strategy to overcome the constraints of Singapore's size and expand its economic space.

3.3.2 Changes in Economic Context: 1997–2006

The Singapore economy recovered quickly after 1986 and by the early 1990s, Singapore had become a Newly-Industrializing Economy, alongside the other fast growing East Asian economies of Hong Kong, Taiwan and South Korea. In 1990, income per capita had reached US$12,000, about 50 per cent that of the US. However economic growth was again being constrained by both land and labor scarcity. At the same time, the end of the Cold War and the fall of the Berlin Wall led to the opening up of ex-communist East European countries. These countries competed for the foreign investment dollar by positioning themselves as efficient but low-cost production centers with the advantage of large, domestic markets. Economic competition was further accentuated by the rise of the Chinese and Indian economies in the first half of the 1990s. The rise of India and China reshaped the international economic balance of power. With their relatively low labor cost and huge domestic markets, these two economies accelerated the flow of investment away from Southeast Asia into South and Northeast Asia.

All these developments demanded adaptability and a rapid speed of adjustment. While Singapore had always been open, the new and continually shifting economic landscape required that policy makers be plugged into these new trends and be agile and flexible enough to respond to events beyond its control but which had significant impact on Singapore. The 1997 Asian financial crisis was a case in point. While the Singapore economy was not in the same boat as the countries whose currencies were attacked, she nonetheless also suffered from the crisis of confidence. While Singapore was affected, its financial system was not jeopardized, and the extent and impact of the meltdown was far less severe. This highlighted to investors differences between Singapore and the other Asian economies in terms of policies, institutions and governance, differences which served Singapore's interests in the longer run. Nonetheless, the event reinforced Singapore's inherent vulnerability and speeded up the search for new sources of growth.

The report of the Committee on Singapore's Competitiveness, formed in the mid 1990s to assess Singapore's competitive position for the decade to follow, reiterated the key role of both manufacturing and services. In view of the susceptibility to increasing competition of manufacturing and its related services, policy makers identified areas in the knowledge-intensive and technology-intensive industries that could form new niche areas of growth. This saw the start of efforts to attract high technology, high value-added industries such as wafer fabrication and petrochemicals. These were not entirely new industries — but now, by identifying the horizontal and vertical linkages, the approach was to integrate both the upstream and downstream industries in each sector.

The new strategy was based on developing and marketing clusters of competencies, and attracting each segment of a cluster to set up operations in Singapore. This way, all the cluster segments would be able to enjoy and exploit economies of scale, creating an advantage to operating in Singapore for the entire cluster segment that would be harder to replicate elsewhere. The idea was to make Singapore a central node, a hub, and part of the broader global network for a range of manufacturing and services-based activities.

Other new sectors like education and medical services came onto the radar. As Asian students began forming large proportions of student populations in established international universities, the potential demand for an expanded education sector in Singapore became clear. However, because of domestic considerations, initial progress was slow. By the late 1990s, INSEAD and the University Of Chicago Graduate School of Business had agreed to set up campuses in Singapore. The World Class Universities initiative announced in 1998 and the open declaration of support from the political leadership cleared the way to attract institutions like Stanford, Waseda, Cornell and Shanghai Jiaotong to establish and jointly run programs with Singapore universities. Additional new areas such as developing Singapore as a medical tourism destination and as a center for creative services, such as media and design, are currently being explored.

Inroads were made into the completely new area of biomedical sciences. The cluster strategy is apparent. First, infrastructure was built. The Biopolis is the new biomedical research hub where researchers from the public and private sectors are co-located, with shared resources and services catering to the full spectrum of R&D activities and graduate training. Five major research institutes are now housed here. Second, top people were pursued to spearhead the key research activities. Then the pharmaceutical companies — such as GlaxoSmithKline, Novartis, Pfizer — were wooed to set up operations. Fourth, the educational institutions, particularly the universities, were encouraged to set up research and degree programs in the biological sciences, biomedical engineering and biochemical engineering, to train up the required manpower. This would be supplemented by other professionals that could be hired from the rest of the world. Fifth, legislation was crafted that would enable researchers in Singapore to pursue research in frontier areas such as stem cell research.

The post-1990 period saw new approaches and strategies to cope with the rapid changes in business models and higher levels of uncertainty precipitated by the sweeping forces of globalization, increased competition and information technology. It was not all smooth-sailing. New levels of competition caught some organizations on the hop. One example was the Port of Singapore Authority (PSA). In 2001, Maersk, which accounted for 18 per cent of PSA's business, moved its operations to the port of Tanjong Pelapas in the southern Malaysian state of Johor after PSA refused to meet Maersk's demands to take ownership of the berths it used at the PSA. Maersk's defection was quickly followed by the Taiwanese shipping line, Evergreen.

While some GLCs or former GLCs floundered in the new economic circumstances, several of them developed themselves into world class companies. Previously government-owned entities such as Singapore Telecommunications (SingTel) and the Development Bank of Singapore (DBS) had become privately owned companies and were embarking on aggressive expansion in the region. Elements of government institutions like the HDB, having developed international reputations, were corporatized; they began bidding and securing contracts to build housing estates in various towns and cities in China. On the national level, Singapore began working to build industrial parks and special economic zones in rapidly developing townships in China and Vietnam. The push to develop an external wing thus proceeded apace throughout the 1990s, with GLCs kick-starting the process — a realization of the earlier vision where GLCs would be a catalyst for new ventures deemed to be in Singapore's long-term interests. This would later pave the way for collaborative ventures abroad by private sector companies.

Being an open economy dependent on international trade and capital flows, Singapore had been a strong exponent of the benefits of free trade and a staunch supporter of multilateral agreements such as GATT and its successor, the WTO. Nevertheless the pace of structural change and the rising incidence of economic dislocation renewed protectionist sentiment in many developed countries. Singapore also embarked on an aggressive policy to maintain and expand its economic space through bilateral free trade agreements, particularly after 1997, and successfully concluded free trade agreements with Japan, India, countries in the Middle East and the USA.

At the same time, the spread of information technology triggered major reconfigurations in business and created new industry value chains that transcended geographical boundaries. In the wake of increased speed of access and the rate of take-up of new technologies in developing countries, Singapore faced the grim prospect of being leapfrogged by developing countries. This was the backdrop for the convening of the Economic Review Committee in December 2001, when Singapore suffered its worst recession since independence with a 2.3 per cent contraction. The chief cause was the bursting of the dot-com bubble in 2000, exacerbated by the contraction of the global electronics industry in 2001. The global economic uncertainty was further compounded by terrorism and related security concerns both internationally and regionally after September 11, 2001. The period after 2001 is significant because the new intense levels of competition forced policy makers to rethink, re-evaluate and reverse many long-standing policy "sacred cows."

The impact of the opening of the Chinese and Indian economies in the early 1990s was felt globally. They became the new favored production bases, not only for those industries needing low-cost production sites but also for companies seeking to tap into the potential of the Chinese and Indian markets. Since 1992, China has been the largest recipient of foreign direct investment in Asia.[38] This development had a major impact on the Singapore economy — its low-cost structures made Singapore highly uncompetitive in many manufacturing industries. After 1990, the shrinkage of the manufacturing sector was palpable. From contributing close to 30 per cent of economic activity in the late 1980s, the second half of the 1990s saw manufacturing's share falling to 19.7 per cent in 2003, nudging up marginally to 20.5 per cent in 2005.[39] With construction accounting for a fairly stable 10 per cent, services-related activities (trade, financial

---

[38] Singapore (2003). *Report of the Economic Review Committee, New Challenges, Fresh Goals: Towards A Dynamic Global City*, Ministry of Trade and Industry, p. 34.

[39] Data provided by the Ministry of Trade and Industry, November 2006.

and business, transport and communications) in the 1990s began to make up about two-thirds of the Singapore economy.

Singapore's development had always been infrastructure-led; this strategy continued with modification in this period as Singapore searched for new sources of growth. High-technology and high value-added industries in search of cost-effective locations, would congregate in locations where infrastructure was already in place, making it quick and efficient to start production. Agglomeration economies were harnessed to great effect in the conceptualization of Jurong Island which, in the 1990s, kick-started the petrochemicals industry. The cluster-based infrastructure approach was adopted for the three areas identified to have the best growth potential in the longer run: biomedical sciences, water and environmental resources, and the digital media and creative industries — all knowledge-intensive industries with high value-adding potential and which, in economic parlance, enjoy increasing returns of scale.

The search for new sources of growth also led to a re-examination of ideas that had surfaced before. The casino industry had been identified prior to this period as one that had potential to boost tourism. But the idea had been put aside by the political leadership several times for fear of destroying the work ethic, attracting related undesirable activities and weakening Singapore's social fabric. The search for new options prompted a serious re-look and this time, the debate was taken to the population. After extensive public debate and consultation with the major religious and civil society groups where numerous concerns were raised, the decision was taken. With Singapore's small size, there were few options. Singapore had a comparative advantage in services. Moreover, policy makers knew that other Southeast Asian countries were also evaluating this issue and perceived there was a first mover advantage.

Apart from identifying new industries and sources of growth, Singapore also adopted a fresh strategy to harness the growth of the Chinese and Indian economies. Singapore started to position itself to exploit new niche opportunities that would inevitably arise by building up linkages, acquiring up-to-date knowledge of developments, and building up Singapore's understanding of the respective business environments. Policy makers understood that the expanding middle class segments in these countries would seek high-end and better quality services — educational, medical and financial — and Singapore was well placed to meet this demand. As major companies internationalized, the government stepped up its initiatives to promote domestic enterprises and entrepreneurship, to augment and expand Singapore's economic base. Small and medium enterprises had been on the economic policy radar since the 1990s but results were less than encouraging. New measures and incentives were instituted to encourage and support innovation and a new Minister was appointed to drive the creation of an entrepreneurial culture in Singapore.

The volatile business environment made it imperative that companies be agile enough to respond and act on fleeting and niche economic opportunities. Attention was thus given to creating a competitive, pro-business, pro-enterprise environment. After a long review, the decision was finally taken to lower corporate taxes to 20 per cent and then lowered again to 18 per cent in 2007. Despite long-standing concerns of Singapore becoming a tax haven, the reduction of the direct tax burden on both companies and individuals was deemed necessary for Singapore to continue to attract foreign investment and foreign talent. Similarly, in line with the objective of reducing costs and to ensure sustainability, the decision was taken to cap the employers' CPF contribution rate at 13 per cent from 2004, and subsequently increased to 14.5 per cent only in 2007.

Greater effort was put into encouraging companies to move from a seniority-based system to one which was more closely linked to performance and profitability. A flexible wage system had first been proposed in 1986 but many companies had not put such a system in place. To avoid crowding out the private sector, the "yellow pages" guideline was instituted: the government should avoid setting up companies to provide services which could be found in the yellow pages of the telephone book.

The intense and accelerated pace of globalization had a major impact on the labor market. As China and India became major recipients of the foreign investment dollar in the early 1990s, they became the new favored production bases, not only for those industries needing low-cost sites but for all companies seeking to tap into the potential of the Chinese and Indian markets. Low skilled workers whose factories had moved found themselves without the skills to get back into the labor market. In the second half of the 1990s, many middle management level white-collar workers also found themselves displaced by those companies which realized they needed to restructure and streamline operations in order to compete. The globalization of the business value chains and the outsourcing of key activities facilitated by IT accelerated the dislocation. For the first time in Singapore's development, the population did not benefit evenly from growth. The figures in Table 3.2 below shows the rise in the number of unemployed among the production level workers in the late 1990s and the later spike in the white collar unemployed in the early 2000s.

Table 3.2. Unemployed Registrants at CareerLink Centres by Occupation Sought 1994–2004

Occupation Sought	1994	1996	1998	1999	2000	2001	2002	2003	2004
Total	1004	2746	7776	5155	3457	9293	15,023	13,916	7749
Professional, Managers, Executives & Technicians	123	316	272	639	494	3625	5112	6972	2284
Clerical & Related Workers	224	1152	1813	1206	767	2007	4173	3129	2245
Sales and Service	302	593	452	510	346	706	1354	1414	754
Production, Transport Operators, Cleaners and Laborers	355	685	4154	2800	1850	2955	4384	2401	2466

Source: Singapore, Workforce Development Agency (WDA). The WDA did not publish this data after 2004.

To help displaced workers cope, there was renewed emphasis on retraining and encouraging them to move to industries where there was demand for workers, e.g., the services industries. But more than simply retraining, policy makers found they had to contend with inertia and entrenched mindsets that slowed down this process of re-tooling. Workers were not prepared to move to industries they were not familiar with, take on shift work or do jobs they deemed "beneath" them. As will be discussed later in this chapter and in subsequent chapters, the emergence of a potential economic underclass would lead to a re-examination of Singapore's approach to welfare and social support.

3.3.3 *Changes in Social and Political Contexts*

Increasing complexity in the economic environment coincided with a period of political transition and social change. The second half of the 1980s was a period of transition — politically, economically and socially. Lee Kuan Yew stepped down as Prime Minister at the end of 1990, preceded by a period of political transition, with the second-generation leadership under Goh Chok Tong assuming de facto control over the reins of the government in the second half of the 1980s. The change in political leadership heralded a change in political style — from Lee's hard driving, task and results oriented approach to Goh's vision for a "kinder, gentler Singapore" and a more consultative style of government. He was a former civil servant — Managing Director of government-linked Neptune Orient Lines — before being elected to Parliament in 1976 and becoming a full minister at the age of 40. Even as he espoused a gentler form of government, Goh's background had been in the "hard" ministries of Defence, Trade and Industry, and Health. His rise in politics was the fastest among the second generation political leaders.

The political transition coincided with what can be termed the gradual political awakening of the Singapore population. The People's Action Party had retained dominance in the political realm in every general election up until the early 1980s when one seat was lost to the opposition in a by-election in 1981. But even though there was one opposition MP in Parliament, he could not initiate a meaningful debate as he could not find another MP to second his motions. In 1984, the Non-Constituency Members of Parliament (NCMP) scheme was launched as a means to provide a voice for the opposition in

Parliament.[40] Goh, who was then deputy prime minister, in proposing the amendment to the Constitution believed that the presence of opposition in parliament would provide a check to the PAP and voice discontent about government policies, which in turn would provide greater legitimacy for the legislature and greater public confidence in the Singapore political system. However this move did not stop the slide in the PAP's votes in the 1984 election held later in the year. The PAP's share of the vote was reduced from 75.5 per cent to 62.9 per cent. The NCMP seat was offered but rejected by members of the opposition parties.

The effort to co-opt alternative non-PAP voices in Parliament continued with the introduction of the Nominated Members of Parliament (NMP) scheme in 1990. This scheme allowed for the appointment of up to six unelected MPs; this was increased to nine in 1997. The idea behind this scheme was to allow citizens without party affiliations to participate and contribute to parliamentary debates without having to go through the electoral process, to beef up the quality of debate in Parliament. NMPs, who cannot be affiliated with any political parties, are appointed by the President for a term of two and a half years on the recommendation of a Select Committee chaired by the Speaker of the House. NMPs and NCMPs can vote on all issues except amendments to the constitution, public funding, votes of no confidence in the government, and removing the president from office.

But these changes were not enough. The loss of four seats in the 1991 election was a strong signal of the restlessness of the population, their desire for a genuine opposition in Parliament and a voice in the country's affairs. Singapore's openness, the free flow of information and the explosion of IT meant that Singapore citizens, particularly the younger generation, were increasingly exposed to the values, mores and practices of the Western developed countries. The Singapore workforce had become increasingly well-educated. Between 1985 and 2001, the average number of years of schooling rose from 5.7 years to

---

[40] Under the NCMP scheme, the top opposition losers who obtain more than 15 per cent of the votes in their respective constituencies are offered the position.

8.4 years, and the proportion of graduates more than tripled from 5.2 per cent to 17 per cent. Sixty-six per cent of the workforce in 2001 had at least secondary education, compared with 46 per cent in 1985. The share of Professionals, Managers, Businessmen and Executives rose from 22 per cent to 42 per cent of the workforce over the same period.[41] Being well-educated and well-traveled, many saw alternative lifestyles and alternative frameworks for engagement between different peoples and their governments. The PAP's directive style of government had worked well in the early years of development when survival had been at stake. However, 25 years of relative peace and prosperity had produced a populace that yearned for a more participative society, a less authoritarian style of government and a relationship between the government and the people that encompassed more dialog and that went beyond legitimacy premised on the delivery of economic growth. Many younger Singaporeans became more critical of policies and developed much higher expectations of government responsiveness and service delivery.

Strong economic growth in the late 1980s and early 1990s had fueled the Singapore dream comprising the "Five Cs": cash, credit card, car, condominium and country club. Yet many segments of the population, where average household income was S$25,000 in 1994, felt this dream to be elusive. In 1992, only about 31 per cent of Singaporean households had cars,[42] due to high car prices, which in turn were the result of high taxes imposed to control the number of cars. Similarly, high-end HDB public housing flats subsidized by the government cost more than S$500,000, and private condominiums and houses cost at least twice as much. In 1994, prices of private residential property rose by 44 per cent over the previous year. High property prices, high car prices, a narrowly meritocratic, highly competitive education system all served to create a sense of disenchantment among many who rued the lack of a middle class quality of life despite a middle class income.

---

[41] Singapore (2003). *Report of the Economic Review Committee, New Challenges, Fresh Goals: Towards A Dynamic Global City.* Ministry of Trade and Industry, pp. 26–27.

[42] Haley, Low and Toh (1996).

The first half of the 1990s saw many families pulling up their roots in search of greener pastures. A major challenge for the public sector was to find ways to engage citizens and to meet their higher expectations.

A series of policy innovations were put in place to try to meet these aspirations. To meet the growing voice for consultation, the Feedback Unit was started in 1988 to obtain the views from the public on a wide range of issues. A new approach to managing car ownership and car usage was developed with the implementation of the vehicle quota system and electronic road pricing (see Chapter 6), under which it became more affordable to own a car but more expensive to run one. In a move to bridge the price gulf between public and private housing, a new type of public housing, the Executive Condominium, was created to cater to the demand for housing with condominium-like finishes and facilities. Prices were set higher than those for standard HDB housing but below those for private apartments. At the same time the government announced measures to curb speculation in residential property, which helped to dampen rising property costs.

But despite these measures, the retention of the local talent pool remained a challenge of the late 1980s and early 1990s. While policy makers went about putting in place these measures, it was clear that the public sector and the political leadership did not accept nor truly understand the reasons that pushed citizens to live and work outside Singapore. The debate on this issue centered around categorizing those who did not migrate as "stayers" and those who did, as "quitters", with questionable loyalty to Singapore. It was not until ten years later that a more productive approach was taken to addressing the issue of Singaporeans who chose to live abroad and to ensure that they kept their links with Singapore. The Overseas Singaporean Unit (OSU) in the Prime Minister's Office was formed in 2005.

The problem of an aging population continued unabated throughout the 1980s and 1990s. As Table 3.3 shows, the median age of the population rose from 24 years to 36 years between 1980 and 2005. Despite campaigns and public education efforts in the late 1980s and throughout the 1990s, Singapore's fertility rate showed no signs of reversal.

Table 3.3. Population Age Profile

1980	2005	2020 (projected)
112,000 elderly	291,000 elderly	575,000 elderly
1 elderly: 14 working-age persons	1 elderly: 9 working-age persons	1 elderly: 5 working-age persons
Median age: 24	Median age: 36	Median age: 40

Elderly: Defined as those aged 65 and above.
Source: Prime Minister's speech in Parliament, published in *The Straits Times*, 14 November 2006, p. H6.

There were several contributing factors. A greater proportion of young people delayed marriage or opted to remain single: the single population rose from 13.4 per cent to 18.1 per cent between 1980 and 1990.[43] In addition, married females had fewer children, with the average number falling from 3.4 to 2.9 children. Moreover, the number of children also fell as the educational qualification of the mother rose. In 1990, married women with no formal qualifications had an average of 4.6 children while those with university education had 1.36 children.[44] This pattern had been cast in the 1970s but did not catch the attention of policy makers until the early 1980s. Caught between low fertility among the best educated and the migration of the same, already small Singapore faced the prospect of not being able to retain a critical mass of talent to support the economy. The initial panic resulted in a couple of early policy mis-steps — the pro-graduate mothers procreation policy in 1984[45] and the granting of permanent residence to Hong Kong residents in 1987. Firstly, the increasingly well-educated population would not tolerate the same level of intrusion as before into what they perceived as personal decisions. Shaping behavior, if it remained at all possible, would require more subtle approaches. Secondly, incentives, particularly monetary and physical, had become less effective in inducing changes in areas where personal

---

[43] Singapore, Census of Population 1990.

[44] Ibid.

[45] For more details, refer to Chapter 5.

preference was generally more critical than financial considerations. This instance was indicative that Singapore society had evolved, and that some problems involving how many children one had and where one lived needed more holistic and sophisticated solutions.

The 1990s witnessed rising income inequality and a widening social divide as the pace of structural change accelerated. Those with the skills and competencies that enabled them to leverage on the globalization of knowledge and information technology enjoyed greater than proportionate returns while those who did not found themselves displaced, with fewer opportunities to bounce back. Unemployment, which had been solved since the early 1970s, returned and it was not just cyclical unemployment but structural. Unlike the early years where all segments of the population clearly benefited from broad-based economic growth, the new kind of growth, driven by knowledge and technology was far less inclusive. Table 3.4 below highlights the widening income disparity since the 1990s.

Table 3.4. Widening Income Disparity

Employed Households	Changes in Per Capita Household Income (% per annum)	
	1990–1997	1997–2005
Lowest 20%	7.2	0.3
Next 20%	7.7	1.6
Next 20%	8.1	2.2
Next 20%	8.5	2.8
Top 20 %	8.8	4.0

Source: Prime Minister's speech in Parliament, reproduced in *The Straits Times*, 14 November 2006, p. H7.

The late 1990s and early 2000s saw efforts directed towards upgrading displaced segments of the population and also finding ways to prevent the development of an underclass. But moves in this direction were hampered initially by the government's conservative fiscal stance where budget surpluses and the accumulation of reserves had been the norm and part of the overall governance approach. Social safety nets and unemployment benefits had long been eschewed for their detrimental effect on the work ethic. But the emergence of uneven growth and its potentially damaging impact on social cohesion demanded a policy re-think. The severity of the situation of some segments of the population — the elderly and the low-income groups — forced a re-examination of long-held convictions. The initial response, through a series of off-budget measures, was tentative. The New Singapore Shares (NSS) were introduced in 2001 to help the low-income group tide over the economic downturn. The Economic Restructuring Shares (ERS) introduced in 2003 were part of the offset package meant to help Singaporeans adapt to the structural changes in the economy, in particular the rise of the GST from 3 per cent to 5 per cent in 2003. Both the NSS and ERS schemes favored the lower income groups but the concept was still one of broad-based disbursement. It was not until Budget 2006 that measures were put in place that reflected acceptance of the concept of targeted assistance. The concept of Workfare will be examined in detail in Chapter 6.

So while sections of the population were suffering the effects of uneven economic growth, it became increasingly clear that Singapore's indigenous population would not grow fast enough to meet the needs of an increasingly globalized economy where success required a critical mass of world-class talent. It was imperative that Singapore build itself up as an attractive and viable place to live, both to retain increasingly mobile and sophisticated Singaporeans and to attract global talent. While this may not have been an issue during the boom years when everyone enjoyed the fruits of growth, pursuing an active pro-foreigner policy in times of economic difficulty and rising dislocation generated strong feelings of resentment. Therefore in stark contrast with the earlier period, new tensions and conflicting pressures such as these made policy-making much more of a balancing act.

The push to attract and retain international talent saw, among other things, policies to reduce personal income taxes and to facilitate the development of culture and the arts, and world class entertainment facilities such as the Esplanade (Theatres on the Bay), dining establishments and an exciting Singaporean nightlife. As a result, the recent annual growth rates of non-residents have outstripped those of the resident population, as can be seen from the figures in Table 3.5.

Table 3.5. Changes in the Resident and Non-Resident Population

	Total Pop.	Av Annual Growth %	S'pore Residents	Av Annual Growth %	Non-Residents	Av. Annual Growth %
1990	3074.1	2.3	2735.9	1.7	311.3	9.0
2000	4027.9	2.8	3273.4	1.8	754.5	9.3
2001	4138.0	2.7	3325.9	1.6	812.1	7.6
2002	4176.0	0.9	3382.9	1.7	793.0	-2.4
2003	4186.1	0.2	3438.1	1.6	747.9	-5.7
2004	4238.3	1.2	3484.9	1.4	753.4	0.7
2005	4341.8	2.4	3543.9	1.7	797.9	5.9
2006	4483.9	3.3	3608.5	1.8	875.5	9.7

Source: Singapore, Department of Statistics, published in *The Straits Times*, 7 December 2006.

3.3.4 *Changes in Security Context*

The complexity of the environment after 1990 was made even more so by the advent of major security issues after 2001. In the first 35 years of development, security had been a key but not a front-burner issue. The Ministry of Defence and the Singapore Armed Forces (SAF) continued to build up Singapore's capabilities quietly. In the wake of the pullout of the British forces, the SAF underwent a period of rapid modernization in the 1970s and 1980s. The emphasis was on deterrence, effectiveness and increasing the indigenous, well-balanced capabilities of the SAF. As with all other key areas, the Singapore Armed Forces developed a reputation for efficiency and effectiveness, premised on a systematic approach to problem solving. The events of September 11, 2001 altered the security landscape irrevocably and the focus of the SAF had to change along with it. Not only did the SAF and MINDEF have to change the way they approached warcraft, the whole concept of defense and security also had to change.

But beyond military defense, the events emanating from 9/11 posed an unprecedented challenge to Singapore's internal defenses and social fabric. The events of 9/11 heralded the start of a new era of global terrorism. In December 2001, 13 men were detained for terrorism-related activities in Singapore, and they were later found to be members of the clandestine organization "Jemaah Islamiyah" (JI). The JI organization in Singapore was part of a larger network with cells in Malaysia and Indonesia, and about half of those detained had trained with Al-Qaeda, the group responsible for the attack on the World Trade Center in New York. Subsequent information uncovered showed that the JI had targeted key installations in Singapore. What was particularly shocking was the profile of those detained. All but one of those arrested had been HDB dwellers. All had studied in national schools in Singapore. Six had completed full-time national service and were reservists. The presence of such extremist elements in Singapore and the fact that the new terrorist threat had an Islamic focus bred new levels of inter-racial suspicion, which in turn posed new threats to the stability and cohesion of Singapore's multi-racial, multi-religious society.

The period after 2001 thus saw renewed efforts to promote inter-racial and inter-religious understanding and open discussion of the threat posed by Islamic fundamentalism. Muslim religious leaders with moderate and inclusive views were encouraged to speak out against violence and to reaffirm the peaceful tenets of Islam. An accreditation scheme for Islamic teachers was launched to prevent a repeat of how the Singapore JI cell leader recruited members — through Islamic classes. Inter-racial confidence circles were established to promote dialog on key issues among all the major religious groups. While terrorism was the main threat, it was not the only one. New diseases, such as SARS and the avian flu whose pathology was unknown, posed new challenges and would demand new types of responses from the government and the people of Singapore.

3.4 The Post 1986 Period: Challenges for the Public Sector

The speed of change, uncertainty and conflicting pressures highlighted the need for adaptability, flexibility and a capacity to deal with the unknown. The new environment also forced the re-examination of mental models and the relaxation of some long-held values and convictions. In contrast with the earlier period when the policy options were more clear-cut, the increased complexity of issues of the post-

1990 period required a careful assessment of policy alternatives and their impacts. Increased complexity also meant that more issues no longer fell neatly within the sphere of a single agency but were cross-agency in nature and demanded integrated solutions.

An example was the issue of meeting the needs of a rapidly aging population, an issue that required input from agencies involved in areas such as health care, community and social services, housing, transport and manpower development. Helping to alleviate the plight of low-income families needed similar coordinated action from the housing, education, finance and community development agencies. External shocks such as SARS and the avian flu tested the country's systems and its crisis responsiveness, and required coordinated government action. Solutions needed went beyond task-based structures that had evolved in the early years and forced the government to develop new processes and structures to meet a new and much more uncertain external environment.

The challenge was reflected in the structural changes in the public sector. While the main functional areas remained unchanged, new areas of focus gradually emerged. Ministries were renamed, closed down, expanded. For example, the Ministry of Community Development started in 2001 as public policy began emphasizing the softer but no less crucial role of developing and encouraging communities with an eye on keeping a ear on the ground for potential social problems. In 2004, the ambit of this Ministry was expanded to include Youth and Sport, again to reflect new emphasis and priorities. A new development was in the increase in the number of cross agency units. Two new units with responsibility spanning several areas were created under the Prime Minister's Office as they did not fit anywhere in the existing ministry framework. These were the Citizen and Population Unit to sell Singapore's immigration policies with a mandate to go beyond the conventional graduates and professionals to attract all kinds of talent; and the Overseas Singaporean Unit (OSU) to help Singapore keep in touch with Singaporeans living and working overseas. The decision to allow Singaporeans living and working overseas to vote in the 2006 General Elections signaled a coming-of-age of Singapore's attitude towards its diaspora.

New problems also forced a re-examination of age-old assumptions and values, one of which has been the case for different treatment for men and women on the premise that the man is the head of household, and that policies should always help affirm and reinforce the family unit. For a long time, singles were not allowed to buy new subsidized flats from the HDB, as this was perceived as potentially undermining the family unit by encouraging single young people to set up their own homes away from their parents. This policy was relaxed in 1991 — singles were allowed to buy flats on the resale market in selected HDB estates. Another policy that was relaxed was the granting of Permanent Resident (PR) status to foreign spouses of Singapore women. Foreign spouses of Singapore men had traditionally been granted PR but not the other way around. The early policy had resulted in many Singaporean women emigrating when they married foreign husbands. The reversal in 1999, a pragmatic response to a pressing problem, is illustrative of the willingness of the government to revise and change its mental models when required. The introduction of the five-day work week in 2005 was another major policy change, a move that had been resisted in the past for the possible negative impression that it may give to investors. But the step was taken to create a more conducive pro-family environment, both to attract foreign talent and to retain local ones. The ability to change and develop new mental models cannot be more clearly illustrated than in the policy decisions to allow the establishment of a casino in Singapore and the launch of the Workfare-targeted assistance schemes.

It is clear from this overview that the vastly different contexts in these two periods demanded very different approaches and capabilities of the public sector. A contrast of the broad differences in context and approach in the pre-1985 and post-1985 periods is provided in Table 3.6. In the immediate post-independence period, survival imperatives demanded efficiency and effectiveness in execution, with the focus on delivery and results. While there were many innovative solutions put in place, the development path and the required policies for a new country with no resources other than her people were nonetheless relatively clear and unambiguous. The focus of the 1960s and 1970s was thus on putting in place systems and structures

Table 3.6. Singapore's Changing Context 1965–2006

1965–1985	1986–2006
Beyond Position: Overcoming Constraints Redefining Purpose: Ensuring Continued Relevance	
Building a New Nation from Scratch: Survival	**Transiting to First World: Sustainability**
Defining the Path	Charting New Paths
Identifying the formula/recipe for growth Creating necessary conditions • Legislating industrial stability • Building institutions • Designing frameworks, systems & structures • Attracting foreign investments • Building up strong state companies	Re-examining a successful system Creating an innovative society • Monitoring competitiveness • Harnessing knowledge and skill • Building a Singaporean identity • Recognizing and boosting the role of private sector • Developing an innovative and entrepreneurial culture
Orchestrating Growth within Predictable International Environment: Internal Focus	Adapting to Competitive and Volatile Global Context: Externally Oriented
• Promoting stability • Regulating internal economic environment to ensure consistency and predictability • Forecasting manpower requirements • Directing the educational mix • Regulating labor market; pacing restructuring • Exploring IT	• Embracing change • Engendering flexibility • Enlarging economic space • Entrenching Singapore in global networks • Exploring emergent opportunities • Encouraging and facilitating enterprise • Expanding educational diversities • Exploiting IT
Efficient Execution of Plans	Handling New Complexities
• Following clear goals, defined strategies • Dealing with basic needs for jobs, housing and education • Building basic physical and social infrastructure for economic growth • Focused-mission statutory boards to ensure efficient execution	• Reviewing assumptions, making trade-offs • Dealing with structural unemployment and income inequality • Building a global city to anchor citizens and attract talent • Integrating solutions requiring coordination across agencies

Table 3.6. *Continue*

1965–1985	1986–2006
<u>Ensuring Social Stability and Survival</u>	<u>Building Unity and Social Cohesion</u>
• Curbing population growth • Prescribing behavior (e.g., anti-littering campaigns and incentives) • Building physical stakes • Providing basic education and healthcare • Ensuring racial and religious harmony • Forging social compact: growth and prosperity in return for hard work, discipline and social order	• Encouraging marriage & procreation • Encouraging diversity • Building emotional stakes, "heartware" and Singapore identity • Meeting higher needs and aspirations of sophisticated population • Ensuring racial and religious harmony • Remaking social compact: even though hard work, discipline and social order remain paramount, government will help those who do not gain as much from growth, but only if they also help themselves.
<u>Presumption</u>	<u>New Reality</u>
Economic growth: necessary and sufficient for stability, development and social cohesion	Reconciling primacy of economic growth with aspirations of a more socially aware population for greater political openness.
Efficiency and Effectiveness sufficient for growth	Continued growth requires speed, adaptability, responsiveness, risk-taking in addition to efficiency and effectiveness: "remaking is essential"
Role: director, regulator, controller	Role: facilitator, convener, aggregator

and building institutions to create the conditions deemed necessary to stimulate and support economic growth and development. The approach was largely directive and the emphasis, on promoting stability and order, accumulating capital resources and managing growth. After 1986, Singapore began looking outward with a more strategic lens whereas before 1985, energies had been largely concentrated on managing the domestic economic environment. The guiding principles post-1986 remained the same but the approach became more open and consultative. For instance economic planning and strategy making before 1985 had largely been carried out centrally within government agencies but the post-1986 period was marked by the highly visible inclusion of other stakeholders, notably senior representatives from industry and businesses, in deliberations. Policy makers began to realize that they did not have all the answers and that better policies could be devised by co-opting those in the know and broadening the ambit and scope of discussions.

The new domestic and external environment of the 1990s thus saw the transformation of the public sector. While the focus of the pre-1985 period was the execution of clear-cut policies, the increasing complexity of issues in the 1990s and 2000s demanded that the public sector develop the capacities and capabilities to design and evaluate policy options and to reassess the relevance of existing policies. It also demanded the ability for rapid response to deal with unexpected turbulence and uncertainty, compared with the emphasis on stability and constancy before 1985. Instead of managing the environment, the approach changed to one of accepting and embracing change and facilitating quick response. Thus instead of tightly regulating the market to ensure consistency, regulations and markets were liberalized to help engender flexibility and responsiveness. In volatile and complex landscapes, it became clear that public sector efficiency was no substitute for private initiative and enterprise. Where the 1970s and early 1980s stressed order and rules, discipline, efficiency and productivity as the drivers of growth, the requirements for the 1990s were flexibility, diversity, nimbleness and adaptability which demanded very different capabilities of the public sector. The lessons of the 1985 recession and the implications of the 1997 financial crisis were laid out by Lee Hsien Loong when he was Deputy Prime Minister after the Report of the Economic Review Committee had been released:

> "… no system works forever. As the external environment changes, and as economies evolve, institutions and policies that used to work can become outdated or even dysfunctional. Countries will adjust incrementally over time to these changes, but eventually incremental change

is not enough. Then it becomes necessary for countries to break the mould and remake themselves... This applies directly to us. However difficult the changes we have to make, the status quo is not an option."[46]

The nature of governance and the relationship between the public sector and the populace would evolve from the prescriptive in the first phase of Singapore's development, to one where the public sector became more of a facilitator and enabler.

While both the political and public leadership recognized that change was necessary, what was even more significant was the acknowledgment that this change would have to be dynamic, a continuing process:

> "The ERC's proposals to remake the economy will not be the final solutions to our problems. Policies will need to be constantly reviewed and updated as situations unfold. New challenges will arise, and we will need to set fresh goals for ourselves. We will need to remake Singapore again, and again. But the more promptly and flexibly we can adjust our policies, the less traumatic and disruptive the remaking will be."[47]

On the social front, the pliant, passive, economy-focused Singapore society of the 1970s and early 1980s evolved to one that was well-educated, more socially aware with higher expectations, and aspirations for greater political openness. This increasing sophistication meant that the directive approach of the early years was no longer possible: the failure of the pro-population policies was testament to that. The 1990s and 2000s would also see policy makers face issues that had no simple straightforward solutions; society would learn that economic growth would not always be the answer, and would

---

[46] Keynote Address by Deputy Prime Minister Lee Hsien Loong at the Annual Dinner of the Economic Society of Singapore, 8 April 2003, "Remaking the Singapore Economy".
[47] Ibid.

begin to question and debate priorities and trade offs. The constraints are no longer purely economic in nature; rather the policy issues that need to be re-examined are largely social and political. Prime Minister Lee cautioned that these issues, if not addressed, could undermine the social consensus needed to pursue rational long-term economic policies:

> "Reform and restructuring is never a purely economic exercise. Success depends critically on social and political factors. Economic reforms are not painless. There will be winners and losers, at least in the short-term. Therefore, there must be political support for the changes, a willingness to accept the pain of the transition, and a confidence that those adversely affected will be helped. This depends on a feeling of shared nationhood, of going through thick and thin together. To maintain social compact, a balance needs to be struck between pushing through needed changes without delay, and spacing them out to reduce the political pain."[48]

3.5 Perception of Position: Impact of History and Geography

Singapore was born in crisis. At independence, the prospects for survival for this minuscule nation state were bleak: there was little land and no natural resources; it was flanked, in particular, by two large neighbors that looked upon this tiny nation with suspicion and hostility; it was heavily dependent on British monies given in exchange for allowing Britain to retain its major military base here. Its population, a mix of immigrant Chinese, Malays and Indians, had survived a tumultuous period of racial and religious conflict, with little sense of nationhood. Singapore's only advantage was its strategic location. Its political leaders concluded that to survive, Singapore had

---

[48] Ibid.

to be tougher, more disciplined, better organized and move faster than other countries. Lee Kuan Yew took stock of what was required for Singapore to survive:

> "I concluded an island city-state in Southeast Asia could not be ordinary if it was to survive. We had to make extraordinary efforts to become a tightly-knit, rugged and adaptable people who could do things better and cheaper than our neighbors, because they wanted to bypass us and render obsolete our role as the entrepot and middleman for the trade of the region. We had to be different."[49]

This was the mindset that developed and which has remained entrenched until the present day. Singapore recognized that it had to be well organized, efficient and internationally competitive to survive. The political leaders understood that this meant that the quality of the government, how it was organized, the way the country was run, and the values and focus of the government and the people had to be aligned and geared towards economic survival and growth.

Today, Singapore's size, with its present 4 million people, is dwarfed by Indonesia's 245 million and Malaysia's 24 million. From time to time, these countries have reminded Singapore of its municipality status. Singapore's relations with Malaysia since independence have been checkered. Singapore depended significantly on Malaysia for its water supplies, and during periods of tension in cross-straits relations, Malaysia invariably raised the issue of water supply to pressurize Singapore. However the most well-known episode was when the former Indonesia President Habibie proclaimed Singapore as "the little red dot" in a sea of green that was Indonesia, when he wanted to remind Singapore of its place in the world and its vulnerability. Free and easy access by air and sea out of and into Singapore depends in some measure on the goodwill of its neighbors. Because of its size, Singapore depends on the goodwill of countries such as the US, France and Australia to conduct military exercises

---

[49] Lee (2000), p. 24.

and to train its armed forces. Thus the constraints of geography have created a siege mentality and a long-standing "sense of reality" in the mindset of the leadership, and this in turn has had significant impact on Singapore's governance and the ethos and culture of the public sector.

3.6 Purpose: Philosophy and Imperatives of Governance

The philosophy of the Singapore government and its approach to public policy formulation were shaped by the circumstances of and the imperatives created by its sudden independence. Singapore had to look beyond and "leapfrog" its immediate region to increase its chances for survival. Its historical experience and its recognition of its dependency on developments in the global economic and security environment shaped its deep sense of vulnerability. Its lack of natural resources focused the leadership's mind on its people as the only strategic resource for the country, and the need to accumulate financial resources from economic growth in order to build buffers for survival during lean years. The perceived vulnerabilities of Singapore's position influenced the leadership's intent and purpose, and the adoption of several strategic imperatives for good governance: economic survival, domestic stability, global relevance, financial prudence, and people development. What constituted good governance?

> "... This depends on the values of a people... As an Asian of Chinese cultural background, my values are for a government which is honest, effective and efficient in protecting its people, and allowing opportunities for all to advance themselves in a stable and orderly society, where they can live a good life and raise their children to do better than themselves."[50]

Three key beliefs drive policy-making in Singapore. First is the belief that a strong economy is fundamental to the viability of all

---

[50] Speech given on 20 November 1992, reproduced in Han, Fernandez and Tan (1998). Times Editions Pte Ltd, pp. 376–383.

other policies, and that continued economic growth is the number one priority. Almost all of Singapore's policy-making is oriented towards ensuring that growth is not compromised, practically to the exclusion of everything else. In response to a query if economic growth was and should always remain the number one priority, Lee Kuan Yew replied:

> "Absolutely. If not that, what are you talking about? You're talking about misery and poverty. You are talking about Rwanda or Bangladesh, or Cambodia or the Philippines. They've got democracy... But have you got a civilized life to lead?
>
> ... People want economic development first and foremost. The leaders may talk something else. You take a poll of any people. What is it they want? The right to write an editorial as you like? They want homes, medicines, jobs, schools. No, no, no, there is no question about it."[51]

More recent demands for greater political openness and consideration of social issues reflect the increasing dichotomy between the aspirations of a better educated and socially aware cohort of Singaporeans and a public sector that was geared primarily to the economy. While it believes that strong economic growth is the precursor for everything else, the public sector is increasingly learning to reconcile economic imperatives and these new aspirations.

Second is the belief that state is central to Singapore's long-term stability. While the private sector is crucial for economic growth and is now contributing a greater share to economic growth, the government's extensive role remains indispensable. Singapore, founded on state entrepreneurship, continues to depend significantly on the public sector some 40 years later. This is a legacy of the thinking of the founding generation of leaders who believed that there was no reason why state capitalism and strongly state-facilitated growth

---

[51] Han Fook Kwang, Warren Fernandez and Sumiko Tan (1998). *Lee Kuan Yew — The Man and His Ideas.* Times Editions Pte Ltd, p. 123.

should in any way deliver inferior results than the private sector. The belief that the best people have to be in the public sector was the direct result of this assumption and that Singapore's survival depended on the government, not just on the private sector. This assumption has been the subject of much debate, both from the ideological perspective and also from the point of view of its impact on the breadth, depth and sustainability of economic growth.

Third is the belief that policy-makers must be future-oriented to be effective. A strong future orientation is a response to the innate sense of vulnerability regarding Singapore — especially its geography, its lack of natural resources, and its small population size. Singapore depended on international trade and investments for its survival, yet its political leaders knew that Singapore would not be able to influence international or regional developments. Its survival depended on it being continuously relevant to the changing global environment. This required a constant scan of current developments and future trends that could affect Singapore, and preparing the country to face the future. The progress and development of the country and a better tomorrow for its people depended on the government's ability to understand the impact of potential future developments, and implement policies to invest for the long term. This was the commitment and motivation that brought the political leaders to seek self-government from British colonial rule, and became the main platform for winning legitimacy and subsequent elections. The same value system was passed to the public sector leaders as they worked closely with the political leadership to build a new nation.

An examination of Singapore's development path over the years reveals that Singapore survived by being open to new ideas, by learning from others, being alert to new opportunities, anticipating challenges and problems. But while patterns emerged over time, there was no clear-cut pre-designed governance framework; as Lim Siong Guan described it, "We were inventing along the way." However it became clear early on what sort of values had to be instilled in Singapore society to ensure that the new state would survive. These values and the principles that defined the nature of governance in Singapore will be described in Chapter 4.

Cultural Foundations: Inculcating Principles of Governance[1]

Dynamic governance comes from the organizational capacity to think and change and is enabled by a supportive institutional culture. The capabilities for thinking ahead, thinking again, and thinking across in the Singapore public service govern its capacity to learn, adapt to change and renew over time. The institutional culture forms the foundation for the development of these capabilities. The capabilities of an organization reside in more than the quality of the leadership and the observable structures and processes; they are also embedded in the culture and the social network, which are manifested in the values and beliefs of the institution, its attitude towards learning and approach to fostering continuous change. Why is there a need to understand the cultural foundations of values, beliefs and mental models? Because learning, development and planned change cannot be understood or be effective without considering how culture may be a source of resistance — since it is shaped by past experiences, culture commonly acts as an impediment to change. We are interested to understand the core values and cultural foundations of the Singapore public service that enabled its dynamic capabilities for change.

We operationalize the cultural foundations of governance in Figure 1.1 of Chapter 1 as the leadership perception of the position of a state, which influences its conception of the purpose and principles of governance. Chapter 3 discussed the contexts that shaped the economic and social development of Singapore since its independence in 1965,

---

[1] The term "Principles of Governance" is used broadly in this chapter to refer to the values, beliefs and strategic imperatives of governance that are derived from the leadership perception of Singapore's position. This usage of the term is different from the official usage of the same term by the Civil Service College, which uses it to refer specifically to the principles of public sector governance.

providing the background for why and how perceptions of a nation's position and its articulation of purpose are derived, which in turn provide the rationale for the principles of governance adopted. This chapter focuses on the principles of governance that have guided the development of the institution's capabilities and the paths chosen to learn, adapt and change. We will describe what culture is, synthesize the perceptions of position and purpose that provide the foundations for the principles of governance, and then describe the main principles that have guided policy-making and implementation in Singapore.

4.1 Understanding Culture

Culture denotes certain group beliefs and values that are shared or held in common, so it can be thought of as the accumulated shared learning of a given community, based on a history of shared experience. The culture of a group can be defined as:

> "A pattern of shared basic assumptions that the group learned as it solved its problems of external adaptation and integration, that has worked well enough to be considered valid and, therefore, to be taught to new members as the correct way to perceive, think, and feel in relation to these problems."[2]

Culture is a product of past successes. As an institution develops and evolves, cultural assumptions become embedded into its psyche and are increasingly taken for granted. These assumptions, based on past experiences, operate as filters on what an institution perceives and thinks about, determine its view of the world and thus influence its policy choices and strategies. Culture consists of patterned ways of thinking, feeling and reacting to various situations and actions.[3] Thus if an institution's culture and past experiences provide the

---

[2] Edgar H Schein (1992). *Organizational Culture and Leadership*, Second Edition. San Francisco: Josey-Bass Publishers, p. 12.

[3] P Christopher Earley and Soon Ang (2003). *Cultural Intelligence*. CA: Stanford University Press, p. 63.

values and mental models to recognize and respond to changes, its culture becomes an enabling foundation for learning and adaptation in periods of rapid change.

What are some manifestations of culture? An organization's mission and espoused values provide the first level indication of culture — defining its reason for being and the manner by which it seeks to achieve this mission. Inherent in these values is its formal philosophy — the broad values and principles that guide its actions. Culture also resides in the behavioral regularities and norms of a group — the implicit rules that govern interaction between different members or groups within the organization and which are a means for internal integration. Moreover, the process of sharing and socialization within an organization fosters common habits of thinking, shared mental models and shared meanings of emergent events. Thus, not only does the culture govern the way groups interact with each other, it also determines the way an organization perceives and interprets external events and, in turn, influences its strategic responses and policy choices.

How do leaders create the culture of an organization? According to Schein, the culture of an organization springs from the beliefs, values and assumptions of the founders of the organization. Founders not only have a high level of self-confidence and determination but they typically have strong assumptions about the nature of the world, the role that organizations play in the world, human nature and relationships, how truth is arrived at, and how to manage time and space. Organizational culture is created when leaders externalize their own assumptions and embed them gradually and consistently into the mission, goals, structures and decision processes of the organization.[4] As the organization evolves and develops, this culture may be moderated or changed by new beliefs and assumptions brought in by new members or leaders.

This is what happened in the case of Singapore. The founding generation of leaders — Lee Kuan Yew, Goh Keng Swee and, to a certain extent, Hon Sui Sen — in their own ways, shaped the ethos

---

[4]Schein (1992), pp. 211–213.

and values of the Singapore public service, and the way it defined and approached its key functions. The leaders created and built the public service based on their beliefs of what constituted a good and effective government that would facilitate economic growth and social development. Retired prominent Permanent Secretary JY Pillay explained how the political leadership played a crucial role in creating a dynamic public sector governance environment in Singapore:

> "In terms of the caliber of people during my time, Singapore did not have more bright people than Malaysia, Thailand or Indonesia — that just goes by the size of the population. The difference is that we were more organized and more coherent and better led by the political system. There was also a sense of mission. The civil service went out of the way to attract a larger fraction of available talent in the country. We had good leadership in the civil service but we were also instigated and aided by the political leadership to remain at the forefront of thinking in terms of policy formulation, of organization structure and strategic thinking."[5]

Over time, changes in the internal and external environments and the changes in the political leadership brought about shifts in the way the public sector operated and led it to redefine and expand its role. Along the way, the culture of the organization was moderated but its underlying values and governance fundamentals have, by and large, remained unchanged. Former Head of the Civil Service Lim Siong Guan elaborated on how political leadership changes influenced the adoption of different governance structures in the civil service:

> "Lee Kuan Yew and his team were very clear on their priorities and values — post-independence, the problems Singapore faced were obvious — unemployment, need for foreign investments, basic housing, education. So the

---

[5] Interview conducted by authors on 11 August 2005.

civil service was set up to solve these problems fast and efficiently. When Goh Chok Tong took over, the nature of government became much more consensual, more participatory — so we had to set up different structures to collect the different ideas that people were putting forward, structures to consult with the citizens and to consider the ideas, and structures to ensure that we had a holistic perspective in the midst of a more messy process."[6]

The culture of a society comes from an accumulation of experience derived from the adaptive, often partial solutions, to frequently encountered problems of the past. The perception of the value of these ideas in the survival and success of a society becomes deeply imprinted in the minds of the people. Over time, a common cultural heritage is formed, reducing the divergence of mental models, and creating a means for transferring these common social perceptions to future generations. This cultural heritage shapes how people think, evaluate, and decide across a spectrum of choices, including governance. The cultural foundations of governance are derived from how leaders perceive the strengths and vulnerabilities of a society's position, which then influence the intended purposes of the governance systems and institutions that are created. Principles are then derived to guide policy decision-making and implementation so that the purposes may be accomplished. The leaders' perception of position, creation of purpose and evolution of principles are the foundations for understanding why and how governance institutions and structures develop over time. At the same time, they provide the internal center and a sense of stability for individuals in a society as it adapts to constant change.

4.2 Values and Beliefs that Shaped a Nation

The essential core of culture consists of historically derived ideas that were selected from positive experience and form the underlying beliefs

---

[6] Interview conducted by authors on 29 July 2005.

and values of a community. Beliefs are assumptions regarding what are needed to achieve the desired results. Values are relatively stable beliefs and emotions that provide a powerful motivational influence on behavior in three ways:[7]

(i)   they describe the desired end-states;
(ii) they prescribe the conduct and behaviors to achieve the end-states; and
(iii) they define and reinforce a sense of identity.

Values act to guide how we present, evaluate and judge ourselves and others. Values reflect our openness to and how we approach new experiences.

The philosophy of the Singapore government and its approach to public policy formulation were shaped by the circumstances and the imperatives created by its sudden independence. In 1965, the prospects for survival for this minuscule nation state were bleak: there was little land and no natural resources; it was flanked, in particular, by two large neighbors that looked upon this tiny nation with suspicion and hostility; it was heavily dependent on British monies given in exchange for allowing Britain to retain its major military base here. Its population, a mix of immigrant Chinese, Malays and Indians, had survived a tumultuous period of racial and religious conflict, with little sense of nationhood. Singapore's only advantage was its strategic location. Its political leaders concluded that to survive, Singapore had to be tougher, more disciplined, better organized and move faster than other countries. The political leaders understood that this meant that the quality of the government, how it was organized, the way the country was run, and the values and focus of the government and the people had to be aligned with and geared towards economic survival and growth.

Its historical experience shaped its deep sense of vulnerability, and its dependency on developments in the global economic and security environment. Its lack of natural resources focused the leadership's mind on its people as the only strategic resource for

---

[7] Earley and Ang (2003), pp. 129–137.

the country, and the need to accumulate financial resources from economic growth in order to build a buffer for survival during lean years. The perceived vulnerabilities of Singapore's position influenced the leadership's intent and purpose, and the adoption of several strategic imperatives for good governance: economic survival, domestic stability, global relevance, financial prudence and people development.

Three key beliefs drive public sector policymaking in Singapore. First is the belief that a strong economy is fundamental to the viability of all other policies, and that continued economic growth is the number one priority. Second is the belief that state is central to Singapore's long-term stability. Third is the belief that policy makers must be future-oriented to be effective. A strong future orientation is a response to the innate sense of vulnerability regarding Singapore — especially its small physical size, its lack of natural resources, and its small population.

Singapore's institutional culture is based on five core values:

(i)   honesty and integrity,
(ii)   people as the main resource,
(iii) results orientation,
(iv)   self reliance, and
(v)   domestic stability.

These core values formed the basis for a set of principles that have shaped how Singapore is governed. The perceived position, purpose and principles of governance in Singapore are summarized in Table 4.1.

4.2.1 *Honesty and Integrity*

An honest and able government was what Lee Kuan Yew set out to create when the People's Action Party assumed control of a self-governing Singapore in 1959. But Lee was under no delusions about the enormity of the task and the aspects of human nature that made establishing an honest government difficult. He had observed the developments in other developing countries that had attained self-

Table 4.1. Cultural Foundations for Dynamic Governance in Singapore

PRINCIPLES *Guidelines for Action based on Values & Beliefs*	Integrity — Incorruptibility People are Key — Meritocracy for best use of talent Results-oriented — Rationality with pragmatism Efficiency — Use of market adjusted for social equity Multi-racial, multi-religious understanding
PURPOSE *Strategic Imperatives of Governance*	Develop people as the key resource Inculcate self reliance through work, not welfare Financial prudence to build buffer for survival Domestic stability to attract FDI and talent Economic growth for survival Global relevance through connectivity and change Build long-term sustainability not short-term political gains Government takes proactive role in development
POSITION *Unique Context & Constraints*	Small, resource-scarce, vulnerable to external trends Diverse cultures and ethnicity, threat to internal harmony Dominant single political party since 1959

government before Singapore, and witnessed time again, the corrupting tendencies of power:

> "The idealism that fired a leader in his early stages, instead of staying with him to the end and making him want to pass the torch on to a younger generation, is corrupted and debased in the process, and leaders lose interest in the future beyond their lifetimes."[8]

In his memoirs, he wrote of his experiences and encounters with students from China who were fired up with the ambition to rid China of the corruption and incompetence of the Nationalist Chinese leaders, and noted that it was disgust with the greed and immorality of these men that made many Chinese school students in Singapore pro-communist. Lee wrote that he and his PAP colleagues were:

---

[8] Speech given by Lee Kuan Yew at a Conference on Youth and Leadership, 10 April 1967, excerpted in Han Fook Kwang, Warren Fernandez and Sumiko Tan (1998). *Lee Kuan Yew — The Man and His Ideas*. Times Editions Pte Ltd, p. 97.

"... sickened by the greed, corruption and decadence of many Asian leaders. Fighters for freedom for their oppressed peoples had become plunderers of their wealth... We were swept up by the wave of revolution in Asia, determined to get rid of colonial rule but angry and ashamed of the Asian nationalist leaders whose failure to live up to their ideals had disillusioned us. ... We had a deep sense of mission to establish a clean and effective government."[9]

Both Lee and Goh were of one mind in identifying incorruptible government as the first precondition for economic growth, followed by the establishment of a good government. Goh Keng Swee stated:

"... it is clear enough what kind of institutions should be created in a society that would encourage economic development. The government must be effective and incorruptible; it should strive continuously to achieve economic growth and should not be distracted by other goals such as national prestige, military strength, the personal fortunes of those in power, or religious sanctity."[10]

A clean government was necessary not only for its own sake; it was deemed critical to building up the moral authority of leaders which, in turn, was key in creating a society that was seen to reward hard work and enterprise:

"Only by upholding the integrity of the administration can the economy work in a way which enables Singapore

---

[9] Lee Kuan Yew (2000). *From Third World to First — The Singapore Story*. Singapore: Times Edition, pp. 182–183.

[10] Goh Keng Swee (1972), (1995), cited in Ian Patrick Austin (2004). *Goh Keng Swee and Southeast Asian Governance*. Singapore: Marshall Cavendish, p. 24.

to clearly see the nexus between hard work and high rewards."[11]

4.2.2 *People as the Key Resource: Reward Hard Work and Performance*

With no natural resources and with Singapore's survival dependent on the ability of her people to work, it was critical that the incentive to strive be maintained, and that society reward and be seen to reward hard work and enterprise. The founding leaders were convinced that good governance depended on getting good people to serve in government, and that those who served in government had to be doing so for the good of the country and not for their own aggrandizement. While the problem of how to identify what he defined as "good people" was an issue that preoccupied the first Prime Minister almost right from the time Singapore became independent until the present, he was very clear about what had to be done to build up a good government. This meant creating systems and devising policies in which:

(i)   practices that could undermine the link between work and reward were actively discouraged;
(ii)   economic incentives were preserved;
(iii) equality of opportunity was guaranteed, but
(iv)   where the principle of "to each according to his ability" was maintained.

4.2.3 *Results Orientation, not Ideology*

Given the circumstances of its independence and the few options available, it is not surprising that policies were adopted not based on ideological considerations but on pragmatic calculations of what would be workable. Singapore policy-making has not been constrained

---

[11] Lee Kuan Yew, quoted in Lim Siong Guan (1999). "Integrity with Empowerment: Challenges Facing Singapore in Combating Corruption in the 21st Century," *Ethos*, August.

by the straitjacket imposed by ideology — the overriding concern has been with the effectiveness of policy and the results. For example, the absence of a viable private sector to drive economic development meant that the state had to take the lead to facilitate the development of the industrial sector. Similarly the absence of alternatives to attracting MNCs to drive growth led to a decision taken in contravention of the prevailing dependency school of thought:

> "We had a real-life problem to solve and could not afford to be conscribed by any theory or dogma… Our duty was to create a livelihood for two million Singaporeans. If MNCs could give our workers employment and teach them technical and engineering skills and management know-how, we should bring in the MNCs."[12]

4.2.4 *Self Reliance*

Ultimately, bound up with pragmatism and the idea of a merit-based society was the principle of self-reliance. The population was constantly reminded that, "no one owes us a living." Singapore's survival depended solely on her people and the quality of the leaders, and their ability to create and take advantage of opportunities. Singapore's experience during the brief time in Malaysia, the hostilities with Indonesia and the British closure of their military bases highlighted that in international relations, there were no permanent friends and no permanent enemies, only permanent interests.

4.2.5 *Domestic Stability: Balancing Interests in a Multi-Racial Society*

While the Singapore public sector is clinical and hard-headed in implementing necessary but less than popular policies, one of the core values of the public sector has been the overarching instinct to

---

[12] Lee (2000), p. 76.

maintain social stability and domestic peace. The public sector has been sensitized to the pragmatic realities of a multi-cultural society. Thus while tough and somewhat unpalatable policies such as directed integration and racial quotas for housing estates were being enforced, the other side of the coin saw initiatives to ensure social stability through dialog, active engagement and consultation with religious leaders on potentially controversial issues and a strict policy on racial equality. Differences in beliefs and cultures were accepted and preserved: an equal number of national holidays were declared for the four main racial and religious groups. While English is the language of business and government, English, plus the language of Malay, Chinese (Mandarin) and Tamil are the four official languages. The government made special effort to establish communication channels with various religious leaders and keep dialog open especially during times of crisis such as the potential fallout from the 9/11 terrorist attacks and the discovery of Muslim terrorist cell groups in Singapore. There are strict laws to guard against acts that could incite hostility against any racial or religious group. Acts that cast aspersion on a particular group are deemed to be seditious and are summarily dealt with by the courts.

4.3 Principles: Defining and Establishing Good Governance

Governance imperatives and principles were not scripted; no one sat down in 1965 and prescribed these fundamentals as the way to run the country. In 1965, the preoccupation was not with principles and theories but with establishing the conditions in Singapore that would attract foreign investment and promote economic development. But there were patterns in how problems were responded to, analyzed and solved. For a long time, these were the underlying, tacit guiding imperatives for policy-making. It was only in the 1990s that these patterns of how the government approached and how policy was formulated were translated into tenets which were subsequently recognized as governance fundamentals. These principles evolved out of the values and beliefs of the founding political leaders, and reflected their assumptions as they developed the frameworks and built the institutions to facilitate economic growth. In so doing, the leaders, in particular Lee Kuan Yew and Goh Keng Swee, also established and created the culture and ethos of the institution, the Singapore public sector, that was responsible for giving shape to and implementing policy.

4.3.1 *Establishing and Reinforcing the Principle of Incorruptibility*

Integrity is defined as the quality of possessing and steadfastly adhering to high moral or professional standards. In the context of government, integrity is typically taken to mean non-corruption and not taking steps to benefit personally on account of the office held. Singapore's drive to establish high professional standards of incorruptibility saw it attack the problem on several fronts — from severe punishment, increasing predictability, minimizing discretion and increasing efficiency in the provision of services.[13]

(i)   *Clearer decision rules*

When Singapore attained self-government in 1959, corruption in the public service was a significant issue. Syndicated corruption was especially common among law enforcement officers. As "(P)etty power invested in men who cannot live on their salaries is an invitation to misuse that power,"[14] systems were revised to make it more difficult to exercise discretion at the lower levels. Official procedures were simplified and opportunities for discretion were removed by having clear published guidelines and, where possible, doing away with permits or approvals. Increased transparency and accountability removed opportunities for corruption and helped members of the public know what they could and should expect, and complain when they did not get it.

---

[13] This section draws from Lim (1999).

[14] Lee (2000), p. 183.

(ii) *Improving efficiency with streamlined operations*

Improved public service delivery removed possible rent from corruption, as efficient and effective services could be obtained without bribes. This was one of the reasons behind the effort to avoid the queuing system in dispensing public services. Retired Head of the Civil Service Andrew Chew explained:

> "One of the things we discovered is that we should never encourage a queue. ... Every time there is a queue you encouraged corruption as people tried to overcome the queue. Let me give you an example. In the old days, TB (tuberculosis) was a big problem — the only way you can get into the hospital is to be put on the waiting list — 3 months, 6 months, 9 months, 1 year. One can see that patients are on the waiting list. Now once you are in the queue, someone close to the system will know that a decision has been made to have a patient admitted next week. He goes to the patient and says, "You waited 6 months, you can get in for a small fee" — and he wanted to get in because he wanted to be treated. So we always tried to get rid of queues."[15]

The push to minimize cash transactions, the encouragement of direct debit and direct payments of salaries into bank accounts were also part of the effort to remove incentives for corruption.

(iii) *Institutional capacity to detect corruption*

The effort to stamp out corrupt practices, especially at the higher levels, was given a strong push with the increased independence given to the Corrupt Practices Investigation Bureau (CPIB). The CPIB, now under the Prime Minister's Office, was set up in 1952 under the British to deal with increasing corruption, especially at the lower and

---

[15] Authors' interview with Andrew Chew, 21 March 2006.

middle levels of the public sector, among those who had extensive contact with the public, e.g., police and hawker inspectors. From 1959 under the new government, the CPIB focused their attention on "the big fish" in the higher echelons of government, and instituted stiff penalties for those who bribed as well as those who received bribes.[16] The anti-corruption laws were amended, expanding the definition of corrupt behavior and enhanced the powers of investigators. The courts could treat proof that an accused was living beyond his means or had property his income could not explain as corroborating evidence that the accused had accepted or obtained a bribe.

(iv) *Swift, severe and public punishment*

All cases of corruption attracted extensive media coverage and served as a constant reminder of the tough stance of the government on corruption. The widespread and adverse publicity given to cases of corruption, particularly those of high-ranking officials or politicians, provided details of the crimes and the punishments meted out,[17] and helped to inform the public about the consequences of corruption. Public shaming through publicity was a key part of the punishment. In the wake of the suicide of the then Minister for National Development who had apparently succumbed to bribery, Lee surmised that, "(W)e had established a climate of opinion which looked upon corruption in public office as a threat to society. Teh (Cheang Wan) preferred to take his life rather than face disgrace and ostracism."[18]

(v) *Strong political will and the example of the political leaders*

The anti-corruption drive was possible only with the strong moral authority and personal leadership of the political leaders. The prosecution of high-ranking officials, particularly ministers, highlighted the standards of accountability that were expected of those in office. It showed that the same rules applied to all, regardless of the level of

---

[16] See Lee (2000), pp. 184–189 for a discussion of some of the high profile cases.

[17] Ibid.

[18] Lee (2000), p. 188.

appointment. Personal incorruptibility became a prerequisite for anyone who aspired to high public office in Singapore.

An instance of personal example was demonstrated by Lee Kuan Yew in 1995 when he was the subject of an investigation with respect to the purchases of two private properties by himself and his son, Lee Hsien Loong. Both the elder and younger Lee had bought a unit each during the soft launch of the property and were given unsolicited discounts. As this was the peak of the property boom and prices shot up immediately after the soft launch, irate consumers who had not been given a chance to buy during the soft launch made a complaint to the Singapore Stock Exchange, as the property company was a listed one. It was rumored that the Lees had gained an unfair advantage on account of the elder Lee's brother being a non-executive director of the company. The then Prime Minister Goh Chok Tong ordered an investigation into the allegations, which found that nothing improper had taken place. Nevertheless, to forestall any perception of impropriety and unfair advantage, Lee Kuan Yew went public on both purchases and their discounts in Parliament. During the debate, both sides of the house, in particular the leader of the opposition who was also a trained lawyer, stated that in their experience, the giving of such discounts was standard marketing practice and there had been no impropriety. That the Lees were subject to the investigation and then publicly cleared, showed the political will and commitment of the leadership to sustain a culture of integrity and incorruptibility.

4.3.2 *Establishing a Culture of Meritocracy*

With Singapore's survival dependent on the ability of her people, it was critical that the incentive to achieve had to be maintained, and the society had to reward and be seen to reward hard work and enterprise. Today, a merit-based system permeates all levels of Singapore society and is viewed as the most efficient method for talent allocation. Lee Kuan Yew and Goh Keng Swee were staunch advocates of the merit-based system, although they emphasized different aspects of it. Lee was convinced that good people lay at the heart of good government and the problem of getting the best and the brightest to serve in government was an issue that preoccupied him almost right from the start.

> "At the heart of the question is what makes a good government? That is the core of the question. Can you have a good government without good men in charge of government? American liberals believe you can … My experience in Asia has led me to a different conclusion. To get good government, you must have good men in charge of government. I have observed in the last 40 years that even with a poor system of government, but with good strong men in charge, people get passable government with decent progress."[19]

The starting point for good government was to ensure a constant supply of good people with ability, integrity and commitment into the public sector. It is clear that Lee expected those in the public sector, particularly the scholars, to perform and he went beyond academic merit. His thinking was reflected clearly in his speech to senior civil servants immediately after independence in 1965:

> "Singapore must get some of its best in each year's crop of graduates into government. When I say best, I don't mean just academic results. His 'O' levels, his 'A' levels, university degree will only tell you his powers of analysis. This is only one third of the helicopter quality. You've then got to assess him for his sense of reality, his imagination, his quality of leadership, his dynamism. But most of all, his character and his motivation, because the smarter a man is, the more harm he will do to society."[20]
>
> "And I want those who believe that joining the government service means automatically you are going

---

[19] Speech in Parliament on the White Paper on Ministerial Salaries, 1 November 1994, reproduced in Han, Fernandez and Tan (2000), pp. 331–342.

[20] Ibid.

to go up the ladder, to forget it. Not with this government. Those who have got the vitality and the grit and the drive and can climb up that rope, well, he goes up. Those who are sluggish and worse, those who have got the ability but think that they have done their life's work by just passing an examination and getting a good degree and now they have got in through the PSC and they are sitting back and not blotting their copy book and so by affluxion of time they will become head of the ministry — I say, forget it."[21]

However Lee was not an organization man; his idea of the art of management was to put the best person to the most urgent task. It was Goh Keng Swee who put in place the structure of advancement based on merit in the public sector. Goh was an economist, an academically brilliant man who has been widely acknowledged as Singapore's economic architect — the man who not only established Singapore's fundamental principles of economic governance but also had a decisive impact on the indigenous public service. He was schooled in the importance of strong economic institutions to a country's development prospects. A pragmatist, his focus was on empirical examination and on problem-solving, rather than elegant development theories.

He understood right from the outset the importance of building institutions of good governance to any country seeking to develop. Many public sector institutions — the Jurong Town Corporation, the Monetary Authority of Singapore, Ministry of Finance, Ministry of Defence and the Ministry of Education bear the stamp of Goh's legacy and influence. Singapore's fiscal prudence, conservative budgetary stance and strong exchange rate policy are all legacies of Goh Keng Swee's approach to economic governance. In terms of the public sector as an organization, the meritocratic and performance based system of talent recruitment, retention and promotion was installed largely by Goh, which in turn was largely responsible for the ability of the public sector to constantly adapt to the rapid changes in its

---

[21] Speech to Senior Civil Servants at the Victoria Theatre on 20 September 1965, reproduced in Han, Fernandez and Tan (2000), pp. 321–323.

internal and external environment. Goh himself had been a member of the British colonial administration and believed in the necessity of a highly elite bureaucracy:

> "In many countries, the top echelon civil servants constitute an important section of the intellectual elite of the country. And this *should* be so, for the task of governing a county is both complex and demanding."

Goh placed a premium on intellectual ability and academic brilliance, rather than experience. So with independence, capable young men and women, the vast majority of them returned scholars, quickly filled up the ranks of the public sector, marking a significant shift from the seniority system that existed under the British.

As Goh had carte blanche to hire anyone from the list of government scholars given to him, he paved the careers of many young officers. While he was open to giving young officers a chance, he was also ruthless in getting rid of them if they failed to meet his exacting standards. Many of the current public sector leaders, e.g., Lim Siong Guan and Philip Yeo joined the public sector during this period, and those who proved themselves capable rose quickly through the system. Lim Siong Guan, for example, was recruited by Goh Keng Swee into MINDEF when he was 23 years old and 18 months later, was appointed General Manager of Singapore Automative Engineering at the age of 24. At the age of 28, Lim returned to MINDEF as Director, Logistics and two years later, moved up to Director, Finance at MINDEF. He was appointed Deputy Secretary at the age of 31, and Permanent Secretary, Defence at the age of 34. This case is not isolated. Many Permanent Secretaries were first appointed to this position when they were in their 30s. The fact that the new young elite joined the public sector almost fresh after university meant that many of them would remain within the public sector for a long period. This stability in the core public sector leadership provided a high degree of continuity and stability in policy direction.[22]

---

[22] Austin (2004), p. 24.

The Singapore public sector operates with very strict and competitive standards for entry. Personnel assessment and promotion decisions adhere to strict procedures and tests for merit. This structure of advancement was formalized when the public sector adopted the Shell system of appraisal that examined not only the performance but the potential of the individual — the Currently Estimated Potential (CEP). The CEP system was introduced as a way to assess staff to evaluate their currently estimated potential and was, in effect, "systematized meritocracy."[23]

The Public Service Commission (PSC) was established to handle the recruitment and appointment of public sector staff and leaders to reinforce the system of meritocracy. Its members are appointed by the President on the recommendation of the Prime Minister. To enforce the separation of the administrative and the political, members cannot be current or past political office holders, and may not be current civil servants. Andrew Chew, the current PSC Chairman, was appointed to PSC only after a 5-year cooling off period after the end of his term as Head, Civil Service. While most levels of public sector recruitment were devolved to the individual agencies in 1995, the PSC remained responsible for all appointments to the Administrative Service, as well as the highest levels of appointment, e.g., Permanent Secretary or CEO of statutory boards. This was subsequently strengthened by requiring all key public service appointments to be subject to the endorsement of the Elected President. The role of the PSC in handling all senior recruitment and appointments helped to protect the public sector from the practice of political appointments and helped to nurture and preserve the impartiality of the service. Many of the PSC members were from the private sector, retired captains of industry and heads of large organizations — individuals with long careers and extensive experience in assessing character, capabilities and performance. As recruitment and appointments were not politically driven, merit became the key criteria.

The merit-based system of the public sector was a reflection of the merit and performance-based values of Singapore society as a whole.

---

[23] Term used by Lim Siong Guan, interview of 29 July 2005.

With Singapore's survival dependent on the ability of her people to work, it was critical that the incentive to strive be maintained, and the society had to reward and be seen to reward hard work and enterprise. Today the merit-based philosophy is one that permeates all levels of Singapore society. For a country with limited human resources, the merit-based system was also viewed as the most efficient method for talent allocation.

Lee believed that a system where just rewards went to those who were capable was the foundation of a successful and economically viable society. He believed that a system where advancement was based on merit would help to build a more cohesive society with few class divisions. As a long-standing observer of British society, Lee recognized the importance of social mobility and of creating a social system where there were no divisions, either by class, race or religion:

> "You cannot have people just striving for a nebulous ideal. They must have that desire to improve, whether it is the scooter, the mini car, the flat, the fridge, the washing machine, the television set, better shoes, better clothes or better homes. You must equate rewards to performance because no two persons want to be the same. They want equal chances in order that they can show how one is better than the other. This is a fact of life that even the communists have had to admit. The constitution of Romania, a socialist country, says that each man shall be rewarded in accordance with what he contributes, not 'to each in accordance with his needs.'
>
> "The... factor which helps us is that we have not got deep class divisions. Social mobility is half the secret of Singapore's success: from rags to riches, from riches down the ladder. When you have social mobility, you haven't got that animosity and antagonism... One of the reasons the communists failed to make inroads into Singapore was they worked in a class hatred that was not there. One of the reasons for the antagonism of the

British worker to management is that he is branded by his accent. You can make a million pounds but you are still Billy Butlin because you talk like one. The workers resent this and they take it out by denying the boss his full day's work. In Singapore, irrespective of your father's wealth, background or status, you enjoy the same opportunities from primary school to university." [24]

4.3.3 *Rationality, Pragmatism and A Strong Results Orientation*

The extensive use of the pricing mechanism reflects the analytical, rational and pragmatic nature of public policy-making. Decisions are made based on "hardnosed, unsentimental calculations of what is right."[25] A large measure of the rationality was forced onto the government when independence was thrust on Singapore, when circumstances meant that there was little option but to eschew political correctness and economic ideology in favor of practical and pragmatic considerations. With reasoned logic and rationality, institutions created by the British — the use of English language, Currency Board system, the Central Provident Fund, the Administrative Service in the public sector — were retained as they were judged to be of long-term benefit to the newly independent Singapore. As Goh Keng Swee summed it up:

"It might have been politically tempting to rid ourselves of institutions and practices that bore, or seemed to bear, the taint of colonial associations. Had we done so we would have thrown away a priceless advantage for the sake of empty rhetoric."[26]

---

[24] Speech at an annual dinner of the Singapore's Employers' Federation, 10 May 1968, excerpted in Han, Fernandez and Tan (2000), pp. 117–118.

[25] Authors' interview with Peter Ho, Permanent Secretary, Foreign Affairs and Head, Civil Service on 11 August 2005.

[26] Goh Keng Swee (1977), (1995), quoted in Austin (2004), p. 16.

This lack of xenophobia was unusual among post-war developing countries where relics of a colonial past were jettisoned amidst post-independence nationalist fervor. For the Singapore leaders then, pragmatic considerations took precedence over any nationalist sentiments.

The rationality was reflected in some of the hard-headed decisions that were taken to create stability in the multi-racial newly independent Singapore. Singapore is probably one of the few countries in the world that addresses racial and religious issues head on in an attempt to forestall the kind of racial and religious conflict that beset the island in the 1950s. Racial integration was enforced during the urban renewal period when families were relocated from the slums areas into high-rise housing blocks with the aim of preventing the formation of racial enclaves. When it became clear that certain racial groups were congregating again, racial quotas were introduced in each housing block. Even though this had the effect of depressing the housing prices for some groups, it was a price thought worth paying for racial harmony.

Unlike many other countries with multi-racial, multi-religious populations, Singapore did not adopt a race-blind policy. Such a policy would have been tantamount to believing that differences between racial groups do not exist. Instead, potential differences among racial groups were acknowledged, taken into account and made public in the course of policy making. Examples include birth rates, educational attainment, drop-out rates, household income levels, and crime rates. Issues that were race-specific were not side stepped. For instance, Malay children were found to have higher drop-out rates from school and to perform less well compared with children of other races. Once this problem had been highlighted, solutions were devised in the form of self-help groups and community-based programs. This approach is unusual — very few governments of multi-ethnic societies would be so open about racial differences. But Lee was a keen observer of behavior and he believed that different groups viewed life differently and responded differently to issues. His view was that these differences had to be acknowledged so that potential problems could be identified and solutions devised. This approach involved dealing with the world the way the world actually was, not the way that one may have wanted it to be or the politically correct way of thinking about the world. Lee believed that only by acknowledging and accepting the reality would there be any chance of devising appropriate economic and social policies. This was a view that would serve the political leadership well when Singapore had independence thrust upon her, and one the political and public sector leadership would later always take in handling tough issues. Many of the policies undertaken by the Singapore government went against "conventional wisdom" — the accepted view but not necessarily the most accurate view. This penchant for taking a hard look at what was going on and understanding the actual reasons for it was critical because it went to the heart of the problem identification. Policy-makers had to be able to identify the problem correctly, understand its underlying causes to be able to craft appropriate solutions.

The rationality and hard-headedness was also reflected in the ability to take tough decisions when necessary. For example, to restore Singapore's competitiveness in response to the 1985–1986 recession, wages were frozen across the board for a period of 2 years and CPF contributions were cut to enable the economy to stabilize. It was a move made possible only because of the strong trust that been built up among the government, the trade unions and the employers through the concept of tripartism and the platform of the National Wages Council. It was a solution born out of a critical appraisal of the problem at hand and recognizing that there was little alternative but to face the realities head-on.

The same hard-headedness was again evident in the policy with respect to foreign manpower. Because of its small population, Singapore had long depended on foreign unskilled and semi-skilled labor to augment its domestic manpower. In the mid-1990s, when it became clear that Singapore's low birth rate was not going to correct itself any time soon, Singapore began courting foreign talent at the middle management and professional levels to augment its labor pool. This kind of open foreign talent policy has always been a political "hot potato" in countries that adopted it. Singapore was no different. In the late 1990s and early 21st century, Singapore, like the rest of world, experienced the fallout from the 1997 financial crises, the post 9/11 loss of confidence, the outbreak of SARS, and faced the full impact of the changes brought about by information technology and relentless pace of globalization. Structural unemployment surfaced. Singapore lost many of its labor-intensive industries to China and India. Jobs at the skilled and technical levels, and middle management were not spared — radiographers, architects and IT professionals found their jobs moving to India. In this climate, it was not surprising that the prospect of a professional foreign talent open door policy was met with a large measure of hostility from many quarters, many of whom openly questioned the value of being a citizen in the face of such an unrelenting drive to attract foreigners. But the policy remained and in 2006, was accelerated. While Singapore policy makers understood domestic concerns, they were also acutely aware of the dangers posed by a declining fertility on the ability of the Singapore economy to continue to grow over the long-term. Given the constraints of Singapore's size, foreign talent was essential to help maintain the critical mass required to sustain economic momentum. Policy makers understood what was at stake and decided on a long-term effort to attract global talent.

Even as policy makers did not bow to populist pressures on this issue, there were indications at the end of 2006 that the concerns on the ground about the value of citizenship had been heard. For much of Singapore's post-independence period, there had not been substantive and significant fiscal privileges accorded to citizens, as the economy depended on and welcomed those who took up permanent residence in Singapore. Non-Singaporean permanent residents enjoyed subsidized education and health care services and paid fees which were only marginally higher than those charged to citizens. While non-Singaporeans permanent residents could not buy subsidized new flats directly from the HDB, they could buy from the resale market. The absence of a significant distinction between citizens and non-citizens was not a critical issue during periods of strong and inclusive economic growth. But in the context of widening economic and social disparities of the early 21st century, it became an issue that needed to be addressed. It was thus announced in December 2006 that subsidies for permanent residents for education and health care services would be reduced, and for foreigners, largely removed.

4.3.4 *Applying the Discipline of Economic Incentives and Markets*

Singapore believed that the best way to ensure the well-being of the individual and of society in the long run was to preserve the incentive to work and to maintain a system where rewards were commensurate with performance. During his student days in Cambridge, Lee Kuan Yew had been an ardent socialist, believing in fair shares for all. It was only later as he observed the results of the welfare-based approach — that it sapped the will to work — that he understood that personal motivation and personal rewards were essential for a productive economy:

> "They went in for compassionate welfare programmes. They paid their unemployed almost as much as the employed when they lost their jobs. They had the right to refuse three or four jobs until the right one came along, commensurate with what they were getting the last time, to their liking. The result was lay-abouts. So finally the Australians gave up, and a Labour government in Australia has struck down unemployment benefits. If we don't learn from other people's errors, costly errors, we would be ruined, wouldn't we? We have got very little margin for error."[27]

Singapore's strong anti-welfare stance, particularly the meager amounts of public assistance, was the result of the imperative to preserve the incentive to work. While the approach to growth is decidedly capitalist, Singapore is not a classic *laissez-faire* free market economy. While recognizing the importance of preserving incentives,

---

[27] Speech during the 1991 Budget debate on 19 March 1991, reproduced in Han, Fernandez and Tan (2000), pp. 390–392.

the founding political leaders also realized that not everyone in society would perform and benefit to the same extent. The state thus had to redistribute the national income on things that improved the earning power of citizens, such as education, and goods that yielded greater societal benefit such as health and housing. With limited resources, public policy makers are under no illusions that anything comes for free. Every service offered to the population has to be paid for, either through user fees, higher taxes, cutbacks in other services or borrowing from the future; every service offered involves trade-offs. The governance fundamentals and the values of the government and the society help to determine the resource allocation process and the trade-offs that are made.

Singapore's governance philosophy — the stress on the link between work and rewards, encouraging self-reliance and the application of rationality and logic to problem solving — and the resulting emphasis on economic principles in policy making, is reflected in the key features of public policy: no inter-generational transfers; no subsidies to consumption, and wherever possible, using the market and pricing mechanism to allocate resources.[28]

Unlike many other countries, Singapore's "social safety net" focuses on investing in housing, education and health care rather than on welfare and subsidies for consumption. For example, during instances when the cost of utilities and public transport rose due to higher oil prices, assistance was targeted in the form of cash transfers to needy households, rather than an across-the-board fuel subsidy which would have distorted price signals.

Singapore's public policy-making abides by the principle that each generation must earn enough to provide for its own consumption, pay for retirement and invest for the future. This principle is clearly reflected in the structure of the CPF retirement scheme, where workers fund their own retirement through monthly savings put

---

[28] These features were highlighted in a speech by Dr Vivian Balakrishnan, Minister for Community Development, Youth and Sports and 2nd Minister for Trade and Industry at 21st Emerging Issues Forum, 6–7 February 2006: "Singapore's Story: Big Ideas in Action," 7 February 2006 at the Institute for Emerging Issues, North Carolina, USA.

aside by themselves and their employers. In stark contrast to the more common pay-as-you-go system where one generation's retirement is funded by the next, Singapore's system is what is called a fully funded one, i.e., self-financing. It helps to foster a mindset of self-reliance and encourages individual responsibility in planning for retirement.

The CPF is also an example of the use of market-based principles in policy making — the retirement funds available are dependent on the amount that has been saved and the prevailing market interest rates. Policy makers utilize market incentives to encourage innovation and enterprise as well as improve resource allocation. Singapore harnesses market forces for resource allocation in many areas, either through the "user-pays" principle for existing services or by creating new markets where none existed previously. Health care and public housing are two areas in which the "user pays" principle has been effectively utilized.

Singapore's public housing program is an integrated govern-ment-and-market based system, aimed at the universal provision of housing without raising it to the level of entitlement. During the tumultuous periods of race riots of the 1950s, Lee Kuan Yew had observed that people who owned their houses took care of them much better than those who lived in rental quarters. It highlighted to him the difference ownership made and that people who had a physical stake in something were likely to do more to preserve it. This was how the home ownership program came about. The cost of flats built by the HDB is subsidized, and the level of subsidy decreases with the size of the flat. Selling prices are set based on affordability considerations. For example, new 4-room flats are priced such that 70 per cent of households will be able to afford them.[29] Flats at the top end of the spectrum are priced at full cost. Market principles are factored into the equation in that the consumption of housing is tied to affordability — the type of flat bought is decided by each household based on what it is willing and able to pay.

---

[29] John W Thomas and Lim Siong Guan (2001). "Using Markets to Govern Better in Singapore," John F. Kennedy School of Government, Harvard University, Faculty Research Working Paper RWP02-010. The number of rooms takes into account the living-dining room and the bedrooms only.

The "willingness to pay" principle is even more clearly reflected in the pricing of health care services. Singapore's health care financing system is a novel hybrid with key elements of the totally free market private insurance-based American system and the British system of tax-funded universal health coverage. What is significant is that while it is accepted that citizens have a right to competent basic health care which the government provides at highly subsidized rates, market-based mechanisms are used to discourage over-consumption and promote individual responsibility. The personal health care savings account — Medisave — which is part of an individual's CPF is funded by contributions by the individual and his employer. It was set up with the express purpose of helping Singaporeans build up sufficient savings for their hospitalization expenses. As these savings belong to the individual outright, he has an incentive to use the funds judiciously. He can also choose the health care provider and the hospital ward type; the more he pays, the greater the level of comfort. Most recently, the government attempted to promote greater competition and improve information to the consumer in an industry characterized by information asymmetry — the publication of the costs of a collection of the most frequently performed hospital procedures. One result of this move has been the effort by hospitals whose costs were significantly higher, to examine their cost structures and bring them into line with other hospitals.

The rationing of foreign workers has also been carried out based on the principle of "willingness to pay." The employment of foreign manpower has been a deliberate strategy to augment Singapore's limited domestic labor resources. However this has been carefully managed, with greater privileges for those who are better qualified and have the potential to add depth and quality to the local talent pool. So while there is an open policy for highly-skilled and professional foreign manpower, there are progressively tighter restrictions on the import of unskilled and lower skilled manpower to moderate the inflow of unskilled workers. One method used has been the levy system whereby employers pay a tax on each unskilled foreign worker hired. The levy helps to ensure that the inflows of unskilled workers do not unduly depress local wages and crowd out local labor, and employers can decide how many workers to hire based on their ability to pay.

The concept of co-payment has been used, even for semi-public goods like education, to drive home the fact that there is a cost to provision. Thus while education is highly subsidized, the level of subsidy falls the higher the level of education. Minimal amounts of co-payment are required for the primary and secondary levels where education is almost 100 per cent subsidized, and the percentage of co-payment rises to about 25 per cent for the university level. To help needy students, there are various loan and financial assistance schemes.

Perhaps the most novel application of market principles has been in the areas of traffic congestion management and vehicle ownership. Singapore was the first country in the world to institute a system of congestion pricing with the Area Licensing Scheme in 1975, which evolved into the current Electronic Road Pricing mechanism. Motorists who travel on certain roads at certain peak periods are charged tolls, which are in effect taxes to reflect the negative external costs generated. To moderate the demand for vehicle ownership, motorists have to bid for the right to buy a new car based on the individual motorist's willingness and ability to pay, within the annual vehicle quotas set by the government.

Markets have also been created within the public sector to stimulate competition and to help minimize wastage and inefficiencies. One such mechanism is the inter-departmental charging system that makes use of pricing to impose incentives and discipline on both the providers and consumers of services. For instance, the public sector's training institute is no longer given a budget to run its courses, an amount it previously received regardless of demand and the quality of the courses it offered. Moreover as government agencies did not have to pay at the point of consumption, there was the danger of over consumption and a lack of incentive to assess the quality of alternative training service providers. Under the current system, the budget originally channeled to the training institute is now disbursed across the various agencies. The training institute now has to earn its budget by charging the agencies the cost of providing training courses; it now has the incentive to ensure that the quality of its courses is up to the mark, while the various agencies have become aware of the cost of sending their staff for training courses.

Part of the reason for the extensive use of market principles has been Singapore public policy makers' long familiarity with market forces. In the course of courting foreign investment especially from the United States, Singapore's leaders learnt that their objective was to find a low-cost offshore production base to compete with the then emergent, low-cost Japanese manufacturers. Singapore's success rested on its being to keep its costs low and to offer investors good and stable long-term investment prospects. Because of its size, Singapore had to be a "price taker" — and so to survive, Singapore's companies had to be able to operate successfully in the international market. Thus Singapore companies and the Singapore public sector learnt very early on about the discipline of market forces and how a competitive environment spurred pro-business practices and efficiencies in resource allocation. This was also true for Singapore's government-linked companies (GLCs), established when the private sector had little capacity; they were set up to run on commercial principles. Many of these GLCs subsequently grew into successful entities operating in competitive markets locally and abroad; their performance was undoubtedly enhanced by their long experience of being subject to the rules of competition and having to respond and react quickly to changes in the business environment.

While market principles have been applied in many areas, what should be noted is that the line between the government and market is not strictly drawn. What makes the Singapore approach unique is that market mechanisms are integrated with public policy and programs, and used in conjunction with public sector regulation to allocate resources. The government tests and determines where markets can deliver the best results in areas where there are social objectives. The decision to use any sort of market mechanism is made only after analysis and assessment of alternatives, and when policy makers are convinced that allocation through the market yields the best results.

Thus the state is central in determining where the market is applied, and in assessing, controlling and regulating the market, in monitoring performance and making adjustments as deemed necessary.[30]

Perhaps the most compelling and controversial application of market principles was the benchmarking to the private sector of the salaries of ministers and senior civil servants starting from 1994. After experiencing several cycles where many good public sector leaders moved to the private sector because of better opportunities, the political leadership devised a market-based formula to peg the salaries of the top public sector leaders and ministers to top earners in selected professions and industries in the private sector. This policy was implemented based on the belief that the way to attract good people into the public sector was the same as in the private sector — to pay them their market value.

This move reflected the political leaders' thorough understanding of economic incentives and a pragmatic understanding that times had changed. They recognized that unlike the first generation of political leaders who entered politics on the backs of a post-colonial passion, the more settled circumstances and Singapore's prosperity had changed the incentives to enter politics and the public sector. Not surprisingly this proposal was controversial as it went against the social orthodoxy of altruism and service in government. The political leadership was also concerned that public servants who were not adequately paid would be more prone to corruption. The system was pragmatic in recognizing that political and public sector leaders were not necessarily motivated differently from bankers and lawyers as far as rewards went. The world and Singapore had changed dramatically from the early days when people were drawn into the political arena by circumstances. Unlike the young in 1965, the young in the 1990s had seen first-hand the fruits of economic prosperity which caused them to shun politics for more lucrative endeavors.

---

[30] Ibid.

4.4 Public Sector Governance Principles in a Political Context

All the above principles — integrity, incorruptibility, meritocracy, rationality, pragmatism, the use of market principles to drive resource allocation and the testing for results — are integrated into the core values and the governance framework for the public sector. If rationality and pragmatism are the basis for policy-making and implementation, then policies that work in Singapore should be easily replicated in other countries. However, public sectors do not operate in a vacuum; on the contrary, public sector institutions and public sector leaders typically function in environments where decisions on which policies are adopted are decided based largely on political considerations — whether the policy will alienate or benefit key segments of the population, and what the likely impact will be on the next election. As Eddie Teo pointed out:

> "We get many visitors from other countries; they ask us "how do you do this?" So we teach them, the structures and the processes and then they go back and try to implement them. But it can only work if the political environment supports it." [31]

While political considerations do of course figure in the Singapore context, the operating environment for the Singapore public sector has been significantly different. The long-standing unbroken dominance of the People's Action Party, the absence of a viable political opposition and strong political lobby groups meant that attention of the political and public sector leadership remained focused on the problems of running the country and planning for the long-term interests of Singapore. This can be seen in the emphasis not on quick fixes but on feasible solutions for the longer term and on the building of strong institutions and organizations to sustain economic development. Unlike countries where the ruling party changes every five to ten years

---

[31] Authors' interview with Eddie Teo, 22 September 2005.

and where policies are enacted with a view to winning elections, policy making in Singapore has not been constrained by this. Moreover the fact that the ruling party is likely to be in power over the long term imposes a strong discipline, as it is likely to be the party that has to manage the consequences of whatever populist or short-term policies it implements. This has also created an environment where the values and priorities of government have remained largely unchanged.

The fact that the PAP has been in power continuously since independence has helped sustain the propensity for decision-making based on rational grounds, a situation that would not have been possible had the government changed regularly. "And because politicians don't change and governments don't change, civil servants do not have to adapt every five years to a new government. The Civil Service can think long term and from the basis of rational grounds rather than political grounds."[32] This is not to say that civil servants were not aware of the political implications of issues; however the public sector did not operate and function based on political considerations.

The absence of cronyism and the practice of political appointments created a public sector that was able to operate relatively free of political pressures. Right from the start, the political leadership put in place structures and processes to institutionalize good practices and to safeguard the integrity of the system. To preserve the impartiality and independence of the civil service, the Public Service Commission established under the British was retained to oversee all recruitment, promotions, appointments and dismissals in the public sector. This strict separation helped to safeguard the integrity of the public sector by avoiding the practice of political leaders making key administrative appointments, which was endemic in many countries.

The above was an early example of the implicit and tacit understanding of what constituted good governance. Even while both Lee and Goh emphasized the overriding need to have good people in government and believed that it was still possible to get decent results in a poor system ably run by good people, much attention was given to

---

[32] Ibid.

establishing systems and institutions that would be above and beyond the actual people running the system, and serve as a check.

The approach to fiscal management that was put in place by Goh Keng Swee is a good example. Goh emphasized prudence in fiscal management — Singapore should never spend more than it saved, especially as whatever reserves Singapore accumulated would be the country's only buffer against any protracted untoward events. As a result, Singapore's approach to budgeting has been conservative. Having observed the predilection of many developing countries for policies that risk runaway inflation, Singapore decided to retain the Currency Board system that had been put in place by the British. By requiring that every unit of currency issued had to be fully backed by reserves, the system imposed discipline in the creation of money and in one fell swoop, negated the possibility of runaway inflation.

What is also noteworthy is the independence of the public sector in the administration and assessment of the budget. The budget allocations to the various agencies are managed by the Ministry of Finance (MOF), and while the final allocation has to be approved by Cabinet, the Permanent Secretary [PS (Finance)] has authority and scope to recommend changes in the structure of allocations.[33] Apart from the budget for the Ministry of Defence, which is allocated on a block basis to preserve confidentiality due to the sensitivity of security, the budget requests of the rest of the agencies are scrutinized by the MOF. The independence of MOF in assessing various budgetary requests and making recommendations can be seen in the story behind the funding processes for the Esplanade, Singapore's performing arts center, in the early 1990s. The Ministry of Information and the Arts, under the stewardship of then Minister, George Yeo, put in a request for S$600 million to MOF to build the Esplanade theaters and concert halls. This was one of the largest building requests received by MOF, whose long-standing practice had always been to accord the building of schools and hospitals higher priority than concert halls and theatres. MOF calculated that even if the capital was provided, its operating

---

[33] One way of changing the structure of allocations is via the Reinvestment Fund which will be examined in Chapter 8.

costs could only just be covered if every seat in the Esplanade was sold every night for S$300 (an extremely unlikely outcome). It used this argument to turn down the proposal. Minister George Yeo, with the support of the Prime Minister, had to go to the Singapore Totalisator Board to get the funding out of its future revenue streams (taxes collected from the turf club) for capital expenditure for the Esplanade, outside of the budget, below the line and over which the MOF had no jurisdiction. As Ngiam Tong Dow described it, MOF was "defeated by this ingenious procedural innovation."[34] This incident highlights the independence of the established public sector systems and procedures and that even Ministers were hard put to override them at will.

The establishment of the position of the Elected President was another key governance initiative. The Elected President's endorsement was needed for appointments to the judiciary and to top public sector posts. His approval was needed for using accumulated reserves from past administrations. The roles of managing the exchange rate and managing Singapore's reserves had been clearly delineated with the establishment of the Government of Singapore Investment Corporation (GIC), and previously any decision to tap into the reserves had to be approved by Cabinet. To make it more difficult for a future renegade Cabinet to unlock the reserves, a second key, in the form of the Elected President's approval, was devised as an additional safeguard.

Thus rational decision-making was possible because the governance system allowed and encouraged it. And it is now part of the public sector culture that rational reasons have to be put forward for things to be carried out. The process of recommendation and decision-making is also formalized in the system of memos to and from the Cabinet. Recommendations from the public sector leaders to the Minister and to the entire Cabinet are documented, as are the Cabinet decisions and the reasons for them. This formal system institutionalized and helped to perpetuate the practice of rational decision-making.

The fact that public sector decision-making is rational and de-politicized has had an impact in the way the government does business.

---

[34] Ngiam (2006), p. 187.

The Singapore Armed Forces/Ministry of Defence (MINDEF) is known to be a very fussy purchaser of military hardware internationally. Many countries look upon MINDEF purchases as a kind of benchmark in the industry, an indicator of sorts. When we put the question to Prof Lui Pao Chuen, Chief Defence Scientist on why this was the case, he said:

> "Firstly there is no politics in our procurement, unlike in many other countries. Our political environment allows this. So we buy based only on value for money. Secondly, our procurement people are professionals; the department is self-sustaining and staffed with bright people. In other countries, procurement is part of the military. These factors allow us to optimize based on transparent considerations, and vendors know this."[35]

Thus a non-political operating environment enabled rationality and pragmatism to function as the basis of decision-making. Yong Ying-I made a similar observation with respect to the process for the consideration of new telecoms licenses:

> "The parties interested in new telecoms licenses were asking themselves whom they should get close to, which minister should they get to know, which civil servants they should know. And we explained to them that the people they were already interacting with were all that they needed to meet. The system doesn't work that way."[36]

4.5 Socialization and the Transmission of Culture and Values

As we examine the core values and principles of the Singapore governance system, it is easy to form an impression of a centrally

---

[35] Authors' interview with Lui Pao Chuen, 2 February 2006.

[36] Authors' interview with Yong Ying-I, 2 November 2005.

coordinated, homogeneous public sector organization. But in reality the public sector is not centralized at all: there are 15 ministries and nine organs of state, with 60,000 employees; the 60-plus statutory boards have another 60,000. Lim Siong Guan acknowledged that this decentralization posed challenges to effective coordination and problem solving across agencies:

> "The government is tied at the Cabinet level, not at the public service level. So if there are big issues to be resolved, they are resolved at the Cabinet level, not by Head of Civil Service. The Cabinet is collegial but centralized. The PSs report to the Minister, not Head, Civil Service. What is the effect of this structure? The issues must be big enough to be brought up to the Cabinet, especially if they are recognized by the PM as national issues... But if only the big issues go to the Cabinet, then the other issues go to individual ministries and may not be resolved in a consistent way. That's why it is very hard to coordinate the resolution of these issues — which may not be major but are still important — across the ministries... There is no central decision-making authority for the whole public sector. If there are no Cabinet decisions, it is very hard to coordinate. So we work on coordinated vision, rather than coordinated action. This will lead to a multiplicity of actions, not necessarily coordinated actions. But the actions are congruent because they subscribe to a coordinated vision."[37]

Given this decentralization and the degree of autonomy of the different agencies, it is not surprising that individual agencies will evolve their own specific culture. The economic agencies, particularly the EDB, developed their distinctive go-getter corporate culture due largely to its critical mission in securing foreign investments for Singapore and the high profile of its leaders. The Ministry of Trade

---

[37] Authors' interview with Lim Siong Guan, 22 November 2005.

and Industry was formed in 1979 out of the Economic Development Division of the Ministry of Finance. However, unlike when they were part of the Ministry of Finance, MTI was given greater latitude and was expected to draw up the direction of economic policy and help other ministries align their own policies with the broad thrust of economic development. Ngiam Tong Dow acknowledged that MTI and EDB officers were considered "pushy" by officers in other ministries.[38] The EDB culture, in particular, is perceived to be aggressive whereas EDB officers pride themselves on their "can-do" spirit, best exemplified by its Chairman from 1986–2001, Philip Yeo. Agencies, by reason of leadership or the nature of their roles, developed different capacities for experimentation and different modes of operation. As Yong Ying-I pointed out, "It may not be necessary to have a common culture across the agencies; each agency may have its own culture that is suited to its objectives. What is necessary is that all the agencies are anchored by a common set of core values."[39]

In addition to coordinated vision, various inter-agency platforms, projects and forums have been created to deal with national issues and to socialize leading members of the public service to core values and shared policy concerns. The socialization process and the dense social networks among members of the Administrative Service have been largely responsible for the transmission of the governance principles and the core values to younger officers joining the public service. The culture and values of the public sector are exemplified by the public sector leaders, who in turn socialize their subordinates and peers within their sphere of influence. How did the public sector develop this culture and values in the Administrative Service in the first place?

- The ability to have a helicopter view was an important criterion for the selection, performance and promotion of officers in the Administrative Service.
- The milestone development programs, particularly the 10-week foundation program for administrative officers, are one

---

[38] Ngiam (2006), p. 175.

[39] Interview by authors, 2 November 2005.

key channel for socialization for new recruits into the public
sector culture and values. The policy focus of these programs
highlighted the constraints and the principles of governance that
were integral to and which guided the formulation of policies.

- The milestone programs also helped forge the social networks that
appear to be critical to an Administrative Officer's (AO)'s ability
to function effectively in the public sector — the whom to call for
what; how to do certain things like write a staff paper. Because
of the small size of the Administrative Service — about 350 at
any one time — these dense social networks are an informal but
powerful coordination mechanism across the different agencies.

- The practice of rotating AOs between different types of postings
and having them serve on cross agency project teams served
to develop their instincts and socialize them to the whole-of-
government perspective.[40]

While there are efforts to inculcate the philosophy of governance
and to build a whole-of-government perspective, what ultimately
determines the effectiveness of a public sector leader is character and
motivation — a leader's personal values and aspirations. And it is
relatively harder to test for these. Through the practice of multiple
postings, some of these values and character attributes can be discerned.
These are supplemented by a system in which high-potential AOs
work directly with the top political office holders. Several of the
current public sector leaders have worked with one or more of the top
politicians at some point in their careers. These postings are a way for
the political leaders to test the character, motivation and values of the
individual officer. The reality is that some bright AOs do not have the
wherewithal to make it as leaders: "We are now starting to look at the
problem of very bright officers who do not have the character or the
values to play leadership roles."[41] While character and values may be
the ultimate determinant of leadership effectiveness, the transmission
mechanisms for these are possibly the most tacit:

---

[40] Authors' interview with Yong Ying-I, 2 November 2005.
[41] Ibid.

"Those of us who started a long time ago, right from the beginning we realized that we were working in a government that believed in meritocracy and incorruptibility. These were values that nobody got out on a piece of paper and wrote, 'This is the kind of government we want'. But as you watched, as you experienced, as you behaved within the service, you realized that these are the values that matter. That is what is unique about the civil service in Singapore — we realize that these things matter, and are vital and you don't step out of line. So when people give you a gift, you declare it. It's a habit now."[42]

4.6 Implications and Challenges of Singapore's Governance Culture

Integrity as the cornerstone of the Singapore governance system has given Singapore many advantages over the course of its economic development, and earned it respect for transparency, professionalism and the ability to deliver. The clarity of the rules, the transparency of the processes and outcomes have created a stable and predictable environment, where the world can be seen in terms of black and white, right and wrong. However, functioning in this kind of environment over a long period may result in a lack of flexibility, a lack of savviness on the part of public sector officials about how to function in situations and environments where issues are not so clear-cut. As the public sector has to continually change and adapt to stay relevant, it is likely that the public sector of the future will have much more interaction with the private sector in order to create new value in a highly competitive global environment. So far it has been able to do this without compromising its values, standards and ethos.[43] As the public sector encourages its officers to be more innovative and flexible

---

[42] Authors' interview with Eddie Teo, 22 September 2005.

[43] Lim Siong Guan (1999). "Integrity with Empowerment: Challenges Facing Singapore in Combating Corruption in the 21st Century," *Ethos*, August.

and as the government moves from being a regulator to facilitator, should public officers have incentives to share in the benefits of their ideas and inventions or intellectual property rights? What happens if their ideas reap large rewards for the government or the private sector? Do these officers get a share of the rewards?[44] If not, would the best talent leave the public sector to pursue their aspirations in the business world? These are some of the kinds of issues that the public sector may face moving forward, and which will have to be resolved without compromising the strong values of the public sector and without having a detrimental impact on the retention of its best people.

This potential ambivalence in dealing with situations which are not clear-cut may be accentuated by the meritocratic system of recruitment, where those who enter the public sector are selected primarily based on their academic credentials, attitudes, and motivation at the age of 18 or 19. While some may argue that an individual's character may or may not have been formed by then, what cannot be disputed is those who enter the public sector do not have the worldly experience that they can bring to bear in handling potential conflicts of interest. Unless this is addressed, the administrative elite that is relatively apart from the rest of society runs the risk of being cut off from reality. In addition, while the merit-based system has served the public sector well in giving it the first choice of Singapore's small pool of talent, some critics argue that the public sector scholarship system has deprived the private sector of its share of talent. This may have the impact of permanently stultifying the development of other sectors of the economy.

The rational and pragmatic decision-making framework has made public sector policy making a clearly articulated and predictable process, with all the attendant benefits. However, rational decision-making in a meritocratic environment has spawned the need to document all parts of the policy debate and policy formulation process. All recommendations from the public sector to the ministers are fully

---

[44] Lim Siong Guan (2000). "Principles of Governance," Talk by PS (PMO) to Senior Management Programme (labeled Confidential).

documented, as are the basis of all cabinet decisions. While this mode of operating has had tremendous benefits in terms of preventing whimsical decision-making, it has created bureaucratic processes and a bureaucratic structure, where little happens before the issues are written down and the paper is submitted.

The absence of ideological constraints in policy making has been a tremendous advantage, enabling policy makers to take the rational approach to evaluating options and a pragmatic approach to problem-solving. While alternatives and options are sought out and evaluated purely on their merits, the ultimate decision is based on what would actually be workable, i.e., on pragmatic considerations. This approach has served the public sector well. But going forward when issues become more complex and appropriate options less clear-cut, this pragmatic approach to governance has the potential to be a weakness in public sector culture. If pragmatism is the ultimate determinant, it then begs the question, are there any boundaries to what should be done? Or is anything and everything possible so long as it works?

A close examination of most of the governance fundamentals will show that the decisive factor has been pragmatism. Integrity was initially valued not so much for its own sake but rather because it served to promote economic growth and differentiate Singapore from many other developing countries at that time. The effort to green Singapore and the development of culture and the arts, were not done solely for the sake of culture but to signal that Singapore was a good place for foreign investment and that Singapore was a good potential home for talented individuals from anywhere in the world. The recent debate on the integrated resort was an illustration of the conflict between the pragmatic and the ideological. Singapore has and can continue to be successful with a dominant pragmatic paradigm. But can Singapore become a great nation based on pragmatic values? Will Singapore hollow itself out when it becomes pragmatic for its skilled and mobile citizens to simply leave when monetary rewards are greater elsewhere? In a crisis, will its citizen soldiers stay to defend the country when it is safer and more pragmatic to get out?

In consistently stressing rational and pragmatic considerations as the basis for decision-making, citizens have imbibed this approach in their evaluation of the value of citizenship and quality of life. In recent years, political leaders have been confounded by the aspiration of many Singaporeans to migrate to other countries, and lamented the apparent lack of rootedness among its citizens. Some have attributed this apparent absence of emotional attachment to citizens' taking a similarly pragmatic, clinical approach in evaluating their quality of life. Their choice of where to live is more bound up with issues such as whether they can buy a bigger house, where the education system is less stressful and where they can make their money go further — purely pragmatic considerations. Softer, more emotive "heartware" issues — such as identity with the country, a deep sense of belonging, the presence of family and friends, the concept of home — seem to count for less. This phenomenon, if not addressed, poses a fundamental challenge to building a national identity and ensuring the sustainability of the nation that is Singapore.

5

Policy Execution: Developing and Implementing Paths

Dynamic governance is essentially about how paths are created, executed, renewed and discarded when circumstances change. Paths include strategic decisions, policy choices, long-term investments and approaches to implementation that are chosen to solve problems or exploit opportunities. The main tasks of leadership involve deciding on what paths to take and how to make them a reality. Execution of paths depends on the quality of people and organizational capabilities, and how they are integrated so that resources are efficiently and effectively deployed to achieve the desired results.

The test of a dynamic governance system is whether paths, strategies and policies remain relevant in the light of changing conditions. Current and potential policies may have to be reviewed, renewed and re-introduced. Under normal circumstances, institutions often follow path dependent trajectories because of legacy investments and infrastructures and the constraining forces of cultural values and beliefs. Path-breaking strategies and policies are made when leaders abandon previous plans and investments to move the organization in a different direction. This may be done in response to a perceived crisis or a new opportunity, or a change in perception, values and beliefs. Although paths are conceptually broader than policies, public institutions tend to think in terms of policies as an umbrella concept that includes strategies, plans and major investments. Thus the rest of this chapter and the next will use the term policies to describe the broad paths taken to govern Singapore in the last 40 years. Policy-making and policy execution are the leadership platforms for governing and effecting change. As shown in Figure 1.1 of Chapter 1, even carefully thought-through and adaptable policies must be executed effectively before dynamic governance can become a reality.

The dynamic governance system in Figure 1.1 of Chapter 1 focuses on policy execution rather than the more conventional approach of policy making. This is a deliberate and important departure. It conveys a critical, yet often overlooked assumption, that polices are made so that they can be implemented. The lack of government effectiveness is often due not to a lack of ideas or information, but the lack of follow-through, to delays and failures in execution. Execution is the discipline of getting things done — "a discipline for meshing strategy with reality, aligning people with goals, and achieving the results promised... a system of getting things done through questioning, analysis and follow-through".[1]

The main secret of Singapore's success, if there is one, is that policies are made to be executed and that they are actually implemented. Observers of Singapore often put it much more simply: "everything works here." Policy options are generated, evaluated and designed with implementation as the main driver. Policies are developed and designed holistically to ensure that long-term goals are met, even if the implementation may be phased. Rigor in policy analysis and realism in policy design are expected standards. Institutions are created to ensure focus and accountability for implementing critical policies. Differences in views among policy makers and feedback from stakeholders are taken into account and reconciled as much as possible so that execution will not be hindered. Accounting for current performance of policy is the basis for budget approval. Leaders are recognized and rewarded for innovative and practical policies that work and deliver results. These execution practices are founded on the principles of pragmatism and meritocracy, and are taken very seriously in the Singapore governance system. Effective execution is essentially about managing people and organizational processes so that knowledge and resources are efficiently converted into desired outcomes.

Understanding the policy execution process is important as it influences the way issues are framed, what options are generated and considered, and how final choices are selected. The execution

[1] Larry Bossidy and Ram Charan (2002). *Execution*. NY: Crown Business.

process describes the people who are involved and how they interact, the kind of information required for analysis and how proposals are justified — all of which are inputs for decision-makers considering a policy change, and they significantly influence what decisions are made and how they are implemented. This is the arena where the public institutions play a critical governance role even though political leaders often front the decisions and announce them publicly. We will discuss how the public sector identifies policy issues, influences policy development and implements policy decisions as part of the policy execution cycle.

Chapter 6 will examine several major economic and social policies and how they have evolved over the years. We will show how the culture of and capabilities for learning and adapting are embedded in the public service as it faces emerging issues in an evolving environment. Both chapters together give insight into how dynamic governance actually works in Singapore — how the capabilities to think ahead, think again and think across are incorporated into the policy process of identifying issues, influencing design and implementing decisions.

5.1 The Political Context of Policy Execution

The public sector is the custodian of the government's reputation and its most important state-management instrument. The effectiveness of the government depends on the public sector's practical ability to solve problems efficiently. When Singapore was given self-government by the British in 1959, then-Prime Minister Lee Kuan Yew recognized that effective execution of policy to serve the people was central to democratic governance. Two months after assuming office, he told civil servants that:

> "You and I have a vested interest in the survival of the democratic state. We the elected Ministers have to work through you and with you to translate our plans and policies into reality. You should give of your best in the service of the people... If we do not do our best, then

we have only ourselves to blame when the people lose faith, not just in you, the public service, and in us, the democratic political leadership, but also in the democratic system of which you and I are working parts."[2]

In Singapore, the major policy decisions are made by the Cabinet of ministers led by the Prime Minister. Policy decisions are ultimately made by political leaders, ministers of specific agencies, or the Cabinet collectively since they would have to garner the necessary political and constituency support for the policies and allocate resources for implementation. The Cabinet sets long-term direction for policy, defines the problems, and initiates search for solutions for the strategic issues it identifies. It acts as an arbiter for conflict resolution, a clearing house for information exchange, and is the repository of legitimate political power and allocation of resources. Within public agencies, the minister overseeing it has the final responsibility to decide and approve policy changes. This is also reflected in the structure of government ministries, where the permanent secretary (PS), the most senior public sector leader, reports to the minister. PSs manage their ministries and oversee the related statutory boards. The organizational structure of the Singapore government is shown in Figure 5.1.

The Singapore public service has been able to exercise a high degree of rationality and judgment in its policy-making and policy execution, and we will describe some of the major processes and practices in this chapter. The political context that enabled the public service to be effective in executing rational long-term policies for Singapore's development and progress is described by Prime Minister Lee Hsien Loong:

"The Government is strongly committed to promoting the long-term interests of Singapore. It has shielded civil servants from political interference, and given them the political backing to see sound policies through. This establishes a political context which gives civil servants

[2] Speech by Lee Kuan Yew, "The Trouble with the Civil Service," at the Opening of the Civil Service Political Study Centre on 15 August 1959.

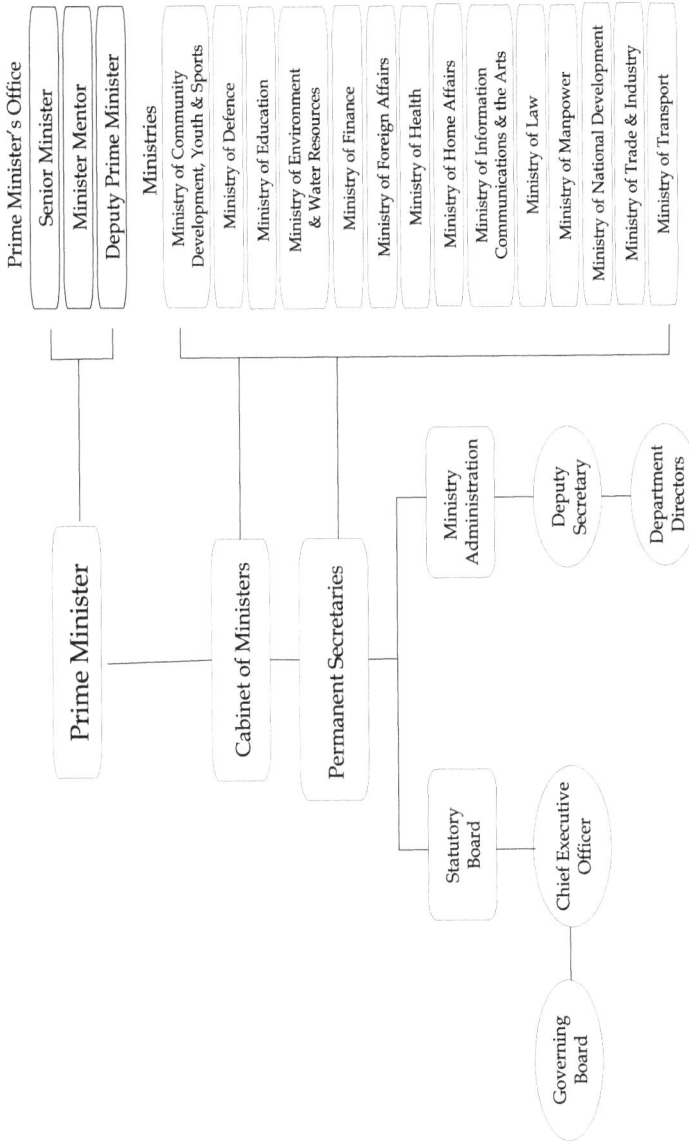

Prime Minister's Office
- Senior Minister
- Minister Mentor
- Deputy Prime Minister

Ministries
- Ministry of Community Development, Youth & Sports
- Ministry of Defence
- Ministry of Education
- Ministry of Environment & Water Resources
- Ministry of Finance
- Ministry of Foreign Affairs
- Ministry of Health
- Ministry of Home Affairs
- Ministry of Information Communications & the Arts
- Ministry of Law
- Ministry of Manpower
- Ministry of National Development
- Ministry of Trade & Industry
- Ministry of Transport

Prime Minister

Cabinet of Ministers

Permanent Secretaries

Ministry Administration
- Deputy Secretary
- Department Directors

Statutory Board
- Chief Executive Officer

Governing Board

*Note: The chart only reflects the Cabinet and the public service. For the sake of simplicity, the judiciary and legislature portions of the government have not been included.

Figure 5.1. Organizational Structure of the Singapore Government*

the space to work out rational, effective solutions for our problems, and to grow professionally. It creates a virtuous circle of sound policies, good government and strong political support.

Thus many countries envy Singapore's ability to take a longer view, pursue rational policies, put in place the fundamentals which the country needs, and systematically change policies which are outdated or obsolete. Even where policies are basically sound we are still not satisfied, and will fine tune them repeatedly so that they work exactly as intended. We should not get overly caught up in fine tuning policies. The world is inherently messy, things rarely go according to plan, and often the hardest solution to find is the simplest. Nevertheless, it is hard to imagine civil servants operating this way in nearly any other country. But in Singapore AOs can practise public administration almost in laboratory conditions."[3]

But the civil service has to be sensitive to the political context in which policies are formed and executed:

"The civil service therefore does not create policies in a vacuum. Policy objectives are ultimately determined in the political arena. Civil servants must shape policies with a view to their political impact, and be sensitive to the politics of the issues you handle. Political leaders must bring out the hard realities of our economy and society for public debate, so that a consensus can be reached, the best way forward chosen and rational solutions implemented. So most often the final policy is the result of many iterations, going back and forth between the ministers and the civil servants, shaping a result which both achieves the political objective and solves the practical problem. This is

---

[3] Speech by Prime Minister Lee Hsien Loong at the 2005 Administrative Service Dinner on 24 March 2005.

obvious to any officer who has dealt with public housing or land transport policies, but it is true of all ministries.

AOs must therefore understand the political context within which you operate. When Singapore first attained self-government, we set up a Political Study Centre to educate civil servants about the political realities and the urgent priorities of the government. Today the Civil Service College runs courses for AOs with a similar objective, and we send AOs to attend Meet the People Sessions, to see first hand how policies are impacting Singaporeans.

While AOs must be sensitive to the politics of the issues you handle, you are not yourselves politicians. You do not make the political judgment whether to proceed with a policy, nor are you the ones who must persuade the public to support it. That is the responsibility of the minister, and ultimately the Cabinet. In advising them, civil servants should never lose your professional objectivity, or second guess the minister and propose only what you think he will find politically convenient. Once you do that, you lose your usefulness and our system will lose its integrity."[4]

Making policy choices thus involves close interactions between political and public sector leaders, and the policy options and decisions are iteratively derived through the interactions. Where there are differences of views among the leaders, broad alignment is achieved through dialog and iterative discussions over multiple cycles of policy framing, analysis, design and decision. New information is introduced, new perspectives are formed and new insights are gained through personal reflection and social learning. It is obviously not a textbook style linear decision process. There are multiple feedback loops and policy options are shaped through these interactions. When a decision is made, it is not just one man's choice but an accepted

---

[4] Ibid.

option that has been shaped by many people who both learn from as well as influence others, both in and out of government. Learning and adaptation continue even after a policy has been implemented. The cultural values of integrity, meritocracy, pragmatism, efficiency and global relevance work through the beliefs and mental models of political and public sector leaders to implicitly influence the policy choices and their subsequent reviews and renewals. Understanding how public policies are formed and executed is central to understanding how governance works in Singapore.

5.2 The Policy Execution Process

5.2.1 *The Discipline of Policy Execution*

The main mission of government agencies is to achieve national objectives through policy execution. Effective policy execution requires three disciplines:

(i)   Discipline of strategic vision and focus in clarifying the long-term vision and goals of a policy;

(ii)   Discipline of confronting reality as it is, not as one hopes it to be — honesty regarding the current realities of the environment, citizens and capabilities of public institutions in the development of policy; and

(iii) Discipline of follow-through — focus in deploying the people and organizational resources to implement the policy and cumulate progress over a reasonable time.

Without the discipline of strategic vision and focus, effort and resources would be spent on the wrong policy issues. Without the discipline of confronting reality, strategic visions would remain as dreams and plans that may be made to impress would remain on the shelf with no practical positive effects on the lives of people. Without the discipline of follow-through, resources would be wasted and opportunities lost, and the capacity for future change would be diminished. In Singapore, the public service shapes policy outcomes through three institutional processes that reflect the three disciplines for effective execution:

(i)   *identifying* and surfacing issues,
(ii)   *influencing* the development and design of policy options, and
(iii)   *implementing* the decisions made.

Public sector leaders are capable of learning and developing independent understanding of social and economic issues, influencing policy development and implementing policy decisions that are made by elected ministers. In managing an advanced economy and modern society where policy problems are more technically and socially complex, the minister often relies on the knowledge, experience and expertise of public sector leaders and officials. Public sector officials and leaders exercise some autonomy to think and act based on their perceived understanding and judgment. They provide the minister with the necessary information, analysis and advice on policy issues, options, and specific detailed plans and programs for implementation. They design and implement systems for collecting, analyzing and reporting information, effectively giving them structural control of the government machinery.

But it does not imply that public officials are totally rational actors relying only on complete information, comprehensive generation of alternatives and objective decision criteria. Rather, human decision-makers are only boundedly rational and often adopt familiar and structured ways to reduce uncertainty and complexity. Our approach in this study takes an institutional view of decision-making and policy execution in the public sector as an institution. Institutional structures and processes inevitably simplify and stabilize the policy process and often become habitual ways of diagnosing and solving problems. They become the established routines that guide behavior[5] and encompass the forms, rules, conventions, strategies and technologies around which organizations are constructed and through which they operate.[6] They may even operate independently of the individuals who execute

---

[5] RM Cyert, JG March (1963). *A Behavioural Theory of the Firm*. Englewood Cliffs, NJ: Prentice Hall, cited in Levitt and March (1988).

[6] Barbara Levitt and James G March (1988). "Organizational Learning," *Annual Review of Sociology*, Vol. 14, pp. 319–340.

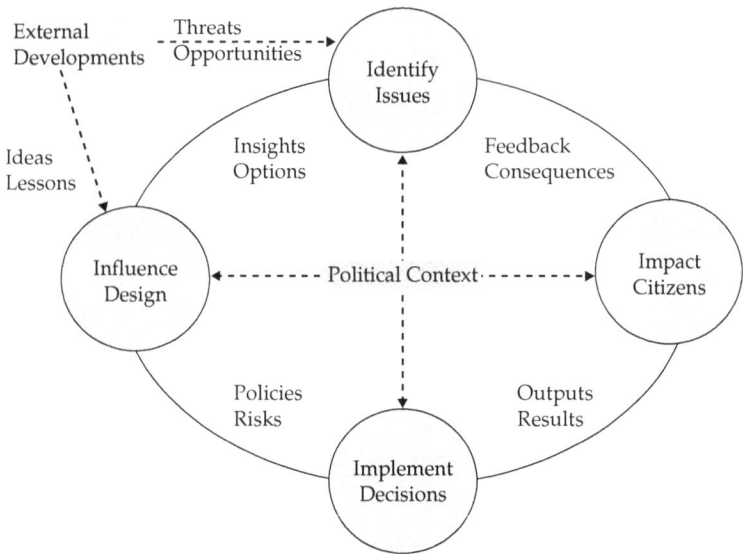

Figure 5.2. Policy Execution Cycle

them.[7] They represent an institution's response system, developed and built up over the years based on what it perceived has worked in the past. These routines, together with the uncertainty already inherent in a changed environment, often discourage organizations from further risking failure by departing from what has been proven to work, leading to path dependency. The policy execution processes influence the actual choices made. Therefore understanding policy execution processes and practices would enable us to appreciate how Singapore has been able to go beyond path dependency to adapt and adjust policies to a changing environment.

5.2.2 *The Dynamics of Policy Execution*

Policy processes are not discrete activities but form an integrated system of interdependencies with closed feedback loops from issue identification to developing policy options, to implementation of

---

[7] J March (1991). "Exploration and Exploitation in Organizational Learning," *Organization Science*, Vol. 2, No. 1, pp. 71–87.

decisions to impacts on citizens and then back to initiation again. These links among the policy processes and their interactive feedback to policy issue identification are shown in Figure 5.2.

External events and developments give rise to potential threats or opportunities that may prompt a policy review. In the design of policy options, external developments provide ideas and lessons that enable conceptualization and generation of alternatives. Policy design is made with a view to execution. Policy decisions are made after weighing carefully a myriad of potential impacts and risks as well as the policy objectives. Internal domestic considerations have to be taken into account throughout the policy cycle to ensure that execution is factored into the policy choice from initiation, and not as an after-thought. The policy process is not a simplistic and linear procedure. Policy issues may surface at each stage of the policy process. In the search for policy options to address an issue, new insights may emerge that may redefine the issue or cause a rethink about the issues that need to be addressed. In the course of seeking to influence policy designs, fresh perspectives from stakeholders may surface that require further study and analysis. The implementation of the policy may have unintended consequences, or surface new issues that may not have been considered, or the impact on the public and their feedback may lead to a re-examination of the problems.

We will describe the main activities underlying each of the three policy execution stages as they have been practiced in the Singapore public sector. These are summarized in Table 5.1.

We will describe the emergence, evolution and embedding of the practices underlying these core policy processes and provide a policy example as an illustration of each of these processes. Emergence suggests that these practices may come from a variety of sources, including prior planning and foresight, learning from others, and external pressure and circumstances. Evolution suggests that these practices may be modified in the process of implementation and may be adapted as a result of trial-and-error experiences. The degree of embedding of a practice within an institution suggests that some of these practices are still person-dependent and may not be performed consistently when there are key personnel changes. There are varying

Table 5.1. Main Activities of Policy Execution

---

1. Identifying issues for policy review
   a. Reacting to external crisis or policy consequences
   b. Identifying improvement opportunities
   c. Surfacing issues from consideration of future scenarios
   d. Identifying and sponsoring strategic issues
   e. Learning from leadership exposure to different views and practices

2. Influencing design of policy options
   a. Setting standards for policy analysis and design
   b. Recommending courses of action through staff analysis and papers
   c. Studying policy options through inter-agency project teams
   d. Engaging external advisers and experts
   e. Forming review committees and conducting public consultations

3. Implementing policy decisions
   a. Selecting key leaders
   b. Structuring an appropriate organization
   c. Planning major strategies and the resources needed
   d. Initiating projects, processes and programs
   e. Monitoring progress and gathering feedback

---

degrees of organizational internalization and reinforcement of these practices, and their continuance may not be assured.

5.3 Identifying Issues for Policy Attention and Review

There are two broad set of circumstances that determine how policy issues are identified: during a crisis and during business-as-usual. In a crisis situation, the perception of the gravity of the situation is borne by external events and there is general consensus that the crisis is real and threatening. The traditional thinking suggests that under these circumstances, the process tends to involve more high-level decision-makers and significant policy changes are more likely.[8] Issue identification and policy initiation during business-as-usual is more ambiguous because of a lack of urgency and perceived threat. It involves policy insiders working with established structures and

---

[8] MS Grindle and JW Thomas (1991). *Public Choices and Policy Change*. The Johns Hopkins University Press.

systems to surface issues and justify the need to put certain issues on the agenda. This tends to take place away from public view and over an extended period of time.

Regardless of the circumstances, the main criterion for execution effectiveness in this policy initiation process is a clear understanding of the long-term vision and goals of a particular policy. This is the discipline of strategic focus. It takes discipline to allocate the best mental capacity and emotional energies to the most strategic issues. Without a clear strategic focus, it would be difficult to overcome the gravitational pulls of path dependency. Why change when a policy is still operating reasonably, when something is not broken, unless we have a vision for something better? Without strategic vision and focus, policy execution can easily degenerate into institutional bureaucracy. Without a deep internalization of the desired strategic directions and outcomes, it would be difficult to assess whether the policies identified for attention and review are indeed the most important issues to be put on the agenda. Effectiveness in execution cannot be achieved if the institution is spending its most important resource, the time and attention of policy makers, in creating a better solution to an unimportant issue.

Policy issue identification and agenda setting in Singapore have been characterized as an "inside initiation" model.[9] Government elites in the ruling political party and public sector believe that they are best able to choose, define and interpret issues and decide if further policy attention is needed. They initiate policy reviews as a normal part of their roles and responsibilities to improve social and economic outcomes and not just during a crisis or for garnering political support.

Policy initiation in Singapore springs more from aspiration than desperation. It is a policy initiative, not a mere policy reaction. Policy initiatives arising from aspirations have a greater likelihood of implementation because there is no external pressure. There is time to think, to design policies with care, to learn and deploy capabilities to achieve the desired outcomes. It stems from a position of strength and resources are available for effective execution.

---

[9] Ho Khai Leong (2003). *Shared Responsibilities, Unshared Power*. Eastern Universities Press.

Policy initiation which arises in the form of reactions to external pressure tends to be skewed toward addressing an immediate pain and are likely to be less balanced in its design. There is less time to think carefully and implement deliberately to achieve long-term objectives. It is short-term fire-fighting and while it may solve an immediate problem, other problems may arise subsequently because there is less care in the policy design. It is a response to a breakdown, a reaction that is required because of weakness. The quality of the policy solution is thus often less than ideal and overall execution effectiveness suffers.

We identify five major practices for identifying potential issues for policy consideration, including

(i)   reacting to external crisis or pressure,
(ii) identifying improvement opportunities,
(iii) surfacing issues from consideration of future scenarios,
(iv) identifying and sponsoring issues,
(v)   learning from leadership exposure to different views and practices.

Only the first practice is a response to a crisis, the other four practices reflect a proactive and systemic approach to identifying issues to be considered before they become threats or crises. They are geared more towards preventing future problems, improving current performance and taking advantage of emerging opportunities rather than reacting to external pressure because of policy failure.

5.3.1 *Reacting to External Crisis or Policy Consequences*

In crisis situations, the policy identification process is characterized by time urgency, pressure to act, high stakes because of public visibility and potentially significant economic or social consequences of both acting and not acting. The process tends to involve more high-level decision makers and significant policy changes are more likely.[10]

---

[10] Grindle and Thomas (1991).

For Singapore, significant policy changes were made in response to two major economic crises during the 1985–86 and 1997–98 periods. When these crises hit, there was widespread public concern as businesses suffered financial losses and workers were retrenched. Wages were frozen, CPF contributions were cut, fees for government services were reduced, financial help was given to those who were in need, and there was widespread public pessimism in the slow process of recovery. Major policy reviews were carried out during these periods. These reviews led to significant changes in tax, wage and social security policies. These were issues that affected the public directly and it would have been difficult to build a consensus for action during business-as-usual circumstances.

The government responded to the 1985–86 economic crisis by setting up an Economic Committee chaired by the Minister for Trade and Industry to review Singapore's economic strategy and policies and recommend changes. The major policy changes included reducing the employer Central Provident Fund (CPF, Singapore's social security system) contribution rate from 25 per cent to 10 per cent, reducing the corporate tax rate from 40 per cent to 30 per cent, freezing wages and initiating wage reform, investing in worker training to improve productivity, and diversifying the economy from an over-reliance on manufacturing into knowledge-intensive services such as information technology.[11]

The Asian financial crisis in 1997–98 triggered economic recessions across many Asian countries. The loss of confidence in Asian currencies and assets led to major sell-offs in financial markets. Although Singapore's fundamentals were strong, it could not escape the financial meltdown. Before the economies could fully recover, the technology assets bubble burst in 2000–01 and the terrorist attack on September 11, 2001 sent Asian economies into a tailspin again. An Economic Review Committee chaired by the Deputy Prime Minister was set up to recommend policy changes to promote further growth and development of the Singapore economy.

---

[11] Singapore Ministry of Trade and Industry (1986). "The Singapore Economy: New Directions." Report of the Economic Committee, pp. 49–63.

The Economic Review Committee recommended changes to remake Singapore into a globalized, entrepreneurial and diversified economy.[12] Major policy initiatives recommended include supplementing the World Trade Organization free trade framework with bilateral Free Trade Agreements, reducing corporate and income taxes to 20 per cent, increasing the Goods and Services Tax from 3 per cent to 5 per cent, refocusing the CPF back to its core purpose of providing for the basic financial needs of Singaporeans, making wages more flexible and linked to economic performance, fostering entrepreneurship, and keeping infrastructural and government services competitively-priced.

Policy reviews may also result from external responses and feedback on implementation, which may have consequences that are both expected and unexpected, regardless of whether these consequences were intended or not. Expected and intended outcomes should be shared and celebrated. For unintended but expected consequences, policies need to be adjusted and fine tuned when there is evidence that the consequences are affecting citizens negatively. These situations are easier to handle as they have been anticipated and policy makers can monitor actual outcomes that may trigger the need to review and adjust policies.

Unintended and unexpected consequences are usually not monitored because they were not anticipated by policy makers. These consequences usually take the form of problems that may be traced to a particular policy decision or implementation or from public feedback and complaints. Because they were not anticipated and thus not monitored, the problems and complaints will take some time to build up before they are large or loud enough to get attention. Even then, the causes of the problems and complaints are not always obvious and may require some analysis to trace them back to the policies that may have caused them.

An example of a policy review resulting from adverse public response to an earlier policy is the withdrawal of priority placement for schools for the third child of graduate mothers that was introduced

---

[12] Singapore Ministry of Trade and Industry (2003). "New Challenges, Fresh Goals — Towards a Dynamic Global City." Report of the Economic Review Committee.

in 1984. Policy makers had earlier noted significantly lower fertility rates among tertiary-educated mothers as compared with their non-tertiary educated counterparts. In an attempt to correct this imbalance and encourage greater procreation among tertiary-educated mothers, their third children were given priority placement in schools. While non-graduate mothers were angry with the policy, as expected, what was not anticipated was the reaction of graduate mothers: they were embarrassed and did not want the privilege accorded by the policy. The adverse public reaction was manifested in a reduced majority for the ruling party in the 1984 general elections. The decision was reversed after the elections and the priority for graduate mothers canceled. Instead, a new policy was introduced giving special income tax concessions to married women for their third and fourth children, and extended beyond university graduates to include "polytechnic, A-level and O-level mothers, enlarging the pool and lessening the sense of elitism." [13]

5.3.2 *Identifying Improvement Opportunities*

Throughout the 1990s, a major policy shift led to a wave of deregulation, liberalization and the introduction of competition in the provision of domestic services such as telecommunications, financial services, media, public transportation and government computerization. They were proactive initiatives to change policies to gain performance improvements and take advantage of new opportunities. The policy reviews were not induced by any external crisis, and in fact implementation often proceeded despite subsequent crises. These policy reviews were not prompted by any failure in the provision of these services to domestic consumers. On the contrary, the dominant players in these industries were already managed efficiently, delivering services at high standards and reasonable prices, and had developed strong brands and reputations. With a small physical island and a small population, over the course of time these companies became viewed as natural monopolies.

---

[13] Lee Kuan Yew (2000). *From Third World to First: The Singapore Story 1965–2000*. Singapore: Times Publishing.

The liberalization program was also not a response to any external pressure, and was initiated years before any free trade agreements required it. Singapore was and is one of the most open economies in the world and there was already limited competition in those industries. The move to liberalize was based on policy makers' beliefs, observations and analyses that with more competition, these incumbent companies would achieve better organizational efficiencies and product improvements, resulting in more innovative services, greater responsiveness to emerging needs and lower prices for consumers. There was also hope that these companies, which were among the largest and most successful firms listed on the Singapore Stock Exchange, would also be better prepared to face the stiff competition when they expanded regionally beyond the local market.

For example, the policy review of the financial services sector began before the Asian financial crisis hit the region in July 1997 and the Monetary Authority of Singapore launched its implementation in November 1997 in the depths of the crisis. The financial services sector had played a major part in Singapore's economic development and by 1997 accounted for 12 per cent of GDP. Singapore had also developed a reputation for high standards of prudence in financial regulation and its local banks were financially sound. In fact, the soundness of Singapore's financial sector was a reason for change rather than not to change. In addition, global trends in banking and finance and new technologies were having significant impact on the sector. When announcing the policy shift, then Deputy Prime Minister Lee Hsien Loong said:

> "The process should start now, notwithstanding the current regional uncertainties. It is a strategic shift, not dependent on the short-term ups and downs of economic fortunes. Indeed by starting now, our financial sector will be more ready to play a significant role as the region recovers."[14]

---

[14] Speech by DPM Lee Hsien Loong, "New Approach to Regulating and Developing Singapore's Financial Sector," at the SESDAQ 10th Anniversary on 4 November 1997.

The review to initiate the liberalization of the financial services sector was the result of observations and interactions that Minister Mentor Lee Kuan Yew[15] had had with international financial services leaders and through his appointment to the international advisory board of the JP Morgan investment bank. He also sought advice from former presidents of the Federal Reserve Bank of New York and the Bank of England. The main objective of the financial sector review and liberalization was to stimulate local banks and other financial services firms to grow and innovate without any loss of regulatory rigor and without any increased risk of systemic failure.

Singapore's financial sector regulatory framework had been characterized by high standards, strict rules and minimum risk-taking. The new direction aimed to keep the first and modify the latter two. The new principles developed to guide the government's policy towards the financial sector were:[16]

(i)   maintain high standards of integrity and sound financial management;
(ii)   shift emphasis from detailed regulation with specific rules to broad supervisory framework;
(iii)   focus more attention on systemic risk rather than protecting individual participants, products or projects;
(iv)   allow investors to judge and take business risks for themselves;
(v)   rely more on market discipline and full information disclosure to protect investors rather than extensive regulation;
(vi)   regulations should provide more transparency; and
(vii) build a closer partnership between the government and the industry.

The results have been dramatic.[17] The financial sector held up well against the full impact of the Asian financial crisis. Seven

---

[15] Lee (2000), pp. 97–102.

[16] Speech by Lee Hsien Loong (1997).

[17] See speech by DPM Lee Hsien Loong, "Financial Sector: Liberalization and Growth," at the Association of Banks in Singapore's 31st Annual Dinner on 17 June 2004, and updates on the MAS website: www.mas.gov.sg.

local banking groups consolidated into three stronger groups and have grown their regional business with acquisitions in Asia. Six international banks were given Qualifying Full Bank licenses. The insurance and stockbroking industries were substantially deregulated. The capital markets have grown in scope and depth. The wealth management industry grew substantially and Singapore emerged as a leading private banking center.

5.3.3 *Surfacing Issues from Consideration of Future Scenarios*

Scenarios are "stories about the way the world might turn out tomorrow, stories that can help us recognize and adapt to changing aspects of our present environment."[18] Scenarios are not predictions of the future. They are useful for learning about the implications of possible futures on today's decisions. A good scenario makes people suspend their disbelief in its stories long enough to appreciate their impact. They can then think through what they would do in each scenario and rehearse their response. This practice sensitizes leaders to early warning signs that may point to the development of a particular scenario and be more timely and appropriate in their response.

Scenario planning was practiced by Shell in dealing with the uncertainty and unpredictability of oil prices in the early 1980s and proved to be effective in preparing decision makers to act under various circumstances.[19] Schwartz[20] outlined the steps for developing scenarios to include identifying the focal issue or decision, identifying the key driving forces in the local and macro-environments, ranking them by importance and uncertainty, selecting scenario logics, fleshing out the scenarios, understanding the implications, and selecting the leading indicators and signposts.

---

[18] Peter Schwartz (1991). *The Art of the Long View*. New York, NY: Bantam Doubleday Publishing Group.

[19] Pierre Wack (1985a). "Scenarios: Uncharted Waters Ahead," *Harvard Business Review*, September–October, pp. 73–89; Pierre Wack (1985b). "Scenarios: Shooting the Rapids," *Harvard Business Review*, November–December, pp. 139–150.

[20] Schwartz (1991).

Singapore develops and considers national scenarios every three years, and these often surface important trends and issues that have policy implications. For example, two national scenarios in the late 1990s surfaced issues relating to "Hotel Singapore" and "Home Divided." The Hotel Singapore scenario relates how highly educated and mobile Singaporeans treat Singapore as a hotel, with no deep roots or emotional bonds to the country, here only to make a good living when times are good, and pack their bags and leave when the situation is no longer as attractive. The Home Divided scenario relates how the increasing income gap between professionals and workers resulted in economic and social disparities, divided the society into the haves and the have-nots, and the economic, political and social problems that could follow. Both scenarios surfaced issues relating to the need to build emotional bonds and social commitment among the educated and professional elite, and the need to ensure that the lower-educated and lower-wage workers were not left behind in the country's progress. These scenarios were presented to agencies which then developed plans and policies that were tested for robustness against the scenarios. Plans were made to weaken and moderate the potentially undesirable driving forces for the two scenarios so they were less likely to arise, and to test for effectiveness under each of the two scenarios should either one occur. The scenario process will be described in greater detail in Chapter 8 when we consider the processes that enable the public sector to change continually.

5.3.4 *Identifying and Sponsoring Strategic Issues*

The Scenario Planning Office in the Prime Minister's Office was reconstituted as the Strategic Policy Office (SPO) in 2003 and broadened to include a Strategic Issues Group (SIG). The focus of SIG is strategic policy issues that cut across several agencies and on monitoring the implementation of accepted policy changes. Proposals for examination of strategic issues may come from political and public sector leaders, scenario planning sessions, strategy workshops, policy forums and individual officers. The SPO works with the initiators to scope the project, provide some background regarding the issue, clarify the objectives and prepare proposals for consideration by a Steering Committee of Permanent Secretaries.

Once approved, an inter-agency SIG project team is formed to work on the project. Team members are assigned to the project on a part-time basis and are drawn from agencies that are interested in or impacted by the issue. The SIG project team meets regularly with overall oversight from the SPO. The recommendations of the project team are sent to the Steering Committee for approval and then formally to the affected agencies for their views and comments before being sent to the Ministerial Committee for approval. Between 2003 and 2005, ten SIG project teams were formed to study various issues including low-wage workers, senior citizens, family and procreation, and immigration. By identifying and sponsoring strategic issues for study, the public sector focuses attention and resources on priority policy areas, and allows teams of officers to understand these issues in-depth and recommend policy options and actions to be considered.

5.3.5 *Learning from Leadership Exposure to Different Views and Practices*

Political and public sector leaders may initiate reviews as a result of their personal observations, reflections, reading, visits to other countries, and interactions with other leaders. Political leaders receive complaints, requests, feedback and comments regularly from their constituents and may request for reviews of policies. There are many forums and informal discussions on policy issues, ranging from tea sessions between Ministers and public officials, to meetings of various committees, to policy forums involving different groups of officials, to parliamentary sessions where specific legislative issues are tabled and debated, and the annual budget debate where the policy agenda of different ministries are often examined by members of parliament. These interactions and debates often surface issues to the attention of public sector leaders and project teams may be formed to study important issues in greater depth.

Government leaders and officials interact with their peers from other countries and often make special study visits to understand and learn how leading organizations in more developed countries handle issues of interest to policy makers. These interactions and visits provide a rich source of ideas because of differences in philosophy, practices, and outcomes. For example, Shell Petroleum was a major investor in Singapore for many years and as a result of interactions with senior Shell executives, the public sector learned and adapted two significant practices from Shell, namely its scenario planning approach and performance appraisal system. Public sector leaders visited Shell to learn first-hand how these practices were implemented and the impacts experienced. A few selected officials were then attached to Shell in London for up to a year each to work with Shell executives so that they understood the practices well enough to know how to adapt them for the Singapore public sector and implement them upon their return.

5.3.6 An Example of Policy Initiation and Review: The Liberalization of Telecommunications Services

The policy approach to implementation of liberalization of domestic services followed a broadly similar approach. The incumbents and stakeholders were engaged and their inputs and feedback obtained — not whether deregulation or liberalization should go ahead but what they would need to do to survive and succeed in a more competitive environment. These dialogs gave policy staff the insights to design the policy to give the incumbents a reasonable time to prepare and build the capabilities to compete. A time-table for phased implementation was worked out, announced and strictly adhered to.

Telecommunications liberalization provides an interesting case of the commitment of policy makers and reliability of policy but not to the point of rigidity and fixation. The timeframe for telecommunications liberalization was developed and communicated in detail in 1992 when the government privatized its only telecom company, SingTel, and offered shares to the public and listed it on the local stock market. An independent regulator was set up for the telecommunications sector and the government approached market liberalization in phases. Mobile and paging services were liberalized in 1997, followed by Internet access service provision in 1998, and international Internet exchange service provision in 1999.

In 1997, as the Internet was transforming and increasing the pace of globalization, an internal analysis convinced the Singapore government that telecommunications liberalization was critical to Singapore's strategic positioning to be an Asian information hub. The time-frame for liberalization needed to be brought forward to ensure that business and consumer access to world-class telecommunications services at competitive prices would be maintained. Accelerated market liberalization of basic telecommunications services was necessary to catalyze the development of a dynamic and competitive telecommunications market. As in the liberalization of the financial services industry described earlier, the policy changes were initiated as a result of proactive internal analysis and judgment rather than because of failure or external crisis.

It achieved policy change in a dynamic environment without eroding the reliability of the policy environment by compensating the two main telcos, SingTel and StarHub, for moving the timeframe forward from 2002 to 2000. The compensation package was about S$1.9b, with S$1.5b going to SingTel, and was meant to cover the expected decline in profits due to earlier deregulation. It was a costly decision for the government but by compensating the telcos for moving forward the liberalization date by two years, it showed its commitment to play by the rules it had set up. More importantly, it demonstrated that its commitment to develop a competitive economy and telecommunications industry to achieve long-term national goals was paramount in its policy review; it would act dynamically but would be fair to the players. This instance of policy initiation was internally driven by a conviction of what was good for Singapore.

Deregulation of telecommunications was the start of a new learning process that would lead to further policy changes. By learning from the experience of others, Singapore avoided some of their costly mistakes, especially in the award of 3G licenses. Minister Lee Boon Yang related the process:[21]

---

[21] From speech by Dr Lee Boon Yang, Minister for Information, Communications and the Arts, Singapore, at the ITU Telecom World 2003 Plenary Forum "Is Market Liberalisation Working?" on 13 October 2003.

"First, we had to transform our regulatory practices from the regulation of an entrenched dominant player, to promoting competition in a multi-player environment. Competition also had to be carefully watched as operators vied for shares of a small pie in a market of less than 4 million people. Of course, there was also the global telecommunications downturn which affected us and which placed additional pressures on our telcos. All these had to be done with little local expertise or practical experience to rely on.

We required our dominant licensee, SingTel, to offer a Reference Interconnection Offer to other service providers. We had to develop a robust set of regulatory principles which include regulation for effective and sustainable competition, open access, consumer protection, technology neutrality and a transparent and reasoned decision making process.

As experience accumulated, we found ourselves better able to adjust to global trends. As an example, we lowered our reserve price for each 3G licence by 33 per cent as the market sentiment for 3G rapidly fell following the earlier spectrum auctions in Europe. This spared our licensees the balance sheet damage that some of the European telcos suffered. Our expectations are that our mobile operators will therefore be in a stronger position to invest in the new 3G services.

We have had our fair share of setbacks. As a result of the global downturn and our small market size, we have seen 4 facilities-based operators leave the scene since we liberalised. Virgin Mobile, a service-based operator, exited the market barely a year after it entered with a big bang. Infrastructure roll-out has also been slow, with operators choosing the 'buy' option over the 'build' option. The implication is that SingTel is likely to remain the dominant player in many market segments for a while to come. This has resulted in more calls for intervention by the regulator from the other operators in the market."

5.4 Influencing Policy Design and Development

If the key criterion for policy identification and initiation is strategic
vision and focus, then the key criterion for policy design and
development is realism. It is the discipline of confronting reality. The
willingness to face current realities squarely and honestly is what
turns visions and dreams into results. If the policy design does not
take into account the realities of the operating conditions, whether
they are the preparedness of citizens, the capabilities of institutions
or the likelihood of support from key stakeholders, then the policy
is doomed. If the analysis does not consider the current operating
realities and demonstrate logically or empirically that the policy
design can work in practice, it is not ready for implementation.
Inadequate depth and preparation in the design and development
of polices cannot be fully compensated by efficient implementation
alone. Actual implementation will surface new problems that may not
have been foreseen or fully comprehended and would require real-
time adjustments by the lead institutions. Effective execution would
be severely hampered if there is inadequate management attention,
standards are not clearly defined and quality is not built into the
policy design.

Once a policy issue has been identified and put on the agenda,
the objectives of the review and the terms of reference are set by
the sponsoring agency and its leadership. Policy design within the
purview of specific agencies is usually assigned to individual staff
officers or teams within the agencies, and the recommendations and
report would go to the Permanent Secretary and then to its Minister for
approval. Public sector leaders exercise influence over policy design
by the standards they set, by the perspectives and parameters they
utilize in defining and framing problems, by the information they use
in explaining the current realities of the problems, by the alternative
proposals they choose to put forward as policy options, and by the
analysis they give to support their recommendations.[22] If policy design

---

[22] Ho (2003).

is where the influence of public sector leaders is greatest, it is also where the reputation of the Singapore public sector is derived. Polices are designed for execution. The ultimate test for a policy design is whether it can be implemented efficiently to achieve the desired results. Execution issues have to be considered during policy design, otherwise implementation would be severely hampered.

While policy elites in Singapore are not immune to concerns over individual career advancements, the competitive positions of their departments, and the adequacy of budgets and resources,[23] the values and ethos of the public service have helped to moderate these by recognizing those who could look beyond these to focus on the longer-term national interests and who could design policy solutions that meet very high standards of analysis and realism. The respect for intellectual brilliance and contributions within the public service goes beyond the initial academic credentials. The ultimate tests are in the policy analysis and design arena. High potential civil servants know that they must get the attention of their peers and superiors through innovation, rigor and realism in their policy analysis and design.

There are five main practices utilized by the public sector in Singapore for developing and influencing policy designs for execution. These include:

(i)   setting standards for policy analysis and design,
(ii) recommending courses of action through staff analysis and papers,
(iii) studying policy options through inter-agency project teams,
(iv) engaging external advisers and experts, and
(v)   forming review committees and conducting public consultation.

Although there is an increasing emphasis on involving the private sector and the public in the development of policy, it is still the internal culture, standards, structures and processes that drive the design of policy options and the attention given to execution considerations during policy development.

---

[23] Grindle and Thomas (1991).

5.4.1 *Setting Standards for Policy Analysis and Design*

The principles of rationality, pragmatism and results orientation described in Chapter 4 are most strongly expressed in the standards used to judge the quality of a policy proposal. The public service adopted the four Shell criteria for assessing the potential of talented individuals (these criteria will be discussed in detail in Chapter 7) but these criteria evolved to become the implicit approach in designing policies and the standard for evaluating policy options and proposals. The four criteria are denoted by the acronym, HAIR:

(i)   H: Helicopter quality, the ability to view issues from a holistic and long-term perspective; not losing sight of the most important issues.
(ii) A: power of Analysis, involving superior intellect, logic, rational analysis and judgment.
(iii) I: Imagination, the originality of the ideas, the ability to imagine and innovate.
(iv) R: Realism, how grounded and realistic the solutions are, taking cognizance of the actual conditions and circumstances.

The HAIR criteria have gone beyond an approach for assessing people; they now encapsulate a philosophy of policy design that ensures vision and rigor, ideas and realism, and are the criteria by which policies are judged for their suitability for implementation. Public officials involved in designing policy options and justifying recommendations are socialized into this way of thinking and have largely internalized these considerations in their approach to policy work. These criteria have become more than a screen for approvals. They have become a guide for generating ideas, collecting data, testing proposals and developing higher quality alternatives in policy analysis and design.

A "helicopter" quality is the ability to determine how a policy is related to the long-term interests of the country and the larger perspective of national development, while simultaneously zooming in on the critical details. A policy that fails this test is not a strategic issue nor a priority and the resources allocated, if any, would not be significant. The rigor and rationality of analysis ensure that policy options are carefully considered and have the potential to achieve desired results. Imagination judges the creativity of the ideas so that a fresh and engaging approach to the problem may be implemented. Realism is a crucial test — does the policy design take into account the realities on the ground? Is it practical? Will it be accepted? Have the potential difficulties, risks and resistance been considered? How would the proposed design deal with these? It is this insistence on realism that makes the policy design amenable to execution.

The attributes of HAIR provide a balanced approach to policy design. They ensure a comprehensive consideration of policy issues and a systematic design of the overall solution, and yet a practical and often phased approach to execution. Coordination of execution is achieved with a shared vision and an integrated policy approach but implementation is agency specific.

5.4.2 Recommending Courses of Action through Staff Analysis and Papers

Public sector officials and staff are expected to be objective, rigorous, thorough and have a national perspective when analyzing policy issues and making recommendations. Most policy review teams consist largely of internal staff headed by a senior official. Even when external review teams or committees are formed, most of the analytical work are done by internal staff and subjected to rigorous internal reviews and approvals.

Staff review teams conduct their own research and collect data to understand the issues and support their recommendations. Where similar problems have been dealt with successfully in other countries, study trips are made to observe and understand first-hand the implementation and impact of adopted solutions. The teams meet regularly to discuss and then prepare a staff paper to describe the issue, the analysis that was done, the recommendations, financial, legal and land use implications, anticipated reactions from the implementation of recommended actions, and a proposed communication plan. The standards that drive policy development discussed earlier are formalized in the expectations of how staff policy papers are written. The format of public sector staff papers for policy design and recommendations is shown in Table 5.2.

For major policy initiatives and changes, a minister would request for a paper to be prepared for final approval by the Cabinet. The Cabinet paper synthesizes the main issues, alternatives, recommendations, financial and legal implications and how the changes would be communicated.

Table 5.2. Format of Staff Papers

---

1. Background: Why paper is necessary.

2. Aim of paper (including the decision required).

3. Main body of paper: left to the discretion of the writer but should include:
   a. Main issues/problems.
   b. Alternatives.
   c. Analysis of alternatives.

4. Compulsory sections:
   a. Consultation with other agencies and their responses.
   b. Financial implications.
   c. Use of land implications.
   d. Legal implications.
   e. Anticipated reactions.
   f. Proposed communication plan.

5. Conclusions.

6. Recommendations.

Public sector staff and officials in policy development teams have significant scope for influencing how a problem or issue is defined, how the research to support the review is done, what data to collect and present, what alternatives to highlight, which proposals to recommend and the arguments used to support them. It is an iterative process of understanding and analyzing an issue, sharing ideas and interacting with other officials in various agencies, refining proposals, gathering feedback and support, and deciding how the issue and proposal would be presented. This iterative process incorporates the views and ideas of many officials, including those not formally represented on the review team, before the paper is finalized and presented to the minister. Even though the minister may be the final decision-maker and would have his input and views represented in the review, it would be difficult for him to ignore objective data and analyses presented by officials and the arguments made in support of or against specific options.

5.4.3 Studying Policy Options through Inter-agency Project Teams

Policy design in a sophisticated economy and demanding society is no longer single issue focused with obvious solutions. The policy issues and solutions are complex and have multiple levels of impact and consequences. The required design is often beyond the scope and expertise of a single agency. A multi-agency approach is thus required for policy execution to be effective. But organizational structures in the public sector were formed according to functional or domain expertise with focused historical missions to solve the policy problems that arose in the past. The public sector deals with these significant and complex policy issues which span multiple agencies by forming inter-agency project teams to study, analyze and design policies that require the cooperation of several different agencies.

Some project teams are formed under the auspices of the SPO as discussed earlier. Projects usually take six to nine months to complete and teams submit their report to the Steering Committee of Permanent Secretaries. When the recommendations are supported by the Steering Committee, the project report and recommendations are sent to the relevant agencies for their comments. The report, recommendations and comments are then sent to the Ministerial Committee for their approval. If approved, the project team will work with the relevant agencies to implement the recommendations. If it is not approved, the project will be filed for future consideration.

The SPO serves as secretariat to the strategic issues inter-agency project teams. The Office recommends team leaders and members to the Steering Committee for appointment to the inter-agency teams, sets the terms of reference for the teams and serves as secretariat to coordinate meetings and record minutes of team deliberations. Its influence on the team's analysis and recommendations is indirect but still significant in providing guidance and direction for the team's deliberations. It also serves as a coordinator to ensure that there is follow-through for implementation when the recommendations are accepted.

5.4.4 Engaging External Advisers and Experts

The public sector's openness to learning from others reflects the leadership's proclivity for better ideas to improve governance. The small size of the country and the population drives the leadership to constantly search for better ways to get more from the limited resources available. Learning from others provides a safer and faster route for progress and avoids the mistakes that others have made. Sometimes external advisers are sought to assure internal stakeholders of the validity and veracity of domestically developed plans and policies. External expertise is also engaged to give independent views and reviews of key areas of development to ensure that current organizational leaders maintain their objectivity and do not unconsciously develop strategic blind spots.

Singapore has historically found significant value in the advisers who provided important inputs in the early development of the country. Dutch economist Albert Winsemius is widely recognized as having provided valuable advice for the economic development and industrialization of the island state in the early 1960s. Similarly, Israeli military advisers helped Singapore plan and build up the armed forces after Singapore became independent in 1965.

In recent years, the public sector appointed advisers to guide its development objectives in many areas, including the formulation of new economic policies, the push into biomedical sciences, information and communication technology development, concepts for new gardens in the Marina Bay area and the development of its universities. Advisers have also helped the public sector with ideas for considering emerging issues such as dealing with complexity, innovation, and disruptive technologies. Advisers may be appointed as consultants to work on specific projects or on advisory panels that meet periodically to review developments in a particular public agency and give their feedback, views and advice on emerging issues.

5.4.5 Forming Review Committees and Conducting Public Consultation

If a policy issue is expected to have significant public impact, to require public support for its implementation, and to need visible expert public inputs, a review committee is formed to undertake the study and develop recommendations for the government to consider. These are appointed by the government, with representatives from groups that would be affected by or have strong interest in the policy. The chairman of the committee is usually a respected business, community or government leader and members are also prominent representatives of various sectors including business, organized labor, community organizations and the public sector. For major complex and controversial issues, the review committee may form sub-committees to propose specific actions or policy changes for the main committee to consider. Examples of review committees appointed by the government to provide inputs and recommendations for policy changes are shown in Table 5.3.

Review committees meet over a period of time to discuss the issues and proposals for change. Public sector officials from relevant agencies serve as secretariat to facilitate the work of the review committees and subcommittees. They work with the chairpersons to set agenda, provide information, coordinate meetings, and record minutes of discussions. They provide background information to the committee, prepare papers on related areas for the committee to consider in their deliberations, gather data or conduct specific studies at the request of the committee, and often prepare draft reports for the committee to consider and adopt for submission to the government. The final report of the committee, containing specific proposals, is presented to the government and released to the public through the media. The government would then consider the recommendations and respond by indicating the proposals that are accepted, those that are not and the reasons for doing so.

Review committees are used to gather feedback and ideas, provide alternative views, develop recommendations, prioritize investments, organize important stakeholders and communities,

Table 5.3. Examples of Policy Review Committees

Year	Review Committee	Chairman
1985	Economic Committee	Minister, Trade and Industry
1992	Library 2000 Review Committee	Chairman, National Computer Board
1996	Committee on Singapore's Competitiveness	Minister, Trade and Industry
1997	Singapore 21 Committee	Minister of Education
1998	Manpower 21 Committee	Permanent Secretary, Ministry of Manpower
2000	Infocomm 21 Committee	Chairman, Infocomm Development Authority
2001	Economic Review Committee	Deputy Prime Minister
2002	JC/Upper Secondary Education Review Committee	Minister of State, Education
2002	Censorship Review Committee	Chairman, National Arts Council
2002	Remaking Singapore Committee	Minister of State, National Development
2005	Committee on Employability of Older Workers	Minister of State, Manpower and Education
2006	Committee on Low Wage Workers	Minister of Manpower

co-opt important opinion leaders and lend legitimacy to proposed policy changes. They prepare important stakeholders to accept the policy changes and engage their support to ensure the success of policy execution. Communicating the work and recommendations of the review committees enables the government to reach a larger portion of the community and provides credible voices of support that prepare the public to accept the policy change and impending implementation. The fundamental analysis and development of policy options for the consideration of review committees are still done by policy staff supervised by public sector leaders. Review committees are really about integrating internal analysis and design with external validation. The value of such engagement is not insignificant — they do result in changes to policy designs and implementation strategies. The engagement usually leads to more effective execution as the

Table 5.4. Public Consultation Framework

Describe	Explain	Consult	Connect
One-way	Two-way	Two-way	Many ways
Purpose: Agency informs stakeholders about its policies.	Purpose: Agency explains the reasons for, and objectives of its policies and responds to queries and feedback from stakeholders.	Purpose: Agency seeks views from stakeholders when developing policies.	Purpose: Agency fosters a network of stakeholders who proactively offer views and suggestions, and help explain policies to other citizens and stakeholders.
Tools: Fact sheets, website.	Tools: Press releases, briefings, surveys, focus groups, web chats.	Tools: Focus groups, taskforces, expert panels, advisory committees.	Tools: Expert panels, advisory committees, civil societies.

review committees and the communities they represent have the opportunity to have their voices heard and their ideas considered. By their involvement, they become more psychologically prepared to work with the government to make the policy changes work and to be a positive force for change in the community.

Public consultation is used to involve and engage a more educated, demanding and vocal population on the policy issues that affect their lives. Public consultation solicits views from the public on policy ideas and proposals before they are approved and adopted for implementation. It is a means to increase public awareness, gather feedback, solicit views, test ideas, sharpen analyses, provide an avenue for voicing concerns, to engage in dialog and debate, discover opportunities, and generate public buy-in for implementation.

Singapore's framework of public participation[24] involves four levels as shown in Table 5.4.

Public consultations have taken many forms, including feedback sessions, meetings with influential opinion makers, town

---

[24] Civil Service College (2006). *A Guide to Policy Development.*

hall gatherings with senior policy makers, letters, postings on e-governmental portals, and web-based discussions. The feedback and comments gathered are then considered by policy makers, who will then decide what and how much of the policy and its implementation approach need to be revised. The level of engagement in public consultations is lower than review committees but the end result is largely the same. A larger and vocal portion of the population is engaged and involved. If the consultation results in substantive changes in policy, they are welcome. But even if they do not, the open channel of communication and the voluntary involvement of those who want to contribute can only improve the overall governance process and pave the way for better implementation.

5.4.6 The Holistic Approach to Policy Design: The Example of Water Management and Security

Singapore's water management is an example of how the public sector designs and executes its policy holistically, considering all the parts of the system. The execution may be phased but cumulative with a clear strategic direction. Having clean water has been a matter of survival for a small, land scarce island without adequate physical capacity to store the water needed by its growing population and economy. Much of Singapore's water is imported from Malaysia's southern state of Johor under agreements signed in 1961 and 1962, and which expire in 2011 and 2061. Singapore's leaders realized that if Singapore became self-sufficient in its water supplies, this would remove a source of perennial tension in its relations with Malaysia. Through a phased, systematic and holistic policy approach, Singapore is now much closer to achieving this objective, so much so that it will not need to renew the water agreement with Malaysia which expires in 2011.

Professor Asit Biswas who won the 2006 Stockholm Water Prize commented in an interview that the two most efficient water systems in the world in the public sector are in Singapore and Tokyo. When asked which feature of Singapore's water practices was the most exportable, he replied:

"What is most remarkable about Singapore is not any of its specific practices but rather the holistic way PUB has gone to manage its limited water resources. Its practices, ranging from an innovative water pricing system that contributes very significantly to water conservation, to issues like overall catchment management, collecting and treating all its wastewater, reuse of wastewater, and raising public awareness, are exemplary."[25]

The comprehensive policy approach to water management and security includes

(i)   formulation and implementation of new water-related policies,
(ii) restructuring institutions to ensure a strategic, broad and long-term perspective in water management,
(iii) the development of new supply sources such as heavy investments in desalination, extensive reuse of wastewater, and enhanced water catchments infrastructure,
(iv) sophisticated water demand management through various tariffs and incentives,
(v)   investing in research and technology development and
(vi) promoting the development of a competitive water industry cluster for both domestic needs and exports

The Public Utilities Board (PUB) was tasked with the execution of the water management policy and now manages the entire water cycle of Singapore. Earlier, PUB was responsible for managing potable water, electricity and gas. On 1 April 2001, the responsibilities for sewerage and drainage were transferred to PUB from the Ministry of the Environment. The consolidation allowed PUB to develop and implement a holistic policy. The country is now fully sewered to collect all wastewater, and the separate drainage and sewerage systems have facilitated wastewater reuse on an extensive scale. PUB has reviewed and restructured water tariffs to reflect the higher cost of water

---

[25]Interview with Professor Asit Biswas, published in *The Straits Times*, on 23 September 2006.

produced with the new sources and to encourage water conservation. The recycling and desalination programs were phased: the potential of these two processes were examined in the 1980s but were not taken up then as the costs were prohibitive. They were re-examined and implemented only 10–15 years later when the technology had developed to an extent that costs became acceptable.

Cecilia Tortajada, Vice President of the Third World Center for Water Management at Mexico, did a detailed study of Singapore's urban water management for 2006 Human Development Report. She commented:

> "Singapore's success in managing its water and wastewater is its concurrent emphasis on supply and demand management, wastewater and stormwater management, institutional effectiveness and creating an enabling environment, which includes a strong political will, effective legal and regulatory frameworks and an experienced and motivated workforce.
>
> The country has successfully implemented what most water professionals have been preaching in recent years. By ensuring efficient use of its limited water resources through economic instruments, adopting latest technological development to produce 'new' sources of water, enhancing storage capacities by proper catchment management, practicing water conservation measures, and ensuring concurrent consideration of social, economic and environmental factors, Singapore has reached a level of holistic water management that other urban centres will do well to emulate." [26]

5.5 Implementing Policy Decisions

Implementing policy decisions effectively is the difference between ideas, plans and results, between vision and reality, between

---

[26] Cecilia Tortajada (2006). "Urban Water Management," in *Asian Water*, April.

policy design and actual progress. From an outsider's perspective, implementation is policy. Outsiders, including citizens, may not be privy to or understand the policy considerations during the decision-making process. Policy is what they see as implemented, whether intended or not. This is the hands-on process of policy execution. It is the discipline of follow-through. It is not about talk and ideas: it is action. It is allocating the resources needed to get the job done. It is ensuring that people with the right skills and motivation are selected and an appropriate organization is created to lead and coordinate the efforts. It is creating processes, projects and programs to transform plans and philosophy into performance, progress and prosperity. It is accountability for appropriate use of resources and for results. It is also about recognizing contributions and linking rewards to performance, sustaining an institutional culture for getting the job done. This is the essence of policy execution. It is the discipline of follow-through of realistic policy designs developed to fulfill a worthy national vision and goal.

Singapore's civil service has a good reputation because it has the knowledge, skills, organization and resources to execute policies in an efficient manner. Implementation considerations begin from the time the policy is being reviewed and developed for potential change. Public officials and staff making recommendations on specific policy proposals and changes are required to meet rigorous standards of analysis and face the tests of reality at the same time. They consult other public agencies and various stakeholders to address implementation issues such as legal implications of the proposals and the key resources (especially finance and land use) needed.

If a policy decision requires changes to legislation, the Attorney-General's Chambers will work with the agency to draft the needed legislative changes and have them approved by Parliament. We identify five main practices from the public sector in Singapore for implementing policy decisions, these include:

(i)   selecting key leaders,
(ii) structuring an appropriate organization,
(iii) planning major strategies and resources needed,

(iv) initiating projects, processes and programs, and

(v)   monitoring progress and gathering feedback.

These are the practical requirements for converting ideas and resources into reality and results. Policy execution requires visionary concepts and realistic design during the development process, as well as efficient deployment of organization resources during implementation. Even with rigorous policy design standards, inappropriate implementation choices and inefficient organization and deployment of resources will result in waste and delays that may threaten the desired policy outcomes or dissipate people's motivation and creative energies.

5.5.1 *Selecting Key Leaders*

Selecting trusted and capable leaders for implementing major policies is a key feature of public management in Singapore. Domain knowledge and expertise are less important considerations. Lee Kuan Yew believed in putting the "best man for the most important tasks"[27] during the critical early years of self-rule and independence and this practice became imprinted into a fairly consistent pattern for implementing changes in public policies. Senior political and public sector leaders identify potential leaders who are able to ensure that policies will be successfully implemented to achieve the desired results and who have the capacity to grow and develop through the assignment. The social network is often used in appointing credible and trusted public sector leaders to lead change in areas that differ from their previous experience; these appointed leaders often in turn appoint managers whom they have worked with previously.

For example, Philip Yeo was a high profile Permanent Secretary in the Ministry of Defence in 1980 when he was given the task of starting up a new statutory board to spearhead Singapore's drive into the IT age. As chairman of the National Computer Board (NCB), he brought in several trusted colleagues from the computer organization of the Ministry of Defence to form the initial management team for NCB. In

---

[27] This was mentioned by several retired public sector leaders during our interviews.

1985, during the worst major economic recession experienced till then, he was appointed by the Minister of Trade and Industry to become chairman of the Economic Development Board (EDB), to increase the quantity and quality of foreign investments to help Singapore out of the recession and to restructure the economy towards higher value-added manufacturing activities. He promoted Tan Chin Nam, then the CEO of NCB to be chairman and also made him the Managing Director of EDB.

When the Ministry of Information and the Arts wanted to review the public library system in 1992, the Minister appointed Tan to chair the Library 2000 review committee. NCB had just released an IT2000 report that suggested that digital libraries would be the direction for the future. When the Library 2000 recommendations were accepted by the government, Tan selected Christopher Chia, his colleague from NCB to be the new CEO of the National Library Board.

5.5.2 *Structuring an Appropriate Organization*

Public sector agencies are created to build the necessary resources and capabilities for executing programs to achieve the strategic intent of public policies. They are responsible for the results of policy implementation and are accountable to the minister who oversees the policy area. Separate organizations devoted to specific missions enable the leadership to have greater focus in deploying resources to achieve desired results. These organizations are created by legislation to be responsible for major government policies, programs and activities. They may take the form of ministries, statutory boards or other state organizations. Statutory boards have their own governance structure and enjoy greater autonomy in managing their human and financial resources, and may generate their own revenue to pursue their given missions.

In proposing changes to policies, an evaluation is also made regarding the appropriate organization structure and form to deliver the desired results and services. A ministry may be restructured to reflect new policy priorities and implement new programs and activities. The Ministry of Community Development was restructured into the Ministry of Community Development and Sports in April 2000, and then again to the Ministry of Community, Youth and Sports in September 2004 to reflect the growing importance of policies and programs for youth and sports.

A new department may be set up to implement a new policy initiative. A new Centre for Shared Services (CSS) was set up in the Ministry of Finance in 2006 to consolidate the processing of the public sector's backroom human resource and finance activities. Agencies transferred these activities and the people performing them to the CSS to enjoy greater economies of scale and efficiency in processing the backroom services. The CSS has the expertise and systems to streamline business processes and redeploy staff to achieve the 15 per cent cost savings promised to agencies.

Existing government departments may be restructured into statutory boards to enable greater focus and autonomy in executing strategies to achieve intended results. The Inland Revenue Department in the Ministry of Finance was restructured into the Inland Revenue Authority of Singapore (IRAS) in 1992 to enable greater flexibility in attracting and retaining the talent needed to transform the agency into a professional tax organization. Internally, IRAS was reorganized from product (tax types) divisions to functional divisions to leverage a process approach supported by a new IT system. Similarly, the National Library was restructured into a statutory board in 1995 to enable it to have greater autonomy in implementing initiatives and programs to achieve its new mission of enhancing the learning capacity of the nation.

Government agencies may be corporatized or privatized if there are existing markets for related services or if there is a strategic intent to allow private sector competition in the provision of similar services. If there are regulatory activities, they are separated and then taken over by existing or new agencies. The Port of Singapore Authority was corporatized in 1997 as the PSA Corporation to allow it to function as a competitive market entity and give it the flexibility to bring in new investors through strategic alliances or a listing on the stock market. The regulatory functions of the port were taken over by a new statutory board, the Maritime and Port Authority.

The operating arm of the National Computer Board was corporatized in 1999 to introduce competition in the provision of IT services to the government. The provision of IT services to the government was initially transferred to a government wholly-owned corporate entity, the National Computer Systems, which was then sold in a private tender to SingTel, the largest local telecommunications company listed on the Singapore Stock Exchange.

5.5.3 *Planning Major Strategies and Resources Needed*

After an appropriate organization is formed or restructured and the key leaders appointed, the leadership team will develop a set of strategic thrusts for implementation and justify the financial and human resources required. These strategic thrusts may be a detailed plan of the policy proposals or review committee recommendations that were previously approved, or may include new strategic directions formulated by the leadership team. Planning rigor is required at this stage so that performance indicators may be developed, targets set and specific human and financial resources requested. After internal deliberations within an agency, the strategic plan and budget is submitted to its parent ministry for support and then to the Ministry of Finance for budget approval and allocation.

The Library 2000 study that was accepted by the government in 1994 recommended six strategic thrusts for the transformation of library services in Singapore, including an adaptive public library system, a network of borderless libraries, coordinated national collection strategy, providing quality service through market orientation, building symbiotic linkages with business and community, and leveraging global knowledge. The new management team appointed to the new National Library Board in 1995 developed specific plans for implementing the Library 2000 vision, including plans for building new physical libraries, renovating existing libraries, investing in a new IT network, enhancing content, improving services, reengineering business processes, and developing the professional skills and knowledge of the librarians. A budget of S$1b, including a development budget of S$611m, was approved in 1996 to enable the Library to execute its plans over eight years.

5.5.4 *Initiating Projects, Processes and Programs*

After obtaining the needed human and financial resources, the restructured agency initiates specific projects, processes and programs to fulfill the desired goals of the policy and achieve the intended results. This is the action phase of the implementation and effective execution is critical to convert plans and resources into capabilities and services for interface with the public and other users. As officials and users learn to interact through the new programs and services, new attitudes and behavior are formed and change in people and organization start to take shape, enabling better performance results to be enjoyed. When projects, processes and programs are properly designed and executed effectively, agency staff can perform more meaningful work while serving the public with more care and speed.

The tax agency appointed a new Commissioner in 1991, was restructured into a new statutory board, IRAS, in 1992 and reorganized internally from tax types to functions. It then initiated a major redesign of its tax processes and a complete redevelopment of its technology platform. For example, tax processing was changed from a manual process based on a tax officer's assessment of individual cases to a pipeline process where the tax officers' accumulated expertise was captured as expert rules and embedded into the new system. Tax assessment is now done automatically by the system and only complex cases are referred to tax officers for their judgment and assessment. The redesigned tax processes and systems, implemented over two years in 1995 and 1996, were crucial in enabling IRAS to eliminate its backlog and complete most of its tax processing in five months rather than two years previously.

5.5.5 *Monitoring Progress and Gathering Feedback*

As new projects and initiatives are implemented, agencies gather feedback from users and adjust their programs and services to ensure that the intended goals are met. They collect data on their performance and progress and review internally to identify opportunities for improvement. These data are included in agencies' annual performance review which form the basis of their budget requests to their parent ministries and to Finance. Where there are significant public interests, the results of the progress may be released to the media periodically.

5.5.6 *An Example of Policy Implementation: Awarding Contracts for the Integrated Resorts*

A recent example of the care and rationality in the design of organizations and processes to implement policies was the evaluation of proposals for the two integrated resorts (IRs) with casinos at Marina Bay and Sentosa. Approval was given for two IRs after much public and parliamentary debate. The Singapore Tourism Board was then designated the lead agency to oversee the implementation of the project. It spent many months discussing with experts and industry players the appropriate process for evaluating and awarding the licenses for the two IRs. A detailed request for proposal document was produced to explain Singapore's purpose of the project, the criteria for judging bids, the process and timing for the bidding and evaluation process, details about the sites, and the requirements of the bid submission. Proposed investors were subject to detailed probity and background checks prior to being qualified to bid for the projects. The criteria and weightage were clearly articulated for each of the two projects, including criteria such as convention attraction, tourism appeal, resort design, amount of investments, and the experience and credibility of the partners.

An overview of the evaluation process for the Marina Bay IR is shown in Figure 5.3. A similar process was used for the evaluation of the Sentosa IR. The evaluation timeline is shown in Figure 5.4. Three separate evaluation committees supported by resource personnel and consultants were formed and their composition are shown in Table 5.5.

The external consultants independently calculated the land price to be charged by the government and assessed the financial projections given by the proposed investors. The design evaluation, consisting of people with architectural expertise, gave their independent assessments of the proposals to the evaluation committees. A tender

```
┌─────────────────────────────────┐
│   TENDER APPROVING AUTHORITY    │
│             (TAA)               │
└─────────────────────────────────┘
                ▲
                │
┌─────────────────────────────────┐
│      TENDER EVALUATION          │
│      COMMITTEE (TEC)            │
└─────────────────────────────────┘
                ▲
                │
┌─────────────────────────────────┐        ┌─────────────────────────────────┐
│                                 │        │   DESIGN EVALUATION PANEL       │
│    GOVERNMENT AGENCIES          │◄───────│            (DEP)                │
│                                 │        │                                 │
└─────────────────────────────────┘        └─────────────────────────────────┘
                ▲
                │  Input
┌─────────────────────────────────┐
│     RESOURCE PERSONS/           │
│       CONSULTANT                │
└─────────────────────────────────┘
```

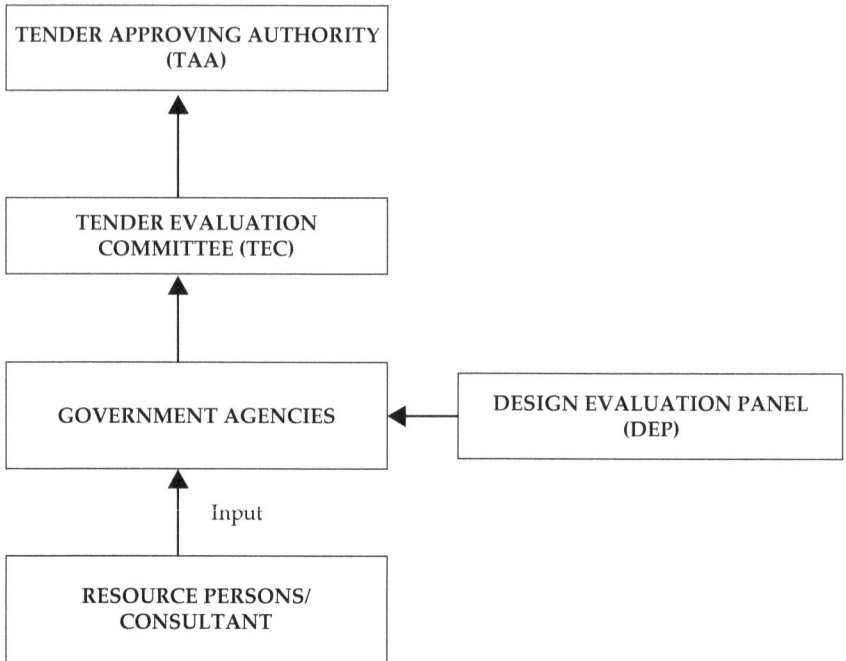

Source: Singapore Tourism Board.

Figure 5.3. Overview of Evaluation Process for Marina Bay Integrated Resort

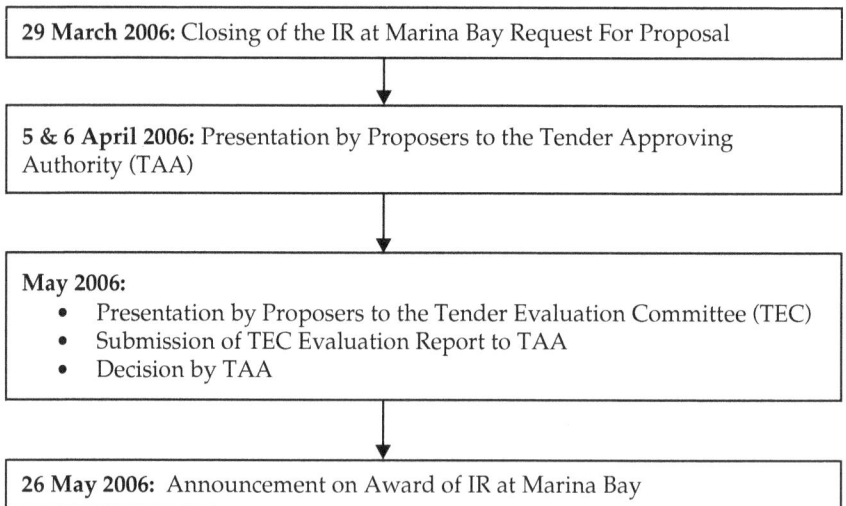

```
┌──────────────────────────────────────────────────────────────────────┐
│ 29 March 2006: Closing of the IR at Marina Bay Request For Proposal     │
└──────────────────────────────────────────────────────────────────────┘
                                  │
                                  ▼
┌──────────────────────────────────────────────────────────────────────┐
│ 5 & 6 April 2006: Presentation by Proposers to the Tender Approving     │
│ Authority (TAA)                                                         │
└──────────────────────────────────────────────────────────────────────┘
                                  │
                                  ▼
┌──────────────────────────────────────────────────────────────────────┐
│ May 2006:                                                              │
│    • Presentation by Proposers to the Tender Evaluation Committee (TEC) │
│    • Submission of TEC Evaluation Report to TAA                         │
│    • Decision by TAA                                                    │
└──────────────────────────────────────────────────────────────────────┘
                                  │
                                  ▼
┌──────────────────────────────────────────────────────────────────────┐
│ 26 May 2006:  Announcement on Award of IR at Marina Bay                │
└──────────────────────────────────────────────────────────────────────┘
```

Figure 5.4. Integrated Resort at Marina Bay Evaluation Timeline

Table 5.5. Integrated Resort At Marina Bay Evaluation Committees

TENDER APPROVING AUTHORITY (TAA)

Chairman Professor S. Jayakumar	Deputy Prime Minister, Coordinating Minister for National Security and Minister for Law
Members	
Mr Mah Bow Tan	Minister for National Development
Mr Lim Hng Kiang	Minister for Trade and Industry
Dr Vivian Balakrishnan	Minister for Community Development, Youth and Sports, and Second Minister for Trade and Industry
Mr Raymond Lim	Minister, Prime Minister's Office, Second Minister for Finance, and Second Minister for Foreign Affairs

TENDER EVALUATION COMMITTEE (TEC)

Chairman Mr Lim Siong Guan	Permanent Secretary, Finance
Members	
Mr Peter Ong	Permanent Secretary, Trade and Industry
Mr Tan Tee How	Permanent Secretary, National Development
Ms Chan Lai Fung	Permanent Secretary, Law

DESIGN EVALUATION PANEL (DEP)

Chairperson Mrs Cheong-Chua Koon Hean	Chief Executive Officer, URA
Members	
Mrs Koh-Lim Wen Gin	Chief Planner and Deputy Chief Executive Officer (Physical Planning and Conservation & Urban Design), URA
Mr Alan Choe	Singapore Institute of Architects Gold Medal Award Winner
Professor Philip Cox	Partner, Cox Group Pty Ltd, Australia
Mr Mok Wei Wei	Managing Director, W Architects, Singapore
Professor John de Monchaux	Professor of Architecture and Planning, Department of Architecture, Massachusetts Institute of Technology, USA
Ms Rita Soh	President, Singapore Institute of Architects

Resource Persons and Consultant

- Dr Chew Tuan Chiong, Chief Executive, Singapore Science Centre
- Mr James Cundall, Chief Executive, Lunchbox Theatrical Productions
- Mr Kwok Kian Chow, Director, Singapore Art Museum
- Bain & Company

Source: Singapore Tourism Board.

evaluation committee comprising top public sector leaders met separately with the bidders and gave their own evaluation and recommendation to but independent of, the tender approval committee made up of ministers.

The design of the entire IR evaluation process was based on an analytical hierarchy process used by the Ministry of Defence in complex military hardware and systems procurement. As shown above, the evaluation process was designed to achieve objectivity and fairness in awarding the license to the bidder with the best proposal to achieve the objectives set out by the Singapore Tourism Board. It required the input of expert knowledge and was designed to ensure independence in assessment, with multiple perspectives brought into the overall evaluation. More importantly, the public sector tender evaluation committee comprising public sector leaders made their recommendation separate from the ministerial approval committee. This separation reinforced the critical role played by the public sector in making and implementing policies in Singapore. The IR evaluation process demonstrated the execution capabilities of the public institutions and the importance of policy implementation rather than just policy talk.

The Marina Bay IR was awarded to Las Vegas Sands which will invest in excess of S$5b into the project. The result was not predicted by earlier public and industry opinion polls. When the details of the award were made public, it became clear that the evaluation had been objective and followed closely the published decision criteria. The Sentosa IR was awarded to a consortium led by Genting International. Two major government-linked property and hotel management groups had formed alliances with international partners to bid for the projects but did not win either of the contracts. Even though the contract sums were large, there have been no charges of irregularities in the process. The elaborate tender and evaluation process was fair, clean, independent and thorough. But there was also a down side. Potential bidders had earlier complained about the slowness and bureaucracy of the process. Balancing thoroughness and speed in execution is difficult and no policy implementation processes will work perfectly. But the importance of careful design of projects, processes and programs in successful policy execution is beyond doubt.

Table 5.6. Policy Development and Change in the Public Service

Phase of Development	Major National Issues	Key Public Sector Leaders
1965–1985 **Implementer:** Make Policies Work & Build Basic Infrastructure	Unemployment Basic Education & Housing Defense and Security	Sim Kee Boon JY Pillay Lee Ek Tieng
1986–1996 **Transition:** Change Mindset & Adapt	Economic Restructuring Better Skills & Productivity Increased Social Expectations	Ngiam Tong Dow Andrew Chew Philip Yeo
1997–2007 **Innovator:** Identify Issues & Create New Capacity	Rapid Change & Uncertainty Aging & Declining Population Unconventional Threats	Lim Siong Guan Peter Ho

5.6 Policy Development and Change in the Public Service

5.6.1 Major Phases of Policy Development and Change

The three policy execution processes of the public sector are also descriptive of the way that the Singapore public sector has developed and changed since independence in 1965. However the phases of policy development and change are in the reverse order of what was described above as shown in Table 5.6.

In the early years following independence from Malaysia in 1965 and the British military withdrawal announced in 1968, Singapore was faced with basic survival challenges: massive unemployment, lack of basic education, health care, sanitation and housing, and building up an armed forces to ensure external security. Political and public sector leaders worked together closely because of the urgency of the problems and the limited talent pool in government. The political leadership was committed and had clear ideas of what needed to be done. The public service was the *implementer*. Civil service leaders made the policies work and built the basic infrastructure needed for a functioning economy quickly and efficiently. The evidence of the success of the policies and the efficiency of the implementation was the sustained economic growth, low unemployment, increased income and better education, health care and housing for the population.

The period from 1986 to 1996 was a *transition* for the public service. The political transition to a second generation of leaders who wanted a more consultative style of government meant that the approach to policy design and implementation had to be modified. Singapore experienced its first major recession in 1985–1986. The public sector had to re-examine its own mindset and adapt to the new changed environment. Economic policies were re-oriented to diversify the economy and to attract higher value-added sectors that utilized more capital and higher skills. Education, health care and housing were upgraded to cater to increasing demands from the population for better quality delivery and services.

The Asian financial crisis that hit the region in 1997, followed by the attack on the World Trade Center in New York in 2001 and then the SARS outbreak in 2003 marked a highly volatile, uncertain and unpredictable period for Singapore. China and India were growing quickly and attracting manufacturing investments that could have come to ASEAN. Previous assumptions and rules were no longer valid. New thinking and new ideas were needed to build an innovative economy. The public sector had to reinvent itself to be an *innovator,* to anticipate the future and develop new capacity to approach emerging issues that were likely to be more complex and multi-faceted. It was a period during which the public sector underwent major changes including the devolution of human resource management and the launch of PS21 (Public Service for the 21st Century) strategy. The main thrust during this period was to be prepared for a fast changing, uncertain and unpredictable future. The public service had to learn to welcome change, anticipate change and execute change.

5.6.2 *Transforming the Public Service*

While the basic responsibilities of government to assure security, build community, provide identity, observe accountability and create opportunity remained unchanged, how it went about achieving these results were transformed. The traditional roles of the public sector as controller and regulator have evolved to new roles as a *nurturer, facilitator, convener and aggregator.* These new roles recognize that the ultimate creator of wealth is the private sector and that government needs to nurture the ideas, facilitate their efficient execution, convene the right set of players to achieve a coherent effort, and aggregate their results to achieve the desired national impacts. The public sector was repositioned so that it became a catalyst for change rather than an impediment to change, a pace-setter rather than a mere follower, and a standard bearer rather than a mediocre also-ran. The Managing for Excellence Framework developed by the Civil Service described the seven patterns of the transformation of the public service as shown in Table 5.7.

Beyond performance to potential describes the practice of looking beyond current performance of an individual to understand and develop that person's potential in a conscious and deliberate manner. Beyond results to process recognizes that good results cannot be sustained without building the right underlying processes and systems. Getting the "most for the input" recognizes the reality that there are more ideas than resources available. Thus the practice had to be one of encouraging creativity to maximize output for the amount of resources given rather than predetermining output and minimizing the input needed ("least for the output"). With limited space and no natural resources, Singapore's success requires its people to continue to innovate just to keep pace with the rest of the world. Beyond improvement to innovation acknowledges the need for the public service to continually re-invent itself if it is to serve the nation well.

Table 5.7. Patterns of Transformation of the Singapore Public Service

1.	Beyond Performance to Potential
2.	Beyond Results to Process
3.	Beyond "Least for the Output" to "Most for the Input"
4.	Beyond Improvement to Innovation
5.	Beyond Agency to Network
6.	Beyond Coordinated Action to Coordinated Vision
7.	Beyond Management to Leadership

Beyond agency to network recognizes that in a more competitive and complex environment, many significant problems and opportunities are interdependent and span the boundaries and responsibilities of individual agencies. The actions of an agency may impact other agencies and local solutions may lead to bigger problems in subsequent periods. Agencies will need to have a national perspective and work together as a networked government to achieve important and significant outcomes. It is tempting to direct actions from the center to ensure coordination of action. Yet that would not be desirable because it would impede the creativity and innovation of people in the network. Therefore, it is more effective to coordinate vision rather than action. With a shared vision and deep understanding of the cause-and-effect links among agencies in the network, the agencies may exercise autonomy in its actions and function in a coordinated networked fashion.

Beyond management to leadership describes the importance of clear vision, strong convictions and ethical values for effective leadership in public service, even though there is often little competition in service delivery and no clear-cut profit numbers for the bottom line. Leadership is needed to raise the aspirations of the public service to serve with integrity and excellence.

The policy processes and practices described in this chapter show how the public service, especially the public sector leaders, played important and influential roles in policy-making and implementation. Though the ministers and the Cabinet make the final decisions on policy and the public announcements regarding policy changes, they depend on public sector leaders to manage critical parts of the policy process, including the selection of team members, the framing of the issues, the collection of data, the analytical methods used, the options considered and the justifications provided. The institutional capabilities for policy-making and implementation are embedded in the civil service and are managed by the public sector leaders. But challenges of effective execution and delivery are constantly evolving and will require the civil service to implement flexibly with good sense while internalizing the deep values of integrity and high standards of public service:

"In Singapore, the challenge will be to retain the virtues of a non-political civil service, while ensuring that it is relevant to the big issues, not just in technical policy advice but also delivery. In such an environment, implementing public policies is more challenging than ever. We are tailoring our policies to a wider range of public aspirations, cutting red tape and making things simpler. Policies have to be clear and firm, but they also need to be implemented flexibly and with good sense. It is not good enough for civil servants just to treat rules as commandments and perpetuate time-tested precedent, without realising that rules may not be perfect, or perhaps circumstances have changed and rules need to be altered.

A competent civil servant who has mastered the art of implementing will know when he needs to hold firm to a policy, when an exception is justified, and when the policy itself needs to be reviewed and changed either by him or his superiors."[28]

The transformation of the role of the public service has enhanced its effectiveness in policy-making and implementation. It still manages the government policy infrastructure and resources but it has broadened its horizons to envision new roles, create a new mindset, define a broad agenda for change and utilize new change levers. While the fundamental policy making and implementation process has largely remained as we have described, it has created new organizational structures, systems and mechanisms that facilitate and induce transformation. These organizational processes, described in more detail in Chapter 8, are more agile and flexible to change. This new platform has given the public service access to new communities and new resources to transit Singapore into an innovation economy, a first world society and a global city. The role of the public service in

---

[28] Speech by Prime Minister Lee Hsien Loong at the 2005 Administrative Service Dinner on 24 March 2005.

dynamic governance in Singapore is now even more important and its potential impact and contributions greater than ever.

Dynamic change capabilities that enable the continuous transformation of the Singapore public sector are possible because of a strong future orientation, long-term systemic perspectives and a pragmatic approach to problem-solving, which in turn are reflected in how it manages its people, processes and chosen paths. The next chapter will describe how several important economic and social policies were implemented over the years and how they were adapted in response to changing needs and circumstances. The process of embedding learning in policy making and implementation will become clearer as we observe how polices are adapted in response to emerging issues in an evolving environment.

6

Policy Adaptation: Embedding Learning and Adjusting Paths

Many public institutions are not able to re-invent and recreate themselves to stay relevant over a sustained period. In business, large and particularly successful incumbents very often lose their premier positions because they are not able to adapt to changing environments. Why do organizations find it difficult to change? In part it arises from the forces of imprinting and path dependence. Successful institutions often continue to reflect the thinking and attributes of their founders and the conditions in which they were formed. The values, beliefs and views of the founders and other dominant leaders define the culture of the organization. The thinking that shaped an organization's period of success often continue to do so even after there is evidence to suggest that conditions have changed. That is why the dynamic governance system in Figure 1.1 of Chapter 1 shows that the dynamic capabilities of thinking ahead, thinking again and thinking across must ultimately lead to adaptive policies that are actually executed before dynamic governance can be realized. This chapter discusses how learning and continual adjustments may be embedded into policies so that they become adaptive and dynamic in a changing environment.

Organizations bear an imprint of their past. An organization's ability and capacity for change is often characterized as being path-dependent, constrained by its heritage and past decisions. The path it has traveled shapes its current position and its paths ahead. The capital and technological assets acquired in the past are legacies that influence the development paths that are open to the organization. Path-dependencies become even more accentuated when there are increasing returns to adoption. Increasing returns may stem from network externalities, the presence of complementary assets and supporting infrastructure, learning by using and scale economies in production and distribution.[1] Likewise as organizations become competent and specialized in a routine that has proved successful, they find it difficult to even experiment with other approaches.[2]

The notions of imprinting and path-dependence may imply that organizations are not able to break away from their legacies, that they are prisoners of the past. But organizations can and do evolve. Organizations do find new direction, adapt to changing conditions and chart new paths, but often only when their survival is threatened. How do organizations break away from the past or path-dependent trajectory? If organizations generally are path-dependent and find it difficult to respond to changed external conditions, then to what extent has imprinting and path-dependence influenced the Singapore public sector? Ultimately, this is a question about institutional learning, adaptation and policy change — how it changes its routines, the processes for search, the acquisition of new knowledge, and how it uses the newly acquired information to change and adapt its paths.

Singapore's ability to shift, redesign and recreate itself time and again to adapt to changing external conditions could have taken place only if policy makers were able to constantly rethink its choices and adapt its paths to keep Singapore relevant. How was public policy able to overcome the formidable pressures of path dependence to chart new paths? How did policy makers perceive the need for change, learn continuously and adapt best practices to Singapore's unique policy environment? How was learning institutionalized and embedded so that goals were refreshed and policies adjusted when circumstances changed?

6.1 Adaptive Paths and Learning for Emerging Issues in a Dynamic Institution

We found in our study an overall pattern of learning and adaptation that made the public sector a dynamic institution. Even though the

---

[1] DJ Teece, G Pisano and A Shuen (1997). "Dynamic Capabilities and Strategic Management," *Strategic Management Journal*, Vol. 18, pp. 509–534.

[2] Barbara Levitt and James G March (1988). "Organizational Learning," *Annual Review of Sociology*, Vol. 14, pp. 319–340, call this the Competency Trap.

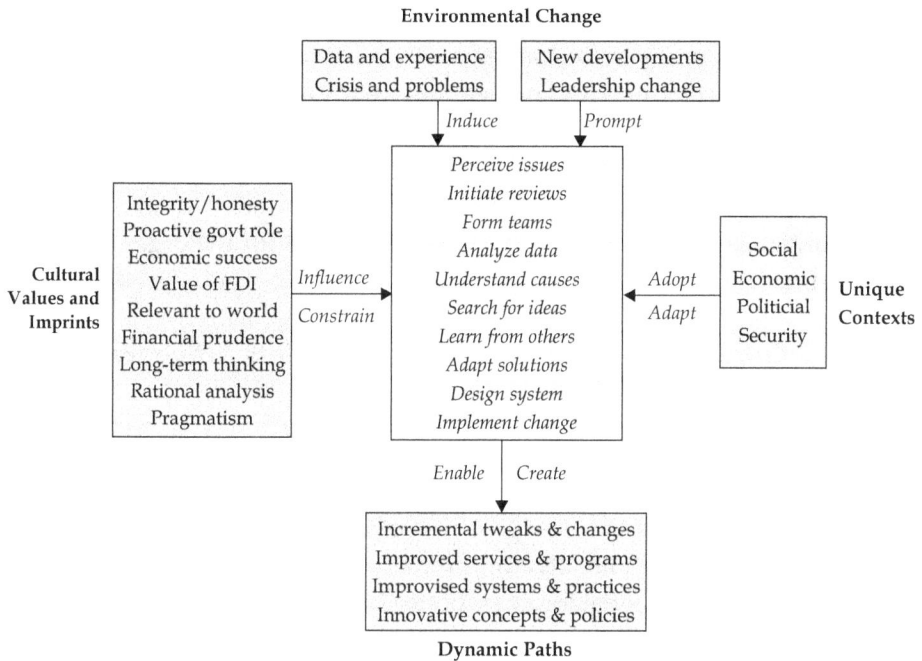

Figure 6.1. Approach to Learning and Adaptation

public sector is still strongly influenced by the founding imprints, these learning patterns and practices enabled the public sector to go beyond these imprints to adapt to a changing economic, social and political environment. These practices and patterns are integrated and generalized into an overall dynamic approach to learning and adaptation that is shown in Figure 6.1.

6.1.1 Changes in the Environment Prompt or Induce Rethinking and Review of Paths

Environmental changes in the form of new events or developments tend not to be obvious and may *prompt* review only if an organization is alert and able to anticipate their potential impact. Leadership changes often *prompt* reviews as the new leaders seek to make sense of the current strategies of the organization and its relevance for the future. Environmental change that has become evident in data and actual experience or which is felt through the problems and consequences of crisis tend to *induce* rethinking of existing paths. An organization needs to be active in scanning external trends and developments and in monitoring data and experiences to be sensitive to changes in the environment and decide if a response is needed. In addition, the results of the monitoring have to be internalized, transmitted to the rest of the organization and the implications of changes for the organization examined.

6.1.2 *Cultural Values and Founding Imprints Influence and May Constrain Path Changes*

Cultural values and founding imprints *influence* how environmental change is perceived and thus may either *facilitate or constrain* change. They also influence the interpretation of data and how the direction for review is framed. Finally, they influence where and how search for ideas is conducted, what ideas get noticed and retained, and the design of the system solution. The public sector's expected proactive role, the primacy of economic success through attracting foreign investments, and the need for financial prudence have influenced the approach to policy analysis and design. Path changes are easier when long-term thinking, pragmatism and rationality are the basis of decision-making. In the Singapore context, these policy making attributes have made it easier to engender policy shifts in response to changing circumstances, as "we do not have the same irreversible attachment to what we have done. That which did us well in the last phase will not do us good in the next 20, 30 years."[3] Organizations that expect to chart new paths should expect change.

---

[3]Speech by Dr Tony Tan, Deputy Prime Minister and Minister for Defence at the Administrative Service Dinner and Promotion Ceremony held on Monday 27 March 2000 at Shangri-la Hotel, "Moving from the Old Economy to the New Economy: Implications for the Formulation of Public Policies," in which he quoted Lee Kuan Yew's speech at the Singapore TechVenture 2000 Conference in San Francisco on 9 March 2000.

6.1.3 *Path Adaptability and Innovation is Predicated on Capable People with Ideas and Judgment, and Confident Enough to Challenge the Status Quo as well as Learn from Others*

The process of learning, adaptation and innovation portrayed in Figure 6.1 was largely tacit and intuitive in the public sector. Yet the process, with inevitable variations, was common practice in the way the public sector sensed, searched and devised strategies in response to threats and opportunities in the environment. The whole process was dependent on capable people with ideas and judgment; good ideas that encompassed new or novel approaches to problems, and good judgment to assess the best approach and design for implementation. The Singapore public sector has made extensive use of the pricing mechanism to allocate resources. What is noteworthy is that the use of the pricing mechanism has been discretionary. The state tests and determines where the market can best achieve the best results and where it has been used, the mechanism has been carefully managed.

The ability to adapt paths is also dependent on the organization's capacity to accumulate and learn from its own experience. A strong organizational memory of what has worked before is necessary in order to be able to adapt successfully. Adaptation requires an in-depth knowledge of what has worked before, and why it worked based on an understanding of how the environment, strategy and implementation all came together, and how environmental changes may make previously successful models seeds of future failure. Leaders need to constantly challenge the status quo and question the mental models and logics of current success so that their organizations can continually create the future.

Leaders who have a strong self-image and are confident of their own abilities are able to learn from past mistakes and the organization's own experience, as well as from the experience of others both in the private and public sectors. When studying the experiences of others and in the search for models, they do not imitate blindly, but are able to assess the value of ideas and how potential solutions are best adapted to suit local conditions. In adapting an external system, understanding the interaction of policy and environment is critical to assessing why some systems work and some do not. Thus a strong appreciation of context is crucial to successful adaptation.

6.1.4 Understanding the Unique Factors that Underlie the Social, Economic, Political, and Security Context Influences the Team in Selecting What Ideas to Adopt and How Ideas May Be Adapted

"Singapore is unique in its demographics, its small size and its lack of natural resources. We cannot become a first world economy simply by following what others are doing. As we look at the successes elsewhere, the critical questions we continuously have to ask are not what they are doing, or how they are doing it, but why they are doing it and why they are doing it that way."[4]

The purpose of searching for ideas and learning from others is to decide how a system can be designed so that it will have the greatest likelihood of acceptance by stakeholders and achievement of desired outcomes. The ability to assess whether certain ideas will be accepted and to anticipate how stakeholders are likely to react requires understanding and internalization of the values, expectations, and circumstances of the major stakeholder groups. At the same time, the system must be designed with the appropriate features so that the policy objectives are achieved. The challenge is to reconcile and adapt the system when the policy features that stakeholders will accept may compromise policy objectives and vice versa, or to build in stakeholder adjustments to the change over time through phased implementation or other migration paths.

Important design choices would include:

(i)   what ideas from other models are likely to be accepted locally, would work well and therefore could be adopted as they are;

---

[4] Lim Siong Guan (2000). "The Courage to be Different," *Ethos*, Civil Service College, January.

(ii) what ideas may need to be adapted to local values, expectations and circumstances, and how they may be adapted;

(iii) what features need to be created from scratch to solve unique local problems; and

(iv) what features need to be designed to integrate the entire system so that the interdependencies of the different features and parts would work seamlessly to achieve the desired outcomes.

6.1.5 *Learning and Adaptive Capabilities Enable Dynamic Leadership in the Implementation of Paths that Create Dynamic Institutions*

Dynamic and flexible paths are the result of learning and adaptation. Some of the paths would be incremental tweaks to existing systems in response to feedback or fine tuned system features to achieve more precise results. Other paths may lead to greater efficiency and improved services and programs for stakeholders. Where long-term solutions are unclear or require significant time and resources to implement, improvised systems and practices may be tried to meet immediate needs while learning and experimentation continue. The disciplined process of search, learning, reflection and integration often also result in the generation of new knowledge, new concepts and innovative policies. These dynamic paths would still be influenced by founding values and imprints but are not totally impeded by them.

As institutions develop, these learning and adaptive capabilities, the flow of ideas and solutions to meet new challenges as they arise become common practice throughout the organization. Feedback and results are used to further improve policies. New ideas and developments are assessed for potential adoption and adaptation. Adaptive change takes courageous leadership, which is crucial for creating competitive, dynamic organizations. Former Permanent Secretary Eddie Teo said:

> "A leader is someone who brings about adaptive, as opposed to technical, change. He makes changes that challenge and upset the status quo and he must convince

the people who are upset that the changes are for their own good and the good of the organization."[5]

This chapter examines the patterns of adaptation, learning and change in Singapore's public policies within the context of an unchanged political leadership. Six major economic and social policies are examined to understand the principles and patterns that have guided the public sector in adapting strategies and paths to emerging policy issues over an extended period of time:

(i)   Economic growth strategy: How the founding imprints guided economic development and how the 1985–86 and 1997–98 recessions induced search for new paths;
(ii) Biomedical sciences development: How the opportunity to innovate in a new industry led to a new approach to development;
(iii) Transportation and car ownership: How the need to solve the road congestion problem resulted in three decades of experimentation, trail and error learning, and innovation;
(iv) Central Provident Fund (CPF): How the original intent of saving for retirement was widened to include housing and health care, and use as a macro-economic tool;
(v)   Health care: How the need to balance quality service provision and costs containment led to innovative paths and continuous learning;
(vi) Working poor: How an anti-welfare imprint constrained policy options for many years and how a new national perspective created the stimulus for systematic search, learning and adaptation.

The six policy areas are selected as case studies to understand the patterns of learning and adaptation in the paths taken to emerging policy issues in an evolving environment. They involve a mix of economic and social issues where significant policy transitions have occurred over the years and which represent some of Singapore's key policy priorities. We describe the historical evolution of policy

[5] Eddie Teo (2003). "Can Public Servants be Leaders," *Ethos*, Civil Service College, September.

responses to each of these issues and the main factors operating in each policy transition. We then summarize our observations about the pattern of policy adaptation for each of the six issues. The examination of these six policy areas show patterns of how founding imprints influence paths, how search and learning are initiated in response to crises, opportunities and problems, and how continual improvements and innovations are embedded in the Singapore public service.

6.2 Economic Growth Strategy

How the founding imprints guided economic development and how the 1985–86 and 1997–98 crises induced search for new paths

Singapore's economic growth strategy is a fitting point of departure for an examination of the themes of imprinting and path dependence in the Singapore public sector, for it is the economy that defines Singapore. The external environment of the early 21st century bears little resemblance to the external environment of the 1960s. Singapore's main trading partners — Japan, the United States and the OECD countries — having to deal with painful restructuring issues in their home economies have become less open and receptive to free flows of trade and foreign investment, a stance exacerbated by the rise of the Indian and Chinese low-cost labor-abundant economies. The impasse in the Doha round of the WTO talks is indicative of the tension. The rise of India and China directly eroded ASEAN's earlier advantage as a low cost production base and new technologies altered the structure of business value chains. Shocks were transmitted across national borders, precipitating large-scale contagion and domino effects. In addition, economic dislocation was compounded by a rise of religious fundamentalism, resulting in the emergence of new terrorist threats regionally and internationally.

What was the Singapore response? On the surface, it may appear that the major thrusts of Singapore's economic development remained largely unchanged despite these drastic shifts in the international economy: the active role of the state in the economy, the key role of foreign direct investment in driving growth, the stress on remaining open to trade and capital flows and the infrastructure-led approach to development. Manufacturing and services continue to be the twin pillars. The emphasis on openness to trade and foreign investment has not diminished; in fact it has expanded to embrace global talent, reinforcing the theme of reliance on non-Singaporean markets, capital and expertise. Yet, the Singapore economy has continued to grow, and the policy makers continued to chart new growth paths.

A closer examination reveals substantive changes in economic strategy. Before the 1990s, economic strategy was based largely on the state trying to identify fast growing industries, using fiscal and other incentives to attract MNCs to locate in Singapore, or growing its own, often state-owned, commercially-run companies. This was how Singapore attracted and grew its electronics industry. This approach depended critically on the ability of the state to perceive "winners" ahead of competitors. With the radical changes in the environment from the 1980s, it has become increasingly difficult to identify in advance fast growing sectors so the strategy of allocating resources beforehand to promote certain sectors was not always as effective. In this new setting, the key to Singapore's survival lay not only in the ability to plan and predetermine what needed to be done, as in the earlier period of development when changes in the external environment had been much more gradual and predictable. The speed of change in the era of globalization and instantaneous communications meant that the ability to see emergent opportunities and to respond quickly to capitalize on them became critical capabilities. Unlike the 1970s when thorough and efficient execution of clearly specified tasks determined success, the transformed business setting meant that success depended in large measure on the alertness and speed in sensing and responding to emerging opportunities.[6] Thus the public sector began to shift its role from planner and controller to being a facilitator, aggregator and convener to enable entrepreneurship and innovation.

The public sector post-1990 was still pro-business — in fact, even more so; however its approach was different from the 1970s and 1980s when it played a direct and active role in the allocation of

---

[6] This draws on the concept of the "sense-and-respond" organization put forward by Stephan A Haeckel (1999) *The Adaptive Enterprise*. Boston, MA: Harvard Business School Press.

resources. Its role had evolved into one of helping and encouraging firms to identify and capitalize on new business opportunities. Recognizing that growth in this new era would not only be MNC-led but also spring from entrepreneurial start-ups nimble and flexible enough to catch the next wave of technological change from a Singapore base, the policy was to create the right conditions to encourage and enable existing companies to change and new ones to emerge. It had to create responsive capital and labor markets to allow innovation and entrepreneurship to thrive, and remove regulatory obstacles to rapid business response. Instead of targeting particular industries and allocating resources, the strategy changed to one of developing and attracting clusters of expertise and talents, and creating the environment to allow increasingly more resources to be attracted to particular areas or companies through the market mechanism. Singapore's value proposition was redefined — a pro-business government, cost competitive conditions, good cluster-based infrastructure — comprising a world-class physical and technological infrastructure, well-trained and skilled workforce, as well as a transparent, regulatory environment with clear enforcement, as a vibrant global city with an attractive living environment together with an open and welcoming stance on global talent. The focus moved from only attracting business with incentives (which assumed the ability to know which industries to plan for) to also attracting business with a flexible, pro-business environment, transparent and consistent policies, and good governance.

How did policy-makers move from its directive, allocative path of the 1970s and 1980s to its current path as a facilitator? How did a state where the government was so dominant a player make this transition? The key to this lies in the lessons learnt from the two major economic crises, the 1985–86 economic recession and the 1997–98 Asian financial crisis. After the 1985–86 recession, the government put in place processes to actively co-opt expertise outside the public sector and to remain open to inputs and experiences of the outside world. While it was a shock, the 1985–86 recession also marked a turning point in economic policy-making.

Path-dependence is predicated on the nature of an organization's search routines and processes, and the triggers to a search process. Because of limited attention and bounded rationality, individuals and organizations seldom, if ever, make decisions based on fully rational theories of attention and search. Decision-makers do not usually consider all possible alternatives in searching for and evaluating possible solutions. Decision-makers usually work on the principle of satisficing, which involves choosing an alternative that meets a specified criterion or target.[7] Satisficing is a de facto search rule — specifying the conditions under which search is triggered or stopped; it directs search to areas of failure. Search is regulated by a comparison between performance and targets — if performance falls below target, search is increased. Viewed in this light, the 1985–86 and 1997–98 economic recessions precipitated periods of policy reflection and crisis-induced search.[8] What were some of the key lessons? How and why did these recessions change the path of economic policy?

6.2.1 *Changes in Economic Strategy: Diversifying the Sources of Growth*

The distortion and the loss of competitiveness caused by the three-year high wage policy highlighted the dangers of trying to manage the labor market. By the early 1970s, unemployment had been eradicated and Singapore began to face labor shortages. Since the success of economic strategy rested on a low labor cost advantage, priority was directed towards maintaining the status quo, even though market pressures were pulling in the other direction. In the wake of the 1973–74, and the 1977 oil shocks, policy-makers felt that Singapore was not ready to restructure away from labor-intensive methods of production. Policies were enacted to maintain a low labor cost advantage until the Singapore economy was ready to restructure. The "orderly wage

---

[7] For example a maximizing procedure for choosing equipment for a new manufacturing facility would involve finding the best combination of features and prices available. A satisficing approach would be to select equipment that fits the specifications and falls within budget. James G March (1994). *A Primer on Decision-Making: How Decisions Happen*. New York: The Free Press, p. 18.

[8] Ibid, p. 28.

increases" recommended each year by the National Wages Council starting from 1972 was an attempt to preserve the status quo. The recommendation for a three-year corrective wage policy from 1979 to 1982 to induce firms to substitute capital for labor did not, as it turned out, give due consideration to the loss of competitiveness with wages outstripping productivity. The experience of having to freeze wages and cut CPF contributions in order to restore competitiveness was an important lesson for the policy makers. Thus once the economy had recovered, the policy-makers proceeded to put in place a system of flexible wages and over the years, with the government as a role model, encouraged the private sector to do the same.

The 1985–86 economic recession highlighted the structural weaknesses and rigidities of the Singapore economy. The Singapore economy was over dependent on manufacturing, especially electronics, which had made the economy susceptible to any downturn in that sector. There was also an over dependence on the construction sector, which had boomed in the years of strong economic growth. Once the issue of over concentration had been identified, the search began for strategies to broaden the economic base. The EDB appointed a new chairman and was charged with implementing a new growth path for the Singapore economy.

The development of industry clusters was defined in the 1991 Strategic Economic Plan (SEP) and reinforced in the 1998 Report of the Committee on Singapore's Competitiveness. Industry clusters, by exploiting horizontal and vertical linkages, would strengthen competitiveness and be less vulnerable to industry downturns. High value-added and capital-intensive clusters with economies of scale and scope, such as petrochemicals, would help to anchor the economy.

There was increased effort to move Singapore up the value chain, to higher value-added, knowledge-based activities. Singapore sensed the impact of knowledge on economic growth in the late 1980s and quickly learnt that the ability to use knowledge within a climate conducive to innovation[9] would be critical in driving economic

---

[9] See the analysis based on Michael Porter's national competitiveness framework in Singapore (1991). *The Strategic Economic Plan: Towards a Developed Nation*. Singapore: Ministry of Trade and Industry, pp. 26–29.

growth.[10] Policy-makers acknowledged that Singapore's economic growth up to that point had been predominantly factor-driven; for growth to be sustainable, innovation-based activities that were highly productive had to become one of the main drivers of the economy. There was thus a strategic push to build up high-level domestic capability in research and innovation-based activities. The National Science and Technology Board was set up in 1990 with the objective of promoting R&D activities in science and technology. However, the initial progress was slow. It was not only until ten years later that these activities were coordinated and slowly began to show results. This effort was further boosted in 2005 by a further allocation of S$10b for R&D activities through the National Research Foundation.

The services sector was developed to complement manufacturing as the second main pillar of the economy. The first step was in the direction of expanding manufacturing-related services such as transport and logistics; it was only in the mid-to-late 1990s that the concept of services was broadened to areas such as education and medical services.

Sources of regional growth beyond Singapore's shores were developed, whereby Singapore companies could relocate labor-intensive activities to Malaysia and Indonesia whilst maintaining the higher value-added activities in Singapore. The initiative to build an external wing gradually evolved to encouraging and facilitating private sector overseas expansion into China, India and the Middle East. This effort was also Singapore's bid to maintain its economic space in light of increasing protectionist sentiments in developed countries. While remaining a staunch supporter of the multilateral free trade framework, Singapore initiated a series of bilateral free trade agreements with key existing and potential economic partners.

The search for new and alternative growth drivers began in the late 1980s and has continued since. The process started with a search to understand why and how Singapore became non-competitive. It identified the structural weaknesses that developed, and built upon

---

[10] Chan Chin Bock (2002). *Heart Work*. Singapore: Economic Development Board, pp. 240–242.

the MNC-dominant manufacturing investments by adding cluster development, local entrepreneurship, R&D and diversification to services to ensure greater economic depth and resilience. The search process did not just take place at one point in time; it became instead a continuing process of identification and evaluation of new strategies as the circumstances changed. At times the search led to a re-examination of options that had been ruled out in the past.

The 1997–98 crisis was initially viewed as a cyclical phenomenon with contagion effects springing from financial weaknesses in neighboring Thailand and Indonesia. Singapore's economic fundamentals were perceived to be strong and belt-tightening was deemed to be the appropriate response until the regional financial crisis blew over. It was only when the crisis persisted and deepened with regional currencies losing a substantial portion of their value, and triggered political upheaval that the impact hit home — Singapore would have to compete in a vastly changed socio-economic and political landscape. At the same time the Internet boom had boosted technology entrepreneurship and global communication networks had vastly altered traditional economic linkages and relationships.

The Economic Review Committee (ERC) set up and chaired by then Deputy Prime Minister Lee Hsien Loong re-examined how Singapore should compete and be successful in the new economic environment. The main theme of the ERC report was the remaking of Singapore into a global, entrepreneurial and diversified economy and its recommendations were announced in phases from 2001 and implementation began even before its final report was released in 2003. The recommended policy directions included enhancing Singapore's hub status by expanding regional ties with countries within seven hours of flying time from Singapore (spanning India, China, Japan and Australia), lowering personal and corporate taxes from 25 per cent to 20 per cent to maintain competitiveness, promoting new service industries in education, health care and professional services, building strong companies through promoting entrepreneurship, attracting global talent, and facilitating economic restructuring through continuous worker education and skills training.

6.2.2 Changes in Economic Policy Making Process

The private sector had a greater involvement in policy review and policy-making process after 1986, a significant departure from the earlier highly centralized government approach. The first economic plan of 1961 was developed by the UN team which recommended the industrialization path, and the second economic plan was developed by the Ministry of Trade and Industry, focusing on how to manage the labor shortage problem and from which emerged the high-wage policy. The economic policy making process changed after the 1986 recession, evolving to a more open, more consultative process with co-opted private sector members involved in policy deliberations.

The private sector involvement had the effect of increasing the diversity of experience and perspective — private sector members provided insights from the business arena into the effectiveness of economic strategies and the impact of government policies. The public sector developed a greater appreciation of the rapid pace of change in the business environment and how firms were affected by the explosion of instantaneous communication flows. Business value chains were being transformed into value networks, where the production process could be disaggregated, with different segments being done in countries offering the best capability and value in that segment. New opportunities would have to be perceived in countries that had not previously been on the radar. While the rise of China and India posed threats, there were also growth opportunities for Singapore companies as these two economies expanded. Policy-makers came to realize that the pace of restructuring could not be managed; Singapore did not have the luxury of biding its time until it was "ready" to restructure, having learnt a painful lesson from the experience of the 1980s. Gains would accrue to those countries that were alert and ready to take advantage of opportunities as they arose. If Singapore was not ready, opportunities would be lost.

Reviews have been conducted in the wake of milestone events that affected Singapore's competitiveness and strategy. The impetus of economic recessions helped to galvanize consensus for major change in economic strategies and paths. The economic planning agencies knew they had to be more proactive in monitoring Singapore's competitiveness and external trends, and developed indicators to monitor both short-term and medium to long-term competitiveness.[11]

The practice of learning from others expanded, especially when the public sector sought expert assistance to help kick-start initiatives to develop sectors entirely new to Singapore. When the EDB was charged to map up a new growth path for Singapore, they used Michael Porter's cluster approach and the imperative to create an innovation-driven economy as the foundation for economic strategy after 1986. When Singapore sought to develop a world-class higher education sector, the International Academic Advisory Panel comprising 12 distinguished international academics, heads of universities and industry, was formed in 1997 to advise the public sector on the groundwork for this initiative. The Biomedical Sciences International Advisory Council was formed in 2000 comprising 17 of the world's top biomedical scientists and industry leaders, to advise on major trends in global medical science research and industry, critique current initiatives and give inputs for improvement not only of research but also on legal and ethical issues. Similarly, the Research and Innovation Enterprise Council was formed in 2005 to advise Singapore on the ways to build up strategic areas of research and to attract enough talent for the long haul. In short, the public sector adopted processes that actively sought inputs and ideas from outside the institution and actively formalized procedures to ensure that it remained open and continued to learn.

6.2.3 Lessons Learnt from the Paths of Economic Development

(i)   *Early success in its economic strategies in the 1960s and 1970s created deep imprints about the economic drivers of success*

The accepted wisdom regarding the drivers of economic success included: a) an active role of the state in identifying selected areas for promotion and development, b) efficient, incorrupt and business-friendly public institutions, c) the importance of foreign investors

---

[11] Singapore (1991). *The Strategic Economic Plan: Towards a Developed Nation*. Singapore: Ministry of Trade and Industry, pp. 82–86.

in bringing in the technology, management expertise, markets and capital needed for driving growth, d) the emphasis on remaining open to trade, capital and people flows and e) investing heavily in efficient infrastructures that would lead to economic development. These were constantly reinforced through public speeches by leaders and became unquestioned assumptions in many internal analyses.

(ii) *These beliefs persisted until a major crisis induced a search for causes, lessons and new paths*

The search for new ideas was precipitated by experience with economic recessions and data that were incontrovertible — negative GDP growth, firm financial difficulties, job losses, wage cuts, and increases in unemployment. The search, usually in the form of review committees, would critically assess the causes of the crisis, discuss a wide range of options and recommend systemic actions that the government should take to ensure the country's future success. It was a systematic and thorough process with teams of officials doing the research and studies needed to support the recommendations of the various sub-committees, and for the main committee to publicly justify its recommendations to the government. Most of the recommendations would be accepted by the government, as would be expected since many senior government officials, including cabinet ministers, were already involved in the committee deliberations. The recommendations that the government did not accept would be explained to the public. The resources needed would be allocated in the budget and periodic reviews of progress reported.

In addition to immediate action to reduce business costs to help firms cope during the difficult economic periods, both the 1985–86 and 1997–98 reviews considered the longer-term economic strategies for Singapore. Both economic review committees did not invalidate the basic economic drivers of success but moderated them by including new important sources of growth that were previously under emphasized. Services were added to manufacturing as the second engine of growth. R&D, local enterprises and start-ups were promoted in addition to MNC investments, and investments in softer infrastructures such as reviews of government rules and human capital development were recommended, in addition to improving the hard physical facilities and communications networks.

(iii) *A strong determination to sustain economic growth and success created an open and pragmatic attitude towards changes in strategies, paths and policies*

The two major economic reviews had a broad mandate to re-examine all policies, even "sacred cows" as long as the changes would enable Singapore to continue to sustain its economic competitiveness and success in the long term. The government has been willing to moderate its economic strategies and change long-standing policies, including major restructurings of the tax regimes and contributions to the Central Provident Fund, because of the importance of economic success to its own legitimacy and credibility. Its pragmatic approach meant that it was willing to consider paths that were previously rejected. The development of Las Vegas-style integrated resorts with casinos was rejected several times previously because of a strong founding imprint to preserve the work ethic and family values. As the need grew for the service sector (including a new emphasis on medical, education, professional and tourism services) to contribute more to economic growth to compensate for a decline in manufacturing, the development of integrated resorts with casinos was accepted as a new competitive necessity. The creation of 30,000 new jobs and significant potential contributions to economic growth were justifications to move early and fast before other countries in the region did so. The pragmatism was also reflected in the imposition of an entry fee on locals to discourage gambling among the population and the steps taken to help those with gambling addictions.

(iv) *Systematic learning took place through changes not only to paths and policies, but also to routines and structures that enabled the new paths and policies to be continually enacted and sustained*

The review committees would only recommend broad changes in strategies and direction. The actual changes in programs, projects and plans were left to the public sector leadership in the respective ministries and agencies. The 1991 Strategic Economic Plan is an example of how the 1986 Economic Committee recommendations were further elaborated for broader and deeper implementation.

Learning is "a systematic change in behavior or knowledge informed by experience."[12] The Singapore public sector underwent a path-changing learning process on several levels starting from the mid-1980s. As a result of the new understanding of how Singapore could survive and continue to add value in the new economy, a different operating framework and new operating routines were established with respect to economic policy-making. In short, operating routines were changed. The process of learning and change in the Singapore approach to economic policy-making illustrates the workings of a dynamic capability, which is the "ability to integrate, build, and reconfigure internal and external competencies to address rapidly changing environments."[13] In this light, a dynamic capability can be thought of as a learned and stable pattern of collective activity through which the organization systematically generates and modifies its operating routines in pursuit of improved effectiveness.[14]

6.3 Development of the Biomedical Sciences Cluster

How the opportunity to innovate in a new industry led to a new approach to development

The effort to develop the biomedical sciences cluster is an interesting case study of how government agencies implemented the new economic strategy of developing innovation-driven, knowledge-based clusters of activity. This strategy to growing new areas of economic activity was developed from the recommendations of the EDB's International Advisory Council, during its first meeting in April 1995. It focused on how Singapore should proceed to maximize the returns from its R&D and technology development efforts.

---

[12] Levitt and March (1998), Cyert and March (1992), cited in Anne S Miner, Paula Bassoff, Christine Moorman (2001). "Organizational Improvisation and learning: A Field Study," *Administrative Science Quarterly*, Vol. 46, No. 2, pp. 304–340.

[13] Teece, Pisano and Shuen (1997).

[14] Zollo and Winter (2002).

The council highlighted the need to integrate the work and achievements of the R&D institutes with the rest of economic development. To be effective, R&D could not be discrete, isolated from the rest of economic activity but had to be assimilated and multiplied. Focusing R&D on existing industries and sectors would complement core manufacturing activities and create clusters of high value-added activity. With several of the world's top pharmaceutical companies manufacturing in Singapore including Eli Lilly, GlaxoSmithKline, Merck, Novartis, Pfizer and Wyeth, Singapore was already the largest pharmaceutical manufacturing site in Asia. In addition, Singapore was also a hub for top medical device makers such as Becton Dickinson and Siemens. Thus production capabilities were already present. The objective was then to build the biomedical science cluster across the entire value chain of industries — from basic and clinical research, to product development, manufacturing, and health care delivery.

The council recommended that in the nature of public-private sector collaboration in high technology development, the government should expect to fund basic R&D and encourage the private sector — both MNCs and local companies — to invest in development work and applications. In addition, R&D should be carried out with technological and socio-economic development in mind.

The Biomedical Science Initiative, BMSI, was launched in June 2000, and a Life Sciences Ministerial Committee was set up with then Deputy Prime Minister Dr Tony Tan as Chairman, and Ministers of Trade and Industry, Education and Health as members. The Biomedical Sciences International Advisory Council was appointed in 2000 to advise the Singapore government on the efforts to develop this sector. The council comprised 17 of the world's top international biomedical scientists and industry leaders, including three Nobel Laureates.[15]

6.3.1 *Building the New Infrastructure*

To facilitate public and private sector exchange and collaboration and to create a dense cluster of biomedical research talent and activities, a

---

[15] Dr Sydney Brenner, Dr David Baltimore and Dr Leland Hartwell.

new biomedical research hub — "Biopolis" — was built with state of the art facilities and co-location of public and private labs. Work on Phase 1, consisting of seven research buildings and two million sq feet of lab space started in December 2001 and was completed in June 2003, 18 months ahead of schedule. The legal infrastructure was put in place. Singapore has banned reproductive cloning but under strict conditions, scientists are allowed to withdraw stem cells from discarded fertility treatment tissue. The regulatory infrastructure and the clear stance on stem cell research were designed based on recommendations by the Bioethics Advisory Committee, which consulted extensively with community, religious, medical and scientific groups. In recent months, new information and privacy laws have been crafted to support clinical testing and trials.

The lead technology agency, A*STAR, began recruiting experts to drive development efforts in this sector. Edison Liu, Director of Clinical Sciences at the US National Cancer Institute was wooed to head the Genome Institute of Singapore. Alan Colman, part of the medical team that created Dolly the Sheep, the first mammal to be cloned from an adult cell, joined ES Cell International, a company that commercializes human stem cell research at the National University of Singapore. Other scientific luminaries were also wooed to set up their biomedical science research work at the Biopolis. The belief was that a concentration of talent creates attractive and effective networks that pull in like-minded experts.

The strategy of setting up both hard and soft infrastructure, appointing an expert committee to provide direction, and depending on foreign talent to provide the technical know-how was part of a well honed template that the Singapore public sector had developed in building up a new industry or sector. The technical know-how in this case, were the international corps of scientists and researchers, and the strategy taken to attract them to work in Singapore was to create the conditions they needed — freedom, funding and facilities, not unlike what Singapore did to attract the MNCs many years ago. The build-up of intellectual and human capital is reflected in the number of researchers, scientists and engineers (RSEs) in the biomedical-related sector. Based on A*STAR's National R&D Survey in 2001, there were

2,055 RSEs in this sector, of which 610 (29.7 per cent) were PhDs. By 2005, there were 4,054 RSEs, which included 1,317 PhD holders (32.5 per cent).[16] So how was this initiative different from what had been done before? The key difference was in the effort to develop indigenous capabilities rather than merely depend on MNCs and foreign expertise. "Before 2000, science and technology in Singapore was focused on servicing multi-nationals. Creating knowledge was an afterthought."[17]

6.3.2 Implementing a New Approach to Development

The new strategy as embodied in the biomedical sciences development approach was for Singapore to be an innovation leader rather than just a fast follower. The intent was to lead in the development of intellectual capital and niche new products rather than merely being a value-added producer. To do so Singapore needed to develop its own indigenous research and commercialization capabilities. A*STAR restructured its organization to have direct oversight over the research institutes it funded, and influenced the direction of R&D beyond academic research towards products and technologies that could be commercialized. New funds were invested and formed in the venture capital industry to diversify into the biomedical science fields. Intellectual capital protection laws were strengthened. Financial support was given to help researchers apply for US patents for the new technologies they developed in Singapore. New organizations such as A*STAR-owned Exploit Technologies were formed to commercialize technologies developed by the research institutes either in conjunction with the inventors or independent of them. The main long-term investment priority was the development of domestic research talent and capabilities to sustain the growth of the industry.

Prior to 2000, foreign scientists had been the sources behind the growth of the innovation and R&D activities. There had been little

---

[16] "Exceptional Growth For Singapore's Biomedical Sciences Industry," Press Release, 6 February 2007.

[17] Edison Liu (2006). "Rise of a Biomedical Dragon," *The Straits Times*, 4 November 2006.

emphasis on developing domestic innovation and R&D capability — in year 2000, only 100 out of the 900 researchers with PhDs in the A*STAR research institutes were Singaporean. This imbalance was addressed in 2001 when new A*STAR Chairman Philip Yeo set out to build up domestic capability to account for half of the total number of research scientists. To build a pipeline of scientific talent, the National Science Scholarships for the Biomedical Sciences (BMS) were launched that year followed by the Science and Engineering Scholarships and A*STAR Graduate scholarships for PhD education at the two local universities in 2002. At the end of 2005, of the PhD population of 751 in the A*STAR research institutes, 251 were Singaporean. In 2006, 102 scholarships were awarded, bringing the total number of scholars supported to 393. Based on current patterns of recruitment, in the steady state, there should be some 500 potential PhDs, with about 50 overseas-trained PhDs a year returning to boost domestic capability in R&D.[18] This pipeline of high potential young scientists will staff A*STAR's biomedical research institutes and constitute a source of research talent to support industry R&D in Singapore.

Given Singapore's small size, the number of Singaporean PhDs will not be sufficient to drive and sustain efforts to build up the R&D industries. It is widely acknowledged that international talent will always be necessary. Nevertheless, this effort to build up domestic capability was a key strategic shift, based on the understanding of the need to embed the skills and competencies for innovation. Top international talent is recruited to help grow the biomedical sciences while Singapore trains its own talent. As Philip Yeo explained:

> "The senior scientists provide the light houses but it is the young up-and-coming ones who will sail out in uncharted waters to find new worlds. A thriving scientific community must have a good pipeline of people — young and old, local and foreign."[19]

---

[18] All figures in this paragraph are quoted from a lecture given by Philip Yeo, "The Basic Foundation for R and D: Human Capital — A Pro-Local/Pro-International Approach," at the National University of Singapore, 20 January 2006.

[19] Ibid.

Thus while building domestic capability is a new path for biomedical sciences, its rapid progress will itself create and reinforce a new path in Singapore's economic development, creating competencies where none existed before. The results of the development of the biomedical sciences cluster have been highly encouraging. Biomedical manufacturing output tripled from S$6b in 2000 to S$18b in 2005 and then again to S$23b in 2006, an unprecedented 30 per cent annual increase. This marks a four-fold increase in output in over six years, with pharmaceuticals accounting for 91 per cent of the total output. The level of fixed asset investment in this sector in 2006 was S$901m, constituting 10 per cent of EDB's total fixed asset investment that year, with a significant portion of the expansion in biologics. BMS investment commitments in R&D and Business Services grew by over a third to S$217m, or 7.6 per cent of EDB's total business spending commitment for the year. Total spending on BMS research grew from S$310m in 2001 to S$888m in 2005, with the growth rate of private sector BMS spending outpacing that of the public sector, accounting for 35 per cent of total spending in 2005, up from 28.5 per cent in 2001. Employment in this sector also grew from less than 6,000 to 10,571 in 2006, of which 62 per cent was in the Medical Technology sector which includes implantable devices and instrumentation systems. Several major pharmaceutical companies have established key research centers in Singapore, and many well-known research scientists have made Singapore their new scientific home.

6.3.3 *Lessons Learnt from the Development of the Biomedical Sciences Cluster*

(i)   *The depth of the imprint regarding the primacy of economic growth prepared leaders to constantly sense and evaluate new opportunities for investment and growth*

Sudden independence in 1965 left a deep imprint among policy-makers of the need for economic growth to ensure its survival, relevance and success. This survival paranoia is a badge of honor for both political and public sector leaders. As a result, they are constantly on the lookout for new ideas to ensure that the growth engine does not stall. The suggestion from EDB's International Advisory Panel to develop the Biomedical Science cluster was thus received by prepared and eager minds. It dovetailed with established criteria and accepted patterns of economic development: state agencies could continue their traditional role to seize the initiative to make investments for growth, the nature of the industry was consistent with a bias for industries based on science and technology, with features that matched Singapore's views of desired industries of the future — high capital intensity in manufacturing, significant knowledge and research content, and high value-added per worker providing economic payoffs that were attractive to Singapore.

(ii) *Established routines for industry development initially guided the approach adopted to growing a new industry*

Even though it was a new industry, the initial approach to development followed established paths — influenced by EDB's approach for attracting MNC manufacturing investments and the local university's norms for funding faculty research. Thus the initial push and promotion effort was undertaken by EDB and resulted in large MNC pharmaceutical and medical devices companies setting up capital-intensive manufacturing operations. The initial research programs supported by the NSTB followed established university norms that favored faculty-initiated proposal and research institutes that were governed within the local university framework. The early approach to the industry's development was a common organizational response to a new project or program — broad adherence to existing structures and processes to implement a new initiative. This was perhaps a necessary learning step but it limited its potential because the established paths were not geared for the full development of the new biomedical sciences cluster.

Leaders who are aware of the limitations of using existing approaches for new initiatives may still use them as a learning step for a limited period of time but would be constantly looking for other approaches or ways to adapt the existing approaches to fit the needs of the new initiative. However, once existing approaches are used and seem to be working, it becomes very difficult to change, and organizations develop blind spots to their drawbacks. A new perspective is required and it often comes from the fresh eyes of new leadership.

(iii) *A greater strategic focus and new leadership significantly influenced the migration to new paths of development*

The BMSI launched in June 2000 gave the development of the bio-medical sciences cluster a new strategic focus with a national objective to make it into a new area of economic growth. This provided the legitimacy and impetus to refocus resources to exploit the economic potential of the cluster. A new Chairman of the NSTB redefined the agency's research agenda from exploration to exploitation, and renamed the agency as A*STAR. All A*STAR funded research institutes, which had previously been governed by one of the two local universities, were placed under its direct management with expected outcomes more clearly defined and greater accountability for results. New units were also formed to commercialize the technologies developed by the research institutes. The Biopolis research park is a visible symbol of the nation's strategic commitment to the development of the biomedical cluster and provided the necessary physical infrastructure and environment for research. The new path of development included an all-out effort to attract global research talent to lead major research programs with generous funding and a supportive research environment. It also involved developing indigenous research capacity through sponsoring selected young scholars for PhD studies at the top biomedical research universities. This new path of development was also consistent with the results orientation and people development approach that its new Chairman had been known for in his previous roles.

(iv) *Leadership credibility and the perceived success of the new paths of development led to their acceptance and enabled them to be embedded institutionally*

The track record and credibility of the new chairman provided the initial social capital necessary to define and pursue a new development path, and the subsequent perceived success of the development led to more widespread support and acceptance. The new paths of development were perceived to be successful because of the visibility of the top scientists attracted to Singapore to lead research institutes and major research programs, the scientific discoveries publicized in the media, the publicity given to the young scholars who had been accepted by and who successfully completed their PhDs at top overseas universities, and the completion of the iconic Biopolis research park. Within the public sector, the development of the biomedical sciences cluster became accepted as a new model for developing intellectual leadership and research capacity in a strategic economic cluster. The approach became institutionalized when a new S$10b was allocated under the National Research Foundation to nurture new potential clusters including water and environmental technologies.

6.4 Public Transportation and Car Ownership Policy

How the need to solve the road congestion problem resulted in three decades of experimentation, trial and error learning, and innovation

Car ownership and public transport are sensitive issues in Singapore's public policy. House and car ownership[20] are status symbols, the manifestations of "having arrived", and part of the aspirations of a large segment of the population. But if left unchecked, rising car ownership and the resulting congestion would impose unacceptably high costs to the whole economy and could act as a deterrent to foreign investment. As the then Prime Minister Goh Chok Tong so graphically described it:

> "Our roads are like our arteries: they carry blood to our vital organs. Our cars are like cholesterol in the blood. You need cholesterol for proper functioning of the body, but too much is not good for you because it clogs up your arteries… In Singapore, the whole city is the economy. If

---

[20] Fock Siew Wah, founding Chairman of the Land Transport Authority, as quoted in Ilsa Sharp (2005). *The Journey: Singapore's Land Transport Story.* SNP Editions, p. 82.

your city is jammed, our productivity and competitiveness will suffer."[21]

Managing the car population was a key policy objective throughout the 1970s and 1980s, when the demand for cars mushroomed amid a booming economy and rising incomes. Singapore's transport management involved two broad aspects: using the pricing mechanism to manage demand for car ownership and usage to minimize traffic congestion on the one hand; and building a good public transport system anchored by the rail system, the Mass Rapid Transit (MRT), and which included buses and taxis on the other.

Singapore's transport and land use vision was articulated in the 1971 Concept Plan for the physical development of the island to 1992. Land use and transport planning were integrated to optimize the limited physical space available. The process of urban resettlement and renewal had generated new travel patterns, with most of the population living in the housing estates in the suburbs and commuting to work. Public transport at that time, comprising warring bus service providers and unlicensed private taxis, did not offer a reliable alternative to cars. The number of cars on the roads doubled. It was clear that some sort of restraint in car demand would be needed.

In 1968, fiscal measures were put in place in an attempt to curb the growth of the car population — import duty, a lump sum registration fee and an additional registration fee calculated as a percentage of the open market value or import price of the vehicle, plus annual road taxes based on engine capacity. The impact on demand was minimal. Even as the bus and taxi systems were rationalized and improved in the early 1970s, congestion worsened, particularly in the central business area. Transport planners began their search for what would form the backbone of Singapore's transport system. The evaluation of the feasibility of and the debate over the building of the MRT system began in 1972. As it turned out, the green light to go ahead with the MRT was given only ten years later in 1982 after an extensive period of evaluation and public debate over the merits of an MRT versus an all-

---

[21] Goh Chok Tong, National Day Rally, 1992 as quoted in Sharp (2005), p. 42.

bus system. Given the size of the investment, transport planners had expected that the final decision would take a long time. Given limited land resources, building more roads in the interim to accommodate demand was not the answer. Traffic congestion, particularly in the business district had to be controlled to ensure a smooth flowing transport environment and high business productivity.

6.4.1 Managing Usage: Road Congestion Pricing

In 1975, during the morning and evening rush hours, traffic in the Central Business District (CBD) — an area of about 5.5 square km was one of the most congested parts of the city — moved at an average speed of 19 km per hour. Road congestion arises because the marginal users of a crowded road consider only the cost to them of using the road and ignore the fact that their vehicles, by slowing down traffic, also inconvenience others. The marginal social cost of one individual using his car is greater than the direct cost to him, his marginal private cost. In this sort of negative externality situation, the standard economic recommendation is for a tax on the use of congested road to increase the individual cost of usage by an amount equal to the external diseconomies imposed by one driver on all the others — in short, increase the price of driving on congested roads to deter road users. The government thus decided that it would try to discourage the entry of cars and taxis into the CBD in the mornings via the imposition of a toll. While simple in concept, this type of experiment had never been done before. Most road tolls in other countries were used to finance the costs of building new roads; thus toll-collection points were built on new roads that were opened — relatively straightforward to implement and easy to understand. Tolls for controlling congestion in the established CBD area needed careful thought and design — the collection of the toll could not slow traffic and add to the congestion, which was a common occurrence in toll roads elsewhere. In June 1975, after a massive public education campaign, the Area Licensing Scheme (ALS) was born.

The ALS started with 28 gantries to mark out the Restricted Zone (RZ) that could be entered between 7:30 am and 9:30 am Mondays to Saturdays only if drivers of cars had bought and displayed a special daily paper license as they entered the RZ through any one of the entry points that would be manned. Vehicles with four or more passengers were exempted from the toll, which was initially set at S$3 a day. The initial results indicated that the toll was successful in reducing congestion — a little too successfully. The total number of vehicles entering the RZ fell by some 43 per cent, far more than the 25–30 per cent reduction originally targeted,[22] reflecting a consequent underutilization of roads in the CBD area.

The ALS was tweaked repeatedly as policy-makers observed and responded to changing patterns of road utilization. The restricted hours and the area under the restricted zone were fine tuned as congestion shifted in time and location. The ALS fees were adjusted periodically. Evening restricted hours were introduced in 1989, and previously exempt vehicles — car pools, buses, commercial vehicles and motorcycles — were now charged. Shoulder pricing was introduced in 1994 to smooth out traffic flow patterns throughout the day. A snapshot of the adjustments to the ALS is given in Table 6.1.

One of the main weaknesses of the ALS was its multiple-entry feature. Once an ALS license had been purchased, the motorist could enter the RZ many times during the day. Thus motorists paid only a one-time congestion charge, instead of paying every time he entered an area and contributed to congestion. Moreover a single license could be switched between vehicles. The system had also become unwieldy with a myriad number of licenses — Whole Day, Part-Day, daily and monthly, and different licenses for different kinds of restricted vehicles. The cost of enforcement increased with the rise in the number of entry points into the RZ and spotting offenders had become increasingly difficult as motorists were not obliged to slow down as they entered the RZ. Policy makers recognized the need to switch to some form of electronic pricing for the system to be sustainable.

Although the ALS was a relatively blunt instrument, it was the first experiment of its kind to charge users for congestion. The whole process of monitoring motoring behavior and patterns of demand

---

[22] Adapted from Phang Sock Yong and Rex S Toh (2004). "Road Congestion Pricing in Singapore: 1975–2003," *Transportation Journal*, Vol. 43, No. 2, Table 2.

Table 6.1. Singapore Area Licensing Scheme and Subsequent Modifications: 1975–1995

Implementation Date	Weekday Hours of Operation	Daily Licence Fee (S$)				
		Private Car	Co. Car	Taxi	Commercial Vehicle	Motorcycle
Initial Scheme						
2 June 1975	7:30 – 9:30 am	3	3	3	0	0
1 August 1975	7:30 – 10:15 am					
Subsequent Changes						
1 January 1976		4	8	4		
1 March 1980		5	10			
1 June 1989	7:30 – 10:15 am					
	4:30 – 7:00 pm	3	6	3	3	
1 July 1989						1
31 January 1990	7:30 – 10:15 am					
	4:30 – 6:30 pm					
3 January 1994	*Whole Day License:* Mon–Fri: 7:30 am – 6:30 pm Sat: 7:30 am – 3:00 pm	3	6	3	3	1
	Part Day License: Mon–Fri: 10:15 am – 4:30 pm Sat: 10:15 am – 3:00 pm	2	4	2	2	0.70
2 May 1995	Restricted hours end at 2 pm instead of 3 pm on Saturdays					

and then adjusting the pricing structure was an extended period of trial and error learning. But the ALS did not exist in isolation. A whole plethora of supporting measures was instituted to discourage entry into the city area — increased parking charges, higher taxes on cars and the construction of new roads to enable motorists to bypass the RZ. The ALS scheme was expanded into a Road Pricing Scheme (RPS) in June 1995, where private car motorists had to purchase a S$1 license to travel on certain sections of an expressway, the East Coast Parkway, between 7:30 am and 8:30 am on weekday mornings. This

RPS was partly an exercise to familiarize motorists with the concept of linear passage tolls. The lessons derived in managing the ALS/RPS were put to good use when technology had developed to an extent that facilitated the introduction of Electronic Road Pricing (ERP) in 1998.

6.4.2 *Electronic Road Pricing: Harnessing Technology for Real Time Congestion Pricing*

Anticipating advances in smart card technology, the government announced plans in 1989 to introduce electronic road pricing. It was almost ten years later, in 1998, that the ERP was formally introduced. The period in between was one involving extensive trials and repeated sessions of going back to the drawing board. The specifications for the system were challenging: it had to be able to cope with cluttered vehicles traveling up to 75 km per hour in a multi-lane traffic pattern with consecutive car passings, lane changes as well as very close parallel passings with motorcycles in between; it would have to distinguish between different kinds of vehicles so as to be able to deduct the right toll since the toll structure would differentiate between buses/lorries, passenger cars and motorcycles; vehicles would not have to slow down (lest this cause accidents); the permitted error rate was 1 error in 100,000 passings; the system had to be active, in that deductions would have to be made on the spot.

This last condition proved prophetic; "passive" systems which simply logged the date, time and where the vehicle had traveled as inputs into monthly billings had been rejected in places such as Hong Kong because of privacy concerns. Toll deductions would be made from a cash card inserted into transponders called In-vehicle Units (IUs), one of which would be permanently installed inside each vehicle, and between the handlebars of motorcycles. Cameras would provide documentary proof of violations but only the car and not the driver would be photographed. Cash cards would be sold by banks and could be topped up at banks and automated teller machines. The system was designed to be convenient for motorists and operationally unobtrusive.

With ERP charges levied each time a vehicle passed through a gantry, it facilitated much more effective congestion pricing. This was borne out by the fall in the number of vehicles in the CBD during the ERP operating hours as compared to the ALS, a result of a reduction in multiple trips that had been made with the same ALS pass. It also enabled flexible pricing. To begin with, there were quarterly rate reviews based on observations of traffic speeds: charges were reduced for various periods at specific points where average speeds were found to have been above the target. Rates were lowered during school holidays when families made fewer trips with many away on holiday. In 2003, rates began to be staggered with smaller increments to discourage motorists from idling on road shoulders awaiting a downward adjustment in the charges, attesting to motorists' very high price sensitivity when it came to usage. Technology enabled further refinement: charges were adjusted according to the speeds registered by a fleet of "probe vehicles" — 7,000 or so taxis fitted with Global Positioning System receivers; the charges rise if speeds slower than 45–65 km per hour (for expressways) and 20–30 km per hour (for arterial roads) are registered for priced roads.[23]

6.4.3 Quotas for Car Ownership and the Certificate of Entitlement

The ALS and subsequently ERP were targeted at car usage; charging for road usage was only one of the pillars in the battle to manage the almost insatiable demand for motorcars. Standard fiscal measures had been in place since 1968 to stem the rising demand for cars — comprising import duties, a flat registration fee, an additional registration fee (ARF) calculated as a percentage of the open market value or import price of the car, as well as road taxes which varied with the engine capacity of the car. In the mid-1970s, the ARF was increased several times — from 25 to 55 and subsequently to 100 per cent of the import prices in successive attempts to further deter ownership. In 1975, the Preferential ARF system was introduced to

---

[23] Sharp (2005), p. 144.

encourage car renewal by reducing the ARF if a car was scrapped every time a new car was put on the road. However the scrap value was pegged to the ARF. As the ARF was successively raised, and with the rising Japanese yen, a perverse result was obtained: the price of some cars rose over time, especially lower priced models within higher engine capacity ranges. The fact that some cars became appreciating assets ended up encouraging car purchases, exactly the opposite result intended by the policy. In the economic recovery years after the 1986 recession, car demand boomed. The ARF was raised to 175 per cent of the import price; road taxes were raised; petrol taxes were raised; car park charges in public housing estates doubled; evening ALS was instituted in 1989. The successive implementation of so many measures within a short period caused much unhappiness among the car owning population. It became a political issue, which ended up dominating parliamentary debate in 1989. It was obvious that the fiscal measures, designed as they were, were not only not effective in controlling demand, they were distortionary and fueled widespread dissatisfaction. It was a less than happy episode in transport policy-making.

It was in the ensuing parliamentary debate that the proposal to impose motor vehicle quotas surfaced.[24] This was not the first time a quantity curb had been put forward. Goh Keng Swee, Singapore's first Deputy Prime Minister had advocated a zero growth rate for private motor vehicles[25] through a system where an old car was scrapped or taken off the roads every time a new car was registered.[26] Other possible systems based on a zero growth policy, such as the transferring of a fixed pool of existing car licenses, were explored, while at the

---

[24] The proposal to use quotas was suggested by a then Member of Parliament and chairman of the Government Parliamentary Committee on Communication and Information, Dr Hong Hai in Parliament on 4 August 1989. Dr Hong then went on to chair the Select Committee for Land Transportation. This section draws from Phang Sock-Yong, Wong Wing-Keung and Chia Ngee Choon (1996). "Singapore's Experience with Car Quotas: Issues and Policy Processes," *Transport Policy*, Vol. 3, No. 4, pp. 145–153.

[25] This idea was originally proposed by Dr Goh Keng Swee way back in 1975 in his article "Zero Growth Rate for Private Motor Vehicles," in *The Practice of Economic Growth*. Federal Publications, 1977, republished 1995.

[26] This was the principle behind the PARF system, described in the preceding paragraph.

same time restricting the number of vehicles. Ngiam Tong Dow, then Permanent Secretary at the Ministry of Finance, preferred a balloting system whereby car owners would be allocated the right to buy a car based on certain criteria. Lee Kuan Yew, in response, suggested that the market should be allowed to price scarce resources rather than rationing by administrative balloting.[27]

In response to the growing unhappiness, an eight-member Select Committee for Land Transportation was appointed on 4 August 1989 to conduct public hearings on Singapore's land transportation policy and to make recommendations to the government. The committee received 71 written submissions; the authors of 28 of them were invited to present oral evidence in public on 2 and 3 November 1989. The Committee presented its recommendations to Parliament on 2 January 1990. Based on a study that showed that the demand for cars in Singapore was more income elastic than price elastic, trying to manage ownership by increasing price would be ineffective during period of rapidly rising incomes, as was shown to be the case. The Committee thus recommended that a quota system be adopted to control car ownership, and suggested that new cars be purchased in one of two ways:

(i)   The scrapping of a used car which can either be the purchaser's own car or one that he buys from the used car market, or

(ii) By bidding for a license to buy a new car through tenders conducted at regular monthly intervals.

Not unexpectedly, the Committee's quota recommendation was debated extensively in the media and in Parliament. On 30 January 1990, the government announced that it had accepted in principle the recommendation for a quota system. The main idea was that the government would determine the number of new car licenses every year, which would be sold via auction. Thus instead of further increasing ownership taxes, the government would only have to decide on the acceptable growth rate of motor vehicle population, auction off the corresponding number of additional licenses and let the market

---

[27] Sharp (2005), p. 143.

determine the price of the licenses. This approach had the advantage of imposing only a one-time cost on ownership; it was politically more acceptable as it was easier to adjust quotas in response to changing road capacities than increasing motor tax rates. The key difference between the policies eventually adopted and those recommended by the Select Committee was that all purchases of new cars required a license — existing owners would not be exempted. It was a system of renewable rights of usage, and the bid price became the rationing mechanism.

Under the Vehicle Quota System (VQS) implemented on 1 May 1990, prospective purchasers of new cars had to secure a ten-year Certificate of Entitlement (COE). Purchasers would have to submit their bids at each quarterly (subsequently monthly) auction; successful bidders need only pay the lowest successful bid price — the price that would exhaust the quota of COEs available at that particular auction — and this lowest successful bid was termed the Quota Premium. To ensure that buyers of smaller cars were not consistently outbid by the wealthy, four vehicle subcategories were established according to vehicle engine capacity. Other categories were established for goods vehicles, buses, and for motorcycles.

The system of transferable COEs and the oligopolistic car market at that time led to several years where the prices of certificates of entitlement hit stratospheric levels, reaching S$100,000 for two categories of cars in 1994. There was a strong public perception that COEs, which to the car distributors represented the right to sell a car, were being hoarded by car distributors and who thereby pushed up COE prices. In response to the public outcry, the system was tweaked — once at the end of 1991, and again at the end of 1994. In November 1994, the Minister for Communications announced that two experiments would be conducted: the first experiment to discourage double transfers and the second was to make all COE bidders pay the amount they bid, instead of the lowest successful price. Prices of COEs across all categories fell after the announcement. The tug-of-war between policy makers and suspected "speculators" was a fascinating period in the annals of car transport policy making; the ingenuity of car dealers in finding and exploiting loopholes in the

COE and VQS system resulted in policy-makers continually playing "catch-up" and demanded much fine tuning to the system.[28]

The government announced in 1997 that additional COEs would be released if the ERP system proved effective in managing congestion. That year, an additional 5,000 COEs were put on the market, and a same number was released in 2002–2003 when the ERP did prove successful. Upon a review of the VQS in 1998, the COE bidding system was made more flexible and transparent. The number of car categories was reduced to two: Category A (less than 1,600 cc), and Category B (above 1,600 cc). The intention to start an Open Bidding system was announced, which would allow online COE bidders to see the progress of the bidding process and to adjust their bids accordingly. A simplified system also enabled would-be car buyers to place their own bids without relying on car dealers to submit bids for them. The online system became fully operational in 2002.

6.4.4 *Catering to Part-Time Car Users: The Weekend Car Scheme*

In addition to congestion pricing and the auction system to ration car ownership, the Weekend Car Scheme (WEC), launched in 1991, was another innovative scheme designed to cater to the segment of the population that aspired to own a car but only for use during the weekends and off-peak periods. Weekend cars would be subject to usage constraints in exchange for tax savings in the price of the car. A separate COE category was added under the VQS. The buyer of a weekend car enjoyed tax rebates on the registration fee, import duty and COE premium, plus a 70 per cent reduction in road taxes. In return for these savings, weekend cars could only be used on Sundays and public holidays, and during off-peak hours between 7 pm and 7 am on weekdays and after 3 pm on Saturdays. A day license costing S$20 had to be bought and displayed if the car was used during the restricted hours. The penalty for using a weekend car during the restricted hours without the display of a day license was a fine equal to half the annual

---

[28] For a detailed discussion of the speculation issue, see Phang, Wong and Chia (1996).

road tax for an equivalent normal car, rising to the full amount of the road tax for subsequent offenses.

Unfortunately the design of the system was flawed: owners of cars with larger engine capacities made net gains from the rebates and offsets, even if they used the day license of S$20 every day for a year. Additional unanticipated savings were realized by car owners exploiting the differences in the COE premiums between normal cars and weekend cars. Instead of being a low cost car option for those who would otherwise not have been able to afford a car, the scheme became one perceived as favoring the rich who could afford more than one car, and larger cars. The WEC scheme was replaced in October 1994 by the Off-Peak Car scheme. Under the revised scheme, the special COE category for weekend cars was removed — bidders for off-peak cars now bid in the same categories as those for normal cars. With the same usage restrictions as the weekend car, off-peak car owners enjoyed the same flat tax incentives, regardless of car engine capacity, a flat $17,000 rebate at the time of registration, and a flat $800 discount on annual road tax.

6.4.5 Lessons Learnt from the Experimentation and Innovation in Road Transportation

(i) *A strong imprint regarding the expected role of policy makers led to proactive actions and interventions to solve perceived transportation and car ownership issues*

Political and public sector leaders see their role as proactively anticipating issues and responding to perceived issues, preferably before the consequences are experienced by the people. The proactive role of policy-makers was manifested both in the forward planning in the 1971 Concept Plan that anticipated road congestion as a future issue by integrating land use with transportation needs, and the constant monitoring of the speed of traffic flow to identify the emergence of actual road congestion. The expected proactive role of the public sector led them to plan ahead, anticipate issues and intervene frequently. They established sensing mechanisms to alert them to issues that needed to be addressed also because they were expected to approach potential issues as rationally as possible, using facts and data to justify policy recommendations, actions and changes.

(ii)   *The accepted practice of using rational and economic principles in policy evaluation and design guided the search toward a market-based approach*

The use of rational economic principles in policy evaluation and design was evident in the preference, wherever possible, for some form of price mechanism rather than direct regulations or administrative rules, to achieve a self-regulating system with market-driven equilibrating mechanisms. Policies were directed at both controlling car demand and increasing supply of road transportation infrastructure and services. The broad policy design to control demand was comprehensive to cover both road usage and car ownership. The ALS and ERP systems controlled congestion (that traffic flows do not fall below desired speed levels) by setting a clearing price for the use of a road during specific periods of time, thereby letting drivers decide if their marginal value of using the road at that time was worth the price charged. The COE system controlled car ownership by setting the annual number of new car registrations allowed and letting potential owners determine how much they were willing to pay to buy these rights. These principles have rational and economic logic that appealed to policy-makers and guided the public sector in their search for policy solutions to emerging issues.

(iii) *Path breaking policy solutions were explored and thoughtfully designed in response to perceived long-term issues and the need to act decisively, even if precedents were not available*

The search for practical solutions would usually lead to the adoption or adaptation of solutions that have worked reasonably well in other countries or contexts. For road transportation and road congestion, path-breaking solutions were explored as policy makers saw the issue as one impinging on business productivity and Singapore's competitiveness as a destination for foreign investments. This triggered a sense of urgency and quickened the pace of search, design and implementation of innovative solutions. Innovation is defined as a deviation from existing practices or knowledge.[29] The Singapore public sector defined innovation as "the creation of new value for the organization through doing things differently and doing different things."[30]

The initial response to road congestion was hardly innovative. It simply followed past practices of raising car taxes to increase the cost of car ownership. When this indirect approach of taxing car ownership achieved only short-term results and as the political costs of raising car taxes increased, the policy emphasis shifted to a more direct, focused control of road usage in the CBD, an area where congestion was perceived to have the highest economic costs. The concept was new and with no precedent to follow, the system had to be designed from scratch. Innovation was required to design a path-breaking initiative that sought to achieve a long-term solution to a knotty problem.

The ALS was the world's first comprehensive congestion pricing system. The features of the system were new and required much thought and creativity to achieve the results for a challenging set of policy objectives. The ERP enabled the congestion pricing system to be extended beyond the CBD, made it more reliable and incorporated the potential advantage of flexible pricing. The technology was complex to design and implement, and concerns over privacy were also addressed. The ERP solution was novel and bold.

Even though road usage control through road pricing worked, it was still not a comprehensive solution. There was still a need to control car ownership while minimizing the political costs of raising car taxes constantly. The COE system was designed to price car ownership as a

---

[29] G Zaltman, R Duncan and J Holbeck (1973). *Innovations and Organizations*. New York: Wiley; A Van der Ven and D Polley (1992). "Learning while Innovating," *Organization Science*, Vol. 3, pp. 92–116.

[30] This is the definition taken from the public sector report titled "Strategy and System for an Innovative Public Service," 7 July 2001. In the paper "The Consequences of Innovation" by Tan Bann Seng (2004), the definition was referred to as the Singapore public service's official position on innovation. *The Public Sector Innovation Journal*, Vol. 9, No. 3.

complement to road pricing. It ensured a sustainable rate of increase in the car population while letting potential car owners decide on how much they were willing to pay to own a car. The weekend car scheme was an innovative approach to lower the cost of car ownership for those willing to restrict the use of their cars to evenings and weekends.

(iv) *Policy innovations were adapted through incremental changes that enabled cumulative learning and ensured that users could cope with the adjustments*

Though the ALS, ERP, COE and the weekend car scheme were designed thoughtfully, rationally and comprehensively, many adjustments and fine tuning were subsequently made through experiential learning. As the ALS was a new initiative, there was little information on how motorists would change their travel patterns as a result of the system. Thus refining the ALS to achieve optimal traffic flows while controlling congestion in the CBD became an iterative process with continual adjustment to rates and fine tuning to time periods. It was an example of trial and error learning.

The ERP system built on the ALS experience and extended road pricing beyond the CBD to major expressways in shorter and more flexible time periods. The ERP is an example of a technological solution that is often preferred and pursued in policy designs in Singapore. Technological solutions build new capabilities into the system to enable better performance and free up the use of scarce human resources. It is almost second nature to the Singapore public sector to migrate a manually operated system, such as the ALS, to an electronic system to enhance system capabilities, consistency, performance and flexibility. Adjustments to rates and time periods are still regularly made but now they are in response to periodic changes in traffic flow patterns. It is no longer trial-and-error learning but real time adaptation to emerging patterns of road congestion and traffic flow.

Similarly, adjustments were made to the COE system in response to emerging patterns of bidding behavior for the new car licenses and to make the system more flexible and transparent. Several changes and refinements were made over a period of time to reduce the types of car licenses to three, shortening the bidding period from monthly to fortnightly and making bid prices, which was initially closed, completely open.

Trial-and-error learning takes place when actions are taken "on-line" and their consequences occur. The process involves observing the outcomes of the system, collecting feedback, understanding the cause-effect relationships and then deciding on actions required. The purpose is either to revise the expected outcomes to fit with a clearer understanding of stakeholder values or to adjust the rules so that the expected results may be realized. The continuous scan and interpretation of feedback from the system enabled corrective actions to be taken to improve the total experience and outcomes desired.

Adaptive learning through such trial-and-error experimentation usually occurs when the objectives of a plan are clear but the workings and results of the chosen method are not, or have unforeseen repercussions. These effects then become inputs for further sense-making that result in the next round of refinement.[31] For such adaptive learning to take place, decision makers must be alert to feedback from the system, infer the reasons why the process was not working as planned, and then fine tuning the rules to influence user actions and behavior.

Equally important is the need to be sensitive to the public response to such frequent tweaking of the system. Without public acceptance of the adjustments, the frequent changes could create confusion and resistance, and they would not have achieved their intended outcomes. Major system changes such as the introduction of the ERP were discussed and debated extensively years ahead of the intended implementation. Once a major new system was adopted, each set of changes was incremental in nature, justified on the basis of data from actual experience, and communicated widely to users. The public now accepts regular changes to ERP rates as a normal way of life in Singapore.

---

[31] Anne S Miner, Paula Bassoff and Christine Moorman (2001). "Organizational Improvisation and Learning: A Field Study," *Administrative Science Quarterly*, Vol. 46, No. 2, pp. 304–340.

6.5 Central Provident Fund (CPF)[32]

How the original intent of retirement savings was widened to include housing, health care and use as a macroeconomic tool

The CPF scheme was established in 1955 and was designed as a savings plan for retirement financed by monthly contributions by both the employer and the employee. It is a fully funded savings scheme, with each working Singapore citizen having his own personal CPF account. Market interest rates were paid for CPF balances with a minimum rate of 2.5 per cent per annum. Monthly contribution rates were steadily increased from the mid-1960s, peaking at 50 per cent in 1985 (25 per cent of monthly salary each from employee and employer) subject to a S$6,000 maximum salary cap. The current rate of 34.5 per cent was last revised in 2007. The principle behind the CPF scheme was that each individual should take personal responsibility and save for his own retirement needs. Excess balances in the CPF accounts, after a minimum sum was maintained, could be withdrawn at age 55, the official retirement age then.

Over the years, the role of the CPF evolved in response to changing demographics, economic conditions and Singaporeans' rising aspirations. There were concerns that the withdrawn funds were used up too fast and leaving little for old age, especially with longer life expectancy. In 1987, a minimum sum of S$30,000 was required to be kept in the CPF account at age 55. From 1995, it was raised by S$5,000 each year to reach S$80,000 in 2003. The minimum sum is used to make monthly payouts to provide a subsistence living during retirement.

In 1978, CPF members were allowed to use their CPF for investments in the shares of the initial public offering of the Singapore Bus Service company. This was extended to commercial property in 1986 and further liberalized in the 1990s to allow individuals to

---

[32] This section draws heavily from Tan Soo San (2004). "The Central Provident Fund: More than Retirement," *Ethos*, July.

invest the CPF funds in an increasing array of shares, gold, and unit trusts for higher financial returns. The CPF system was widened to include other social objectives such as housing, health care and education. Adjustments to CPF contribution rates were also used as a macro-economic tool to improve competitiveness by lowering the cost burden on employers. With each extension and adjustment, it has been necessary to weigh and balance policy trade offs between social and economic goals.

The Economic Review Committee in 2001 sought to refocus the CPF on the basic needs of retirement, health care and home ownership. The changes made in 2003 included lowering the contribution rate for older workers, lowering the income ceiling for CPF contributions, limiting withdrawals for housing to 120 per cent of the value of the property, and to increasing the CPF minimum sum to S$120,000 over ten years.

6.5.1 *Expansion into Housing and Health Care*

The first extension of the use of CPF was for public housing in 1968. Working class families were allowed to use the CPF Ordinary Account (OA) to pay for their monthly mortgages when they bought subsidized flats built by the Housing and Development Board (HDB). This enabled families to own their apartments, as many did not have to use their monthly take-home pay to service their mortgages. This served the national objective of giving the largely migrant population a physical stake in the young nation. The scheme was further extended for purchases of private residential properties in 1981, investment of non-residential property in 1986 and for upgrading costs in the 1990s. From 1968 to 1977, two-thirds of all CPF withdrawals were for housing. The magnitude of the withdrawals prompted the creation of the Special Account (SA) in 1977. A portion of the monthly contributions was deposited into an individual's SA, which was meant for retirement and could not be withdrawn for housing or other purposes.

From 1 April 1984, the CPF system was further modified to include a new Medisave Account (MA), to which 6 percentage points of each worker's monthly contributions were credited.[33] Medisave funds could be used to pay for hospital, surgery and doctor's fees as well as approved outpatient treatments such as chemotherapy. The thinking behind this approach was that since Medisave monies belonged to the individual who paid at the point of consumption, each individual would have the incentive to save and use his Medisave funds judiciously. As Medisave funds that were not used remained part of the individual's savings for retirement, the system discouraged over-consumption of health care. In 1990 a new Medishield catastrophic insurance scheme was implemented and CPF members could use their Medisave funds to pay for their insurance premiums.

As CPF members began drawing on their Medisave funds, there was a concern that the fund balances might be not be adequate for medical needs during retirement. A Medisave Minimum Sum was introduced in 1988 to ensure that there would at least be some funds available to cover medical expenses during the retirement years. The minimum was increased from S$16,000 in 1988 to S$25,000 in 2003.

6.5.2 CPF as a Macro-Economic Tool

When the CPF contribution rates were going up, cost competitiveness was not an issue since the economy had been growing at about 9 per cent per annum for 20 years. However, high labor costs were a significant factor contributing to the loss of competitiveness which triggered the 1985–86 recession. Adjustments to CPF rates were then used as a macro-economic tool for the first time. The employer's contribution rate was cut from 25 per cent to 10 per cent of monthly incomes and the peak rate of 50 per cent was brought down to 35 per cent. As the economy recovered, the rate was slowly restored to 40 per cent (20 per cent each from employers and employees) in 1991. It was cut again to 30 per cent in 1999 in the aftermath of the Asian financial crisis, and then increased to 32 per cent in 2000, 33 per cent in 2003 and 34.5 per cent in 2007. In using the CPF rate

---

[33] This 6 per cent rate of contribution was considered adequate to meet the basic hospitalization needs of the average Singaporean based on the charges in the most highly subsidized wards. The rate was later increased to 8 per cent for older Singaporeans.

adjustments as a macro-economic tool, the belief that economic growth and competitiveness had to be sound before social objectives could be achieved was reaffirmed. It reflects how Singapore juggles its social, economic and political imperatives to meet citizen's needs and aspirations without weakening the economy's capacity and fundamental basis for future growth.[34]

6.5.3 Lessons Learnt from the CPF's Evolutionary Path

(i)   *The CPF system was imprinted with the governance principles of promoting self-reliance, a traditional family support structure, thrift and positive incentive to work and a commitment to a non-inflationary economic environment*

Although the CPF scheme started under the British colonial administration, the founding leaders of independent Singapore continued with it and infused it with their personal beliefs and values. Cultural values may not have been formally articulated then but they were practiced and reinforced, and socially transmitted to subsequent generations of policy makers which in turn deepened the commitment to these shared values that govern policy decision-making and choices. It demonstrated the commitment of policy-makers to what they believed to be crucial foundations for the success of Singapore. Their focus and conviction were very firm and amply expressed in both the policy and system design of CPF. The CPF system design has been recognized by the IMF:[35]

> "Both employees and employers are required to contribute, which discourages any notion that benefits are a free good. The minimum sum scheme ensures that at least part of the retirement benefit is taken in the form of a pension and cannot be consumed rapidly. Finally, because

---

[34] Tan (2004).

[35] Robert Carling and Geoffrey Oestreicher (1995). "Singapore Central Provident Fund," Paper on Policy Analysis and Assessment, Southeast Asia and Pacific Department, IMF, December.

the plan is mandatory, pressures for budgetary social
security outlays are largely avoided, and broad coverage
of the population is achieved at low administrative
costs."

(ii) *Once the CPF system was established, it became a ready solution
whose usage was widened to meet other social objectives, and its
original objectives for retirement were broadened to include housing
and health care*

The policy-making milieu is not just about problems to be resolved
but also how to broaden the usage of available and working solutions.
How problems and solutions are connected depends on the ingenuity
and perceptions of policy-makers. As long as the objectives are
reinforcing, widening the scope of application leverages the power
of the system. However, if it is just a convenient solution, then the
intended goals may be compromised to the detriment of both the
original problem and the new issues at hand. Once the CPF system
was institutionalized as a regular compulsory savings plan for every
working Singaporean, it became a solution that could be applied to
long-term social objectives that required financial contributions and
investments from citizens. Housing, health care and education are
long-term needs that are not inconsistent with the financial security
needs for retirement. The CPF model has evolved into an institution
that takes care of many aspects of a Singaporean's life. It has become
a central component of the complex social contract between the
government and the people it serves.[36]

(iii) *Despite best efforts, policy-makers could not anticipate fully all the
impacts of the design of the CPF system — sequential fine tuning was
a natural response to a better understanding of the impact of policy
choices as they occurred*

Although the policy goals of the various CPF changes were clearly
thought through and articulated, it was difficult to fully appreciate

---

[36] Tan (2004).

and anticipate all the consequences of policy changes, especially second and third order effects in a complex social system. Alertness to the implications of a policy change during its implementation is crucial to the process of continuous improvement and change. The use of CPF for housing was extended and widened in response to public enthusiasm and demand. When the amounts withdrawn became large and accelerating, limits were introduced. For health care, the amounts to be set aside have been increasing in response to rising aspirations and cost of quality health care. Over the years, contribution rates have been adjusted up and down in attempts to balance the long-term social objectives with the need to maintain cost competitiveness for economic growth. The CPF experience demonstrates the need to understand the impact of policy changes and to gather feedback from affected stakeholders in order for the system to be adjusted to adapt to changing circumstances and balance competing requirements.

(iv) *While making adjustments and changes to the system, policy-makers did not lose sight of the purpose of the CPF and took periodic reviews to ensure that retirement needs were met*

The danger of constant adjustments is that the system may become a mixed bag of inconsistent rules and programs that may dilute the intended outcomes, or worse, become self-defeating. Over time, the policy goals may become so convoluted that it loses its purpose and energy. Yet the rules and programs often continue to be perpetuated and a big bureaucracy is a common institutional result. The CPF has avoided this dysfunctional pattern even though many system adjustments and changes have been made because policy-makers never lost sight of the original purpose of providing for retirement needs. Ideally the policy goals should be simultaneously optimized in the course of making adjustments in response to changing circumstances. In reality, the pressure and urgency to make changes to respond to emerging issues usually create a situation that may cause policy-makers to place greater priority in solving the current problem. Thus continuity of direction is only done sequentially at best. Policy-makers who recognize this reality and seek to avoid dysfunction degeneration due to constant changes should build into the system periodic overall reviews to ensure that the original policy purpose is still relevant and not lost by default, and that there is some coherence in the changes made at different times by different people under different circumstances.

6.6 Health Care Policy

How the need to balance quality service provision and cost containment led to innovative paths and continuous learning

Singapore's current health care system is the result of a long process of incremental improvement and innovation based on an enhanced understanding of the characteristics of health care provision and delivery. Health services have significant positive externalities, which are often cited as grounds for government intervention. The challenge is how to balance the provision of quality health care and the cost of health care delivery to manage potentially unlimited demand. Singapore's approach to health care financing is based on a mix of public and private sector provision and the innovative use of market principles and pricing mechanisms to reflect the cost of providing health care services. Health Minister Khaw Boon Wan said Singapore's health care policy is focused in five areas:

> "First, we work on the basis that health care cost will continue to rise. Second, we believe that the health care market can work better under competition. Third, we must empower patients and get them to take greater responsibility for their own health. Fourth, we must revive the important role played by the primary health care sector. Fifth, we should exploit globalization to help lower cost." [37]

6.6.1 Introducing Co-payment for Health Care Services

Singapore inherited a nationalized system of free hospital care and subsidized clinics from the British. This was a tax-funded system of

---

[37] Speech by Khaw Boon Wan reported in *The Straits Times* on 19 September 2006, "Five Steps to Keeping Health Care Affordable."

universal health coverage where patients bore little or no responsibility at the point of consumption. Whilst this was in keeping with the socialist leanings of the founding political leadership, it quickly became clear to them that this approach encouraged over consumption, resulting in rationing by queuing. The approach adopted by the US was a free market system based on health insurance with little state intervention. This led to spiraling costs and inconsistent quality of care, with rationing by access as high health insurance costs gradually shut out those who could not afford to pay. Singapore leaders realized that neither of these were the solution to the problem of how "to give all Singaporeans proper access to efficient health care services at a cost the individual and country can afford."[38] Continuous learning and innovative experimentation were necessary to evolve a working model.

The crux of the problem — under both the tax-funded universal coverage and the health insurance models — was that the consumer did not see or feel the direct link between his health care choices and the costs involved. Thus the policy approach was to discourage over consumption by making the patient pay, at least in part, the cost of his health care at the point of consumption. The civil service set the pace for employers by revising the health care benefits to introduce co-payments by its employees. This also meant that each consumer had to save for his own health care costs.

To make this practice mandatory, health savings accounts were built into the CPF system. From 1 April 1984, 6 percentage points of each worker's monthly contributions were credited to a new account called Medisave, which became each individual's personal savings account for health care.[39] As the contribution rates were not large, concern grew that Medisave would not be able to cover expenses of prolonged hospital stays and catastrophic illnesses. In response, the health care financing system was expanded in 1990 to include

---

[38] The then Second Minister for Health, Mr Goh Chok Tong, Parliamentary Debate, 30 August 1983, cited in *Singapore Economic Review* (1986), "Report of the Central Provident Fund Study Group," Vol. 31, No. 1, p. 63.

[39] This 6 per cent rate of contribution was considered adequate to meet the basic hospitalization needs of the average Singaporean based on the charges in the most highly subsidized wards. The rate was later increased to 8 per cent for older Singaporeans.

a national insurance component called Medishield to cover the cost of prolonged serious illnesses for all unless individuals opted out. Medishield, a low-cost, high deductible co-insurance program, is run on actuarial and not social principles where the premiums and benefits are determined by the actual health risk factors in the population. So unlike most national health insurance schemes, there is no cross-subsidy across age bands and the healthy do not subsidize the unhealthy. Those in the higher risk category pay higher premiums. Finally, a health care endowment fund, MediFund, was set up with surpluses from the budget: income from the fund could be used to pay for the medical costs of the people who could not afford to pay. Medifund is administered by a separate government-appointed committee that determines if a person is eligible for support and the amount that will be given.

6.6.2 Differentiating Health Care Services through a Tiered System

On the supply side, the government subsidizes hospitalization costs through a four-tier system (A, B1, B2 and C wards), with higher subsidy levels for rooms with less comfort. For example, Class A wards comprising single-bedded rooms, TV, attached bathroom and air-conditioning are charged at full cost with no subsidy while Class C wards which are open, dormitory-like wards with no air-conditioning are subsidized at about 80 per cent of the cost. The level of medical care across all the wards is provided by the same medical staff and the medical facilities in the hospitals (such as operating theaters and specialized equipment) are shared across all the wards; the only difference is that patients in Class A and in the four-bedded Class B1 wards can choose their own doctors. Thus patients can self-select into an appropriate class ward according to their willingness to pay. Private hospitals have a wider range of variety in ward and service delivery structures but there are no government subsidies for health care provided at private hospitals.

The rationing principle in the Singapore health care financing system is not based on queuing (as in the British National Health

System) nor on access (as in the US free market health insurance-based system); it is rationed largely on consumer choice and on ability to pay.[40] Consumers who wish to opt for better coverage of hospitalization expenses can opt for Medishield or Medishield Plus or private health insurance. Similarly consumers who are able and willing to pay the cost can opt for private hospitals and private medical care. Private hospital beds account for some 20 per cent of total hospital beds and patients can use Medisave (up to the same $ limits as public hospitals) to pay for their treatment. The capping of Medisave withdrawal limits according to the type of expenditure for inpatient and outpatient treatments demanded that hospitals provide a breakdown of costs to the patient to enable the patient to choose the quality of ward.

6.6.3 *Providing Information and Introducing Competition in Service Delivery*

One of the characteristics of health care provision is the problem of information asymmetry between the provider and the patient, as patients rely heavily on doctors and hospitals for advice. This problem is compounded by a general lack of comparative information on the actual cost of health care services. Elements of competition began to be injected into the public hospital system starting in the 1980s — first with the restructuring of public hospitals into corporate entities and later by the creation of two vertically integrated delivery clusters, Singapore Health Services and the National Health Group. The restructuring created an environment for competition between clusters and collaboration within cluster. Hospitals can rationalize their services within each cluster and harness economies of scale in the purchasing of common goods and services. The most radical move towards greater transparency and competition was the 2004 mandate to hospitals to disclose the average bill sizes for various procedures and conditions based on class of ward, together with the number of such procedures performed by each hospital each year.[41] A few hospitals

---

[40] Rationing is also effected through the imposition of withdrawal limits for both inpatient and outpatient treatments.

[41] These are now published on the website of the Ministry of Health.

were surprised at how far above the norm their average bill sizes were and were compelled to review their processes and cost structures. This initiative was unprecedented, a radical attempt to increase the level of transparency and to help consumers make a better choice through the provision of better information. This information-based approach has now been widened to include service levels and waiting times in each hospital.

6.6.4 *Going beyond Inpatient Treatment to Structured Disease Management*

One of the features of Medisave prior to 2006 was its coverage of predominantly in-patient treatment, except for specific treatments like chemotherapy. For more than 20 years, the public sector had balked at expanding out-patient care coverage, fearing the consequences of a more unrestrained use of Medisave funds for out-patient treatments that might not be necessary or of doubtful effectiveness. In 2004, this long-held stance was reviewed in light of developments in the outpatient treatment of several common chronic conditions. Structured disease management programs had been developed for conditions like diabetes based on the concept of patients taking co-responsibility for their care by receiving structured evidence-based treatment by good family physicians working in partnership with hospital specialists. For example, if diabetes was well managed through good control of blood sugar by patients working together with their doctors and nurses, they would more likely be able to avoid the serious complications arising from diabetes such as kidney failure or foot amputation. By taking action early and complying with such disease management programs, patients were likely to achieve better health outcomes and avoid the severe cost of delayed treatment for complications once they had set in. The benefits of good disease management programs had been demonstrated overseas and MOH itself undertook a trial through public hospitals and the polyclinics to gauge the effectiveness of this approach in the local context. Given the well-documented benefits of this structured approach both locally and internationally in terms of the enhanced health outcomes and savings in costly medical treatment in the future, the decision was taken to allow the use of Medisave funds to help defray the cost of this type of out-patient treatment, but with a deductible and co-insurance element and an annual cap on withdrawals. This significant change illustrates the constant review-and-improve cycle in public sector policy making, which in this case was triggered by the development of new treatment protocols.

6.6.5 *Exploring Emerging Health Care Policy Issues*

Current health care policies continue to evolve a holistic health care delivery system. There have been increased efforts to encourage Singaporeans to live healthy lives through education and promotional programs on personal hygiene, diet, exercise, and regular health screenings. Investments in new medical facilities, including new hospitals and specialized institutes, and comprehensive medical record systems have been announced. More doctors and nurses are being trained and a new graduate medical school has been set up between the National University of Singapore and Duke University. Medical research, pharmaceutical product development, clinical trials and health care delivery are being aligned as part of a larger vision to make Singapore a biomedical hub for the region. The export potential of medical services is attracting greater attention.

One of the emergent practices in the process of public policy-making has been the use of "feelers" to gauge public opinion to controversial issues as inputs into policy-making. This method was employed in the wake of the 1997 financial crisis when the prospect of a cut in the CPF was mooted repeatedly for months before the actual decision to cut was taken, by which time it had become a non-event. A similar method was utilized to gauge public sentiment to a proposal to introduce means testing in charging for subsidized inpatient treatment. A Health Feedback Group had proposed that subsidies be directed to the neediest; that health care subsidies be tied to a patient's financial status, instead of the type of hospital or class of ward. This in effect meant linking hospital charges in subsidized wards to a patient's ability to pay. Dropping "feelers" on this issue enabled policy-makers to explain the implications of the policy and why such a policy was being considered. It allowed different points of view and arguments and concerns to be surfaced. It was an informal method of public consultation, a way to sound out the public on potentially explosive issues, a way to meet the expectations of the public to be consulted on the major issues that affected them. As it turned out, various stakeholder groups highlighted the potential pitfalls of means testing, such as the difficulties in assessing a patient's ability to pay, the possibility of an enlarged administrative burden on hospitals, and the possibility of inadvertently pushing up health care costs by forcing better off patients into higher class wards. After taking into account these views, it was recently announced that means testing in hospitals would be introduced within a year.[42]

The quality and outcome of health care in Singapore is equivalent to those available in the developed countries while expenditure for national healthcare is about 4 per cent of GDP, which is significantly lower than that of developed nations. In the latest World Health Organization study in 2000, Singapore's health care performance was ranked 6th out of 191 countries.

6.6.6 Patterns of Learning and Policy Adaptation in Health Care

The management of health care policy in Singapore involved a combination of market forces and government intervention to manage demand and supply. Demand is moderated through co-payment to ensure personal responsibility and supply is enhanced through continued investments in medical facilities and technologies and the training of doctors and nurses. The following patterns of learning and innovation are evident:

(i) *Tensions among different policy objectives and realities induced decision-makers to search for and develop innovative concepts in health care systems design*

---

[42] *The Sunday Times*, "Means Testing in Hospitals Within a Year," Sunday, 8 April 2007.

Government leaders view health care as fundamental to a good standard of living and economic productivity, and have always regarded the provision of good and affordable health care services as one of its core responsibilities. The reality was that providing quality health care was expensive and constituted a major and increasing portion of the national budget. Policy-makers were also determined that individuals should take personal responsibility for the cost of health care they consumed even as they recognized that individual demand for health care was potentially insatiable. Though the British heritage of a universal free health care coverage was aligned with the social leanings of the founders of modern Singapore, breakdowns such as over-consumption and rationing by queuing in similar health care systems in other countries served as warning signals that initiated search for new policy designs.

The tensions among these policy objectives made the search for a solution difficult and complex, but also unleashed creativity that led to the development of innovative concepts that have underpinned the design of the health care system for more than 20 years. Key concepts that were integrated into the health care financing infrastructure included individual co-payments, Medisave accounts, a tiered delivery system based on patient comfort without compromising medical treatment, costs transparency to facilitate consumption choices, competition among government hospitals and expanding Medisave coverage to include outpatient disease management. These are innovative approaches, incorporating elements of both the free market and socialist systems, with consumption rationed largely through the pricing mechanism. It was an effective system for health care provision that integrated both national objectives and personal responsibility.

(ii)   *A comprehensive approach to public policy required that both demand and supply dynamics be considered in the design and implementation of health care provision*

While co-payment and the use of Medisave, Medishield and Medifund were aimed at dynamic demand management that gave consumer choices, the supply was also managed so that there were indeed differentiated selections without compromising minimum standards of medical care. Dynamic supply management was achieved through a range of health care services (primary, tertiary, specialist) provided by both the private and public sectors which offered alternatives in terms of the panel of doctors and surgeons as well as the type of medical facilities and equipment available. Within the public hospitals, the four-tier system provided different levels of ward support and comfort while sharing common hospital medical facilities and ensuring that a minimum standard of medical care was provided. At the same time, the public hospitals were organized into two groups so that an element of competition was introduced to drive efficiency and service levels without degenerating into senseless rivalry. The public sector calls this "guided competition."

(iii) *Continuous learning and system improvements are the drivers for success in areas of sensitive social policies that affect people's lives*

One of the features of Singapore's public sector policy-making approach is its pragmatism, that it has never been fixated with any particular policy design. Policies are crafted based on its merits within the context at a particular point in time. When there are indications that the circumstances have changed, policies are reviewed. The process of policy execution and adaptation in health care has been one of continuous learning and constant improvements through regular review, incremental changes as well as radical innovation, based on a thorough understanding of the issues and the forces operating in the health care market. Although there were missteps such as the decision taken in 1994 to reduce the number of doctors arising from a fear of supply-induced demand for medical services — a policy which has since been relaxed — health care policy has been distinctive in its unique integration of the free market and socialist systems, buttressed by an unprecedented level of transparency and disclosure of health care costs to spur more informed consumer choice.

6.7 Tackling the Issue of the Working Poor[43]

How an anti-welfare imprint constrained policy options for many years and how a new national perspective created the stimulus for systematic search, learning and adaptation

Where the focus in health care policy was the creation of new concepts and system designs to overcome weaknesses experienced elsewhere in the provision and financing of health care, many a time the problem is how to deviate from an existing path or overcome a very strong imprint. This was the situation faced by the taskforce examining the plight of the working poor.

6.7.1 *A New Perspective of an Old Issue*

The problem of the working poor was surfaced by grassroots organizations and the Ministry of Community Development, Youth and Sports (MCYS) in 2004. Based on a preliminary study that year, the Ministry of Finance (MOF) felt that the issue warranted closer scrutiny. A study team was formed in the MOF at the end of 2004, which later evolved into a Taskforce on Vulnerable Workers comprising officers from the MOF, MCYS and MOM (Ministry of Manpower). The taskforce focused on the lowest deciles and the lowest quintiles of the population. Due diligence was done; the incomes and household expenditure patterns of these groups were examined — there were households whose wages were not keeping up with average wage increases and for some, their wages were not even keeping up with inflation.

Why did this issue warrant study at this time? The unemployed and low-income households have always existed and the stance of the political leaders remained unchanged: Singapore had succeeded because it believed in the principle of self reliance, hinged on a strong work ethic. Citizens had been constantly reminded that in socialist countries, the welfare state had bred a culture of entitlement, the cost

---

[43] This section on Workfare draws from an interview with Jacqueline Poh, Director (Fiscal Policy), Ministry of Finance on 16 June 2006.

of which was not only debilitating but which had wreaked havoc with the work ethic. As a result, the public sector extended no automatic unemployment benefits[44] and the handouts under public assistance schemes were paltry — the philosophy was to give little and demand little. The anti-welfare stance had persisted through the effects of the recession in 1985–86 and the one following the Asian financial crisis in 1997. The anti-welfare, "no-one owes us a living" mindset was a very strong imprint on Singapore society. One reason for the eventual change was a different perspective articulated by a new Prime Minister.

In his first National Day Rally speech in 2004, the new Prime Minister Lee Hsien Loong positioned Singapore as a Land of Opportunity. But by then, there was clearly a group of Singaporeans for which this was obviously not the case. The restructuring of the economy to higher value-added knowledge-based activities had caused severe dislocation: those with few skills and little education saw their jobs disappear as low-skilled labor-intensive jobs moved to low labor cost destinations. Their lack of qualifications and skills impeded their move to jobs that were opening up in new higher value-added, knowledge-based industries. Whereas dips in employment in the past had been cyclical, this time they appeared to be more persistent for a certain group. While efforts were put in place to help the dislocated retrain for new jobs, the process was slow. Age was also a factor, with most of the lower-income and lower-skilled being 45 and older, who found it harder to retrain. Thus the pressure to extend and expand the scope of public assistance to those families experiencing protracted dislocation increased throughout the 1990s. The initial response to pressing needs from grassroots organizations was the establishment of the Community Care (ComCare) Fund in 2004. ComCare was intended as a safety net of last resort for those in permanent need, those who could not help themselves, and for those who needed temporary help. But ComCare had a strong needs-based

---

[44] There were some assistance schemes to extend temporary help to the unemployed in periods of economic downturn which extended a limited period of financial support contingent on seeking jobs. But there was nothing for structural unemployment.

focus at the time and there was concern that a well-intended and well-meaning initiative could breed a mentality of welfare and entitlement. Equally important, policy makers appreciated that in those families who suffered extended periods of unemployment, uncertainty and low wages, there was a danger that the negative attitudes and mindsets of discouraged workers could well be transmitted to their children, doing irreparable harm to the work ethic and attitude of the next generation. Thus a change in the perception of political and socio-economic contexts prompted action.

6.7.2 Searching for Ideas and Learning by Discovery

However the taskforce did not set out with any preconceived idea of how exactly to deal with the issue. Their only guiding principle was that some sort of operating framework was needed to manage the group of vulnerable workers, to pre-empt an inadvertent slide into welfare. The group thus began looking for models and systems of welfare, which they felt were instructive. Their search through the literature turned up the system in Hong Kong, a model in Wisconsin, USA written up in an article in *The Economist*, and a description of welfare reform in New York in ex -mayor Rudy Guiliani's memoirs. The taskforce then visited these states to see their systems first hand. The team found the systems in Wisconsin and New York broadly similar.

The taskforce identified five major thrusts of Wisconsin Works (W2):

(i)   Under the W2, job readiness determined whether an individual who was otherwise eligible for assistance would actually receive income support. If an individual was deemed fit to work, he was automatically defined as ineligible for welfare. This job-readiness test of eligibility marked a change from the approach where assistance was extended based on entitlement, and resulted in a significant reduction in the number of people receiving welfare payments.

(ii)   Work was a precondition of aid. Work was broadly defined to include activities related to employment seeking, taking state-approved courses and undergoing approved self-improvement directly related to finding a job. Community service jobs such as maintenance of public parks also counted as work. Moreover there was a time limit for participation in W2 — a lifetime limit of 60 months.

(iii) The fundamental approach was to treat W2 participants who received grants just like they were working. To simulate actual working conditions, the W2 grant structure was flat, akin to a salary structure. This was one major difference from the system that had existed previously which had been a needs-based entitlement system. Under entitlement-based systems, those with more children received more assistance based on "need" than those with fewer children. This ran counter to the objective of simulating a normal work environment where those with more children were not paid more than those who had no or fewer children. Like normal work, new mothers under W2 had to go back to work after maternity leave. There was a sanctions system: if W2 participants did not turn up for work three times, they were disqualified from the W2 system.

(iv) The W2 classified jobs into four tiers:

- Unsubsidized jobs — those eligible to take up these jobs received help with case management services, e.g., employment search, improving employability etc.
- Trial jobs — these were targeted at those with basic skills but without sufficient work experience to meet employer requirements. Employers agreed to provide on-the-job work experience and training in exchange for wage subsidy. Trial jobs were expected to lead to permanent employment.
- Community service jobs — those capable of holding these jobs received direct cash assistance;
- W2 Transitions — direct cash aid was given to those with mild disabilities but who still worked for at least 28 hours a week.

Thus individuals had to do something to qualify for aid under all of these tiers. Available aid schemes included those pertaining to food, medical care, childcare assistance to work or attend training, and job access loans. In the spirit of the work-oriented approach, doctors certifying cases of individuals with disabilities now had to attest to the level of capacity instead of the level of incapacity.

(v) To encourage work, the government had to be seen to support work. Thus childcare, health care and transport services were extended and expanded to the entire low income working population. The premise was that welfare recipients should not be treated better than the low income group; if the unemployed on welfare were treated better than the low income working group, there would be little incentive for welfare recipients to find work. Therefore services had to be expanded to help all those in the low-income group. This point struck a particular chord with the taskforce.

Administratively, W2 participants needed help that was provided by a range of government departments. To make the system work, co-ordination was thus required; each W2 participant had a financial and employment planner who would help the participant determine his eligibility, provide employment services etc. All these services were put under the Department of Workforce Development, not Welfare. The taskforce also noted the role of the private sector in administering the program. Private sector for-profit or not-for-profit organizations were invited by the state government to compete with government departments to provide these services. Those that ran job centers operated with very clear KPIs (key performance indicators); they were paid by the state according to certain criteria, e.g., length of placement.

New York and Wisconsin had similar models. The taskforce noted that the New York "America Works' model was even more performance driven — providers were given a payment for the caseload and then a performance component, which was measured by indicators like job retention and wage gains. In the New York model, it was found that it cost the state about US$5,000 to place a person into a job whereas maintaining them on welfare cost US$15,000. Such a work-based system was thus compelling.

6.7.3 *Evaluating Practices and Adapting them to the Local Context*

Adaptation is defined as the adjustment of a system to external conditions.[45] In the current context, we also take adaptation to mean the tailoring of an external system to local conditions. The Singapore public sector has been keenly aware of Singapore's context and has always worked on the basis of the need to adapt any policy to local conditions. While Singapore has always sought to learn from the experience of others, it has not transplanted policies and initiatives wholesale. Integration of successful practices elsewhere into the local context is the standard practice adopted by the Singapore public sector, which, in effect, helped to transcend the usual tendency of local search for solutions. This in turn contributed to the capability of the Singapore public sector to overcome path-dependence.

On their return, the taskforce talked through and evaluated the key findings of the programs they had seen and debated which features were applicable to Singapore and which could be adapted to the Singapore context. All the members agreed on the key principle that any cash support had to be based on work. However they understood that the contexts for the Wisconsin initiative and the one they were trying to craft for Singapore were very different. In Wisconsin, the motivation for moving to the work-based system was the widespread entitlement mentality, which had resulted in some 300,000 out of a population of 5 million on welfare. Singapore did not have a big welfare bill so no case could be made based on this argument. In addition, most Singaporeans did not have an entitlement mentality and there was no significant problem with the work ethic. So how did they make the case to move to a work-based system of assistance?

The taskforce took a leaf from the experience in Hong Kong which they also visited. It brought home to them what the consequences could be if a firm work-based philosophy was not established right from the start. The British had left behind a system of welfare entitlements and the Hong Kong administration was trying to make the system

---

[45] Miner, Bassoff and Moorman (2001).

more conditional on work but found the entitlement mentality hard to reverse. Thus even though an entitlement mentality had not yet taken root in Singapore, the taskforce believed it was important to make a stand at that point, while addressing the problems of the low income. So the case for the work-based system was made based on the need to reinforce the work ethic of future generations.

While the taskforce believed that there were merits to private sector provision for these sorts of services, they felt they need not push for it at that point because there already existed the network of Community Development Councils (CDCs), the purpose of which was to disburse financial and social aid to citizens. A number of existing programs could also be rationalized to fit into the new framework. So the taskforce recommended that scheme be administered by the Workforce Development Agency under the MOM, which in turn would pay the CDCs to run work placement activities.

There was a lengthy debate within the taskforce over the definition of work and whether to include community service-type jobs in the scheme. W2 had included community-based jobs based on the belief that even community service job participants would get to understand what having a job entailed and benefit from the experience. However in Singapore, the few community service type jobs available were usually filled by foreign workers. So the taskforce decided that if the objective was to encourage people to work, it would be real work which paid market wages. The community service element was left out.

Another element that was cut after discussion was that relating to single mothers. In the W2, single mothers were mandated to go back to work after their maternity leave and the state would help with childcare. While the taskforce also wanted to emphasize that single mothers in Singapore should also go back to work, after some debate, the members agreed that this element would be too radical in Singapore's current context, given the lack of social consensus with respect to the extent of societal acknowledgment of the plight of single mothers. Moreover pushing this aspect might have sent the signal that the government thought that state care was better for babies than their mothers — a stand the government was not ready to take.

The taskforce found there was relatively little emphasis on training in the W2 — the focus was on placement. In Singapore, the opposite was true — the focus was on training with perhaps less attention on placement. The W2 philosophy was that once a person was in a job, he would be better able to see the meaning in training. While the taskforce acknowledged the merit in this argument, it also noted the key differences between the target groups of the W2 and in Singapore. The W2 target group was the younger age group with a negative attitude whilst the target in Singapore were the over-40s with a skills gap. So some differences in the approach to training were necessary. But nonetheless, there has been a shift from the train-and-place to a place-and-train approach.

To demonstrate the support for work, the taskforce also recommended the extension of the range of support services to families of low wage workers. They examined the drop-out rate in the schools and came to the conclusion that better kindergarten and preschool education would make a difference. The taskforce thus recommended enhanced financial assistance to children from vulnerable families to help ensure that they had access to and completed their education. They also recommended an expansion of vocational training to help youth acquire skills that increased their employability.

The taskforce made their recommendations and completed their report in mid-2005, at about the same time the Ministerial Committee on Low Wage Workers was appointed by the Prime Minister, with Minister for Manpower Ng Eng Hen as Chairman. The final package, named Workfare, was unveiled during Budget 2006 and incorporated all the key elements put forward by the taskforce. A workfare bonus provided income support for those aged 40 and above earning less than S$1,500 per month and distributed in mid-2006 benefiting about 330,000 workers. MCYS put in place a new Work Support program. Higher childcare and student care subsidies were provided. MOE and ITE enhanced and upgraded the program at the Vocational Training Centre to customise it to students' learning styles, and help equip them with relevant skills for life-long learning. An additional housing grant of S$20,000 was given to low-income families.

More study was conducted into the labor market effects of wage supplementation. In November 2006, the Prime Minister announced that Workfare would be formalized as part of the permanent support structure to help the needy and low-wage workers, and a major plank would be the Workfare Income Supplement (WIS) scheme.

The WIS scheme was officially unveiled in Budget 2007 on 15 February 2007. It was acknowledged as a major policy change as it would be the first time the state would be supplementing the market wages received by low-income workers. The WIS will be given to low-income workers who have worked at least three months in any six-month period in a calendar year, or at least six months in a calendar year. The income supplement would not be fully in cash but would be split between cash and Central Provident Fund top-ups in the ratio 1:2.5. The eligible group for WIS was expanded to those aged 35 and above earning less than S$1,500 but those aged 45 and above with less than S$1,000 a month would get the largest supplement.

6.7.4 Adaptation Process for An Emerging Issue

The policy design and implementation regarding the issue of the working poor showed in some detail how the public sector learned and adapted principles and practices that worked in other countries to fit the unique values and conditions in the Singapore context. The pattern of adaptation process is summarized below:

(i)   *Sensing and perceiving: The initial perception of the need arose from actual experience from an examination of data*

The issue was surfaced by grassroots organizations and MCYS, a ministry whose mission it is to care for and develop communities. The given role of MCYS enabled the perception of the issue from the experience and data collected as part of the normal course of work. The MOF's role in leading the study team is interesting as it required them to share similar social values, to be able to perceive how the previous policy stance aimed at avoiding a welfare mentality was no longer adequate, and to view the impact of this issue on the long-term aspirations of the nation. The ability to sense the issue and to

initiate the study was helped by an earlier public sector exercise that
identified the need to raise aspirations by positioning Singapore as
Opportunity[46], and by the new Prime Minister's public articulation in
his opening of Parliament in 2005. The adoption of this perspective of
Singapore's future allowed a re-perception of a perennial issue when
it was again surfaced.

*(ii)   Interpreting the data and defining the problem involved analysis of the
long-term trends and patterns, which the problem groups were, and
how the problem had come about*

The sensing of the need and its importance initiated the study to
understand the issues more deeply and to search for ideas and
solutions. The situation was reassessed from a new perspective and
the new analysis then pointed to the need that some sort of solution be
found. It can be seen that the taskforce did not have any preconceived
idea of what exactly the solution was. It was guided only by a set of
imprinted values and principles — to set up some sort of operating
framework to prevent a slide into welfare and the entrenchment of an
entitlement mentality. The tension between these concerns and how
Singapore could be viewed as a land of opportunity for this group of
low-income citizens that seemed trapped in a poverty cycle made the
team realize the need to search for ideas and learn how others had
dealt with similar issues.

*(iii)   Search and discovering: The search process was open and fluid, as the
team sought to identify other working models and to learn directly
from the actual experience of others*

In their search, the team looked at models and systems that had been
successful, as well as others that had been less so, on the basis that
success and failure both held important lessons. Their objective was
to see what could be adapted to Singapore's context, not to port over
solutions or systems wholesale. They therefore looked not only at the

---

[46] Lim Siong Guan (2005). "Is There a New Role for Government?" *Ethos,* Civil Service
College, January–March.

details of the specific practices, but also why they were designed the way they were, the implementation process and the intended and unintended consequences experienced. The team studied available documents and went on field visits to understand the practices first-hand and interacted with the people who developed and implemented the systems so that they could glean tacit knowledge not articulated in the documents.

(iv) *Interpreting, deciding and adapting: The process of interpreting and deciding what to adapt was based on a process of dialog, debate and discussion*

The taskforce was mindful that the group that needed assistance in Singapore — older, lower-income, lower-skilled workers — was different from the target groups of Wisconsin Works and other schemes which were predominantly single mothers and younger workers. The process of adaptation took this difference into account. Members of the taskforce, and later their supervisors, examined which elements were "us" and which were "not us," and decided what to include or what not to include accordingly. The decision on which elements to include and which not to, was based largely on judgment and an understanding of Singapore's particular context, societal values and norms. Existing systems and structures were used wherever possible, e.g., the Workforce Development Agency and the CDC framework, and new structures were created if it seemed appropriate, e.g., the financial employment manager. A phased approach was adopted: the extent to which the private sector should be involved was left open (to be taken up again at a later time); but at the same time, CDCs were given targets in their placement activities, in a bid to enhance the performance component. To cater to Singaporeans' aspiration to own homes and be consistent with the overall policy to encourage home ownership, an element relating to helping low-wage workers own their apartments — through the provision of a housing grant — was later included.

The adaptation process went beyond adjusting an external system to suit internal conditions. This initiative also saw an adaptation of the framing of the problem. Because the very idea of welfare had long been anathema in Singapore, the problem had become one of how to give assistance without undermining this anti-welfare, pro-work ethos of Singapore society. The reframing of the context of the assistance — from welfare to Workfare — provided an acceptable alternative framework to what otherwise remained for all intents and purposes, public assistance to low-income households.

(v) *Negotiating and adjusting: Even with framing the issue as workfare rather than welfare, negotiating and adjusting were still needed to address concerns over costs by policy-makers with a strong imprint of financial prudence*

Sending a signal that the state valued work and would provide social support for work based on the W2 model would be a costly affair. Singapore's welfare bill at the time was not big so there was some initial resistance to the perceived need to make the switch to a workfare approach at the time. The counter-argument was it was necessary to make a stand before the situation worsened: Workfare was a necessary pre-emptive move. And because the workfare bonus was a signal to encourage work, it made sense for the workfare system to be a long-term one. However there was resistance to this. So in the end, a compromise was reached — the Workfare bonus would be given, in the first instance, for two years.

(vi) *Announcing, adapting and implementing: For a new initiative, adaptation was a continuous iterative process of receiving feedback, perceiving the potential impact and refining the system so that intended results may be realized*

The Workfare Bonus and the strategies to help vulnerable workers were announced in Budget 2006. The bonus was contingent upon the worker having worked for at least six continuous months in the preceding year. Feedback from the community indicated that some workers could not meet the continuous employment condition due to the nature of their jobs, e.g., odd-job workers. Based on this feedback, the Workfare criterion was revised: workers who had worked a total of at least six months in the preceding year would be eligible.

This particular initiative is an example of the public sector perceiving, anticipating and thinking ahead, surfacing and identifying the problem, and working with the political leadership in the crafting of the solution. The process of adaptation rested upon tacit knowledge among public sector leaders and though not explicitly articulated, had become common practice in dealing with emerging issues. It is a process that has similarities to sense making in organizations,[47] which involves perceiving and placing emerging issues within a new perspective, comprehending their significance, constructing meaning from analyzing the data, and interpreting the patterns to develop understanding. The intervention to sense an emerging issue is often grounded in the establishment and maintenance of an organization's identity, in this case, the role of MCYS in caring for and building communities, and MOF in making "Singapore as Opportunity" real for all. The issue was acted upon by MCYS and MOF when they determined that it was important to pay attention to it. The inclusion of MOM was important as the issue was reframed as workfare, since long-term employment and employability was a central mission of the MOM.

The WIS announced in Budget 2007 took the adaptation and refining process even further: while those over 45 years of age and with income of less than S$1,000 would get the most assistance, the eligible age was lowered from 40 to 35 years and the income eligibility criterion raised from S$1,200 to S$1,500. Payouts would be made twice a year and those who had worked for three months in any six-month calendar period would now also be eligible.

This graduated payout structure and other adjustments were in response to the feedback on the previous year's experiment with the Workfare Bonus. Policy-makers were wary of breeding a dependency mindset, even though these payouts were contingent upon work. While the Bonus payouts in 2006 did not require applicants to furnish supporting evidence of employment, only those workers who contributed to CPF and to their Medisave accounts would receive a

---

[47] Karl E Weick (1995). *Sense Making in Organizations*. CA: Sage Publications Inc.

WIS payout. Unlike the Workfare bonuses of 2006 which were paid in cash directly into workers' bank accounts, the WIS payouts would be split between cash and CPF, with the ratio 1: 2.5; 70 per cent of WIS payouts would go into workers' CPF accounts. The framework and proposed workings of the WIS package reflected the long-standing principles of governance — the emphasis on self-reliance and saving for the future — by requiring workers' contributions to CPF and Medisave. In response to concerns that the mandatory CPF contribution requirement, and the high proportion of the WIS being paid to workers' CPF accounts instead of directly in cash might deter many, particularly those in the informal sector or who were self-employed from signing up for the WIS, policy-makers conceded this possibility and undertook to monitor, review, adjust and refine the process and requirements as necessary. It was thus acknowledged that adaptation and continual adjustment would very likely be needed.

The institutionalization of the Workfare Income Supplement reflected the deep-seated sense of pragmatism, a realization that abiding by long-held assumptions about the unacceptability of state-supplemented assistance was no longer tenable, that the status quo was not acceptable and that definitive state action was necessary to prevent a widening income gap and preserve social cohesion. Even though it had been announced in 2006 that the Workfare bonus would be a two-year experiment, the fact that it was institutionalized after just one year was a recognition that the problem of structurally displaced low-income older workers was one that demanded a timely, permanent and structural response.

The main expressions of dynamic governance are policy execution and policy adaptation. Chapters 5 and 6 have shown how the Singapore public service has been able to achieve both. They are also the continuing challenges going forward, as articulated by head of civil service Peter Ho:

> "The hallmarks of the civil service remain those of pragmatism, seeing opportunity in challenge and excellence in implementation and delivery. These attitudes are deeply imprinted in the DNA of the civil service. What

is important is that in the early days, it was quite easy to pluck the low-hanging fruits. The guts and gumptions may still be there but most of the low-hanging fruits have already been plucked. I think you need policy innovators, you need policy implementers. Both need to exist in the civil service.

The brave new world is one full of uncertainty and risks. The solution? Have a sensible approach that anticipates, reduces and tries to manage risk, but is not paralyzed into inaction by it... the biggest mistake we could make in the civil service is the sin of inaction because we fear failure and we fear risk. Rather than a command and control structure which presumes that hierarchical superiors have the total picture, 'search and discover' may be a better modus operandi, as this allows for acting in the absence of complete information."[48]

---

[48] Chua Mui Hoong's interview with Peter Ho reported in *The Straits Times* on 17 November 2006, "Wanted in Public Service: Guts, Gumption and Risk Taking."

7

People Development: Recruiting, Renewing and Retaining Leaders

Singapore's ability to bring about changes in policy paths arises from a relentless pursuit for improvement and a constant drive to learn, adapt and innovate. The mode and method of adaptation are dependent on the nature and urgency of the issue, resulting in a multitude of learning and adaptation processes. In some cases public sector leaders thought ahead and enacted policies in anticipation of the future. In others, policy-makers re-examined existing policies and assumptions for their appropriateness and adequacy in light of changed circumstances. In many of these instances, the common practice was to scrutinize the practices of other countries and assess the relevance of their experiences for Singapore. The abilities of the public sector to think ahead and anticipate, to think again existing policies and to think across to extrapolate and interpolate lessons from different contexts are central to dynamic governance. These capacities for change largely come from people, especially the leaders, in the public sector. Only people have the innate capacity to think, to rethink, to feel, to make choices and to develop the personal and organizational capabilities to change. Able people in leadership are shown in the dynamic governance framework in Figure 1.1 of Chapter 1 as the main drivers of dynamic thinking, policy adaptation and execution. Recruiting, renewing and retaining able people especially those in leadership are the heartbeats of developing dynamic governance capabilities.

7.1 Framework for Managing People for Dynamic Governance

Dynamic capabilities embody the ability to change as circumstances warrant, and the ability to make judgment and choices premised on certain unchanging values and beliefs despite the circumstances. The

Singapore public sector used many different ways to learn and adapt, each choice reflecting the judgment of those involved in the process. It is clear that these dynamic governance capabilities reside first and foremost in the organization's human capital. Of all the factor inputs that go into the making of an organization, only people have the ability to make independent decisions and effect choices. All the other inputs, instituted processes, systems and structures are the result of leadership decisions and choices. People are the main drivers behind the development of any organizational capability — only people have the ability to think independently, to decide to act and change, to overcome constraints. That Singapore overcame its geographical and physical constraints at independence to create livelihood for its two million people was the result of the decisions and choices made by her founding political leaders. The fact that it was subsequently able to continue to survive in a changing global environment is testimony to the astuteness of her leaders in taking the right, if not always, popular decisions at each stage. As Lee Kuan Yew stated succinctly in an interview, "Singapore is man-made."[1] Whether or not there is dynamic governance depends on people, especially the leaders.

An organization's leaders are thus the most important determinant of dynamic capabilities. Leaders' decisions and choices affect the other two determinants of dynamic change capabilities, the paths that will be taken by the organization and the design of organizational processes that in turn affect the potential reconfiguration of resources. It is the interaction of all three factors that enable transformational change. Dynamic capabilities in people are developed by how an organization recruits the needed talent from the marketplace, how it continuously renews the skills and knowledge of its people, and how it retains and deploys the crucial expertise for creating and implementing its strategies. Figure 7.1 shows the overall framework of the public sector human capital management system comprising the philosophy, policies and practices that govern its approach.

---

[1] Interview of Lee Kuan Yew by the *New York Times* on 3 August 1995, cited in Usha CV Haley, Linda Low and Toh Mun-Heng (1996). "Singapore Incorporated: Reinterpreting Singapore's Business Environments Through A Corporate Metaphor," *Management Decision*, Vol. 34, No. 9, pp. 17–28.

Figure 7.1. People as Key to Dynamic Governance

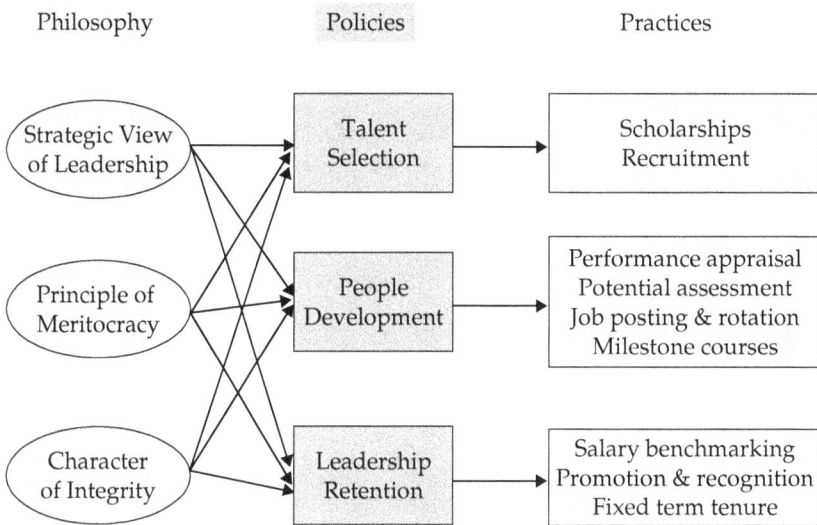

Philosophy	Policies	Practices

Strategic View of Leadership	Talent Selection	Scholarships Recruitment
Principle of Meritocracy	People Development	Performance appraisal Potential assessment Job posting & rotation Milestone courses
Character of Integrity	Leadership Retention	Salary benchmarking Promotion & recognition Fixed term tenure

The people management philosophy in the Singapore public sector is underpinned by strong beliefs in:

(i) the strategic importance and crucial role of talent and leadership for good governance,

(ii) meritocracy as the basis for their selection, deployment, promotion and retention, and

(iii) a fundamental requirement that leaders have to be people of integrity and honesty.

These core beliefs are manifested in signature practices in the selection, development and retention of leaders: recruiting based on academic performance, the extensive use of scholarships with bonds, assessing both performance and potential, developing potential leaders through job rotations and milestone programs, and retaining leaders through market-based salary benchmarks, promotion and recognition, and fixed-term tenures. This chapter describes how the public sector people management system emerged from its historical roots in the British colonial administration, its core principles, policies and practices and some lessons that we can learn and apply from the emergence, evolution and embedding of these principles, policies and practices.

7.2 The Public Sector People Management Philosophy

In Chapter 4, we explained how integrity and meritocracy were instituted as fundamental principles governing Singapore society. Integrity and honesty are basic character values required of public leaders. There is no tolerance for a lack of honesty in public leadership. The founding political leaders believed that no degree of competence or contribution could compensate for a lack of honesty in public office. Without a character of integrity, capable leaders could easily direct resources to self-serving ventures rather than serve the nation, and would ultimately destroy a society. Beyond assessing for an individual's dynamism, vision and competence, it was deemed important to appraise "… his character and motivation, because the smarter a man is, the more harm he will do society."[2] With limited human resources, it was imperative that the available talent be put to the best possible use.

Lee Kuan Yew had a strategic view of leadership — he was convinced that the good people lay at the heart of good government. Getting the best and the brightest to serve in government was an issue that preoccupied him:

> "Can you have a good government without good men in charge of government? American liberals believe you can… My experience in Asia has led me to a different conclusion. To get good government, you must have good men in charge of government. I have observed in the last 40 years that even with a poor system of government, but with good strong men in charge, people get passable government with decent progress."[3]

[2] Speech by Lee Kuan Yew during the debate on the White Paper on ministerial salaries on 1 November 1994, reproduced in Han Fook Kwang, Warren Fernandez and Sumiko Tan (1998). *Lee Kuan Yew: The Man and His Ideas*. Times Editions.
[3] Speech in Parliament on the White Paper on Ministerial Salaries, 1 November 1994, reproduced in ibid, pp. 331–342.

For Lee, the starting point for good government was to ensure a constant supply of good people with ability, integrity and commitment into the public sector. His strategic thinking was reflected clearly in an impassioned speech to senior civil servants immediately after independence in 1965:

> "Every year, we are going to take the best in. I am tired of having first-class honours graduates coming out, doing a bit of dabbling in the Attorney-General's chambers... They get a bit of money, then they learn a bit of law and learn how to practice and after three years, they go out to private practice, leaving the second-class honours man... The second-class honours man goes to court to prosecute a case and the man defending is a first-class honours man. Now if the law of evidence is loaded against the prosecution plus brains of the defendant being loaded against the prosecution, then thieves, rogues and vagabonds get away. That is not my idea of good government... I don't want second-raters and the third-raters in and first-class men outfighting us, because that is a stupid way of running the country. I want first-class men prosecuting... I have watched all this and this will not do... I want them inside — better than those outside. That way, this place will hum. And I want those who believe that joining the government service means automatically you are going to go up the ladder, to forget it. Not with this government."[4]

While Lee's management practice was to put the best person to the most important task, it was Goh Keng Swee who put in place the merit-based structure of advancement in the public sector. Goh was an economist, an academically brilliant man widely acknowledged as Singapore's economic architect — the man who established

---

[4] Speech to senior civil servants at the Victoria Theatre on 20 September 1965, reproduced in ibid, pp. 321–323.

Singapore's fundamental principles of economic governance. It is less widely known that the public sector's meritocratic and performance-based system of talent recruitment, retention and promotion was installed largely by Goh.

The approach to leadership development consisted largely of three overarching principles: get the best people into the public sector, give them challenging work and pay them well. Economic uncertainty at the time of independence elevated the status and prospects of a government job which helped encourage the best brains to enter the public sector. There was less appreciation of the need to help public sector personnel develop skills and competencies to enable them to better carry out their jobs or for the need to create an environment to retain good people. Two factors in the late 1980s and early 1990s forced the public sector to re-examine its approach: the first was the coming of age of a younger generation with higher demands and different aspirations, and who viewed a career in the public sector as just one of a myriad of employment opportunities open to them; the second was the increasing complexity of issues arising from the rapid pace of change which in turn changed the demands on public sector leaders. The move to a more integrated and coherent personnel management policy began in the early 1980s and gathered pace throughout the 1990s. The rest of this chapter focuses on how the strategic view of leadership and principle of meritocracy are expressed in policies and practices that develop the people and leadership capacity for effective and dynamic governance.

7.3 Evolution of Public Sector Personnel Management System

In 1955, Singapore's constitutional status was transformed from a crown colony to that of a ministerial form of government under the structure recommended by the Rendel Constitution.[5] The reorgani-

---

[5] In 1953, Sir George Rendel was appointed to chair a commission to devise a new political and constitutional structure to enable Singapore to function as a self-contained and autonomous unit. The structure recommended by the Commission became known as the Rendel Constitution. Lee Boon Hiok (1989). "The Bureaucracy," in Kernial Singh Sandhu and Lim Chong Yah (eds.). *Management of Success: The Moulding of Modern Singapore*. Singapore: Institute of Southeast Asian Studies, pp. 90–101.

zation of the government departments into ministries formed the basis of the new Civil Service structure and redefined the relationship between civil servants and ministers. A key development was the creation of the position of permanent secretary (PS). The PS was to be responsible for the day-to-day administration of the ministry, for the formulation of policy recommendations for the minister's consideration and for ensuring that the decision of the Minister was put into effect.[6]

This separation of the executive and administrative branches of government created much uncertainty and resentment among serving civil servants who had operated as both the administrative and political masters of colonial Singapore. The uneasy relationship resulted in a rising tension between the political and the administrative arms of government. With the achievement of self-government in 1959, the newly elected People's Action Party established the Political Study Centre in 1961 to reorientate the mindsets and values of civil servants, to make them more aware of the new developments in Singapore and the rest of Asia, and to socialize them to the requirements of building a new society. Then Prime Minister Lee said at the opening of the center:

> "You and I have a vested interest in the survival of the democratic state. We the elected ministers have to work through you and with you to translate our plan and policies into reality. You should give of your best in the service of the people. Whatever your views on socialism, capitalism, liberalism, communism, whether they be progressive or conservative, your task and mine for the next five years are exactly the same... It is in our interest to show that under the system of 'one-man-one-vote' there can be an honest and efficient government which works through an efficient administration in the interests of the people. If we do not do our best, then we have only ourselves to blame when the people lose faith, not just in

---

[6] Ibid, p. 92.

you, the public service, and in us, the democratic political
leadership, but also in the democratic system of which
you and I are working parts."[7]

Many who could not accept the changed conditions resigned.
While the resignations resulted in a serious depletion of expertise
across all ranks, particularly the senior ranks, the relatively clean slate
paved the way for the development of a new, politically sensitive
but neutral public sector, one whose vision and values were closely
identified to those of the ruling PAP, yet not belonging to any political
party. It opened the promotion doors for young officers and provided
the government with an opportunity to put in place a structure of
advancement, which was based on merit rather than on seniority, a
legacy that continues until today — the public sector today is openly
meritocratic where advancement and remuneration are performance-
driven.

The public sector personnel structure is based on the
recommendations of the Trusted Commission in 1947, which devised
a system based on four separate divisions, organized according to
skills, education and responsibilities.[8] The profile of the civil service
by divisional status is shown in Table 7.1.

Entry into Division One is open only to graduate officers. It
comprises the Administrative Service, where its officers focus on
national policy-making, and officers in the professional services.
Grades in Division One are divided into timescale and superscale
officers, with permanent secretaries and deputy secretaries making up
about half of the latter group. The increasing quality of public sector
manpower is reflected in the steep increase in the number of graduate
officers. From comprising just 5 per cent in 1970, they rose to form 50
per cent of the manpower strength by 2006.

---

[7] Speech by Lee Kuan Yew at the opening of the Civil Service Political Study Centre on
August 15, 1959, from Han, Fernandez and Tan (1998).

[8] Seah Chee Meow (1985). "The Civil Service," in Jon Quah et al. (eds.), *Government and
Politics in Singapore*. Singapore: Oxford University Press.

Table 7.1. Civil Service Strength by Divisional Status 1970–2006

Year	Division I		Division II		Division III		Division IV		Total
	No.	%	No.	%	No.	%	No.	%	No.
1970	2,873	5.3	14,808	27.3	16,076	29.7	20,438	37.7	54,195
1975	4,415	7.5	17,542	29.8	20,277	34.5	16,543	28.2	58,777
1980	7,796	11.0	23,051	32.4	24,892	35.0	15,342	21.6	71,081
1985	10,158	14.6	22,915	32.9	22,369	32.1	14,188	20.4	69,630
1990	12,348	19.5	21,095	33.3	20,150	31.8	9,799	15.4	63,392
1995	16,654	28.3	18,081	30.7	17,426	29.6	6,715	10.6	58,876
2000	24,400	38.5	18,939	29.9	14,993	23.7	4,984	7.9	63,316
2004	28,638	46.6	16,086	27.0	12,250	19.9	4,020	6.5	61,516
2006	32,412	50.2	16,668	25.8	11,582	17.9	3,875	6.0	64,537

Figures cover only manpower in ministries, government department and organs of state and not the statutory boards. *Source*: Public Service Division.

7.3.1 *Centralization of People Management Functions before 1995*

The early personnel management system was highly procedural in orientation. Recruitment of all public sector personnel in the ministries was carried out centrally via the Public Service Commission (PSC). The PSC was set up on 1 January 1951 as the agency "to meet the staffing requirements of the Government in accordance with the merit principle"[9] in the recruitment, selection, appointment, compensation, training, promotion, performance evaluation and disciplinary control of all civil servants. The PSC was responsible for all confirmations, emplacements, promotions, transfers, dismissals and discipline of all public officers within the civil service. It also administered and awarded top-tier undergraduate scholarships, which was and continues to be the public sector's main recruitment channel for administrative officers.

The role of the PSC to ensure the separation of the administrative and the political branches of government was enforced largely through

---

[9] Republic of Singapore (1984). *The Budget for the Financial Year 1984/85*, Singapore National Printers, as cited in Jon ST Quah (1984). "The Public Bureaucracy in Singapore 1059-1984," in You and Lim (eds.), p. 301.

the composition of the commission. Its members, appointed by the President on the recommendation of the Prime Minister cannot be current or past political office holders, or current civil servants. Andrew Chew, the current Chairman, was appointed to PSC only after a 5-year cooling off period after the end of his term as Head, Civil Service. Many of the PSC members have been and continue to be from the private sector, retired captains of industry and heads of large organizations — individuals with long careers and extensive experience in assessing character, capabilities and performance. This separate mechanism effectively prevented the practice of political appointments endemic in many developing countries, helped preserve the impartiality of the service and reinforced the separation of the executive/political and administrative branches of government.

However the degree of centralization created many problems, exacerbated by the diffusion of personnel management functions across agencies. Before 1972, public sector personnel management functions were divided between the PSC and the Establishment Division of the Ministry of Finance, which was responsible for all civil service personnel matters not handled by the PSC. Between 1972 and 1980, the Personnel Administration Branch (PAB) of the Budget Division of the Ministry of Finance took care of job classification and terms and conditions of service, while the Establishment Unit of PMO dealt with career development and training of Division 1 officers, a function, which they handed over to PSC in April 1981. It was a highly convoluted system which, not surprisingly, resulted in overlapping responsibilities, divided policy direction, and uncertainty and confusion for public servants. A centralized system had reduced the responsiveness of the system to changing circumstances in terms of its ability to recruit and promote officers at a pace sufficient to keep up with changing needs and demands. It also resulted in a lack of agency ownership, with personnel management being seen as a compliance with rules instead of the management of people. This created a disjoint in agencies, which were accountable for results but had little control over people hiring.

1982 saw the beginning of a more systematic approach to the development of civil servants. Strong economic growth had created an open market for talent and against this backdrop, the government recognized a need to ensure that those recruited found their jobs satisfying, and that a more coherent approach to personnel management was needed to attract, motivate and retain talented staff. That year marked the start of a new employee-centered personnel management approach, particularly in recruitment, training, career development, job matching and succession planning. A new agency, the Public Service Division (PSD), was formed to be responsible for formulating and reviewing all personnel policies in the public sector and to ensure that such policies would be consistently implemented. With the set-up of the PSD, the role of the PSC was refocused towards ensuring impartiality in the appointment, promotion and disciplinary control of civil servants.

But the problems remained. PM Lee Hsien Loong, who became Deputy Prime Minister in 1990 under Goh Chok Tong and concurrently Minister-in-charge of the Civil Service recalls:

"We were struggling with the civil service for many years. It was different from the private sector. The civil service was rule bound. We had fixed annual increments, salaries that were tied more to seniority and internal relativities between services than to the officer's performance or market benchmarks, a personnel system overly centralised in the Public Service Commission ... We found it a very difficult system to work."[10]

A two-pronged approach was taken to address the problem — the first was "cutting off pieces from the system" — converting government departments into statutory boards or corporatizing them outright where it was viable — and the second, overhauling the system.

The first prong involved spinning off entities from the civil service, either by corporatizing them or converting them into statutory boards. For example, Singapore Telecommunications (SingTel) was spun off

[10] Authors' interview with PM Lee Hsien Loong on 17 January 2007.

from the Telecommunication Authority of Singapore into a full-fledged corporate telecoms entity in April 1992 and was publicly listed the following year. Similarly, the Inland Revenue Department (IRD) was reconstituted into a statutory board, the Inland Revenue Authority of Singapore, in September 1992. The problems that bedeviled the IRD were symptomatic of the malaise of the civil service at that time:

> "IRD could not offer competitive salaries, could not fill their estab (establishment) posts. They lost many good people. MOF (Ministry of Finance) wanted IRD to computerize, but IRD could not. We just could not get anywhere… it was messed up. IRD became a statutory board IRAS when Koh Yong Guan became Commissioner and he was prepared to make the system work… It was quite controversial but we overrode objections and made it happen…"[11]

While this approach alleviated the situation, it did not address the core problems of a centralized, uncompetitive system and a severe misalignment in people management responsibilities. The system clearly needed overhauling:

> "… the salaries were not competitive. We argued that tenure and the iron rice bowl made up for this. But the revealed preference of the better officers was that they were not valuing their tenure or their pensions — we were so uncompetitive they were leaving… Ministries had little influence over the promotion and advancement of their own people. Personnel management was over-centralized, under the PSC … The question was how to break that mould without affecting the objectives for which we originally set up the PSC system."[12]

---

[11] Ibid.

[12] Ibid.

Because of internal resistance and a fear of negating the key role of the PSC, a tentative — what PM Lee termed "half-hearted" step at overhauling the system was taken in the late 1980s. Aimed at increasing the level of ownership for the two largest branches of the civil service, the Education Service and the Uniformed Services Sub-commissions were formed under the PSC, chaired by its Deputy Chairman. But because consideration and evaluation of promotion remained centralized in the sub-commissions, officers were considered for promotion only once every three years to enable the sub-commissions to cope with the interviews! It became clear that the problems could be solved only if the "mold was smashed" which took place with devolution in 1995.

7.3.2 Devolution of People Management Functions in 1995

1995 saw the devolution of powers and responsibilities for personnel management from the PSC to the ministries to enable PSs and line managers to recruit and promote deserving officers. While most levels of public sector recruitment were devolved to the individual agencies, the PSC remained responsible for all appointments to the Administrative Service, as well as the highest levels of appointment, e.g., as PS or CEO of statutory boards. Different functions were devolved to different extents but discipline control was retained with PSC. The responsibility for recruitment was devolved the most, to give immediate superiors greater say in recruiting the skills and people they needed. Promotion was devolved to a more limited extent as there were equity and morale issues involved. Promotion for the rest of the grades shifted to the various Personnel Boards. However, even with personnel boards, individual ministries' recommendations for promotion of their own staff were still constrained to an extent by the need to maintain some parity with other ministries within the same personnel board cluster.

With devolution, the PSD took over the management of the careers of Administrative Officers (AOs), coordinating the deployment of AOs to key posts in ministries and statutory boards, ensuring that

Table 7.2. Personnel Management Structure under Devolution

Structure	Jurisdiction
Public Service Commission (PSC)	Officers in Superscale D and above (e.g., Permanent Secretaries, heads of large divisions and departments)
	Revised role • Recruitment into the Administrative Service and Administrative Service (Foreign Service Branch) • Promotion of all officers to Superscale D and above • Award of undergraduate scholarships • Disciplinary cases • Appeals
	Chair: Andrew Chew Members: Members of the private sector All Appointments by President on advice of PM
Special Personnel Board	Superscale officers up to E1 and timescale officers in the Administrative Service (e.g., Senior Managers) Chair: Head, Civil Service Members: PS, PMO, three other senior PSs
Senior Personnel Boards (6)	Division I officers (graduate officers) Each board oversees Division I officers in a group of ministries. Chair: Appointed PS Members: PS of the ministries covered by the board
Personnel Boards (24)	Division II, III, IV (non-graduate officers, e.g., supervisory, technical, clerical and secretarial staff) Each ministry has at least one Personnel Board Chair: Superscale officer of ministry Members: Division I officers Appointed by PS, PMO

Source: Information collated from Commonwealth Secretariat (1998). *Current Good Practices and New Developments in Public Service Management: A Profile of the Public Service of Singapore.* The Public Service Country Profile Series No. 8.

all had proper career paths and that key posts were filled with suitably qualified officers. This marked a turning point, the start of an integrated approach to management of key personnel in the civil service. Under the devolved authority model, the division of responsibility is shown in Table 7.2.

In addition to managing the careers of AOs, the PSD also continued to define the personnel framework for the public sector. There was still pressure for consistency, and thus central direction, in key personnel policies by virtue of the public sector being the single largest employer in the country. With devolution, ministries obtained fairly extensive autonomy in recruitment: they were now at liberty to offer salary packages that recognized candidates' special attributes or experience without needing PSD clearance except when the proposed package was way beyond the guidelines. Statutory boards had an even greater degree of flexibility regarding pay, and were free to deviate from the central guidelines for annual leave. In performance appraisal, agencies were free to include other criteria in their own systems but they were not allowed to subtract from the criteria established by PSD. Nonetheless, the PSD continued to set the tone for the entire public sector for policies where there was a national objective and when the public sector needed to take the lead. Some of these included the medical benefits system, the flexible wage policy and the imperative to hire older workers.

Thus, public sector personnel management approaches and policies evolved and were refined over time, often in response to changing circumstances. It appears that the "harder" aspects of personnel management — the belief in hiring the best people and paying them well — were understood and implemented much earlier than "softer" aspects such as career planning, training and development. But one consistent theme that has underpinned the personnel management system has been the focus on the selection, recruitment, remuneration and development of the public sector leadership echelon, the Administrative Service.

7.4 The Public Sector Leadership: The Administrative Service

The Administrative Service is the apex of the civil service hierarchy. Administrative officers are the interface between the political leadership and the machinery of government. While the first generation political leadership saw the Administrative Service primarily as the executors of policies with responsibility for their successful implementation, the second generation leadership wanted the Administrative Service to "help the political leadership spot trends, meet needs, maintain standards and formulate and implement policies for the security and success of the country."[13]

> "Administrative Officers will remain the main interface between the political leaders and the machinery of government. Your responsibility is to provide Ministers with reliable, comprehensive data and analyses on which policy decisions will be based. You will also have to ensure that these decisions are properly, fairly and sensitively implemented. Policies and regulations which have served their purpose, should either be modified or discarded. As senior civil servants, you should take a proactive role in reviewing these policies and procedures."[14]

While AOs are part of the public sector graduate officer ranks, their identification, selection, promotion, development, salary scales and expectations of their performance and contributions are very different from the normal graduate officers. There are about 30,000 graduate officers with university degrees in the ministries alone, not counting the statutory boards. These officers are inducted into the professional services where they perform functional specialist work in their respective ministries or statutory boards. AOs on the other hand are policy experts in the general business of government, and therefore not attached permanently to any agency. They are instead rotated to various agencies through postings that constitute part of their development program. While professional officers are expected to contribute predominantly to their parent agencies, high potential AOs are groomed to take on public sector leadership positions and contribute to the formulation, implementation and review of policy at the national level. To this end, the development program for AOs is far more extensive and centrally structured than for graduate officers

---

[13] Speech by Prime Minister Goh Chok Tong at the Fifth Administrative Service Dinner at the Oriental Ballroom, Oriental Hotel, on Friday, 30 July 1993.

[14] Speech by Prime Minister Mr Goh Chok Tong at the Third Administrative Service Dinner at the Marina Mandarin Ballroom on Friday, 5 July 1991.

in the professional services, and their career progression is monitored more closely by PSD to ensure that high potential officers gain the breadth and depth of exposure to the various aspects of public sector work. Commensurate with the different performance expectations, the salary scales for AOs are higher than for graduate officers in the professional services.

Table 7.3 shows that AOs form less than half a percent of the total manpower strength, thus forming a highly elite group in the public service. Goh Keng Swee himself had been a member of the British colonial administration and he believed in the necessity of a highly elite bureaucracy:

> "In many countries, the top echelon civil servants constitute an important section of the intellectual elite of the country. And this *should* be so, for the task of governing a country is both complex and demanding."[15]

Goh placed a premium on intellectual ability and academic brilliance, rather than experience, and as such, he put in place the system where merit and performance became the key criteria for recruitment and retention.

Table 7.3. Administrative Service Strength 1980–2006

Year	Staff Strength
1980	221
1985	191
1990	191
1995	179
2000	181
2004	189
2005	181
2006	184

Figures do not include the Management Associates and Dual Career Officers. *Source*: Public Service Division.

---

[15] Ian Patrick Austin (2004). *Goh Keng Swee and Southeast Asian Governance*. Singapore: Marshall Cavendish, p. 24.

The emphasis on merit and academic brilliance is reflected in the profile of AOs. They are drawn from the top 1 per cent of each educational cohort and are selected based on the promise of high "helicopter quality."[16] Officers with the potential to make it to the Administrative Service are put under a rigorous training and assessment regime, given challenging opportunities, appear before ministers and work under the direct supervision of the permanent secretary. Only those officers with potential to make the higher echelon superscale grades are confirmed. The stringent requirements mean that usually less than 10 officers are selected each year for the Administrative Service but once confirmed, AOs are rotated across a wide range of jobs and work with many permanent secretaries to ensure that they are versatile, adaptable, able to learn and to produce effective results. Only AOs who live up to their potential become deputy secretaries and only the best become permanent secretaries.

So how has the public sector managed the officers of the Administrative Service? What are the key elements in the systems of recruitment, development, performance management and retention that have contributed to the continued effectiveness of the Administrative Service as leaders, agents of continued change and a dynamic public sector?

7.4.1 *Generating a Pool of Potential Leaders through Scholarships*

The vast majority of the officers in the Administrative Service are recruited through the public sector scholarship system. Scholarships are the tools to identify and groom talent for policy development and other key positions in agencies. Every year, the public sector, both centrally via the PSC and through the individual ministries or statutory boards, offer an array of prestigious scholarships to attract the cream of the GCE A-level examination cohort. Because the task of running the country was deemed "both complex and demanding", attracting

---

[16] Speech by Prime Minister Lee Kuan Yew at the First Administrative Service Dinner on Tuesday 19 December 1979 at Mandarin Hotel, Singapore.

the best and the brightest was thus imperative. Currently, 10.6 per cent of those who hold degrees in the ministries are scholarship holders, while the figure is 16 per cent in the statutory boards.[17]

The PSC began awarding scholarships for local and overseas study in 1961, based on candidates' A-level examination results and the PSC's assessment of their leadership potential. This process meant that only those who had excelled academically by the age of 18 had any chance of qualifying, and excluded those who were late bloomers. This selection at the age of 18 persists until today and possibly constrains the pool from which potential leaders are selected. In 2002, the PSC refocused its attention on the top tier scholarships and delegated second tier scholarships to the ministries. While scholarships offered by individual ministries and statutory boards are part of each individual agency's recruitment for their own staffing requirements, PSC scholarships are targeted at recruiting for critical public service functions and, in particular, for the Administrative Service.

There is no fixed number of scholarships offered each year. If there are more applicants who meet the PSC scholarship criteria, more scholarships may be offered. While there is no quota, projections of the number of future Deputy Secretary and Permanent Secretary positions that have to be filled, as well as the attrition rate, are taken into account. Nonetheless, the actual number of scholarships awarded is based on merit. Table 7.4 shows the number of scholarships offered every year since 2001. Scholars who are tied to specific schemes of service (e.g., teaching, foreign service, education) will be deployed to their respective parent ministries when they graduate. "Open" scholars are given a choice of ministry or statutory board postings but final postings depend also on service needs. The allocation of scholars since 2001 is set out in Table 7.5. Over the years, the PSC has widened the range of disciplines for which scholarships are applicable (Table 7.6). There is some leeway for scholars to choose disciplines of study to match their future career aspirations, but ultimately, PSC scholarships have to meet the needs of the civil service.

---

[17] *The Straits Times*, 15 February 2006, p. H4, "Parliament."

Table 7.4. Types and Numbers of Public Sector Scholarships

Types of Scholarships	2001	2002	2003	2004	2005	2006
Singapore Armed Forces Overseas Sch.	7 + 1*	5 + 1*	3 + 2*	5 + 2*	6 + 1*	3 + 2*
Singapore Police Force Overseas Sch.	3	3	2	2	3	1
Overseas Merit Scholarship (Open)	41 + 2*	30 + 3*	30 + 1*	11	21 + 1*	21
Overseas Merit Scholarship (Teaching)	6	7	6	7	5	3
Overseas Merit Scholarship (Legal)	-	1	2	2	2	3
Overseas Merit Sch. (Foreign Service)	2	1	2 + 1*	3	4	1*
Local/Overseas Merit Scholarship (Open)	6	1	-	1	1	1
Local/Overseas Merit Sch. (Teaching)	1	2	-	1	4	1
Local Merit Scholarchip (Open)	-	-	1*	1	1*	2 + 1*
SUB-TOTAL (TOP SCHOLARSHIPS)	69	54	50	34	49	39
Singapore Govt Scholarship (Open)	36	-	-	-	-	-
Singapore Govt Sch. (Teaching)/ Education Merit Scholarship.	20	14	12	18	17	18
Singapore Govt Sch. (Foreign Service)	4	3	1	2	4	7
Singapore Govt Sch. (Home Affairs Uniformed Services)	-	1	6	10	8	7
Singapore Govt Sch. (Ministry of Community Devt, Youth and Sports)	-	1	-	-	2	1
Local Merit Scholarship (Open)	20	-	-	-	-	-
Local Merit Scholarship (Teaching)	81	44	-	-	-	-
Min. of Educ. Teaching Sch. – Overseas	-	-	14	24	19	30
Min. of Education Teaching Sch. – Local	-	-	27	50	55	79
Local Merit Sch. – Accounting/ Auditing	4	-	-	-	-	1
Local Merit Sch. (Ministry of Community Devt, Youth and Sports)	1	2	-	1	1	2
Local Merit Sch. (Home Affairs Uniformed Services)	18	7	7	5	11	8
Overseas Study Award (Teaching)	-	5	-	-	-	-
Overseas Study Award (Paramedical)/ Health Science	-	17	11	15	19	27
SUB-TOTAL (OTHER SCHOLARSHIPS)	184	94	78	125	136	180
GRAND TOTAL	**253**	**148**	**128**	**159**	**185**	**219**

Source: Public Service Division, Prime Minister's Office (* are President Scholarships).

Table 7.5. Allocation of scholars to ministries and statutory boards

Year Deployed	Ministries	Statutory Boards	Research/Academia (e.g. A*STAR, Universities)	Total
2001	68	35	2	105
2002	83	15	3	101
2003	102	29	5	136
2004	98	15	12	125
2005	89	27	3	119
2006	69	11	2	82

Source: Public Service Division, Prime Minister's Office. At the time of publication, the 2006 deployment exercise has not been completed.

Table 7.6. Public Service Commission Scholarships: Disciplines of Study

Field of Study	2001	2002	2003	2004	2005	2006
Economics/Philosophy, Politics and Economics (PPE)	13	17	10	10	12	9
Engineering	27	13	8	9	8	7
Science	12	7	9	8	8	5
Other Humanities and Social Science	9	13	17	4	17	10
Law	3	3	3	3	3	5
Others (Accountancy, Applied Science, Architecture, Education, Medicine, etc)	5	1	3	0	1	3
Total	69	54	50	34	49	39

Source: Public Service Division, Prime Minister's Office.

7.4.2 *Selecting Potential Public Sector Leaders*

While scholars account for only 10 to 15 per cent of all graduate officers in the ministries and statutory boards, the majority of officers in the Administrative Service are scholars. The process for identifying AOs has evolved somewhat. Before 2002, returned PSC scholars were interviewed by the PSC to determine if they should be posted directly to the Administrative Service. This system was inadequate, with scholars being selected on the basis of one interview. In 2002, PSC scholars were recruited under the Management Associates Program (MAP), a career development program tailored to give scholars a management career track in the public sector upon their graduation, either in the Administrative Service or the professional services under the various ministries. This created another track for scholars and gave PSD more time and greater leeway to identify potential candidates for the Administrative Service. Under the MAP, scholars with second-class upper honors are posted to Ministries under two two-year postings during which time they work closely with senior staff and the PSs and receive training and development opportunities just like AOs. MAs with potential for the Administrative Service are surfaced via recommendations from the permanent secretaries and are then interviewed by the PSD. Alternatively, MAs can also opt to return to their parent ministries or join other ministries if they prefer. On average, around 10 AOs are recruited every year.[18]

What are the selection criteria into the Administrative Service? It is commonly believed that academic excellence is the overriding criterion. The public service acknowledges that while sterling academic credentials are necessary to gain entry into the Service, they do not guarantee attainment of leadership positions. It has been pointed out that there have been instances when officers with impressive academic qualifications did not make it to the top and those at the top did not always have the best academic results.[19] So while academic excellence was a necessary condition, it was not sufficient, as pointed out by Lee Kuan Yew:

> "Singapore must get some of its best in each year's crop of graduates into government. When I say best, I don't mean just academic results. His high O-levels, A-levels, university degree will only tell you his powers of analysis. That is only one-third of the helicopter quality. You've then got to assess him for his sense of reality, his imagination, his quality of leadership, his dynamism. But most of all,

---

[18] Singapore (1994). "Competitive Salaries for Competent & Honest Government: Benchmarks for Ministers and Senior Public Officers," Cmd. 13 of 1994.

[19] Eddie Teo (2003). "Can Public Servants be Leaders?" *Ethos*, September.

his character and motivation, because the smarter a man is, the more harm he will do society."[20]

While the candidates' values, performance and character determined whether they ultimately made it to the top of the public sector leadership ranks as deputy secretaries or permanent secretaries, excellent academic results were indeed necessary for entry. This merit-based selection and recruitment system attracted and surfaced individuals who were "technocrats" — individuals who were strong in analysis, reasoning and problem-solving, who could discern and challenge implicit and explicit assumptions, who were comfortable learning and assimilating information from many sources and adapting to suit the local context. In the early years of Singapore's development, not only did Singapore's manpower development programs emphasize the training of technical and engineering skills, scholarships and recruitment into the administrative service also favored the hard sciences and engineering. Most of the second generation public sector leaders were engineers by training, and they brought their hard sciences' perspectives to bear on policy-making. For instance, the officers who worked with Goh Keng Swee in the late 1970s to overhaul the education system were systems engineers. The predisposition for officers with these sorts of backgrounds and attributes buttressed the highly rational, analytical, problem-solving approach to policy-making displayed by the first generation of political and public sector leaders. The systems approach, which translates into what can be termed holistic policy-making as reflected in areas as diverse as water conservation and management to setting up the biomedical industry to managing car ownership and traffic congestion, is no doubt an imprint of engineers into policy-making. These qualities became essential to the development of leadership in the public sector and were reinforced by the strong policy focus of the training and development programs of AOs.

---

[20] Speech given during the debate on the White Paper on ministerial salaries on 1 November 1994, reproduced in *Lee Kuan Yew: The Man and His Ideas*, Times Editions, 1998.

The scholarship system of recruitment worked well in the early years but has come under increasing pressure as a result of enhanced economic opportunities in the private sector and the changing aspirations of a younger generation. In the days when Singapore was just embarking on its development path, a PSC scholarship was the only way for talented students from poor families to go to university. Obtaining a scholarship to study at a university also meant a secure job after graduation during a period when good employment was an uncertain prospect. Being the recipient of a government scholarship was a source of high prestige and the bond of six to eight years was viewed as a necessary obligation, in return for job security, free medical benefits and a good pension system. Rising standards of living changed these perceptions. The current generation of young people value freedom to choose their careers and many loathe shackling themselves to a bond at the age of 18. Many more companies and statutory boards now offer scholarships to good universities and many more Singaporeans are studying overseas without scholarships. Taking up a scholarship with a bond has become a much less compelling option. Along the same lines, many scholars left the service immediately after serving their bonds or bought out their bonds with the help of private sector organizations. In addition, the MA program, while increasing chances of better fit, creates uncertainty as to whether a returned scholar will eventually make it to the Administrative Service. To supplement the pool, PSD also draws from other sources for potential public sector leaders. In-service scholars, i.e., those in the professional services in the Ministries are surfaced from time to time for review and possible induction into the Administrative Service. However these number less than ten a year.

With the scholarship system as the main recruitment mechanism, those recruited began their careers in the public sector in their early 20s after completing their degrees. Thus after independence, the public sector was staffed by capable young men and women, the vast majority of them returned scholars, marking a significant shift from the seniority system that existed under the British. Goh Keng Swee played a significant role in nurturing the second generation of public sector leaders. Goh had *carte blanche* to hire anyone from the list of government scholars given to him and while he was open to giving young officers a chance, he also had high performance standards. Those who proved themselves capable ascended quickly up the system. Current public sector leaders like Lim Siong Guan and Philip Yeo joined the public sector fresh out of university, were spotted early and mentored by Goh, given challenging assignments and autonomy to act, promoted quickly, and reached the highest ranks of the public sector. Their cases are not isolated — many PSs were first appointed to this position when they were in their 30s. The fact that the new young elite joined the public sector almost fresh after university meant that many of them would remain within the public sector for a long period. This stability in the core public sector leadership provided a high degree of continuity and stability in policy direction.[21] We describe briefly the careers, leadership styles and management philosophy of Lim Siong Guan and Philip Yeo to illustrate how their different talents were appreciated and deployed in the public sector. Both men were bestowed the nation's highest honors in the 2006 National Day Awards in recognition of their lifetime of achievements in the public sector.

Lim Siong Guan

Lim Siong Guan has spent his entire career in the public service. For 25 of his 37-year career, he was Permanent Secretary of key ministries: Defence from July 1981 to May 1994, Prime Minister's Office from June 1994 to July 1998, Education from April 1997 to June 1999 and Finance from June 1999 to September 2006. In addition, he was the first Principal Private Secretary to then Prime Minister Lee Kuan Yew from May 1978 to June 1981, and Head of the Civil Service from September 1999 to March 2005. An engineer by training, Lim was awarded the President's Scholarship to study at the University of Adelaide, Australia, from which he graduated with First Class Honors in Mechanical Engineering in 1969. He attained a Postgraduate Diploma in Business Administration from the National University of Singapore in 1975.

---

[21] Austin (2004).

Lim Siong Guan is credited with introducing a plethora of new ideas, policies, programs and projects that kept the civil service at the forefront of change and innovation. From the Ministry of Defence, to the PSD, to the Ministries of Education and Finance, he built deep foundations for change and innovation, new cultures and structures in those institutions that sustained their impact long after he had left. Among his many contributions are the introduction of scenario planning first in MINDEF and then the Civil Service at large, the devolved personnel management system, the limited-term tenure for public sector leaders, personnel and financial innovations in MINDEF, the PS21 strategic initiative for the civil service which gave every civil servant a 100-hour training commitment per year, the refocusing of the education system during his time at the Ministry of Education, major budgeting reforms in the Ministry of Finance that included the Reinvestment Fund (to be discussed in the next chapter), and elevating the e-government initiative to a more strategic and integrated platform. He has been called a "one-man think tank"[22] for the civil service.

Lim is respected for his leadership, strong values, deep insights, long-term perspective, focus on people development and commitment to public service. He is widely regarded for his humble, approachable and unpretentious style, preferring to work behind the scenes and letting his ministers have the limelight. He served with distinction under all the three Prime Ministers and is credited by many of his PS colleagues as being the man responsible for the dynamism and transformation of the civil service. His younger colleagues respect him as a man of ideas, a leader with deep convictions and a sharp intellect, who communicates passionately and believes in people. He calls himself "an organization man," one who believes in building structures, systems and processes so that change efforts may be sustained.

"Systems and a systems orientation are paramount because this is the test of whether anything is around

---

[22] *The Straits Times* , 9 August 2006, p. 3.

after you leave. The process is more important than the results."[23]

He is known to be publicity-shy and speaks little to the media. He is at his best when sharing his views, ideas and convictions to individuals and small groups of officers, and challenging them to take responsibility and initiative for change.

Throughout his career, Lim focused on developing and putting in place ideas, concepts, structures and frameworks to help to build organizational capability and capacity. He believed that developing organizational capacity meant building an organization that embraced change:

> "We need an organization that is open to change all the time. The best way to build up organizational capacity is to create an environment where everyone accepts and expects change."

It was in Defence where he made his first concerted move to implement this philosophy of change. Besides overseeing the introduction of the CEP system[24] and the "Total Defence" initiative to raise the image of the SAF, Lim was the force behind the WITS (Work Improvement Teams) and SSS (Staff Suggestion Scheme) initiatives, which are now thought of simply as part of the public sector productivity movement. But the premise of SSS and WITS was much more fundamental, and their development and implementation reflected Lim's philosophy and work in building organizations that would be sustainable over time:

(i) Getting people involved

Lim stressed the inherent capacity of people — that people wished to do their best, wished to contribute, and that each individual was

---

[23] Author's interview with Lim Siong Guan, 29 July 2005.

[24] The system to measure Currently Estimated Potential (CEP) will be discussed in the next section.

the best person to suggest improvements to his work and had the creative ability to do so. He believed that the task of a leader was to create the kinds of organizations and processes that allowed this. The key was to get the people actively involved in the effort to build a culture that supported the objectives of the organization. In this vein, the SSS and WITS were introduced in MINDEF and the SAF as a way to get people thinking about what they were doing, which in turn would help to develop nimble, quick-thinking soldiers. To him, this was the key process — to get everybody thinking. Lim believes that the way to achieve organizational excellence is by getting people to think about what they are doing, in a way that supports the objectives of the organization.[25]

(ii) Focus on the purpose of the organization

Thus, he believed that even if leaders did not know everything, they could make themselves useful by constantly asking, "What is the purpose of this organization?" and "What can you do to help people do their jobs?" This was a philosophy that guided him during his time at the Ministry of Education:

> "I knew nothing about the theory of education. But I talked to the teachers and principals and listened to them. I just gave expression to their dreams and created the structures to make it happen. They wanted to do a good job, but did not have the authority and resources to make it work. I created a way in which they could get involved."

As a result of this approach, his tenure at MOE saw teachers and educators defining their role as "Moulding the Future of our Nation."

> "My way of operating is always to help people discover a higher purpose for their actions."[26]

---

[25] Author's interview with Lim Siong Guan, 29 July 2005.
[26] Author's interview with Lim Siong Guan, 22 November 2005.

This mode of thinking was apparent in his conceptualization of e-government. Originally premised as the process of simply bringing IT into government, he believed that the larger objective of an e-government initiative should be to make ordinary Singaporeans comfortable with IT. This was why he advocated teaching older folks to start using the ATMs to do their banking and the Internet to access government services, and in so doing, build national facility for IT, which would in turn help give Singapore a strategic competitive advantage.

(iii) Good processes and systems are necessary for sustained good results

To Lim, capability was embedded in people, but this capability had to be reinforced and sustained via systems and processes.

> "It is critical to emphasize process. Good processes will lead to sustained good results, whereas good results by themselves cannot assure sustainable performance."[27]

He started the scenario planning process — to establish dialog between political and public sector leaders so that there would be alignment in vision and concerns. Under the old guard in the immediate post-independence period, political and public sector leaders shared a joint vision and values as requirements were clear and immediate. In the 1990s, as circumstances changed and government became more consensual and when issues and solutions had became less clear-cut, new structures and processes were required to forge a common understanding with political leaders as to what the future might turn out to be. He deemed this necessary to ensure a continuity of the joint vision and values that had been key to Singapore's early success. Similarly, the crux of the PS21 movement was the establishment of structures and processes to ensure that the public sector as an organization was ready to cope with the greater uncertainty in the

[27] Lim Siong Guan (2003). "Government that Costs Less," Speech given at 5th Global Forum on Reinventing Government, 3–7 November.

environment and would be able to change and respond in good time to continue to be a competitive edge for Singapore.

Philip Yeo

Philip Yeo's career has not been that of a typical public sector bureaucrat. His brash, brusque and unconventional style has made him one of the best-known civil servants in Singapore, but as he himself acknowledged:

> " ... I never envisaged myself becoming a civil servant!
> Some people say that I am neither civil nor a servant in
> my working habits."[28]

Born in Singapore in 1946, he went to the University of Toronto on the Canadian Government-funded Colombo Plan scholarship and Harvard University on the US Government-funded Fulbright Scholarship. He joined the Administrative Service in June 1970 and became Permanent Secretary for Defence in September 1979. The imprint of Philip Yeo is evident in many areas — from defense technology and weapons, IT, disk drives, semiconductor, petrochemicals to biomedical sciences to foreign investments in Singapore, particularly Singapore's relations with the MNCs.

Yeo was the visionary behind the computerization of the Singapore public sector, which in turn helped push the information communications revolution to the rest of Singapore. To circumvent a government-wide policy at the time that forbade individual agencies from purchasing their own computer hardware, he purchased them by clandestine means. In tender documents, minicomputers were classified as "small business machines" and IBM mainframes, "intermediate business machines." When he was appointed chairman of the executive committee of the Defence Science Organisation, a mini supercomputer was purchased under the label of "calculating machine." Later as founding Chairman of the National Computer

---

[28] Philip Yeo, "Passion Drives," in Chan Chin Bock (2002). *Heart Work.*

Board in September 1981, Yeo successfully completed the task of computerizing all ten ministries — at one go with a budget of S$100m, with no external consultants and within a five-year time frame with an army of fresh young in-house trained IT staff.

His strong business sense and "take-no-prisoners" style were evident during his Chairmanship at the Economic Development Board, an appointment he assumed in the midst of the first recession in 1986. He leveraged on the downturn, with a memorable advertisement in the international press titled "Who would be mad enough to invest in Singapore in a recession?", endorsed by the Chairmen and CEOs of companies such as Apple, National Semiconductor and Motorola. During his tenure, Singapore diversified its economic growth base, becoming a hub for manufacturing-related services. Inward investment soared. From 1986–2000, EDB attracted more than S$70b of fixed asset investment, which in turn generated more than 230,000 manufacturing sector jobs; total business spending in terms of manufacturing-related services rose to more than S$12b, bringing with it another 44,000 jobs. Many of these investments were in industries such as semiconductors, aerospace and chemicals, which Yeo had identified and pushed for and which later became key industries in the Singapore economy.

His penchant for innovative solutions to apparently insurmountable constraints is illustrated in his vision of creating an island for the petrochemical industry by reclaiming the seas around seven tiny offshore islands to form a Chemical island. This island created a plug-and-play environment for petrochemical companies, without compromising safety and the environment in Singapore. Five years after the concept paper, Jurong Island had investments totaling more than S$20b from 60 companies.

Just as he made the petrochemicals industry a reality, Yeo was the key driver for Singapore's push into biomedical sciences.[29] In February 2001, Yeo took over the National Science and Technology Board, refocused and renamed it A*STAR, the Agency for Science, Technology and Research, and went on to seed and incubate Singapore's then fledgling biomedical sciences industry. Over a period of five years,

---

[29] This area covers pharmaceuticals, biotechnology, health care and medical technology.

he recruited a crop of top international research talent, nurtured and mentored local talent, initiated scholarship and outreach programs, and established biomedical research institutes that have enhanced Singapore's basic science expertise. He built Biopolis, Singapore's new epicenter for biomedical research to help foster interaction and collaboration between different disciplines. His energy and focus were primary reasons for the surge in the contribution of biomedical sciences to output which tripled to about S$18b between 2000 and 2005; its contribution rose from practically zero to about 5 per cent of output in 2005,[30] with employment rising about four fold over the same period.[31] His relentlessness in pursuing and attracting many of the top research talent was the same drive he displayed in creating new niche industries when he was with the EDB in the 1990s.

Yeo has been a strong advocate of scholarships and an outspoken proponent of the need to build up domestic capability. This belief was evident in his priorities when he was Chairman of the Executive Committee of the Defence Science Organisation (DSO) in the 1980s:

> "You develop your people through scholarships... We are not only keeping them for the organisation, we are developing our population, building our national capability. Even if they don't stay in DSO, we are building up the asset in our country. That is my belief."[32]

Scholars have been one of his legacies in all the organizations he has helmed. In SembCorp where he was Chairman from 1994 to 1999, he grew 75 scholars. In the Singapore Technologies Group and National Computer Board, there were over 330 and 120 scholars respectively. In the 1960s and 1970s, EDB had received a significant share of government scholars in the 1970s, but this had changed in the

---

[30] Figures from *TODAY*, 19–20 August 2006, p. 2.

[31] Philip Yeo (2006). "The Basic Foundation for R and D: Human Capital — A Pro-Local/Pro-International Approach," lecture given at National University of Singapore, 20 January.

[32] Interview with Philip Yeo, in Melanie Chew and Bernand Tan (2002). *Creating the Technology Edge: DSO National Laboratories, Singapore 1972–2002*. Epigram.

1980s by the time Yeo became chairman. Yeo found a unique solution — he convinced key investors to fund scholarships as their way of giving back to Singapore. Glaxo put in S$50m for 30 scholarships per year in engineering and economics beginning in 1990 and over a 15-year period, this program nurtured more than 300 Glaxo-EDB scholars and is the reason why in EDB, one in three officers today is an ex-Glaxo scholar. Mobil, now part of Exxon-Mobil, donated S$20m for the development of EDB Managers through MBA and Executive Education programs in INSEAD, Harvard, MIT Sloan and Stanford Sloan Business school programs.

His strong advocacy of developing local capability was evident from his time in MINDEF. Unlike many in the SAF who preferred to purchase what was required, he gave priority to developing local capability to produce:

> "Of course, SAF prefers to go out and buy. My argument to them is that 'you want to buy, they want to sell'. That's too simple. How are you going to build up? So even if you buy, you should carry on developing... So we develop, we buy, we know everything about what we buy. We can improve on it. We can take it apart... To sit down and tinker, that is not easy. But when you tinker, develop yourself and you know more, your capability grows."[33]

This focus on people and developing local capability was the distinctive feature of Singapore's approach in developing biomedical sciences, and this was Yeo's trademark. Alongside recruiting world-class international research talent, developing local research talent was his priority.

> "... we are not short of labs or state-of-the-art equipment. What we are still short of are well-trained, globally-exposed, eager and committed English-fluent scientists. The senior scientists provide the lighthouses, but it is the

---

[33] Ibid.

young and upcoming ones who will sail out in uncharted waters to find new worlds."

To realize his vision, he aggressively recruited local scholars and set high performance benchmarks. As a result there are now more than 600 PhD scholars in A*STAR. His personal mentoring of his scholars is legendary.

His first comments on his new appointment as the Chairman of Spring Singapore in April 2007, the agency in charge of promoting the development of local small and medium enterprises, reflects the consistency of his priorities:

> "... for our SMEs (small and medium enterprises), the way to grow, it's not just money, markets and know-how, but people who can lead and take the company to the next level. And that is the greatest challenge today — it's leadership."

Yeo is well known for his confrontational, combative working style and has not been above going head-to-head with members of parliament on issues he felt strongly about. When he was asked why he never entered politics despite being asked, he said,

> "If I went into politics, I would have offended all my voters. Over half of them would not vote for me. So, better not. I have a very different make-up."[34]

7.4.3 *Developing Public Sector Leaders: Assessing Potential*

Performance appraisal and the assessment of potential are now the cornerstones of the promotion and development process for public sector leaders, but it was not always the case. In the 1960s and 1970s, the leadership selection and development of public servants was ad

---

[34] *Weekend TODAY*, 19–20 August 2006, p. 2.

hoc, depending on whether or not their work and performance were noticed by the right people. As the business of government became more complex, it became critical to be able to assess the potential of those recruited to ensure that the public sector had individuals of the required caliber to eventually take on the top leadership roles.

The formal system of appraisal began with the introduction of the Potential Appraisal System (PAS) in 1983, adapted from the system used by the Shell Petroleum Company, which was one of the earliest investors in Singapore. Shell developed its PAS in the 1960s to enable the company to identify those employees with potential for senior management.[35] Shell's PAS was based on the work of Professor Van Lennep, an industrial psychologist at the University of Utrecht in Holland, who concluded that the four basic qualities critical for predicting employee potential were: "helicopter quality" (an individual's ability to examine a problem or issue taking all important factors into account), "power of analysis," "imagination" and "sense of reality." These four criteria are denoted by the acronym HAIR. Shell employees were ranked against each characteristic and then against all four; these rankings could then be used to predict which employees would be best suited for senior positions.

The qualities encapsulated in HAIR were discussed briefly in Chapter 5. The *helicopter* quality (H) is the ability to look at things from a higher vantage point while simultaneously being able to zoom in on the critical details; A is the ability to rationally and rigorously *analyze* the issues; vision, *imagination* (I) and creativity to develop fresh approaches to a problem, to see ahead and to break new ground which must co-exist with a sense of *reality* (R), an ability to integrate vision and imagination with realities on the ground and the capacity to execute well. The HAIR criteria became so entrenched that in addition to being the assessment framework for individual performance, these criteria are now also the barometer for evaluating the design and workability of policy recommendations, as was examined in Chapter 5.

---

[35] The discussion on the Shell PAS is drawn heavily from Sarah Vallance (1999). "Performance Appraisal in Singapore, Thailand and the Philippines: A Cultural Perspective," *Australian Journal of Public Administration*, Vol. 58, No. 3, pp. 78–95.

What elements of the Shell system appealed to the Singapore public sector?[36] The focus on qualities and attributes that were not job-specific was considered appropriate for the purposes of identifying public sector leaders, and the prescriptive set of potential assessment criteria facilitated standardization and comparability of assessment. Requiring the appraisers to assess and rank officers according to the appraisal qualities encouraged appraisers to get to know their officers well and note the process by which officers went about achieving their targets, thereby enabling recognition for officers with targets which were more qualitative. The fact that the appraisal ranking was done by a team, and that the ranking panel members would undergo exhaustive discussions in ranking individual officers relative to others based on first-hand experience against clearly defined criteria, made the process more rigorous and objective. Knowledge of an officer's long-term potential would enable more meaningful and appropriate training and development opportunities to help him maximize his potential, and in so doing, would also help the public sector organization in its own manpower planning to ensure that there would be sufficient staff of various potential to fill up key positions vacated as each generation of officers retired.

Officers are evaluated and promoted based on their performance and potential: those deemed to have the capacity to reach the key leadership positions are given special development opportunities. How fast officers are promoted depends on their estimated potential. An officer with higher potential will be promoted faster than someone with lower potential. But whether officers are actually promoted depends on their performance. A high-performing, high potential officer will be promoted faster and rise to the top at a relatively young age while a high-performing, low potential officer will also be promoted, albeit at a slower pace.

The appraisal consists of two parts: the Work Review and the Development Assessment. The Work Review requires qualitative comment on the employee's work performance. The intention behind this section is to enable the employee to contribute to the appraisal

---

[36] These reasons were provided by the Public Service Division.

process, and focuses on the positive aspects of the employee's performance. Based on the tasks for the year ahead, supervisors comment on the training and development needs of the employee and make an overall assessment of employee potential. The Development Assessment is closed. In this section, officers are assessed on the qualities that give an indication of the employee's "Currently Estimated Potential": the HAIR criteria together with results orientation and leadership qualities. The list of the constituent factors is set out in Table 7.7. Appraisers have to rate the officer against each of the qualities, with the scale ranging from "High" to "Exceeding" to "Meeting" to "Below." In addition, employees are rated on other qualities such as "Commitment to Job," "Integrity," "Resource Management," "Developing Others" and "Teamwork." The most significant part of the appraisal is the section where the appraiser has to make an assessment of the employee's Currently Estimated Potential (CEP) by indicating the officer's highest potential job level and salary grade. Moreover, within the Adminstrative Service, the appraiser has to assess the probability of the appraisee becoming a permanent secretary, comment on the appraisee's development prospects and make recommendations for training.

Table 7.7. The Potential Appraisal System for Division 1 Officers: Qualities influencing "Currently Estimated Potential (CEP)"

Helicopter Quality	Broad perspective Long-term view
Intellectual Qualities	Power of analysis Imagination and innovation Sense of reality
Results Orientation	Achievement motivation Socio-political sensitivity Decisiveness
Leadership Qualities	Capacity to motivate Delegation Communication and consultation

Source: Vallance (1999) and Public Service Division, Singapore.

The public sector adapted the Shell system by instituting a system of ranking of officers on the basis of performance and potential to fine tune assessments and fitness for promotion. An officer with higher potential can expect to move faster and go further but no officer is promoted solely on the basis of potential.[37] Each appraiser makes his assessment of the officer's potential independently of the officer's previous appraisers and it has been observed that an officer's assessed CEP generally stabilizes after about five years in the service. An AO whose CEP is below that of a Deputy Secretary by the time he is in mid-30s will be counseled to leave the service. The principle of ranking on the basis of both performance and potential, and the focus on the assessment of Currently Estimated Potential underscore the competitive, meritocratic approach of the public sector, an approach described by Lim Siong Guan as a "systematized meritocracy."[38] It is a highly rigorous system aimed at identifying and targeting the best, in terms of performance and value system, for development for the top echelon of leadership.

The focus on getting the best and brightest into the public sector has given rise to a unique problem. Because of Singapore's small size, a large number of those recruited into the Administrative Service come from only a handful of top local schools and overseas universities. The public sector is aware of the danger of getting leaders "cut from the same bolt of cloth" and the need to recruit talented individuals with different perspectives and experiences to add diversity to the Service. Diversity was needed to pre-empt "group-think" that was highly likely given the similarity in the AOs' exposures and educational backgrounds. This was the reason behind the initiative to recruit mid-career professionals from the private sector into the Administrative Service, but this move to inject diversity has had only limited success.

[37] Eddie Teo (2002). "The Singapore Public Service: A Development-Oriented Promotion System," *Ethos*, Vol. 8, No. 1, pp. 10–15.
[38] Authors' interview with Lim Siong Guan, 29 July 2005.

7.4.4 Developing Talent: Training Staff and Investing in Milestone Programs

The infrastructure for the formal training and development of public sector leaders was developed only in the 1990s. In the early years, training for civil servants was limited to fairly ad hoc attendance of courses and on-the-job training. Moreover, much of the training provided was functional in nature that aimed at increasing efficiency and productivity. It was only in 1995, under the tenets of PS21 that training became part of the systematic development system for civil servants. That year, a civil servant spent an average of 2½ working days a year or 1.1 per cent of his time on training. Under the PS21 framework, each officer became eligible for 100 hours of training a year which they could use to take up formal courses and workshops, such that on average each officer would spend 5 per cent of his working time on training and development.

Similarly, up to the early 1990s, training and development for Administrative Officers took place mainly through job rotations and postings to positions that required officers to develop different sets of skills and competencies. Apart from the foundation courses for AOs, there were very few courses for senior officers. Teo Chee Hean, current Minister for Defence and Minister-in-charge of the civil service conceded that "… until the mid 1990s, we were not doing a good job in training."[39]

Prior to the mid-1990s, there were no common platforms for AOs to come together to forge relationships. Singapore AOs hailed from a diversity of socio-economic backgrounds and came together only because of the system of meritocracy and public scholarships. Once they entered the Service, each was routed to different postings and they were sent individually for advanced management programs overseas. Concerns gradually grew that the absence of a commonality of experience and social ties would have a detrimental effect on the identity and cohesiveness of the group of top public administrators. The lack of identity and esprit de corps within the Service was

---

[39] Authors' interview with Teo Chee Hean, 29 December 2006.

reflected in the relative weakness of institutional values. This was in stark contrast to the elite services in countries like Japan, France and Malaysia where rites of passage, similar educational backgrounds and milestone programs helped forge common experiences and bonds.

The Service thus began establishing rites of passage to enhance the identity and sense of belonging to an elite service.[40] The annual Administrative Service dinner, established in 1989, was one such rite; the occasion marked the career milestones for AOs — confirmation in the service, entry into superscale grades and substantive appointments as permanent secretary.[41] But the most important instrument for building up identity and cultivating and transmitting institutional values was the milestone programs that were to be run by the Civil Service College.

The Civil Service College (CSC) was established in 1993 to run courses in policy and strategic planning, management and leadership skills for senior civil servants. While it conducted requisite functional courses, it also aimed to build esprit de corps, imbue senior civil servants with a strong sense of public service, raise level of service orientation and inculcate a practical approach to public administration.[42] Its courses were initially targeted at senior civil servants but the plan was to eventually incorporate participation from statutory boards, government-linked companies and the private sector to encourage networking. Specifically, the Civil Service College sought:[43]

(i)   To develop among civil servants an understanding of the key factors which were the cornerstones of Singapore's continued survival and success. These fundamentals were to be debated and internalized and from time to time, changed to fit changing

[40] Speech by the Prime Minister at the First Administrative Service Dinner on Tuesday, 19 December 1989 at Mandarin Hotel, Singapore.

[41] "Govt to Set Up Civil Service College," Business Times, 11–12 July 1992.

[42] Speech by Mr Richard Hu, Minister for Finance at the Fourth Administrative Service Dinner at the Sheraton Towers Ballroom on Friday, 10 July 1992.

[43] "Top Govt Officers Must Take Courses before Promotion," The Straits Times, 20 April 1993.

circumstances, so that civil servants shared the same goals and values;

(ii) To build a value system, a sense of esprit de corps, camaraderie and a sense of tradition among senior civil servants, so that they would have a shared spirit of service to the nation, competence, dedication and integrity, such that the public should continue to expect this of them;

(iii) To bring officers up-to-date with the latest ideas, thinking and trends in a world of rapid change;

(iv) To work together with the private sector to continue to make Singapore successful.

The training program was designed to play roles not only in developing the potential of high caliber officers but also to serve as the platform for the inculcating of public sector values and the forging of relationships and social networks. Teo Chee Hean, current Minister for Defence and Minister-in-charge of the civil service explained:

> "In the CSC courses, we not only do functional training but we train officers on how the government works, the ethos, values, and what we want officers to be able to do together, get people to know each other, know each other's strengths and weaknesses and how to work together as a team. That's the reason we ask everyone to go to OBS (Outward Bound School) together."[44]

The civil service drew upon the model in MINDEF in designing of formal training and development program for AOs:

> "In MINDEF, there were induction courses for new staff, courses for middle management staff level and then command courses for senior management. We then used this structure for the CSC courses."[45]

---

[44] Authors' interview with Teo Chee Hean, 29 December 2006.

[45] Ibid.

The first key milestone program for AOs and potential AOs is the **Foundation Course**. This is a ten-week induction course to equip new AOs with the basic concepts of governance and public administration, and the necessary skills and knowledge to work in the public sector. The focus is on the challenges facing the public service and the public sector's response to these challenges. In addition, the course also teaches new AOs how to lead and manage teams and resources. While management skills are included in the training, these courses have an overwhelming policy and governance orientation. The AOs are immersed in the Singapore policy-making environment, schooled on the impact of Singapore's history, geography and multi-racial society on policy-making and the principles that have been crucial to governance in Singapore. All key policy initiatives, whether successful or not, are dissected and the lessons and implications discussed at length. That AOs would review policies with a critical eye and adapt them to changing circumstances was an expectation conveyed and reinforced during the training process.

It was recognized that AOs needed to have political sensitivity and that successful policy formulation and implementation demanded that policy-makers had empathy for and were able to factor in reactions on the ground. Senior civil servants needed to have the right political instincts and they had to learn to acquire these instincts by keeping in close touch with ground sentiments and their dealings and contacts in neighboring countries. To give new AOs a dose of what was required, the Foundation course includes a community involvement component where AOs are posted to various types of grassroots organizations as part of their induction. In recent years, attachments at government-linked organizations and organizations like the United Nations General Assembly have been created, together with longer-term attachments in private sector companies.

The training program for AO and potential AOs was refined significantly in 2002 and reflected the investment the public sector was willing to undertake to develop and groom potential leaders. All AOs and potential AOs (Management Associates starting from year 2002) are put through a structured development program comprising seminars, exchange programs, policy forums, overseas trips and study visits. These programs inculcate in the scholars an appreciation of

Singapore's geopolitical context and the limitation of resources within which Singapore must function. There is also a Gap Year option. Before they are deployed, scholars are also given the option to embark on a six-month to one-year internship in a public or private sector organization, designed to allow MAs to get first hand experience of business operations.

In addition to the Foundation Course, there are two other milestone programs: the **Senior Management Program** (SMP), a six-week course targeted at officers in the middle management level who are about to enter the superscale grade, including those in the statutory boards. It aims to broaden and deepen their understanding of Singapore's principles of governance and policy. Officers are exposed to managing people, building teams and handling the media. There are also two country visits as part of international exposure.

The **Leaders in Administration Program** (LAP) is a five-week program to prepare senior public sector leaders at the Deputy Secretary level for top leadership positions, and to challenge their understanding of Singapore's approach to governance. In addition, postgraduate awards are made to high caliber officers who are identified by the PSD.

Milestone programs like these help AOs, MAs and other public sector leaders forge social networks and build a sense of esprit de corps. The small size of the Administrative Service — less than 300 — has resulted in a tightly networked AO circle. These networks have facilitated coordination and a speedy response to events. In recent years, technology has reinforced the flow of information through these networks.

> "In today's situation, with all of us so wired up, being connected is a blessing as well as a curse on us but with technology available, you are able to know what is happening in other parts of the world… on the specific issue of integration, you are able to tie things up with this kind of networking."[46]

---

[46] Interview with Chiang Chie Foo, Permanent Secretary, Ministry of Defence, 6 February 2006.

Apart from the milestone programs, AOs are expected to regularly attend development workshops and seminars to continually upgrade their skills and knowledge. In addition, regular policy forums for senior public officers are held to build up a common understanding of public sector concerns and to think and act from a whole-of-government perspective.

7.4.5 Developing Leaders through Job Postings and Rotations

The other main mode of development for Administrative Officers is through postings. AOs are rotated through different types of postings in different agencies for them to gain exposure to different kinds of issues and challenges. This is one major difference in the development opportunities between the scholars who are groomed for the Administrative Service, and graduate officers who are in the professional services recruited directly by the agencies. Those recruited directly by individual ministries and statutory boards become the staff of those agencies and are expected to develop their careers within that agency. In contrast, for scholars recruited by the PSC and who are groomed for the Administrative Service, rotation of duties and postings is an integral part of their career development. Each posting is about two years, long enough to give officers a sampling of the domain area, and for the Public Service Division to gain an idea of the strengths of each officer. For more senior Director-level positions, postings are for three to five year-periods to create a balance between fresh ideas and stability. AOs are rotated not only across domain areas, i.e., different ministries, but are also exposed to a broad spectrum of policy, supervisory and operations work. Management Associates assessed to have potential to become public sector leaders thus receive far greater and deeper exposure and training opportunities than those in the professional services track. Officers in the Administrative Service are paid on a higher salary range than similar ranks in the professional services.

Even though AOs were rotated regularly as part of their career development, in the past, they had little choice in their postings. This was largely the result of the need to ensure that AOs obtained exposure over a wide range of areas to enable them to hone their instincts in different areas. As JY Pillay once said:

> "… an administrative officer is required by the terms of his calling to behave almost like a Jesuit: To serve where he is required to without demurring. The unwritten motto of the Service is 'never refuse, never volunteer.' That is not to say that initiative, a vital ingredient in leadership, is not valued, but that presumptuousness is frowned upon."[47]

This system of directed postings became less popular with a younger generation of AOs who wanted a greater say and more choice in their postings.

The Open Posting System was set up in year 2000, where AOs and Ministries met up to market themselves to each other. This system by and large resulted in better talent management by the agencies and better job matches. While this system accords weight to the preferences of AOs and the Ministries, PSD still has to oversee the allocation to ensure that each officer has exposure in different types of roles, that less sought-after officers are rotated and that all key positions are filled. Nonetheless, the open posting system has been effective in identifying good officers within the Service.

In addition to fresh postings, in recent years, AOs have had another outlet for development — cross-ministry project teams. The increasing prevalence of issues that do not fall under the purview of a single agency has necessitated the formation of project teams that cut across agencies to review the issues and come up with recommendations for action. Being on an inter-ministry project team exposes AOs from one agency to the perspectives and concerns of other agencies, encouraging them to look for and to take a whole-of-government view to issues. Work on project teams is over and above the regular workload of AOs but they are excellent opportunities for them to stand out and be noticed by the Permanent Secretaries.

---

[47] JY Pillay (1996). "Modern Singapore: The Role of the Civil Service," speech given at the NUS Convocation Ceremony on 27 August 1996, published in *Ethos*, January.

The wide spectrum of developmental opportunities translates into high performance expectations and the retention standards are stringent. For the Administrative Service, there is a "potential threshold." If an officer's CEP is estimated to be below that of a Deputy Secretary by the time he reaches his mid-30s, he will be counseled to leave the Administrative Service, either by transferring to the professional services or leaving the public service altogether.[48]

The recruitment process, selection criteria and development programs all worked together to produce a public sector leadership that comprised some of the country's best analytical minds, all applied to the business of policy-making, problem-solving and governance. The system produced technocrats who were trained to think in terms of Singapore's best interests, who were disposed to be innovative, outward-looking and pragmatic in their approach to problem-solving, to be critical in evaluating the effectiveness of policies and in assessing their continued relevance in the face of changing circumstances. The system selected individuals with high IQ but not necessarily with the skills and EQ to be an effective manager. The public sector leadership has recently recognized this — that management skills were just as important as analytical skills to an AO's success as a leader. Results from a pilot 360-degree feedback exercise with a group of 30 timescale officers, and later rolled out to all superscale officers gave support to this concern. AOs were perceived to be effective with a high degree of integrity but were perceived to be less effective in coaching and motivating others.[49]

7.5 Talent Retention: The Public Sector Compensation System

The Singapore approach to public sector compensation is quite distinct from that taken in many other developing countries. A key difference has been the principle of paying public servants competitive wages.

---

[48] Eddie Teo (2001). "The Singapore Public Service: A Development-Oriented Promotion System," *Ethos*.

[49] Opening Address by Lim Siong Guan at the Fifteenth Administrative Service Dinner on 28 March 2003 at the Grand Ballroom, Grand Copthorne Waterfront Hotel.

Strong economic growth had created a competitive market for talent right from the early 1970s and there were almost annual salary reviews to ensure that the civil service pay for the various services did not lag too far behind the private sector. As Singapore's largest employer, the public sector's compensation approach has had to reflect market conditions, take into account national objectives and adapt to the changing desires and aspirations of a younger, more educated and more demanding workforce. Public sector compensation rests on five core principles:[50]

(i) *Paying competitive rates commensurate with abilities and performance*

The public sector recognizes that good administration is premised on good people and that it needs to pay market rates to retain talent. Annual salary reviews are carried out, particularly for the professional services, with comparisons based on equivalent job markets or equivalent qualifications. Whether adjustments are made depends on the health of that particular service, i.e., staffing levels and retention rates. While paying competitive rates, the working principle has been that public sector should mirror but not lead the market. Civil service pay rises usually follow strong economic growth, as was the case in year 2006 when strong wage growth in the private sector resulted in an increase in public sector attrition rates.[51]

(ii) *Paying flexible wage packages*

This was one of the key lessons learnt from the 1985–86 recession when a lack of wage flexibility reduced the ability of firms to respond quickly to changes in demand without cutting employment. Salary packages of civil servants now have a fixed and variable component, with the latter forming about 40 per cent of annual compensation. To further

---

[50] This section draws from Lim Soo Hoon (2005). "Remuneration in the Singapore Civil Service," Executive Program for Kazakhstan Agency for Civil Service Affairs, Singapore, Public Service Division.

[51] As a result of strong economic growth, the attrition rate for graduate officers in the first 10 months of 2006 was 8 per cent, compared with 7.4 per cent for the whole of 2005. *The Straits Times*, Saturday, 25 November 2006, p. 1.

encourage flexibility and discourage the retention of non-performing or under-performing staff, the British pension system was gradually replaced by the CPF system. Currently, about 85 per cent of civil servants are on the CPF system, whereby the government's financial liability for its officers is fully discharged upon their retirement. Similarly the public sector medical benefits system encourages individual responsibility for medical insurance and coverage with the payment of an additional 1 per cent into the staff's Medisave account every month, from which staff can draw to pay medical insurance premiums. Having a greater flexible component enabled the public sector to reward staff according to the performance of the economy without locking in large wage increases. In 2006, two days after the economic growth forecast for the year was revised upwards from between 6.5 to 7.5 per cent to between 7.5 to 8 per cent, the public sector announced a bumper bonus for all its officers of 2.7 months, a significant increase from the 2.15-month bonus for 2005 when economic growth had been less robust.[52]

(iii) *Performance-driven pay*

The performance bonus system was introduced to senior civil servants in 1989 and extended to all officers in year 2000. This strong link between pay and ability enables the system to differentiate between outstanding, average and under-performing staff, reinforcing the meritocratic ethos.

(iv) *Recognizing potential*

Good graduate officers are eligible for merit increments. As opposed to the previous fixed increment system, the ability to pay merit or variable increments allows good performers to be rewarded with higher increments. While the quantum of the performance bonus is determined only by the officer's performance, increments are determined by both the performance and potential of the officer. High performing, high potential officers can thus receive much higher

---

[52] *The Straits Times*, Thursday, 23 November 2006, p. 1.

increments, helping them to ascend the career ladder at a much faster rate. This is in recognition of the fact that good young officers are no longer content to wait a long time to be promoted and face the prospect of peaking in their careers just before retirement.

(v) *Paying clean wages*

Public sector salary packages translate as many benefits as possible into cash. This reduces the number of hidden perks and increases transparency and accountability.

The public sector compensation framework is clearly merit-based. The strong performance and potential-driven elements ensure that talented individuals rise quickly through the ranks, to reach their peak in their mid to late 30s. This has been part of a concerted strategy to reward and retain its top talent, which has been a key challenge since the 1970s.

7.6 Retaining Public Sector Leaders: Benchmarking Salaries

From the above, it is clear that Singapore has been one of the few countries in the world that stressed the need for competitive public sector salaries and this has been most evident in its compensation policy for public sector leadership:

> "The public sector needs a fair share of the best brains to tackle the complex economic and social problems Singapore will face in the next two decades. The thrust of our economy will continue to depend on the entrepreneurial vigour and business acumen of our private sector but its management will require sophisticated skills and administration in the public sector... The findings of the income comparison between graduates in the public and private sectors suggest that while the average officer in the Administrative Service earns as much as the average officer in the private sector, the

remuneration of the outstanding Administrative Officer is much less than that of the top five per cent of the salaried graduates in the private sector… the immediate problem is not one of inadequate financial rewards for the average Administrative Officer. It is the problem of gross disparity between what the outstanding graduates are earning in the private sector compared to what high-flyers are earning in the Administrative Service."[53]

As those in the Administrative Service comprised a high proportion of the most able people in the country, the private sector was willing to pay a premium to hire one or two of them for their organizations. Since the early 1970s, public sector leadership salaries had been reviewed and adjusted often to try to keep pace with the private sector. However salaries of top private sector wage earners surged so much due to strong economic growth that public sector salary adjustments, already facing a time lag in terms of implementation, could not keep up. The impact of the growing wage differentials was clear: outflow from the Administrative Service was more marked during periods of strong economic growth, to rebound only slightly immediately in the wake of salary revisions. In his speech at the Administrative Service dinner in 1994, then Prime Minister Goh Chok Tong highlighted how the periods of the most serious outflow from the Administrative Service followed periods when public sector leadership salaries significantly lagged behind the private sector: Between 1976 and 1981, there was an average of 18 resignations a year; the 1982 salary revision reduced resignations to an average of five a year for the few years immediately following. The years immediately following the 1989 salary revisions saw moderate resignation rates of four a year each but this surged to seven by the first half of 1993. Goh noted that "economic growth has been so strong, and the private sector moves so fast, that every few years, the problem recurs. Each

---

[53] Ministerial Statement on the Singapore Administrative Service made by the Minister for Trade and Industry on behalf of the Prime Minister in Parliament on Tuesday, 15 May 1979.

time this happens, the service is severely depleted and the quality and efficiency of our administration is affected. Succession in key posts becomes a problem."[54] In the mid-1990s, the rise of the regional economies — India, China, Vietnam and ASEAN — exacerbated the problem. More opportunities opened up, not only for young officers but also for senior officers already in the superscale ranks. Table 7.8 is a snapshot of the outflow situation over a 25-year period.

Table 7.8. Administrative Service Strength and Outflow 1980–2006

Year	Staff Strength	Outflow	
		Number	% of Strength
1980	221	7	3.2
1985	191	5	2.6
1990	191	12	6.3
1995	179	7	3.9
2000	181	21	11.6
2004	189	8	4.2
2005	181	20	11.0
2006	184	13	7.0

Figures do not include the Management Associates. *Source*: Public Service Division.

In the political leadership's view, paying top talent well was necessary not only to attract them to stay but was also instrumental in preserving the integrity and upright reputation of the public sector leadership. The soundness of this policy was acknowledged by the World Bank, which noted that "in bureaucracies, as in nearly everything else, you get what you pay for." It further observed, "(In) general, the more favorably the total public sector compensation package compares to compensation in the private sector, the better the quality of the bureaucracy", and identified the following principles for building a reputable civil service:

• Recruitment and promotion must be merit-based and highly competitive;

[54] Speech by Prime Minister Goh Chok Tong at the Fifth Administrative Service Dinner at the Oriental Ballroom, Oriental Hotel on Friday, 30 July 1993.

- Total compensation, including pay, perks and prestige, must be competitive with the private sector;
- Those who make it to the top must be amply rewarded.[55]

It explicitly pointed out that, "Not surprisingly, Singapore, which is widely perceived to have the region's most competent and upright bureaucracy, pays its bureaucrats best."[56]

To address what had become a perennial problem, a radical decision was taken in 1994 to benchmark the salaries of Ministers and public sector leaders to designated groups in the private sector, such that salary revisions for those in political and public sector leadership positions would be automatic, moving in tandem with the private sector according to a specified formula. The White Paper on "Competitive Salaries for Competent & Honest Government: Benchmarks for Ministers and Senior Public Officers" sets out two benchmarks for both the political and public sector leaders. The benchmark for Ministers and Senior Permanent Secretaries was set at Staff Grade 1 (MR4 grade), while that for director-level appointments was set at Superscale G (SR9 grade), the first superscale grade for the Administrative Service, a grade good Administrative Officers would reach by age 32. The other salaries were to be set by interpolating or extrapolating from these two points.

At the MR4 grade, the grade for senior permanent secretaries, the benchmark is defined as two thirds of the median principal earned income of the top eight earners in six professions — bankers, accountants, engineers, lawyers, employees of local manufacturing companies and MNCs.[57] The benchmark ("2/3M48 income") was set

---

[55] "The East Asian Miracle: Economic Growth and Public Policy," A World Bank Policy Research Report published for the World Bank by the Oxford University Press, 1993, p. 175.

[56] Ibid, pp. 175–176.

[57] The top six professions excluded owners of banks, expatriates and those in speculative activities such as foreign exchange dealing and stockbroking. The benchmark was originally set as the mean salary of the top four earners across the six professions and principal earned income included stock options but excluded dividends, perks and overseas income, which are not fully captured or declared to the IRAS. In a review in year 2000, the formula was modified: the base was expanded to the current top eight earners of the six professions, stock options were discounted by 50 per cent and the median was adopted rather than the mean to reduce the effect of outliers.

at a discount to the private sector to ensure that those who served in high office did so with a motivation for public service and were willing to make a financial sacrifice to do so.

At the SR9 grade, the benchmark was set at the average of the principal earned income of the 15th person aged 32 years belonging to the same six professions ("15P32 income"). The bonds of many officers in Administrative Service expire when they are in the late 20s and early 30s and it is at the juncture that they will consider alternative career options. These are the officers who are the most mobile and most likely to be drawn to the private sector. Thus unlike the benchmark for Ministers and Senior Permanent Secretaries who would have been at the top of their professions had they remained in the private sector, the SR9 grade benchmark was not set at a discount to the corresponding private sector figure as it was "unreasonable and unfair to expect civil servants to make a financial sacrifice compared to their private sector peers, in order to enter public service."[58]

This thinking is reflective of the values of Singapore's first generation political leaders. "Civil Service salaries should not lead private sector incomes, but must keep pace with them."[59] This formula was intended to make it such that subsequent revisions to the salaries of Ministers and top civil servants would be automatic, linked to the income tax returns of the private sector. By pegging the salaries of public sector leaders to their private sector counterparts, it meant that public sector salaries would rise in tandem with private sector salaries. However this also meant that when private sector salaries declined, those in the public sector declined accordingly; when private sector salaries declined in 1995, salaries of public sector leaders were reduced in 1997.[60] However, the mechanism did not work fully as intended.

In 2000, steps were taken to close the gap between the actual salaries then and the prevailing benchmarks for the MR4 grade over

---

[58] Singapore (1994). "Competitive Salaries for Competent & Honest Government: Benchmarks for Ministers and Senior Public Officers," Cmd. 13 of 1994.

[59] Ibid.

[60] Lee Kuan Yew (2000). *From Third World to First: The Singapore Story: 1965–2000*. Times Editions.

a three year period.[61] But in the wake of the 9/11 terrorist attacks in 2001 and the SARS crisis in 2003, ministers and senior civil servants took 10 per cent pay cuts each time, which were only restored in July 2004 and January 2005. In the meantime the benchmarks, particularly for MR4, had moved due to strong economic growth. The next review and adjustment was carried out in April 2007. In 2007 MR4 salaries were 55 per cent of the benchmark, based on private sector income earned in 2005, compared to 71 per cent in 2000. Given the size of the gap, the plan was to close the gap in two stages — half by end of 2007 (to 77 per cent of the benchmark, again in two steps), and the other half by end of 2008.

The first increase to close the first half of the gap was effected in April 2007. Annual salaries for MR4 grades and above rose by an average of 25 per cent, from an average of S$1.2 million to S$1.6 million, which brought MR4 salaries to 73 per cent of the benchmark. The second increase, to take effect on 1 January 2008, would raise MR4 salaries to 77 per cent of the benchmark. Table 7.9 sets out the benchmarks and the quantum of the adjustments for the two grades carried out in April 2007:

Table 7.9. Salary Benchmarks and Adjustments in 2007

Grade	Benchmark	Benchmark Level (YA 2006)	Actual Salary (2006)	Revised Salary (2007)
Senior Permanent Secretary (MR4)	2/3M48	S$2.2 million	S$1,202,600 (55% of benchmark)	S$1,593,500 (73% of benchmark)
Entry Superscale Grade for Admin Officers (SR9)	15P32	S$361,000	S$371,900 (103% of benchmark)	S$384,000 (106% of benchmark)

Source: Ministerial Statement by Mr Teo Chee Hean, Minister-in-charge of the Civil Service, on Civil Service Salary Revisions, at Parliament on 9 April 2007, Annex 3.

[61] The gap for MR4 prior to the revision in 2000 was 71 per cent of the benchmark. The gap for SR9 in 2000 was 67 per cent of the benchmark and SR9 salaries then were adjusted to close the gap fully.

In addition to the upward revision for grade MR4, a greater proportion of the salaries was made variable, dependent on individual performance and the performance of the economy. Before the revision, the norm GDP Bonus was two months if the economy grew by 5 per cent, no bonus if GDP growth was 2 per cent or less and a maximum of four months if the economy grew by 8 per cent or more. With the revision, the norm payment would be three months if the economy grows by 5 per cent. No bonus will be given if economic growth is less than 2 per cent but the maximum will be increased to eight months if the economy grows by 10 per cent or more. To strengthen the link between pay and performance, the norm performance bonus was increased by two months, to a norm of seven months. With the changes, almost half (47 per cent) of the annual package of MR4 grades and above will be variable, compared with about 34 per cent prior to the revision — 20 per cent of the annual package will be dependent on the GDP bonus, another quarter of the package will be performance dependent. Table 7.10 sets out the changes in the monthly and annual packages for the two grades, along with the projected ranking of these grades compared with the earnings of professionals across all sectors.

Salaries for those in the professional services in the Ministries are pegged to their equivalent counterparts. The Public Service Division works with about 20 to 30 benchmark salary scales for the different services. These benchmarks are reviewed once every five to six years but salaries are reviewed every calendar year. Whether or not an adjustment is actually made depends on the health of that particular service.

According to observers, this benchmarking to private sector salaries was "a most revolutionary alteration" to the way good men in government would be rewarded. It provoked a strong negative response from the public at large who found the notion that public servants could be paid so high, offensive. However as Lee Kuan Yew concluded when he participated in the debate on this issue: "I don't think we can afford to be inhibited by conventional attitudes."[62] He

---

[62] Speech given during the debate on the White Paper on ministerial salaries on 1 November 1994, reproduced in *Lee Kuan Yew: The Man and His Ideas*, Times Editions, 1998.

Table 7.10. Changes in the Monthly and Annual Salary Packages for Senior Administrative Officers 2000–2007

	2000 Revision			2006			2007 (New)				
	Monthly ($)	Annual ($)	Ranking	Monthly ($)	Annual ($)	Ranking	Monthly ($)	% Increase over 2006	Annual ($)	% Increase over 2006	Ranking*
Senior Permanent Secretary (MR4)**	37,900	968,000	367	42,790	1,202,600	769	52,420	22.5%	1,593,500	32.5%	438
Entry Superscale Grade for Admin Officers (SR9)**	17,500	363,000	> 1000	17,530	371,900	> 1000	17,530	0%	384,000	3.3%	> 1000

* How the projected 2007 salary compares to the 2006 earnings of professionals across all sectors and professions.
** The salaries of those at the SR9 grade, typically young Administrative Officers at director level, are pegged to the 15P32 benchmark; the salaries of those at the MR4 grade are pegged to the 2/3M48 benchmark.

stressed that the world had changed and that it was no longer possible to depend on men who were motivated solely by a desire to serve the country while being paid a pittance. Teo Chee Hean, the Minister-in-charge of the Civil Service summed up the thinking in 2007:

> " ... we know financial rewards cannot and should not be the main motivation for those in the public service. There are many intrinsic rewards that come from working in the public sector. However that does not mean that we do not need to pay them market-competitive salaries. We don't want pay to be the reason for people to join us. But we also don't want pay to be the reason for them not to join us, or to leave after joining us."[63]

This was a pragmatic and hardheaded solution to the issue of attracting and retaining talent in the public sector. But in the ensuing debate, it was clear that paying private sector equivalent market wages for top civil servants and ministers in an era where the bottom deciles of the population were struggling to make ends meet, where income inequality was rising and when the GST had to be increased to pay for Workfare and other support programs[64], was going to be a hard proposition to sell and would entail loss of political capital. But it was one of the tradeoffs deemed necessary to attract and retain the talent required to keep the government pushing the boundaries to keep Singapore on top of the game.

While this benchmarking of salaries is well known, what is less well known is the fact the public sector retained the pension system as the retirement scheme for top public sector leaders. The CPF, with its system of portable individual savings accounts, facilitates labor market flexibility and avoids saddling employers with a long-term burden when their employees retire. The latter is the main reason why 85 per cent of the public sector moved to the CPF system in the 1970s.

---

[63] Ministerial Statement by Mr Teo Chee Hean, Minister-in-charge of the Civil Service, on Civil Service Salary Revisions, at Parliament on 9 April 2007.

[64] As announced in Budget 2007.

The other 15 per cent, which includes the top public sector leadership, remains on a pension scheme. The reason is strategic: to encourage the core top leadership to take a long term view of their careers in the public sector and a long term view of their role in public policy making and governance. However to manage the long run costs of these pensions, all salary increases since 1994 for eligible officers have not been pensionable.

7.7 Balancing Retention and Renewal: Managing Leadership Tenure

To further facilitate the retention of capable young AOs and to ensure a renewal of new talent and ideas in the top echelons of the public sector, a system of "flow through" fixed term appointments was established for all public sector leadership (PSL) positions. PSL positions include Permanent Secretaries, Deputy Secretaries, CEOs of major statutory boards and heads of key departments and some of the posts one level below the top.

Under the traditional framework, individuals who achieved public sector leadership positions in their forties could expect to remain in their jobs until they retired at age 62. Two factors made this arrangement increasingly untenable in the 1990s. The speed of change made it imperative that the public sector remain fresh, with a constant flow of new ideas and perspectives to tackle increasingly complex issues. To maintain organizational vibrancy, there had to be regular renewal of officers appointed to the PSL posts. In addition, the need to retain high potential young AOs behooved the organization to provide some realistic opportunities for them to attain PSL positions by the time they were in their mid-40s. At the same time, this need for organizational renewal and retention of high potential young talent had to be balanced against the need to maintain sufficient predictability and security in AOs' career paths to enable them to continue to take a long-term view on the job.

Since 2000, AOs who made it to PSL posts were appointed for fixed ten-year terms. For example, an officer appointed to the PSL post of Deputy Secretary could expect to be DS for ten years. The same situation applied to those officers appointed as Permanent Secretary.[65] At the end of their terms, these officers will have to assume non-PSL jobs if they are available or leave the service altogether. There is no formal emplacement mechanism outside the Service. Most PSs therefore expect to step down from their positions in their mid-fifties but the increasing number of young PSs assuming their positions in their late 30s and early 40s[66] will result in even earlier retirement.

This enforced renewal process mirrors the policy within the Singapore Armed Force where senior officers are retired in their mid-40s to enable younger officers to rise through the ranks quickly. In the early years of implementation, retiring SAF generals were eased into second careers as heads of statutory boards and government-linked companies. This was changed after 1997 when compensation packages were revised in the SAF. To make up for the early enforced retirement, an SAF officer earns in 25 years what he would have made if he had worked in other branches of the public sector. This revision probably came about due to difficulties in emplacing retired generals and the mixed results of those actually emplaced. It is likely for this reason that there was no undertaking to emplace retiring PSLs. Of the six Permanent Secretaries who retired up to 2005 since the new PSL framework came into operation, three became ambassadors and three took up positions on various boards.

This enforced early retirement has been criticized as a waste of valuable resources. While it has been pointed out that this is not unlike the system of fixed term appointments for CEOs in the private sector, there is a difference: the relative dearth of talented individuals good enough to provide leadership in the public sector in Singapore makes it sensible to retain them for as long as possible. Some have also observed that the pressure on PSL appointments is the result of the absence of alternative career paths within the public sector. Thus in

---

[65] Speech by the Prime Minister Lee Hsien Loong at the 2005 Administrative Service Dinner, 24 March 2005.

[66] Yong Ying-I, PS (Health) became PS at age 38. Tan Ching Yee, PS (Education) and Leo Yip, PS (Manpower) became PS at ages 40 and 41 respectively. Ong Ye Kung became the CEO of the Workforce Development Agency, a statutory board, at the age of 35. *The Straits Times*, "Super (Scale) Men: Up, Out … and a Waste?" Saturday, 19 November 2005.

devising an apparent solution to the problem of retaining young AOs, another problem was created, one for which no appropriate solution has been found.

In summary, dynamic capabilities in the public sector leadership have been fostered by a competitive merit-based system that stressed not only performance and delivery of results, but also good instincts in policy-making, and a systematic renewal process that ensured a constant flow of new ideas and perspectives. Singapore's public sector leadership core, by virtue of its small number, is a tight network which operates with an unusually high internal discipline. Even though officers in this network are evaluated on a predominantly individual basis, there appears to be a strong peer and team-based mentality, and a common set of values and principles which help to explain its continued effectiveness over 40 years.

7.8 Lessons on Having Able People as Leaders for Dynamic Governance

What lessons can we learn from the Singapore public sector experience in ensuring that it has leaders who are competent and honest, which ultimately is the source of dynamism in governance? We outline five key principles that we have discerned from Singapore public sector practice that we believe are applicable beyond this context.

7.8.1 *Dynamic Governance Requires a Strategic View of People and Leadership, and a Holistic Approach to Their Development*

Dynamism in governance is impossible without capable and committed leaders of character. Only leaders who are committed to the vision and values of the institution would constantly be on the look-out for signals that existing policies and programs may no longer be good enough because of changed circumstances. Able leaders with dynamic capabilities are required to adapt policies, projects and programs and to innovate to achieve the intended results even as needs evolve and new opportunities emerge. Making choices and taking action to change before you are forced to require commitment, character and capabilities. Dynamic governance is impossible without dynamic, moral leadership. This strategic view of leadership is the key lesson from our study of public sector governance in Singapore.

Singapore's political leaders understood right from the beginning that their ability to govern well, grow the economy, improve lives and combat the communists depended on the ability of the civil service to implement policies and achieve results. Good governance is impossible without good leaders. The strategic recognition that the quality of those in leadership would determine the quality of government made leadership issues top priority. It spurred significant investments in attracting and recruiting talent through scholarships, developing high potential officers, creating and giving opportunities to able leaders, and the constant effort to ensure that their compensation kept pace with the private sector. The approach taken was holistic and covered recruitment, development, deployment, reward, renewal and retention of leaders. This strong belief in leadership led to a number of practices, including:

(i)   deploying the best leaders to the most important tasks,
(ii) projects did not start until the right leaders were found,
(iii) autonomy was given to leaders to develop their strategies and achieve results,
(iv) strong accountability for results, and
(v)   promotion and progress were dependent on performance and potential.

7.8.2 *Manage People Development as a long-Term Investment*

Leadership development cannot be isolated from a larger commitment to people development on a long-term basis. It is not a one-time project or an ad hoc program. Organizations need to take a long-term view of developing the right people with the right capabilities for the strategic needs of the future, not just for short term performance improvements. Only such an organizational commitment can develop leaders with a long-term view to strategic and policy issues. The business of government is complex, multi-faceted and with many interested parties. Leaders develop their abilities to understand and deal with social and political nuances and subtleties over the long term. It is thus crucial that human resource policies retain adequate numbers of leaders for an extended period without jeopardizing the need for leadership renewal.

The Singapore public sector employed several policies and practices to encourage leaders to take a long-term view to policy issues, including retaining the pension scheme for Administrative Officers, rotational postings to expose officers to different issues from a national perspective and creating a strong social network with leaders who are committed to Singapore's interests in the long term. These practices were supported by a concerted career planning system and a reward structure that provided the appropriate incentives.

7.8.3 *The People Management System Must Be Based on Performance and Potential*

Cronyism demoralizes capable leaders and ultimately drives good people away from the organization. A good people management system must thus be based on merit, with clear and legitimate criteria of what constitutes performance, leadership potential and an accepted process for evaluation. The public sector continued with the assessment of potential even though its original proponents, Shell, in recent years moved away from it. The public sector's system gives financial rewards on the basis of current performance but requires an assessment of a person's potential before the individual is promoted to a leadership position. This is an interesting approach that is not usually practiced even in the private sector. That is why the Peter Principle is still so prevalent — people are promoted to their point of incompetence. When a person reaches his point of incompetence, his performance suffers and he is fired. An individual's career may be destroyed and an organization loses a staff who would have otherwise been a good performer. If a person is performing well in the current job, he should be rewarded and continue in the current job. He should be given a bigger leadership role only if he has the attributes and capabilities (i.e., potential) for the new job. When an assessment of potential is made before a leadership appointment, much pain in people management can be avoided.

Merit would involve an evaluation of an individual's performance and contribution but may go beyond that. When a subjective criterion such as potential is included, it should be defined clearly and the process of assessing potential, objective and valid. Beyond the specified criteria for performance, potential and an accepted process, people ultimately judge a human resource system by decisions that are made and the results that are achieved. Selection, promotion and appointments must be based on, and seen to be based on, critical factors of ability, performance and potential and not ideology, political leanings, experience or affiliations with existing members of the organization. Only then will committed and talented people be attracted to stay with the organization, and give of their best to achieve the desired outcomes.

7.8.4 People Issues are the Most Complex and Complicated, Requiring Constant Innovation rather than One-Time Clean Solutions

Determining the appropriate processes and systems for recruiting, renewing and retaining able and committed people within the public sector leadership is an unending journey of learning, adaptation and innovation. Constant monitoring of outcomes and refining of the system are crucial for dynamic governance as people issues are never completely solved. Dilemmas and unintended consequences are part and parcel of new ideas and innovative approaches. Solutions and schemes may work for a period of time, and then unexpected and unintended results may surface, requiring further innovation and change. The Singapore public sector provides many examples.

The PSC was created to ensure some independence of the civil service from the political leadership. But it became a big and lumbering bureaucracy so much so that its functions had to be decentralized. At the same time, key leadership appointments in the public sector not only continued to come under the PSC's jurisdiction — the process became more stringent when the Elected President's endorsements were made mandatory for such appointments. In response to complaints about a lack of flexibility in the centralized posting system for AOs, the PSD created an open market system to allow AOs to select their postings. However this created mismatches in the demand and supply of jobs available, and resulted in less balanced development paths for some officers. The system was later fine tuned to give PSD a greater voice in the deployment of AOs while still taking in account AO preferences. Market salary benchmarks to keep talent should go hand-in-hand with rigorous performance appraisal and judgment as in the private sector, yet the public sector does not want to be a hire and fire organization. The formula for benchmarking salaries is controversial: though it has been adjusted over time in response to feedback and its impact on turnover, it will always have its critics, whose suggested solutions themselves are problematic. Retention of leaders is desired but not at the expense of leadership renewal. But where does an organization strike a balance? Scholars are sent to top overseas institutions for greater exposure to broaden their development and help them build social networks with other future leaders but this practice undermines the objective to build local universities into world-class institutions. There is current debate over a range of people issues including the fixed-term appointments for leaders, whether scholars should be sent to local universities, why the recruitment of mid-career managers into the Administrative Service has proven to be difficult, and the desirability to expose high potential people to experiences beyond the public sector.

Constant monitoring and review of human resource policies and practices are needed to ensure that talent continues to be attracted, developed, deployed, rewarded and retained. The market for talent is dynamic and the competition for talent is intense. People management issues are never completely or cleanly resolved. New challenges and issues will arise from unexpected quarters. Ensuring that an organization has a good share of the talent available for key functions and roles will determine its ultimate success.

7.8.5 Leadership Should Be Selected on the Basis of Values, Performance and Potential with Freedom for Diversity of Leadership Personalities and Their Expressions

A good leadership system should select people imbued with values consistent with the organization's objectives, with a track record of credibility and performance and who have the potential to do well in new leadership opportunities. These leaders should then be given freedom to contribute to the organization in their own ways without being penalized for deviating from what are deemed to be the norms. A diversity of talent and a multiplicity of perspectives are needed for governance that is dynamic, governance that is constantly reviewing, perceiving, adapting, changing, innovating, and learning.

The diversity in public sector leadership is reflected in the careers and nature of the contributions of two of the top bureaucrats in the Singapore public sector — Philip Yeo and Lim Siong Guan — described earlier in the chapter. Both men started out in MINDEF but made different contributions — Lim Siong Guan led innovation in organizational and administrative processes, systems and structures while Philip Yeo led innovation in people and technological capability building. Lim went on to deepen organizational capacity in PSD, MOE and MOF while Yeo created new visions and spurred entrepreneurship, dynamism and the development of new capabilities in NCB, EDB, A*Star and a number of government-linked companies. In their own ways, they epitomize the dynamism of the public sector. But despite their different personalities, modes of expression and leadership styles, they share many attributes and values — both are highly intelligent and capable, strongly committed to public service, driven by their beliefs in developing people and building strong organizations, trusted by their political leaders and highly regarded by their people, peers and partners. They were able to make significant contributions because the system gave credence to these abilities and values rather than their personalities, and was flexible enough to allow them to make impact in their own ways. Because of this, the Singapore public sector and the Singapore economy now bear the imprint of both men.

The public service values the attributes of commitment, courage, conviction, conceptualization and contribution, and is willing to accept differences in approach to problem-solving. In a recent interview, the current Head of Civil Service illustrated the latitude the public sector is willing to give to those who think rationally and who can convince others of their ideas:

> "I will be more tolerant of (mavericks) but only up to a point. And this is because a maverick is only a maverick if he's fighting the establishment. So a person must believe enough in his ideas to be able to have the courage and conviction of his beliefs to push them through even against resistance… You come up with an idea and say 'I've got an idea,' then in one sentence 'Do this.' Why should I accept it? So there must be some ability to conceptualise the idea into a proper proposal and enough argument to make me look at it a second time."[67]

Above all else, Singapore's dynamic governance is the direct result of committed leadership of character in both the political and public sector arenas. The public sector people management system is the result of endless adjustments and changes in attempts to select, develop and retain the best talent and leadership who can help shape Singapore society as it faces the challenges of survival and success in an uncertain, unpredictable and fast changing global environment.

---

[67] *The Straits Times*, Friday, 17 November 2006, p. 41.

8

Process Innovation: Creating Agile Structures and Systems

People and processes are the main drivers of dynamic governance as shown in our framework in Figure 1.1 of Chapter 1. While the commitment and competencies of people in leadership ultimately determine the effectiveness of governance, it cannot just depend on specific individuals. Governance that depends solely on the motivations and capabilities of individual leaders would be too risky and too vulnerable. The survival of countries is too important to be subject to such risks. Effective governance has to be institutionalized to be sustainable. For dynamic governance to be effectively institutionalized, organizational processes must be designed and implemented so that the governance system can still continue to function even when there is a change in leadership.

"The key to understanding what makes an organization more or less effective is how it does things... its various processes."[1] The quality of competencies of individual leaders, while crucial for effective performance, does not define the entirety of an organization's capabilities. Individual competencies are derived from a person's attitudes, knowledge and skills in performing important tasks and activities. Organizational capabilities are embedded in processes that coordinate, combine and integrate the performance of various workers and units, enable learning and absorption of new knowledge, and induce continuous reconfiguration and transformation. Dynamic governance capabilities thus require the development of distinctive organizational processes.[2]

---

[1] Edgar H Schein (1988). *Process Consultation: Its Role in Organizational Development*. Reading, Massachusetts: Addison-Wesley, p. 15.

[2] DJ Teece, G Pisano and A Shuen (1997). "Dynamic Capabilities and Strategic Management," *Strategic Management Journal*, Vol. 18, pp. 509–534.

Processes define the required input resources, the tasks needed to be performed, the people responsible for performing the tasks, the required output, how the tasks and people performing them are to be coordinated and integrated to produce the required output, the rules governing its performance and management, and the customers who are to receive the output. They also define how quality and performance are measured, how errors are detected and corrected, and how improvements and changes are made.

Garvin identified three categories of organization processes: work processes, behavioral processes and change processes.[3] Work processes accomplish the operational and administrative requirements of an organization by defining activities that transform input into output. Behavioral processes are widely shared patterns of behavior and ways of acting and interacting that infuse and shape the way work is conducted by influencing how individuals and groups behave. Change processes describe how organizations adapt, develop and grow, and eventually alter the scale, character and identity of the organization.

This chapter's focus on creating dynamic capabilities through organizational processes would encompass all three categories of work, behavioral and change activities. We identified three major organizational processes in the Singapore public sector that together created the capacity that enabled it to continue to transform itself: anticipating the future, allocating financial resources and applying systemic discipline. Each process includes work, behavioral and change structures and activities that collectively induce the public sector to continually learn, improve and adapt.

These processes, as shown in Figure 8.1, show the key dynamic outcomes that may be potentially created by organizational processes: reframing of leadership perception, renewing of organizational activities, and redesigning of structural linkages. The three processes we found in our study work through different practices to influence the nature, direction, and pace of change:

[3] David A Garvin (1998). "The Processes of Organization and Management," *Sloan Management Review*, Summer, pp. 33–50.

(i)   anticipating the future utilizes future scenarios and strategies,
(ii) allocating financial resources works through the budget mechanisms and value assessments, and
(iii) applying systemic discipline focuses on enabling integration, engaging change and enhancing service.

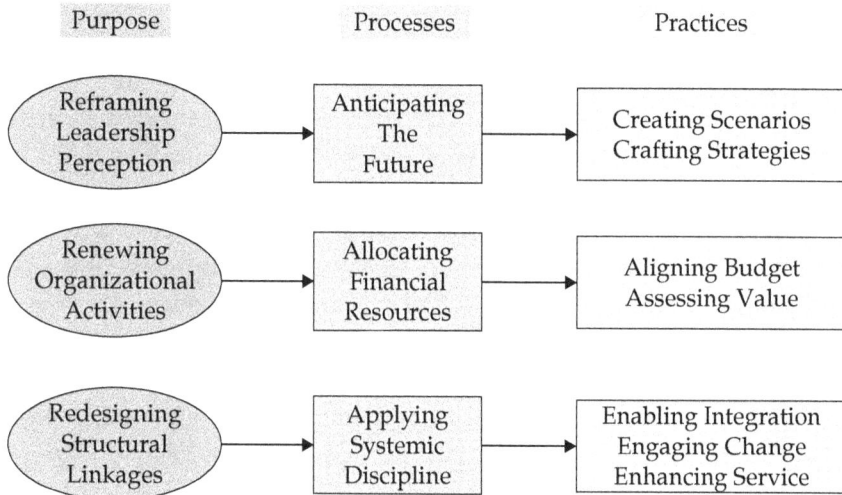

Purpose	Processes	Practices
Reframing Leadership Perception	Anticipating The Future	Creating Scenarios Crafting Strategies
Renewing Organizational Activities	Allocating Financial Resources	Aligning Budget Assessing Value
Redesigning Structural Linkages	Applying Systemic Discipline	Enabling Integration Engaging Change Enhancing Service

Figure 8.1. Creating Processes for Dynamic Governance

Organizations often change only when the pain of a crisis is felt. The need for change is then clear — however in a crisis, leaders have little time, less resources, and fewer options. Many organizations do not survive a crisis. The challenge for organizations is how to recognize the need for change and move before a crisis hits. The goal of anticipating the future is thus not merely to make future plans but to influence the perceptions of decision-makers.[4] Anticipating the future in the public sector is a process of engaging the leadership and reframing their perception of the emerging issues that may have significant impact on the success of a country's strategies and policies. This process of crafting future scenarios to challenge assumptions and

---

[4] Arie de Geus (1988). "Planning as Learning," *Harvard Business Review*, March–April, pp. 2–6.

creating strategic responses to them builds the organizational flexibility needed for survival in an uncertain and unpredictable environment. It also enables the organization to prepare for the future by reviewing policy changes that may be needed, initiating investments in long-term infrastructure, building new capabilities, and preparing contingency responses to specific possible developments.

Allocating financial resources is a process of inducing the desired changes in organizational activities by ensuring that adequate resources are allocated and reallocated to fund both on-going operations and new programs and activities. The process of allocating resources should be aligned to the process of anticipating the future so that the latter will not degenerate into a mere intellectual exercise with no real resources to effect required change in the organization. It also provides a platform for assessing the value of existing expenditure and induces the change required for greater efficiency and effectiveness.

Applying systemic discipline is a process of designing structures and systems to ensure that organizational change becomes a sustained effort of continuous improvement, and not merely a one-time change that will lose its relevance over time as the future unfolds in uncertain and unpredictable ways. It is easy to change and do something differently when there is leadership attention and adequate financial or human resources. However, without carefully designed structures and systems, changes in activities, choices and values cannot be sustained and will lose momentum when leadership attention in a particular activity is inevitably reduced to focus on other important issues. In a complex and dynamic environment, systemic structures and linkages have to be redesigned to expand organizational capacity, enable integration across agencies, engage people at every level for continuous change, and enhance service to customers and citizens.

The three processes individually and collectively build organizational capacity for continuous change as leadership perceptions are constantly challenged, as resources are reallocated to new programs and activities, and as change-sustaining systems and structures are implemented. The rest of the chapter describes the processes and practices that are followed by the Singapore public sector and show how these have built the dynamic capabilities that enabled it to continually change in response to new challenges.

8.1 Anticipating the Future — Reframing Leadership Perception

We know the future will be different from today, but we do not know in what shape and form the future would take — it is uncertain and unpredictable. "To operate in an uncertain world, people needed to be able to reperceive — to question their assumptions about the way the world works, so that they could see the world more clearly."[5] The purpose of anticipating the future is to gather and transform information of strategic significance into fresh perceptions. The real value of thinking about the future comes from the interactions among those who must decide and act. Learning occurs when leaders understand and challenge their shared mental models of their environments and their institutions and become better equipped to respond to inevitable surprises.[6] The desired end result is not necessarily a more accurate picture of the future, but better mental sensitivity to and interpretation of signals of future developments and increased agility of response when future events occur.[7]

Hamel and Prahalad[8] identified four patterns of corporate failure that reflected inabilities to escape the past and invent the future:

(i)   complacency with current performance as a result of a track record of success,

(ii) abundant resources in an organization substituting for its creativity,

(iii) vulnerability to new rules of the game as a result of deeply etched routines and recipes, and

(iv) mistaking momentum for leadership that led to a failure to reinvent the organization.

---

[5] Pierre Wack (1985). "Scenarios: Uncharted Waters Ahead," *Harvard Business Review*, September–October, pp. 73–89, and "Scenarios: Shooting the Rapids," *Harvard Business Review*, November–December, pp. 139–150.

[6] de Geus (1988).

[7] Peter Schwartz (1991). *The Art of the Long View*. New York, NY: Bantam Doubleday Publishing Group.

[8] G Hamel and CK Prahalad (1994). *Competing for the Future*. Cambridge, MA: Harvard Business School Press.

Staking out new competitive space requires an understanding of how competition in the future will be different from the present and is a process for finding and gaining insight into tomorrow's opportunities. "What prevents companies from creating the future is an installed base of thinking — the unquestioned conventions, the myopic view of opportunities and threats, and the unchallenged precedents that comprise the existing managerial frame."[9] Good insight and foresight do not guarantee future success, but without them one cannot even begin the journey.

In Singapore, the need to anticipate the future stems from an innate sense of its vulnerability — arising from its small physical size, its lack of natural resources, and its small population size. Singapore depends on international trade and investments for its success, and thus is significantly impacted by international or regional developments. Yet Singapore cannot influence or control events. Its only option is to change to remain relevant — thus the critical need to anticipate the future. It needs to be able to respond fast, flexibly and frequently. Survival and success require its leaders to have a deep understanding of plausible future developments, the impact of such developments, and what policies and investments would be needed for Singapore to stay relevant and effective in the changing global environment. The Singapore public sector's approach to anticipating the future and reframing leadership perceptions takes two main forms: creating scenarios that challenge assumptions and crafting strategies to face the future.

8.1.1 *Creating Scenarios that Challenge Assumptions*

Scenarios are "stories about the way the world might turn out tomorrow."[10] It is a tool for reframing leadership perceptions about alternative future environments in which important decisions might be played out. Scenarios are not predictions of the future. They are useful for learning about the implications of possible futures on today's decisions. "In a scenario process, managers invent and then

---

[9] Ibid, p. 61.
[10] Schwartz (1991).

consider, in depth, several varied stories of plausible futures... the point is to make strategic decisions that will be sound for all plausible futures. No matter what future takes place, you are much more likely to be ready for it — if you have thought seriously about scenarios."[11] Scenarios as stories give meaning to events, open leaders to multiple perspectives and help them cope with complexity. An essential step in the process is rehearsing the implications for each scenario and how one would act to achieve the desired outcomes.

The Ministry of Defence was the first public agency to use scenarios in 1990 to think about the future and surface issues that required attention. The civil service began learning about scenario planning in 1991 with support provided by the Ministry of Defence and a Scenario Planning Office was set up in the Prime Minister's Office in 1995. Scenario planning was adopted by the public sector as a strategic tool to anticipate change by providing a structure to clarify thinking about the future, understand the key drivers of change, challenge the underlying assumptions, and interact over possible options in each scenario. Strategic plans were tested for robustness using the scenarios and inherent risks were made more explicit. Decision-makers developed sensitivity and alertness to changes in the environment and were better prepared to take action in response to change.

The Scenario Planning Office conducted workshops for agencies to equip them with the tools and methodologies for doing scenario planning and acted as a coordinator for the development of national scenarios. It created a suggested agenda for approval, selected the team members, developed the broad methodology, coordinated the activities of the team, helped to connect different ideas into a coherent framework, influenced how the scenarios were put together, prepared reports and papers for approval, shared the scenarios with agencies, and facilitated agencies' strategic responses to the scenarios. Four sets of national scenarios were developed in 1997, 1999, 2002 and 2005. Each scenario development cycle took about a year, broadly following an approach learnt from Shell.

---

[11] Ibid, p. xiii.

First, the scope and agenda for the scenario exercise were agreed between the scenario office and the committee of permanent secretaries. For example, a recent exercise sought to understand the key challenges that Singapore would face in 2025. Second, a scenario project team was formed with 20 to 25 young officers each with three to four years of public sector experience in the various agencies. The team gathered information and interviewed decision-makers in the public and private sectors, academics and journalists to gather a range of viewpoints. The main questions posed were of the form, "What keeps you awake at night and why?" The driving forces of change were identified, researched and examined. These driving forces included external elements such as developments in China, India, the Middle East and the neighboring countries, developments in technology, energy prices and security threats. They also included internal elements such as rising expectations among the young, plight of low-income workers, and needs of senior citizens.

Third, these critical issues were summarized into a three-page paper and submitted to the Cabinet for approval. This early engagement of the political decision-makers was carried out to initiate conversations that would lead to a shared view of the issues important for Singapore's future. Fourth, these critical issues were developed into scenarios and plausible stories of the future. Fifth, strategic responses were sought and developed for each scenario. The central question was of the form, "What will you do if this scenario happens and why?" All national scenarios were sent to the Cabinet for approval. Priorities for the country were identified and formed the strategic themes for development for the future.

Finally, the national scenarios were presented to public sector agencies to enable them to understand the key issues affecting Singapore's future. These scenarios were used by the agencies as input for their strategic planning processes. Agencies had the autonomy to assess the implications of the scenarios on their strategic priorities and decide on the issues they deemed as important to be incorporated into their annual work plan. Although many agencies used the scenarios to identify important issues, they were not obliged to formally report to the Scenario Planning Office on how the scenarios were used.

Their strategic planning is decentralized and approved by individual ministries rather than by the Scenario Planning Office.

Scenarios are used in the Singapore public sector to engage government leaders in conversations about the future and stimulate a re-examination of policies and assumptions rather than as a formal planning mechanism for consolidation into an overall plan. With formal follow-throughs intentionally left to the agencies, it is inevitable that not all agencies take scenarios as seriously as they should. The purpose for using scenarios in this manner is to preserve the strategic nature of the conversations without allowing it to degenerate into a form-filling and report-generation exercise. This approach in the use of scenarios in anticipating the future focuses attention on the substantive issues and keeps the interactions organic and informal. The Scenario Planning Office has fewer than ten staff who serve as expert facilitators and do not rely on top-down bureaucratic mandates to direct the agencies. Participation in scenario teams is viewed by public officers and agencies as significant development opportunities. The teams have to ensure that their work is substantive, interesting and credible enough to engage the agencies and to motivate the agencies to consider the scenarios seriously in their own strategic plans.

8.1.2 *Crafting Strategies for the Future*

As the role of the public sector changed from controller and regulator to nurturer, facilitator, convener and aggregator, its focus changed from monitoring current activities to creating strategies for future development. Strategic planning by public sector agencies went beyond their own annual work plans, extending to the strategic development of the sectors under their preview or their related clusters. These sectors included economic industries such as retail, tourism and manufacturing, and social sectors such as the arts, sports, and education. In a typical strategic planning process, agencies anticipated the future by studying economic, social and technological trends affecting their missions, assessed the achievements to date, evaluated the capabilities needed for exploiting new opportunities or countering threats, and developed migration paths to achieve their strategic intent. Teams involving internal staff and external stakeholders were formed to study the key issues and brainstorm for ideas within broad strategic frameworks developed by the agencies in consultation with international experts.

As an important part of the planning process, the teams would study potential role models and exemplars in other countries for ideas, motivation and risk mitigation in the implementation. The study process involved teams scanning and identifying potential role models that may stimulate thinking about potential outcomes and development paths, visiting the sites to interact with the managers, understanding how results were achieved and how the implementation was managed, identifying what Singapore might learn from these exemplars, and incorporating the learning points into proposals for development.

The study teams then consolidated findings from their research, discussions and visits into specific strategies and proposals for development. These proposals were then presented to different stakeholders for feedback and support, and revised in an iterative process. The proposed strategies for development were then submitted to the permanent secretary and minister for approval. Resources required for the development and implementation of the strategies would be requested in the annual budget submitted to the Ministry of Finance.

In recent years, several agencies have crafted strategies for long-term development of key sectors. The Infocomm Development Authority crafted strategies for growing the computer, software and telecoms industries, attracting investments from leading global players, developing needed skills through new training programs, and promoting ICT (information and communications technologies) applications and usage by businesses, government and citizens. Similarly, the EDB developed a strategy to make Singapore an educational hub by attracting ten world-class universities to set up campuses and offer their programs to Asian students. The Agency for Science, Technology and Research crafted a comprehensive strategy for building a world-class biomedical cluster in Singapore. Starting from scratch in 2000, it attracted many leading pharmaceutical and biotech companies to invest in R&D and manufacturing in Singapore, created a new infrastructure for biotech R&D in the Biopolis, funded research centers in key areas of biomedical sciences, attracted leading researchers to spearhead major research programs and sponsored selected young talent to enroll for PhD programs in the top biomedical science programs in the US and Europe.

The strategic planning process complemented the scenarios process in enabling the public sector to anticipate the future with both intellectual rigor and practical actions. While the scenario process was done from a national perspective, strategic planning was usually spearheaded by individual agencies and focused on specific sectors or clusters. The scenarios served as important input for the strategic planning process and challenged the study teams to develop rigorous strategic responses that addressed the issues surfaced in the scenarios. While the scenario process was kept fairly informal with an emphasis on reflective conversations, strategic planning was a more formal process with specific accountabilities, timelines and formats, milestones for deliverables, strategy papers required for various approvals, and formal publication of strategic plans. These plans were used as a basis for developing budgets and implementation schedules and subsequent measurement of progress. Scenarios and strategies together integrated the public sector's intellectual, social and organizational response to an uncertain and unpredictable future. A judicious mix of both informal interactions and formal processes has enabled the public sector to focus on substantive issues without losing the formal accountabilities required to achieve desired outcomes in a large and complex institution.

Recently, the civil service led a national effort involving many ministries and agencies to generate new ideas for Singapore's future growth in a more competitive and connected world. In April 2007, the government announced a new growth strategy for Singapore based on integrating the ideas of trust, knowledge, connectedness and life into a catchy name, "World.Singapore".[12] The effort which began in 2005 involved 19 teams, each with 10 to 20 members and led by

---

[12] Speech by Minister Teo Chee Hean at the Opening of the EDB's International Advisory Council meeting on 19 April 2007.

a permanent secretary[13]. The teams visited seven global cities and interviewed many people, including those who were not currently engaged with Singapore. More than 90 ideas were proposed and ten of these have been approved and funded by the Ministry of Finance for execution, including S$45.5m to enhance Singapore's nightlife scene through better night lighting and infrastructure, and S$21.3m to fund exchange programs and overseas attachments for students.

8.2 Allocating Financial Resources: Renewing Organizational Activities

Reframing leadership perception to prepare for the future is important in overcoming a natural tendency of denying current problems until they reach crisis proportions and fostering new mental models regarding threats and opportunities. A prepared mind makes the organization more able to recognize early signals of change and more able to respond appropriately to counter the threats and take advantage of new opportunities arising from change. However, a change in strategies, policies and activities in a resource-constrained environment require a reallocation of existing resources to fund new projects, programs and experiments. While it may be easy to agree to new programs, it is more difficult to decide what existing programs and activities to stop or reduce in order to free up resources for the new activities. Leaders and organizations are often over-invested in the status quo, and a reallocation of resources to effect change is an intensely political process.

> "Legacy strategies have powerful constituencies; embryonic strategies do not. In most organizations, a manager's power correlates directly with the resources he or she controls — to lose resources is to lose stature and influence. Moreover, personal success often turns solely on the performance of one's own unit or program. It is hardly surprising, then, that unit executives and program

---

[13] *The Straits Times* report on 20 April 2007, "19 Civil Service Teams' Task: Ideas to Spark S'pore Growth," by Lynn Lee.

managers typically resist any attempt to reallocate their capital and talent to new initiatives — no matter how attractive those new initiatives may be." [14]

Further, while most organizations require new programs and activities to be carefully evaluated and justified, no such requirement is made of existing programs and activities, resulting in many projects being perpetuated beyond their relevance and usefulness. These existing programs tie up resources and make the funding of new activities much more difficult. "Allocational rigidities are the enemy of resilience... it can maximize the efficiency of existing programs... and yet fail to fund the unconventional ideas that might yield an even higher return." [15]

Allocation of financial resources in expenditure budgets are subject to problems of information asymmetry, agency and moral hazard. [16] A government department has access to more information about their financial needs than would ever be communicated to the Ministry of Finance (MOF) because of both local departmental specialization and MOF's limited ability to monitor the amount and quality of the information provided. This creates agency problems because the department may use the resources to take risks and implement programs that are sub-optimal. Moral hazard arises when departmental actions and behaviors cannot be closely monitored to ensure that allocated funds are used efficiently. These resource allocation problems are compounded in the public sector by the intangible nature of both public policy input and output, and by the difficulty in accurately measuring costs and benefits. As a result, resource allocation processes in the public sector are subject to budget gaming, timid goals, resource hoarding and spending sprees.

Fiscal policies in Singapore are designed to achieve objectives of enhancing economic competitiveness, managing social demands, and

---

[14] G Hamel and L Valikangas (2003). "The Quest for Resilience," *Harvard Business Review*, September, pp. 52–63.

[15] Ibid.

[16] RS Kaplan and AA Atkinson (1998). *Advanced Management Accounting*, 3rd Edition. NJ: Prentice-Hall.

responding to short-term cyclical downturns. Fiscal prudence has been a core principle for the government since Singapore's independence. Being a small economy heavily dependent on international trade, there is little scope for generating domestic demand when there is a drastic drop in global trade. Since the country has no natural resources, financial reserves accumulated from budget surpluses are the only means available to cushion the adverse impacts of an economic recession.

MOF has adopted an organizational renewal approach to the budget. It sees the budget as more than a statement of how financial resources are distributed to different agencies. It envisions the budget as a statement of Singapore's perceived future, governance philosophy, chosen strategy, proposed outcomes, people's expectations, and resource availability. These purposes are summarized in Table 8.1. The budget shows the government's priorities and how it intends to develop the country.

Table 8.1. Purpose of the Budget

1. Statement of Perceived Future
2. Statement of Governance Philosophy
3. Statement of Chosen Strategy
4. Statement of Proposed Outcomes
5. Statement of People's Expectations
6. Statement of Resource Availability

Budget principles and practices are used to stimulate public agencies to renew their priorities and activities while maintaining an efficient operational core. Cognizant of the problems associated with information asymmetry, agency and moral hazard, the MOF has implemented a number of innovative practices to induce flexibility, change and renewal while ensuring financial accountability. It seeks to influence the ministries' goals and priorities during the budget cycle so that adequate resources are channeled to the most important projects without direct bureaucratic dictates. It engages the ministries through a series of three strategic conversations during each budget cycle.

At the start of the budget cycle, MOF meets with each ministry in an Annual Strategic Review (ASR). Through the ASR meeting, MOF discusses with each ministry its strategic priorities in the medium term (next five years), and reviews the alignment of the ministry's desired outcomes with national outcomes. The ministry is also engaged on its new strategic thrusts and made aware of how their priorities fit into the larger picture of national priorities.

Sectoral Budget Meetings (SBM) are then held with permanent secretaries from each of the three major sectors (economic, social, and security/governance) to generate cross-agency synergies, ideas and programs that are aligned with national whole-of-government outcomes. The SBMs facilitate consensus building (amongst peers) on the priorities for each sector, surface gaps and duplications across ministries' programs in each sector, and consolidate ideas for possible cross-agency cooperation. Agencies are encouraged to develop joint funding proposals for cross-agency projects that would be strategic to the country.

After the ministries have submitted their initial budget proposals to MOF, Budget Review Meetings (BRMs) are held with each ministry to focus on how each ministry intends to manage its strategic initiatives and on-going operations with the proposed budget resources. During the BRMs, MOF officials engage each ministry on their past performances, in the desired outcomes and design considerations of new projects and in ideas for improving the efficiency and effectiveness of on-going operational activities. While the ASRs engage the ministries on the question, "Are we doing the right things," the BRMs go further by engaging the ministries on the question, "Are we doing the right things efficiently and effectively?" The financial year for the public sector runs from April to March. The annual budget cycle is shown in Table 8.2.

Once the budget is approved, the ministries manage their own execution without interference from the MOF. On an annual basis, MOF measures the performance of the ministries relative to their own goals and in comparison with other ministries. It is a delicate balance to try to influence the ministries without affecting their autonomy to decide and act. The approach adopted by MOF seeks to encourage

Table 8.2. Annual Budget Cycle

Budget Activity	Time Frame
1. MOF determines the planning parameters for the budget	April to June
2. Annual Strategic Reviews with ministries	May to June
3. MOF informs ministries of planning parameters and seeks comments and proposals from ministries	July
4. Sectoral Budget Meetings (economic, social, security)	August
5. Ministries submit budget proposals to MOF	September to October
6. Budget Review Meetings with ministries	October to November
7. MOF informs ministries of budget decisions	November
8. MOF consolidates and finalizes government budget	December
9. Cabinet approves budget	January
10. Minister of Finance presents budget to Parliament	Mid-February
11. Budget debate in Parliament	End February to Mid-March
12. Parliament approves budget and passes the Supply Bill	Mid-March
13. President endorses the Supply Bill	End March

Table 8.3. Budget Principles and Financial Practices

Establish Budget Limits	Maximize Discretion	Account for Full Costs	Seek Value for Expenditure
Budget Caps - By Ministry	Block Budgets - Operations - Development	Resource Budgeting and Accounting	Best Sourcing
Reinvestment Fund	Net Budgeting	Net Economic Value	Shared Services
Cost Norms for government buildings (e.g., for government buildings/ rental rates)	Budget Flexibility - Advances - Rollovers - Carry Forwards	Inter-departmental Charging	Economy Drive - Cut Waste - Cut Red Tape
Development Projects Committee			

the best possible outcome by the agencies for the financial resources allocated. The framework includes establishing limits, maximizing discretion, accounting for full costs, and seeking value in financial expenditure.[17] The budget principles and financial practices that induce organizational renewal are summarized in Table 8.3.

8.2.1 *Establishing Budget Limits*

To achieve fiscal prudence, Singapore's constitution limits the total expenditure of each elected term of government (usually four to five years) to within the operating revenue collected and net investment income from reserves available to the current term of government. The fiscal discipline is meant to prevent an elected political party from over-spending in order to win elections. Such a fiscal formula might compound budget difficulties resulting in big swings from overly conservative expenditure budgets at the beginning of an elected government's term to excessively liberal budgets toward the end. To overcome these potential problems, MOF establishes a transparent formula of budget limits for each ministry that give agencies a sustainable level of expenditure that enables them to plan strategically, build capabilities, respond to new needs, and improve efficiencies over a medium term.

Since financial year 2003, sectoral and ministry budgets have been capped to a percentage of a smoothened GDP, defined as a weighted six-year average of the past three years and the projected GDP of the next three years. The caps take into account the ministries' actual historical expenditure levels at the time of formulation, reflecting national priorities at that point in time. Adjustments to the capped percentages are made systematically, in line with fundamental shifts in national priorities and social-economic factors, e.g., population profile, that require long-term shifts in expenditure budgets for the different sectors and ministries. There is also a built-in adjustment to

---

[17] The material for this section comes from the authors' interviews with the Permanent Secretary and other senior officials from the Ministry of Finance and from an article written by Lim Siong Guan (2004). "Government that Costs Less," published by the Civil Service College.

the budgets based on GDP growth or decline. The expenditure and budget allocations as percentages of GDP to different ministries in the last six years are shown in Table 8.4.

The sustainability of budgets with established limits, which assures agencies of funding over several years, also leads to status quo continuation of existing programs and activities in some agencies. But direct intervention by MOF in specific activities in public agencies is undesirable (since it is based on a questionable assumption that

Table 8.4. Sectoral and Ministry Budget Allocations

Ministry	2001–2006 Total Expenditure as a % of GDP	2007 Total Budgeted Expenditure as a % of GDP[a]
Economic Development	**1.75–2.61**	**1.83**
Trade and Industry	0.75–1.21	0.88
Transport	0.84–1.26	0.84
Manpower	0.10–0.14	0.11
Social Development	**5.93–7.89**	**6.22**
Education	3.06–4.16	3.13
Health	0.89–1.21	1.01
National Development	0.63–1.43	0.89
Environment & Water Resources	0.47–0.86	0.39
Community Development, Youth & Sports	0.41–0.50	0.57
Information, Communications & the Arts[b]	0.24–0.29	0.24
Security & External Relations	**5.96–6.73**	**6.04**
Defence	4.65–5.17	4.70
Home Affairs	1.12–1.41	1.16
Foreign Affairs	0.15–0.18	0.18
Government Administration	**0.57–0.86**	**0.57**
Finance	0.25–0.35	0.26
Law	0.13–0.27	0.11
Prime Minister's Office	0.08–0.12	0.10
Organs of State	0.10–0.18	0.10
Total Government Expenditure	**14.26–17.96**	**14.66**

Source: "Budget Highlights" from the 2007 Budget and Singapore Department of Statistics.
[a] 2007 GDP is based on 5 per cent growth over 2006 GDP.
[b] Includes info-communications and media development.

Table 8.5. Reinvestment Fund

Year	Percent of Budget
2004	1.28%
2005	3.28%
2006	5%

MOF knows more than the agencies themselves) and undermines the ownership, commitment and incentives of staff and officials in the agencies to pursue the best possible outcome for their agencies.

In 2004, MOF introduced a reinvestment fund that engendered rethinking of existing expenditure patterns in each agency and drove the reallocation of resources for investment in synergistic programs, creative projects and new opportunities. A certain percentage was deducted each year from each ministry's budget and pooled into a reinvestment fund, from which ministries could bid for funding for their new, synergistic and innovative programs. The percentage deducted from each year's budget and pooled into the reinvestment fund for reallocation is shown in Table 8.5.

The reinvestment fund mechanism prompted ministries to reconsider and improve their existing activities, and to develop new ideas for creative experimentation and pilot testing to further their strategic objectives. With their budgets reduced by the reinvestment fund percentage, ministries had to improve the productivity of existing programs (by the percentage deducted) if they wanted to continue with the existing portfolio of activities, cut some activities to live with a reduced budget, or obtain additional budget resources by introducing creative ideas, innovative projects and new activities to achieve their strategic goals aligned with national objectives.

8.2.2 Maximizing Discretion

Traditionally, budgeting involves protracted negotiations between MOF and the ministries over the costs needed for pre-specified programs or outputs, with predictable outcomes — a political game played with ministries asking for more, MOF trying to give less, and a compromise reached between the two numbers. Over the years, as the budget allocations moved towards predetermined limits based on a percentage of GDP, the budget process evolved towards giving ministries greater autonomy, discretion and incentives to obtain the maximum value from resources allocated to them.

Rigid line-by-line control of expenditure items was changed to a more flexible program budgeting in 1978. This was further liberalized in 1989 into a block-vote budgeting system that allowed ministries flexibility in managing allocations across programs. In 1996, a budgeting-for-results system was introduced that shifted emphasis from programs to output. This approach created incentives for ministries to improve efficiency and achieve the lowest costs for agreed output targets. Ministries were accountable for results rather than program activities, and efficiency savings could be used for other programs. A block-budget system was implemented in 2001 that gave ministries maximum discretion in the use of allocated resources to find the best means to achieve desired results. Ministries could reprioritize their spending needs, including the movement of funds between operating and development expenditure, as circumstances changed and as new needs arose during the year.

Net budgeting was implemented to encourage agencies to recover some of the cost of public services through fees and financial charges especially if there were some commercial benefits attached to the use of the services, and generally to prevent over-use of free services. Ministries' budgets are adjusted annually in line with revenue collected from these services. Ministries thus have to carefully manage these services because any variances from the net budget would be funded from their own operating budgets.

Budgeting is done on a financial year basis for accounting purposes but the timing of expenditure for new projects and initiatives may not fit neatly within a financial year. MOF developed a budget utilization framework that gives some flexibility in the use of resources without excessive hoarding. The three main budget flexibility mechanisms are summarized in Table 8.6.

A ministry is allowed a roll-over of 5 per cent of its operating budget to the following year to reduce the tendency for a spending

Table 8.6. Budget Flexibility Framework

Flexible Mechanism	Limit	Purpose
Roll over	5%	Reduce tendency for end-of-year binges
Advances	10%, repaid within 3 years	Allow rational financial decisions without undue constraints imposed by time periods
Carry forward	3 years	Enable accumulation of funds for larger projects

binge at year-end. If a ministry under-utilizes its budget by more than 5 per cent, its following year budget would be adjusted downwards to better reflect their real needs. This is to ensure that each ministry budgets properly and asks only for the required amount rather than to overstate its requirement. If a ministry requires more funds in the current financial year, an advance of up to 10 per cent of the budget could be given by MOF, and the advance has to be repaid with interest over the following three years. Finally, any block budget allotments not taken up in any year could be carried forward for three years to enable ministries to accumulate funds to undertake larger projects and to minimize incentives to overstate budget requirements.

The budget process has become more sophisticated as the MOF sought in a nuanced approach to create greater autonomy and flexibility without loss of financial accountability and control. The budget innovations liberated the budget process from being a bureaucratic mechanism to being a set of flexible tools that enabled agencies to optimally manage their financial resources to achieve their strategic objectives. The budget has moved from being a preserver of the status quo to being a tool for provoking organizational renewal — change capabilities created in the public sector as a result of innovations in financial processes.

8.2.3 Accounting for Full Costs

Many governments, including Singapore, have traditionally allocated budgets on a cash basis and accounting for fund usage also, typically, has been done on a cash basis. However, cash accounting did not provide adequate information for economic decision-making because of the exclusion of non-cash items that have economic consequences and timing differences between benefits obtained and cash flow. MOF introduced resource budgeting and accounting to supplement the traditional cash budgeting and accounting.

In a resource accounting system, ministries are required to keep their internal accounting records on an accrual basis to include non-cash items such as depreciation, cost of capital and imputed rental, as well as record expenditure when incurred rather than when cash was paid. In resource budgeting, ministries are required to budget for these non-cash items and ensure that they have enough funds on a total resource (i.e., including the provisions for the non-cash items) basis. The effect of resource accounting and budgeting is to reflect the full costs of all resources in providing public services and in implementing new projects and programs.

Net Economic Value (NEV) accounting, equivalent to the concept of Economic Value-Added, has been introduced to induce public sector efforts to get the most value from the resources allocated. NEV, which measures revenue less operating costs less the cost of capital, has been negative for most agencies. MOF has thus set the improvement target as the incremental rather than absolute NEV (less negative from year to year) to encourage public agencies to continually evaluate possibilities for recovering some costs of services provided (thus increasing revenue), improving efficiency of operations (thus reducing costs) and more prudent capital management (thus reducing capital costs).

One weakness of public sector decision-making is the lack of a financial bottom-line to motivate managers to act in the interests of the stakeholders who are citizens and may not have the knowledge, time nor the access to question managers of public agencies. With the implementation of resource budgets and accounting and NEV, MOF adapted best practices for financial measurement from the private sector and gave ministries the economic information needed to make rational decisions. The lack of a financial bottom-line is no longer an impediment to optimizing financial resources. Public agencies have the financial tools and information to maximize output to achieve strategic objectives, whether the decisions are about building or renting facilities, outsourcing activities or performing them in-house, or the extent of private sector involvement in funding and operating capital projects.

8.2.4 *Seeking Value in Financial Expenditure*

MOF introduced several practices to public agencies that helped them stretch the financial resources allocated to them. These practices did not determine the block budgets allocated to ministries but they had to show in their review meetings with MOF, how they were implementing these practices to stretch the money allocated to them. The main practices introduced were best sourcing, shared services, and economy drive.

In best sourcing, ministries were required to differentiate between their strategic and non-strategic activities and then perform a market test for their non-strategic activities. It was not an outsourcing policy per se but a discipline to continually evaluate internal non-strategic activities against benchmarks set by external providers. In a market test, ministries obtained service proposals from private sector providers to perform their non-strategic activities, evaluated the private sector proposals against internal costs and standards, and justified whether the non-strategic activities should be outsourced or continued to be performed in-house. Since April 2004, the public sector has market-tested about 230 or 18 per cent of its non-strategic functions. Seventy per cent of these functions were subsequently outsourced with an aggregate contract value of about $1.8b, yielding an annual operational cost savings of at least $34m. Some of the activities that have been outsourced included data center operations, library services, car parking enforcement, fishery port operations, laboratory support, call centers, maintenance and cleaning services, and logistics operations.

As part of the best sourcing framework, a public-private-partnership (PPP) approach was adopted to engage the expertise and resources of the private sector to provide services to the public. Government agencies used to own and operate the facilities required for delivering public services. In the PPP approach, the public sector purchased services from the private sector that were then delivered to the public. The private sector has since developed, owned and operated needed assets such as water treatment plants, higher learning institutions and sports facilities.

The shared services function was implemented in April 2006 within MOF to consolidate the backroom finance and human resource functions of public agencies to achieve economies of scale and process improvements. These backroom functions and the staff performing the activities were transferred to a new department under MOF, called Centre for Shared Services (CSS)-Vital.org. Agencies that participated in the shared services initiative were promised a similar level of service and cost reductions. CSS-Vital.org expects to reduce the annual operating costs of these functions by an estimated 15 per cent after stabilization. The first phase involved agencies that shared the same financial and human resource systems as MOF and pooled together about 300 staff. The intent of the shared services function was to streamline and reengineer the backroom processes by adopting best practices to achieve higher standard of performance with lower costs. Staff were trained with skills to perform and manage the new operational processes. The number of staff is expected to be reduced after the consolidation is completed.

The public sector Economy Drive campaign sought to inculcate an attitude of efficiency and cost savings among officials so that social and economic benefits of the budget may be maximized. Cost savings from the economy drive ranged from S$602m to S$738m in each of the years 2003 to 2005, representing about 2 per cent of the public agencies' budgets.[18] Two major initiatives (Cut Red Tape and Cut Waste) were launched to review internal practices and solicit ideas for reducing waste and bureaucracy in the public sector.

The Smart Regulation Committee under the civil service's Cut Red Tape initiative was implemented in 2000 to review and remove bureaucratic rules and regulations in public agencies. The committee ensured that all agencies had reviewed 95 per cent of their existing

---

[18] Ministry of Finance Statement, "Economy Drive Saves the Government $602m in FY2005," 8 June 2006.

rules and as a result, 12 per cent of the rules were removed and another 24 per cent were updated. Another result was the removal of 60 of the 173 statutory declarations required by different agencies. Three panels were also set up to respond to feedback for reducing public sector bureaucracy from business (Pro-Enterprise Panel), residents (Zero-In-Process) and public sector employees (POWER — "Public Officers Working to Eliminate Red-tape"). The Pro-Enterprise Panel received almost 1,600 suggestions and accepted more than half of them for implementation. The Zero-In-Process received about 8,000 suggestions from the public and resolved more than 108 cases. POWER received 350 suggestions from public sector employees.

The Cut Waste Panel, whose members comprise representatives from the public and private sectors, and the public at large, was set up in 2003 to seek feedback from ordinary residents on ways to reduce wasteful practices, inefficiencies and unnecessary frills in the delivery of public services. The panel examined an agency's response to public feedback regarding their practices and if it was not satisfied with the response, the panel asked the agencies to justify its response or reconsider its practices. From September 2003 to May 2006, 3,108 suggestions on cutting waste were received and the agencies agreed with 84 per cent of the suggestions. Of those suggestions that agencies agreed with, 96 per cent of them were already being done by the agencies, or had already been addressed in some other way. Four per cent were new suggestions that are being or will be implemented by the agencies. The cumulative cost savings arising from implementing new and unique suggestions amounted to S$11.4m.[19]

The four sets of financial principles and practices collectively built institutional capabilities that facilitated continuous change in the public sector. Establishing sustainable budget limits with a pooled reinvestment fund compelled public sector leaders to plan and build organizational capacity for the medium term and yet constantly renew the organization by re-examining existing activities and introducing new projects. Maximizing discretion gave agencies the autonomy, flexibility and incentives to continually adapt their plans in a realistic

---

[19] Ibid.

manner to meet their strategic objectives. Accounting for full costs provided the agencies with the economic information they needed to make rational decisions to get maximum results from scarce resources. Seeking value from financial expenditure gave agencies common frameworks and tools to stretch the financial resources allocated to them by continually reviewing and improving their operating and financial processes. Financial processes became more than mere allocation and accounting tools. They were imbued with a strategic purpose, embedded with new structures and implemented in a new capacity to spur continuous improvements and change in the public sector.

8.3 Applying Systemic Discipline: Redesigning Structural Linkages

Systems thinking is the capacity to see the structures, or the pattern of inter-relationships among key components of the system that underlie complex situations.[20] Systemic structures influence behavior. "Recognizing the congruence and complementarities among processes, and between processes and incentives, is critical to the understanding of organizational capabilities."[21] But systemic inter-relationships are difficult to observe because the results may not be obvious or immediate due to time lags, mediating factors, and spatial separation in the cause-and-effect relationships among the key variables.

The potential of an organization's tangible and intangible assets, including the knowledge and expertise embodied in people and software, would not be fully realized unless there were structures and processes to coordinate and integrate their deployment to generate desired outcomes. When placed in the same system, people, however different, tend to produce similar results. Even well-intentioned or skilled people often become exasperated when they try to do things in a system that does not support them or worse, constantly makes it difficult for them to do their best. When good people work

---

[20] Peter Senge (1990). *The Fifth Discipline: The Art and Practice of the Learning Organization*. NY, NY: Doubleday/Currency.

[21] Teece, Pisano and Shuen (1997), p. 520.

in a dysfunctional system, their performance suffers and potential achievements are limited. Yet people in an organization often feel powerless to change the system. Organizational leadership is required to mobilize the energies and expertise, and structure the relationships, authority and resources to effect change to organizational systems.

Applying systemic discipline to any large organization involves redesigning structural linkages — how people, resources and activities are grouped into units, how these units relate and how their work is coordinated — so that new behaviors may be enabled and sustained.[22] Redesigning structures and processes fundamentally is about rethinking the flow of information and work, the linkages among the work flows, the operating policies whereby people translate perceptions, goals, rules, and norms into decisions, and the technology applications that facilitate and support the actions.

Public sector leaders in Singapore view their main organizational responsibility as putting in new systems and redesigning existing structures and processes so that new behaviors may be encouraged, enabled and sustained to achieve desired long-term outcomes. The hallmark of the dynamic capabilities created in the public sector is the development of holistic system-based competencies that leveraged intangible assets such as knowledge, skills and technology to design structures, processes and systems that delivered continuous improvement and innovation. Leadership-induced change can only be sustained through carefully designed organizational systems and processes. Otherwise, the organization tends to revert back to old behaviors over time when the leadership attention inevitably shifts to other needs and priorities. New behaviors can be sustained only as new structures and systems continually provide the information and incentives that reinforce desired behaviors and highlight deviations that encourage self-control and self-monitoring.

We identified four sets of systems-based competencies that have been developed by the public sector: systems for expanding the capacity of critical resources, systems for enabling mission focus and integration across agencies, systems for engaging the organization for

---

[22] Henry Mintzberg (1993). *Designing Effective Organizations*. NJ: Prentice-Hall.

Table 8.7. Systems-Based Competencies in the Public Sector

---

1. Systems for Expanding Capacity: People and Financial Processes
   • People Systems
   • Financial Systems

2. Systems for Enabling Focus and Integration: From Vertical to Horizontal Structures
   • Statutory Boards
   • Inter-Ministry Committees
   • Cross-Agency teams

3. Systems for Engaging Change: The PS21 Framework
   • Lead People
   • Manage Systems
   • Serve Citizens and Customers

4. Systems for Enhancing Integrated Service: Many Agencies, One Government
   • Goals: Connecting Citizens, Delighting Customers, Networked Government
   • Services: Publish, Interact, Transact, Integrate

---

change, and systems for enhancing integrated service to the public. These systems-based competencies are summarized in Table 8.7.

8.3.1 *Systems for Expanding Capacity: People and Financial Processes*

Most government bureaucracies have been stereotypically viewed as inefficient, slow, and unresponsive, characterized by deeply etched practices and fixed routines based on traditions in a closed environment where national borders are paramount. The Singapore public sector understands that people and finances are the two critical resources for achieving its strategic objectives, expanding capacity and invigorating dynamism in such a large and complex institution.

Significant attention and resources have been invested in developing people to realize their potential and in deploying financial resources to maximize desired results. Systems for managing people in the public sector included structures and processes for recruiting and deploying talent, renewing their capacity through appraisal and development, and retaining leaders through competitive compensation.

Systems for managing finances included structures and processes for engaging agencies on strategic priorities, establishing budget limits, maximizing discretion, accounting for full costs and seeking value in expenditures. These people and financial systems were described in detail in Chapter 7 and earlier in this chapter. We found people and finances to be the most important systems for creating dynamic capabilities in the public sector. They were the key levers for strategic development and change. Without effective systems for the two fundamental resources of people and finances, other systems we described in this section would not have worked well.

8.3.2 *Systems for Enabling Focus and Integration: From Vertical to Horizontal Structures*

"Structure follows strategy" is the conventional wisdom in business management. "Effective policy requires structural innovation" is the corollary in the public sector. Since independence, the Singapore public sector has continually developed new organizational designs and structures to implement national priorities whenever existing structures and systems were limited in their capacity to deliver the desired results. When the civil service systems were slow in handling urgent issues of mass housing and severe unemployment in the early 1960s, statutory boards were created to develop and implement strategic solutions speedily.

Statutory boards are public institutions that are created through legislation, have focused missions, more independent governance, and are given autonomy in managing their finances and human resources. They have relatively more freedom to employ the necessary human expertise and use financial resources to implement projects and programs than their parent ministries, which are subject to normal civil service rules and practices. They are governed through fairly independent boards that include respected representatives from the public and private sectors. Statutory boards have gained a reputation for fast and efficient operations in achieving their given missions and are used extensively for focused attention on strategic national issues that fall outside the traditional scope of government ministries.

Statutory boards are structural innovations that have been created to exist in parallel with civil service departments. It is a pragmatic approach to achieving results in critical policy areas when the civil service structures are inadequate. Necessary civil service reforms would take some time to achieve. Statutory boards are structural innovations that overcame then civil service rigidities and are highly effective vehicles for important policy implementation and change. The statutory board organizational model is the basis for subsequent civil service reforms to enhance responsiveness, accountability and quality. Statutory boards show the importance of having the appropriate organizational structures for effective policy implementation. The creation of statutory boards is an organizational innovation developed to enable effective policy delivery.

Over the years many specialized statutory boards were formed to implement important national objectives ranging from helping local firms regionalize to delivering specialized education to nurturing the arts and protecting the environment. The first statutory boards created were the Housing Development Board in 1960 to build low cost housing and the Economic Development Board (EDB) in 1961 to attract foreign investments to create jobs. The industry financing department in EDB was later spun off as a separate statutory board, the Development Bank of Singapore, in 1968, and later privatized as a full-fledged commercial bank with a pan-Asian ambition. Similarly, a new statutory board, the Jurong Town Corporation, was formed to take over EDB's functions in industrial infrastructure development.

Here we see how structures evolved to meet new needs as new opportunities arose from the success of earlier policy initiatives. Structural innovation enables effective policy execution and creates new opportunities. New opportunities that were not foreseen may arise as policies are implemented effectively requiring further structural evolution. That is the essence of how structures and systems can contribute to dynamic governance. Many organizations view structures and systems as constraints to change and are resigned to adopting only incremental steps that may be implemented within existing structures. The Singapore public sector showed how innovations in organizational structures are necessary to implement substantive policy initiatives. That is the difference between dynamic governance and a mere public bureaucracy. Further, leaders need to recognize that today's organizational innovation is tomorrow's legacy system unless there is a commitment to constantly think ahead, think again and think across to learn from others.

A statutory board represents a vertical collection of knowledge, expertise and resources within a single agency for focused attention and fast implementation of solutions to a specific set of problems. However, as the country developed, issues became more complex and multi-faceted in their economic, social and security implications. Resolving these issues required knowledge, skills, expertise and resources that were spread across many agencies. A single agency such as a statutory board within a single ministry may no longer be adequate or able to implement the needed policies on its own. Here we see how an organization innovation such as the statutory board that worked so effectively in the past may become the new structural impediment for change — that is the reality that makes dynamism in governance absolutely critical and yet so difficult to achieve.

New structures and processes are required for synergizing across many agencies to achieve effective integrated policy outcomes. These more complex policy issues require an inter-ministry, inter-agency approach that bring together the requisite resources, albeit on a temporal basis, to ensure a broader and more comprehensive perspective in identifying the right causes, discussing different policy alternatives, and coordinating policy implementation across several agencies. Further, a permanent configuration of agencies is not sufficient in a fast-changing socio-economic environment. Different configurations of agencies are needed depending on the nature and complexity of the policy concerns. In addition to vertical structures of specialized agencies, temporary horizontal network structures are needed to link appropriate agencies in teams for policy review, change, and implementation. An agency is now represented in several horizontal teams that are constantly being reconfigured. Depending on the issues involved, each agency makes different contributions to the team on the basis of their expertise, experience and network. The differences between a typical vertical structure and a horizontal structure are shown in Table 8.8.

Table 8.8. Structural Characteristics

Vertical Structure	Horizontal structure
Permanent	Temporary
Fixed resources	Configurable resources
Focused on its mission	Multidimensional perspectives on issue
Single agency	Multiple agencies
Hierarchical	Network
Implement policy directly	Coordinate implementation across agencies
Fast and efficient	Comprehensive and effective

Examples of a typical vertical structure include designs such as a government ministry, department or a statutory board. Such structures tend to be long-lived, with fixed resources that are fairly permanently assigned to achieve its focused mission within a single agency. These vertical structures are hierarchically organized for implementing specific policies and programs efficiently and speedily.

Table 8.9. Examples of Horizontal Structures in the Public Sector

Horizontal Structures	Purpose
Strategic Issues Group	Ad hoc group formed to review and recommend policy changes for issues surfaced during Scenarios and Strategic Planning
Inter-Ministry Committees	Ad hoc committee to study national issues identified by Inter-Ministerial Committee
Committee of Permanent Secretaries	Standing committee that regularly surfaces and reviews issues that cut across agencies
Sectoral Committees	Standing committee to coordinate sharing and understanding of issues across agencies within sector such as economics, social and security
Inter-Ministerial Committee	Ad hoc committee of ministers to consider major national policy issues
National Security Coordinating Committee	Standing committee to coordinate inter-agency responses to national security issues
National Research and Innovation Committee	Standing committee to coordinate development and investments in strategic research areas

The public sector has been using more horizontal structures such as inter-ministry committees or cross-agency teams for more complex and multi-faceted security and social issues such as counter-terrorism, low-wage workers, population growth, and aging society. These horizontal structures involved representatives from multiple agencies whose views and expertise were needed, worked on important issues for a period of time and were disbanded when the project was completed. Some of the horizontal structures may be standing committees if they relate to long-term issues such as security that require close and constant coordination. The teams worked as networks of professionals based on their knowledge and expertise rather than as a hierarchy of line relationships. Their purpose was to develop comprehensive and effective solutions, and if necessary to coordinate the implementation of accepted policies by multiple agencies. Examples of horizontal structures used in the public sector are shown in Table 8.9.

The public sector developed both focus and integration as crucial capabilities for effective execution of policies. Focus was necessary for fast and efficient implementation of urgent national policies that had fairly obvious causes and well structured solutions. Dealing with urgent bread and butter policy issues required an efficient vertical structure that could mobilize resources quickly to implement predetermined solutions. Many national issues in the early days of independence such as providing the population with mass housing, basic health care and simple jobs were amendable to the vertical structural innovations such as statutory boards. As basic needs were increasingly being met, social demands became more complex and sophisticated with causes that were more subtle and solutions that were not obvious, the critical policy capabilities required shifted from efficient implementation of predetermined solutions to sensing needs, understanding problems, identifying causes, and finding possible solutions.

Focused vertical agencies would only find solutions within their own domains, which is not good enough for more complex problems. Speed in rushing to implement simple solutions becomes risky when the real solutions are non-obvious and are likely to have unintended second and third order consequences. Efficient execution was no substitute for developing effective solutions. An integrated perspective in finding good ideas and a coordinated approach to implementing a multi-pronged solution became necessary for success. Thus horizontal networks, temporary and reconfigurable teams, were required for engaging the right perspectives to find the right solutions and coordinating their efforts in a network fashion. Although recent developments in the public sector were mostly in the formation of horizontal networks, they did not substitute for vertical organizations, which were still needed for housing functional resources and delivering basic services efficiently. Horizontal organizations added new capabilities for intellectual and social coordination for policy effectiveness in a more demanding and complex society.

8.3.3 *Systems for Engaging Change: The PS21 Framework*

PS21 (Public Service for the 21st Century) was launched in 1995 to instill a sense of urgency for change in the public sector so that it would be prepared for an uncertain and unpredictable future. It was a holistic approach of engaging all levels of the public sector for organization change — anticipating change, welcoming change and executing change. According to former Head of Civil Service, Lim Siong Guan, major policy reviews and changes were still largely the domain of the Administrative Service and the higher echelons of the public sector — "the big ideas were still going to come from the top, but we need PS21 to prepare the staff at all levels in the public sector to be responsive and able to change when needed, and to propose and effect change at their level wherever possible."[23] The motivation for the PS21 movement was "how do you bring people to the stage where they see the need for change, are willing to change and want to change... a framework by which you can draw everyone in... a central idea is that everyone at every level should be thinking all the time about what they are doing and how they can do better." [24]

---

[23] Authors' 2005 interview with Lim Siong Guan, who was Permanent Secretary of the Public Service Division when he initiated PS21.

[24] Lim Siong Guan (2005). "Catalyst for Change," *Challenge*, Vol. 11, No. 10, November.

PS21 was launched as a grassroots movement grounded on a conviction that public sector staff would be more ready to respond positively to change when they were themselves actively involved in learning and looking for improvements all the time, even if their ideas for change were purely operational in nature. "PS21 is most useful in getting junior and lower level officers to feel that they can make a difference, that they have a voice, that their views matter and that they can and should speak out... If you have 120,000 persons always on the lookout to improve things, you will have an awesome public service."[25] The fundamental emphasis of PS21 "is not about chasing results, it is about values, about organizational and leadership philosophy, about capacity."[26] The basic philosophy and approach of PS21 is summarized in Table 8.10.

PS21 built upon earlier efforts in productivity improvement and extended the reach and participation to all staff in the public sector. Tools such as work improvement teams and staff suggestion schemes were integrated into a holistic and integrated approach to create positive attitudinal change in public sector staff and organizations — from being fearful of change to being open to change and seeing change as an opportunity. The Enterprise Challenge was launched in 2000 to seek innovative ideas for major improvements in public service. Between 2000 and 2005, more than 900 proposals were received and 41 of them have been trial-tested and implemented.

Investments in staff training and involvement in work improvement equipped public sector employees with needed knowledge, skills and attitudes that contributed positively to change. In 2004, each public sector employee spent an average of 12.3 days in training and about 35 per cent of all staff completed at least 100 hours of training. In the same year, 71 per cent of the 120,000 public sector staff submitted an average of 3.27 suggestions, 84 per cent of which were implemented, resulting in cost savings of S$184m.[27]

---

[25] Eddie Teo (2005). "Reflection on 10 Years of Change," *Challenge*, Vol. 11, No. 10, November.

[26] Lim (2005).

[27] The latest information may be found on the Ministry of Finance website: www.mof.gov.sg.

Table 8.10. Basic Philosophy and Framework of PS 21

Theme	Continuous change in the public sector
Reason	Unending uncertainty in the environment
Beliefs	Ideas for change can come from anywhere Staff want to improve and do a good job Leaders help staff in their efforts to achieve objectives
Means	Harvesting creativity of everyone
Outcome	In time for the future
Strategic Thrusts	Organizational excellence Innovation and enterprise Openness, responsiveness and involvement
Functional Programs	Staff well-being Continuous enterprise and learning Quality service Organizational review
Structures	PS21 executive committee chaired by head of civil service Committees on (i) people, (ii) systems, (iii) customers/citizens PS21 office within Public Service Division Public Sector Centre of Organizational Excellence
Improvement Tools	Work Improvement Teams (WITS), Staff Suggestion Scheme (SSS), The Enterprise Challenge, Singapore Quality Awards (SQA), People Excellence Award, Singapore Innovation Class Awards, Singapore Service Class Awards

Both formal structures and informal mechanisms were utilized to implement PS21. Three public sector committees chaired by two permanent secretaries each focused on the key areas of people and systems, and customers and citizens. Each agency has similar committees to build the needed capacity to achieve the objectives of PS21 within the agency. The PS21 executive committee was chaired by the head of the civil service and considered issues and proposals surfaced by the three main PS21 committees. The entire PS21 effort was coordinated by the PS21 office within the Public Service Division in the Prime Minister's Office. Four functional programs — staff well-being, continuous enterprise and learning, quality service and organizational review, were designed and implemented to foster an environment that welcomes change.

The Public Service Centre of Organizational Excellence served as an informal mechanism and support network for facilitating sharing and learning within the public sector. It provided informal networking and promoted organizational excellence benchmarks such as the Singapore Quality Award and the Singapore Innovation Class. These awards recognized organizational excellence for Singapore-based organizations and were open to both the private and public sector. These awards were managed separately by Spring Singapore (an agency dedicated to promoting productivity, quality and innovation in Singapore) with independent award committees and assessors. At the end of 2005, eight public agencies had won the Singapore Quality Award, three had won the People Excellence Award and one had won the Singapore Innovation Award.

PS21 was an organization-wide framework that immersed staff in the thick of the public sector transformation experience. The aim was to change the mindset and attitudes of staff so that they worked together with their leaders to implement change. The end result is an observing, thinking and learning organization that is open to new ideas for improvement. The tangible output and measurements were viewed as a way to assess progress, not a quantitative target to justify the effort. Public sector leaders viewed PS21 as an on-going journey, not a completed destination. They admitted without hesitation that after 10 years of implementation, the internalization of PS21 values was still not consistent throughout the public sector — it was still highly dependent on the commitment and energy of leaders in each agency. Still, PS21 was an innovative framework with structures and processes that enrolled all levels of staff to participate in support of and accept change as a way of life. It added a different dimension of change capabilities to the public sector — a system that energized the organization to keep looking for improvements in every area — which ultimately affected the scope and pace of change that the public sector could undertake. That many organizations had not paid as much attention to this dimension of change capability is a testimony to the far-sightedness and systemic thinking that underlay the foundation for transformation in the public sector. The capacity to manage PS21 as a perpetual work-in-progress illustrated the conviction among the leadership that processes, structures and systems are foundations that sustain change capabilities throughout the public sector.

8.3.4 Systems for Enhancing Integrated Service: Many Agencies, One Government

Excellence in service requires customer needs to be met in a fast and convenient manner. As the country developed, citizens have become more sophisticated, expecting and demanding ever higher levels of service from the public sector. Yet service often failed to meet customer expectations because of timing differences, spatial separation and fragmentation in information, processes and organizations. Since the 1980s, the public sector has embarked on several initiatives to enhance service to the public: offices have been renovated to create a more pleasant physical environment for serving customers, frontline staff have improved their skills through customer service training, agencies have developed and published service standards, and every agency appointed a senior official as a quality service manager to respond to public feedback and complaints.

A major strategic thrust was the use of ICT and the Internet as key enabling technologies for integrating organizations and information, and speeding up processes to enhance public service. The public sector developed e-government strategies, infrastructure, and systems as a platform for re-inventing government around the needs of customers and citizens to achieve a vision of "many agencies, one government." There was a conviction that comfort and confidence in the use of ICT applications among the population is an issue of national competitive advantage. Thus the national mandate was to maximize the use of electronic channels to deliver service, and provide assistance to those who needed help to learn and use the electronic channels. The goals of e-government initiatives were three-fold: connected citizens, delighted customers and a networked government.[28]

---

[28] Singapore e-Government Brochure, Version 3, published by IDA, March 2005.

E-governance utilized ICT applications that supported Singapore's nation-building efforts and enhanced relationships between citizens and government in policy review, development, and implementation. E-service delivery systems overcame the constraints on available people, time and space and transformed the public sector into a networked government that delivered accessible, integrated, and value-added e-services for the changing needs of customers living and doing business in a dynamic global city. The networked government infrastructure enabled agencies to collaborate, share information and leverage on their collective knowledge to provide seamless service to the public.

A single web access portal (www.gov.sg) was created for all government information and services. These were organized to cater to the needs of four customer groups: government, citizens and residents, business, and non-residents. Services for citizens and residents were further segmented according to common needs: security, housing, transportation, culture and recreation, health, family and community, education and employment. By October 2004, the e-citizen portal was already getting about 24 million hits a month. By May 2006, 1600 services were available online, comprising 98 per cent of public services that could be delivered electronically. Eighty-six per cent of all residents used e-services at least once a year and 85 per cent of users were satisfied with the overall quality of electronic services.[29]

An e-government maturity framework[30] guided the public sector in the development and deployment of e-services and e-governance toward higher levels of sophistication. In e-services, the maturity framework defined five levels of e-services; from simple publication of information, to initiation of transaction, to completion of multiple transactions with a single entry and interface, to integrating multiple transactions across both public and private sectors. By May 2006, 15 integrated multi-agency e-services were implemented that enabled a more seamless service and reduced needed interactions with the

---

[29] e-Government Customer Perception Survey, conducted by MOF and IDA, 2005.

[30] Singapore e-Government Brochure, Version 3, published by IDA, March 2005.

government by 50 per cent. An example was the Online Business Licensing Service that will be described in more detail later.

In e-governance (see the consultation portal at www.feedback. gov.sg), agencies were encouraged to go beyond informing citizens about its policies to include explanation, consultation and connected involvement. Citizens were encouraged to be involved in policy deliberations by giving their views, comments and suggestions to consultation papers and by giving feedback on the implementation of policies. In the three years to 2006, 100,000 public responses were received for policy consultation exercises, half of which were received online.

Over the years, Singapore's e-government strategies, programs and systems were widely acknowledged to be among the most advanced in the world and have won many international awards. The major awards received in 2005 are listed in Table 8.11.[31]

Table 8.11. Singapore e-Government Awards and Accolades

- Singapore ranked 2nd in e-Government Participation and 7th in E-Government Readiness in 2005 United Nations e-Government Readiness report

- The Online Business Licensing Service was awarded the UN Public Service Award in 2005

- Singapore ranked 1st in the 2005 World Economic Forum Global IT Report

- Singapore was ranked 3rd in 2005 Annual e-Government Leadership Study of 22 countries by Accenture

- Singapore ranked 2nd in the 2004 Global e-Government Study by Brown University

---

The e-government journey[32] began in 1980 with the creation of the National Computer Board that led in civil service computerization and the development of IT professionals needed for the exploitation

---

[31] For awards in earlier years and an updated list, see www.egov.gov.sg.

[32] *e-Government: Accelerating, Integrating, Transforming Public Services*, published by IDA, 2001.

of ICT for increasing productivity. As part of the response to the economic recession in 1985, a national IT strategy was implemented to build network systems that enhanced business competitiveness and to promote the IT services industry. In 1992, a concerted effort was launched to build a national information infrastructure that improved personal and social lives as part of the IT2000 vision for Singapore to be an intelligent island. A parallel effort deregulated and introduced competition in the provision of telecommunication services and broadcasting. In the late 1990s, the National Computer Board was privatized and government computerization was opened to private sector IT services providers on a competitive basis. A new agency, the Infocomm Development Authority (IDA) regulated telecommunications and promoted ICT usage in both government and the private sector. From 2001, the focus was on connecting and involving citizens in policy feedback and review and in providing integrated services to customers. There is a current effort to develop a new strategic vision and roadmap, codenamed IN2015, that seeks to recreate Singapore as an intelligent nation by 2015. The e-government journey from 1980 to 2006 is summarized in Table 8.12.

Table 8.12. The e-Government Journey

Period	Focus	Scope
1980–1985	Computerization of basic functions to increase productivity	Government agencies
1986–1991	Communication networks in economic value chain to enhance competitiveness	Business firms within key economic sectors
1992–2000	Content of information to improve quality of life	Schools and individuals
1995–2000	Competition in provision of information and communication services to gain efficiency and innovation	Telecoms, broadcasting, government computing
2001–2006	Citizens connect to build relationships Customer service to meet needs fast and conveniently	Policies and feedback Cross-agency integration

The e-government vision was implemented through a comprehensive action plan[33] that included projects that integrated all e-services into a single access point, increased awareness of e-services, provided convenient access through self-service terminals and e-helper programs, instilled confidence in e-services, generated positive e-service experience, engaged citizens through virtual communities, transcended organizational boundaries through common architecture and standards, enhanced security, innovated through technology experimentation and exported e-government expertise and capabilities to other governments. In October 2005, Citizen Connect was implemented — a new program that gave residents free access and personal help to use the Internet to interact with the government in their neighborhood community clubs. Five centers were set up by May 2006 and this will be expanded into a network of 25 centers island-wide.

The e-government action plan II included an investment of S$1.3b from 2003 to 2006. A new iGov2010 master plan would invest a further S$2b over five years to transform back-end processing to achieve front-end efficiency and effectiveness. The emphasis of iGov2010 would be on "transcending organizational structures, changing rules and procedures, and reorganizing and integrating the government around customers' and citizens' needs and intentions." [34]

There were three levels of leadership for e-government implementation as summarized in Table 8.13. The overall owner of e-government strategy and policy was the Ministry of Finance. This is aligned to the role of MOF in allocating resources for government-wide initiatives and ensuring an optimal use of allocated budget resources. There was a shared belief within the public sector leadership that ICT enhanced the effectiveness of scarce human and space (land) resources. The public sector chief information and technology officer was the IDA. It led in strategic planning for ICT exploration and exploitation in both the public and private sectors. For the public sector, it performed the

---

[33] Singapore e-Government Brochure, Version 3, published by IDA, March 2005.

[34] Speech by Second Minister of Finance, Raymond Lim, at the launch of iGov2010 on 30 May 2006.

CIO function in recommending ICT policies, standards and procedures for adoption across agencies, and managed shared public sector ICT infrastructure and major e-government development projects. For the private sector, it worked in partnership with both business users and IT services providers to exploit innovative ICT applications that enhanced Singapore's competitiveness in key economic sectors.[35]

Table 8.13. Leadership for e-Government

1.	Overall Owner: Ministry of Finance • Decide public sector ICT policies • Oversee centralized ICT infrastructure and services • Sponsor e-government initiatives
2.	Government Chief Information Officer (CIO): IDA • Provide technical advice • Recommend ICT policies, standards and procedures • Perform ICT master-planning • Manage central ICT infrastructure and projects
3.	Ministry/Statutory Board CIO • Articulate vision and plan for exploiting ICT • Align ICT policies, standards and investments to organization's needs • Provide leadership for development of ICT projects • Manage people and financial resources for ICT initiatives

At each agency, there was a separate CIO function that articulated the vision for exploiting ICT and managed the development and implementation of ICT projects. Reporting to the permanent secretary of each ministry or CEO of a statutory board, the CIO function aligned the agency's ICT policies to its organizational priorities and the central policies adopted by the public sector.

Three different governance structures have been formed to oversee the implementation of e-government as summarized in Table 8.14. The public service ICT committee comprised the top leadership of the public sector and met quarterly to review strategic direction and progress of e-government initiatives. It acted as a forum for resolving

---

[35] *Connected Singapore: A Blueprint for Infocomm Development*, published by IDA, 2003.

all significant issues in the implementation of e-government projects. The e-citizen council facilitated the collaboration of agencies across the public sector to go beyond agency-specific services to provide citizen-centric e-services that were coordinated and integrated according to eight broad areas called e-towns: business, culture and recreation, education and employment, defense and security, family and community, health and environment, housing, and transport and travel. Finally, an e-government advisory panel comprising prominent representatives of the public and private sectors provided feedback on the implementation of e-government projects and advice regarding overall trends.

Table 8.14. Governance Structures for e-Government

---

1. Public Service ICT Committee
    - Members include top leadership of ministries and statutory boards
    - Meets quarterly
    - Strategic direction for public sector transformation through ICT
    - Advice on implementation of e-government initiatives

2. e-Citizen Council
    - e-Town mayors and deputy mayors from major ministries
    - Overall direction and policies for e-Citizen portal
    - Development of 8 e-Towns

3. e-Government Advisory Panel
    - Representatives from public and private sectors
    - Feedback on implementation of e-government projects
    - Advice on global trends in e-government and their impacts

---

An innovative e-government application[36] that was implemented to achieve the vision of "many agencies, one government" was OASIS (Online Application System for Integrated Services). It has an Online Business Licensing Service (OBLS — see https://licenses.business.gov.sg) which won the UN Public Service E-government Award in

[36] The information summarized here is taken from a detailed case study of OASIS by Pelly Periasamy and Sia Siew Kien (2005). "Delivering Cross-Agencies Integrated e-Services through OASIS," Working Paper, IMARC, Nanyang Business School, Nanyang Technological University.

Table 8.15. Development and Implementation of OBLS and OASIS

Project Initiator	Pro-enterprise panel and Action Community for Entrepreneurship
Project Leadership	Ministry of Trade and Industry and IDA
Project Funding	S$10m funded by Ministry of Finance
Project Timeline	Four years from August 2001 to August 2005
Project Scope	154 business licenses administered by 30 agencies
Project Structure	Steering Committee co-chaired by MTI and MOF Core team of officials from MTI and IDA Task forces to review and re-engineer licensing processes Pilot and project development awarded to private IT firms
Project Implementation	11 licenses removed 2 licenses converted to one-time lifetime licenses 5 licenses reduced in scope of need for the licenses 7 grouped into class licenses 82 licenses from 18 agencies integrated into OBLS 80% of new start-ups can apply for needed licenses online
Process Time Improvements	Average license processing time reduced from 21 days to 12.5 days 43 licenses processed within 3 days 42 licenses processed within 7 days New business registration reduced from 5 days to 2 hours
Results	55,000 applications used OBLS from Jan 2004 to May 2006 Estimated savings of S$11.4m in first year OBLS/OASIS won 2005 UN Public Service Award

2005. Starting a new business often required multiple regulatory approvals and licenses involving a tedious, complex and time-consuming process. For example, starting a public entertainment outlet required licenses approved by at least seven agencies regulating business registration, use of premises, food hygiene, liquor distribution, fire safety and tax collection. The project was initiated as a result of input from business entrepreneurs to the pro-enterprise panel regarding the problems associated with application of business licenses. The project was led by the Ministry of Trade and Industry and IDA with about S$10m funding from MOF. The main features of the four-year development and implementation of OBLS and OASIS are summarized in Table 8.15.

Task forces were formed to fundamentally review and re-engineer the processes involving 154 licenses from 30 different agencies. Twenty-five licenses were either removed or reduced significantly in scope. Eighty-two licenses were simplified, rationalized and integrated for implementation into the OBLS portal. As a result of the OBLS implementation, 80 per cent of all start-ups could apply for and obtain the required licenses online through OBLS. Eight thousand businesses used OBLS in the first year, saving an estimated S$11.4m. From January 2004 to May 2006, 55,000 applications were made using OBLS. The average time to obtain the licenses has reduced from 21 days to 12.5 days, with new business registrations now approved within two hours compared to five days previously.

8.4 Creating Innovative Processes for Dynamic Governance: Key Lessons

8.4.1 *Creating Dynamic Capabilities in Processes Goes Beyond Creating Change Processes*

When leaders consider managing change, they seek to identify what different directions to take, what new programs to launch, and how to get their organizations moving to implement them. It is usually a one-time effort in response to a crisis, a new business opportunity or a change of leadership. Once the change is implemented, the organization repeats them as routines and returns to an equilibrium state until the next external jolt is given. Change is seen as a discrete activity and change processes are treated as off-the-shelf routines that are activated only whenever leaders think that change is needed.

These types of change processes are important to ensure that organizations can alter its paths to new directions to survive and succeed. They can become organizational capabilities if there are strong execution skills and resources to achieve desired results when needed. However, these types of change processes are separate from the organization's regular processes and tend to be managed as special projects and initiatives. They are not integrated into the normal operating activities of an organization. The change capabilities we described in this chapter go beyond these discrete change processes to how the public sector created the capabilities for change through its on-going operational and management processes.

8.4.2 *Sustaining Change Requires Integrating Change Capabilities into Operational and Management Processes*

One-time change via the adoption of specific programs and projects is easier to achieve because of the management mandate, attention and resources usually focused on these efforts. Sustaining change is more challenging because it requires the engagement of people at all levels within the scope of their work routines. It aims for continuous improvements even when management attention is not specifically focused on them. It goes beyond changing specific actions and behavior to changing mental models, goals and values. Sustaining change requires new ways of thinking, new goals and new values to be constantly reinforced and practiced through their incorporation into operational and management processes.

Our study of the Singapore public sector showed how change capabilities were embedded into management processes for anticipating the future, allocating financial resources, and applying systemic disciplines. These are not unique processes by themselves. Nor are they the only processes with the potential to be embedded with capabilities for change. Most organizations have processes for planning, budgeting, organizing, and controlling activities — but like most operational processes, they are targeted at producing specific output such as a work plan or budget. In many organizations, these processes are often repeated in a bureaucratic manner merely to produce the required reports without fully engaging the mind and heart — degenerating into mere organizational forms but without substance. What is unique about the public sector is that it managed these activities as processes for sustaining change.

Creating change capabilities in management processes have enabled the public sector to sustain and deepen organization change cumulatively over many years. Any specific change proposed and implemented may be only incremental, but the cumulative effects of continuous incremental changes sustained over many years and across many agencies have been substantial. There were no silver bullets for building an adaptive and innovative culture overnight. Specific programs and activities may be helpful to generate interest, focus attention and give people the basic skills. But unless the new goals, values and thinking were built into management and operational processes, change would be superficial and would not last. Creating change capabilities in processes thus required strategic intent, deliberate redesign and continuous learning.

8.4.3 *Creating Change Capabilities in Processes Requires Strategic Intent, Deliberate Redesign, and Continuous Learning*

Strategic intent provides the direction, drive and dynamism to management processes such as planning or budgeting to become organizational change capabilities. Without strategic intent, these processes would be mere organizational routines. Strategic intent comes from the vision, insight and foresight of organizational leadership. In our study, public sector leaders visualized strategic outcomes from organizational activities and made investments to build processes into change capabilities. "We believed that continuous change sustained over time is strategic."[37] Their strategic perspectives and intentions provided the organization with the edge, exemplars and energies to execute systems that enabled continuous change.

Since operational and management processes normally were not geared toward continuous organizational change, they had to be deliberately redesigned so that they were imbued with change capabilities in addition to their routine output. The public sector chose to focus on several processes — planning processes for anticipating the future, financial processes for renewing activities, people processes for developing talent, and organizing processes for integrating agencies,

---

[37] Authors' interview with Lim Siong Guan.

engaging staff and enhancing service. Deliberate redesign of these processes involved rethinking their objectives, activities, performance measures, desired output, coordinating structures, and incentive systems. Deliberate process redesign is the systemic application of the best knowledge, expertise and insight available to inject new ideas and thinking to create new organizational models of work. Deliberate design does not guarantee smooth execution or perfect results. But it does create an organizational framework for sensing and learning in its implementation.

These organizational innovations require continuous sensing, learning and adaptation during implementation to ensure that strategic goals and objectives are achieved in a fast changing environment. Many of the deliberate designs were new and experimental and required sensitive monitoring of feedback and impact so that they could be effectively adapted. For example, the reinvestment fund was initially designed as a productivity dividend to ensure that the public sector kept pace with national productivity trends. During the implementation, MOF officials observed that some agencies reconfigured their activities in response to the 3 per cent budget reduction for the reinvestment fund, and some agencies were enthusiastically making proposals for new activities that they could not consider previously because of the budget lock-in. The reinvestment fund was then de-linked from the national productivity dividend to induce change in organizational activities through substantive re-allocation of resources. Continuous sensing, learning and adaptation enabled the reinvestment fund to go beyond its original design and goals to achieve the strategic intent for using financial processes for organizational renewal in the public sector.

Sustaining Dynamic Governance: Lessons and Challenges

This book explains the development of a dynamic governance system and the lessons that we can learn from examining the role of the public service in Singapore. Our framework for dynamic governance comprises the foundation of a supportive institutional culture and the development of proactive organizational capabilities. The institutional culture is based on a set of values, beliefs and principles shaped by how leaders perceived the position of their country and what purposes they pursued. These cultural beliefs and principles were not mere abstract concepts or elegant statements. They molded the way issues were perceived, and shaped the approach to policy execution. In some instances, these beliefs constrained the direction of change to those consistent with the beliefs, confronted solutions that were not aligned, or catalyzed the design of innovative policies that accomplished the desired objectives. Path-breaking change can only happen when external pressures and crises cause values to be reformulated or reinterpreted, when beliefs are adjusted as a result of new knowledge and experiences, or when strong leaders with different values and perspectives abandon past practices and convince their society to redefine the requirements for survival and success.

Dynamic change without a crisis requires leaders who keep learning, adapting and innovating. Proactive organizational capabilities need to be developed to ensure a country's institutions' continuing relevance and effectiveness. Three cognitive capabilities were defined: thinking ahead to prepare for the future, thinking again to improve current performance, and thinking across domains to learn from others. These capabilities make chosen paths, policies and strategies dynamic by incorporating into the governance system new thinking and learning that foster continuous improvement, adaptation and innovation. The main drivers for the development of dynamic governance capabilities are able people who lead the institutions that design and implement public policies, and agile processes that promote organizational renewal and change. The new thinking and learning are manifested in policies that are adaptive, innovative, contextualized and effectively executed to achieve the desired results. It is an interactive and iterative system of governance.

A recent book[1] by a former director of the IMF Training Institute in Singapore, Henri Ghesquiere, described the inter-relationships among the different elements of the Singapore system that made it effective:

> "… economic outcomes, policies, economic and political institutions, attitudes, values and leadership in Singapore are closely interwoven. Their exceptionally strong internal coherence and mutual reinforcement, over a long period of time, account for the impressive results obtained… the overarching emphasis on achieving sustained prosperity has itself provided a powerful rationale for nation-building and other development ideals. The Singapore authorities have preached the secular religion of public pursuit of prosperity for all. The path to this nirvana ran through export-led industrialization by inviting MNCs to locate in Singapore. This necessitated political and social stability, which in turn required ethnic and religious harmony and sharing benefits by providing equal opportunity. Judicious policies created incentives and opportunities for superior performance, allowing Singapore's elite and the population at large to prevail and thrive."

In this concluding chapter, we highlight the perspectives of a few key leaders in the public sector on why and how the governance system works in Singapore, why and how Singapore developed a

---

[1] Henri Ghesquiere (2007). *Singapore's Success: Engineering Economic Growth*. Thomson Learning Asia, pp. 5, 7.

first-class public service which, in PM Lee Hsien Loong's view, is the country's most sustainable, enduring competitive advantage.[2] We then discuss the continuing challenges of the public service, and its leaders readily admit that there are many areas where improvement and change are still on-going struggles. We then distill the main lessons of the development of the Singapore governance system as a whole. Finally, we provide some guidelines on how the principles and insights described in this book may be extended and practiced beyond the Singapore public sector and applied in other contexts.

9.1 Perspectives of Policy Insiders: Public Sector Leaders and Ministers

First we view the public sector itself through the eyes of four of its key leaders and the two ministers who had oversight of its development in recent years. Though we interviewed many public sector leaders and have quoted them on various aspects of governance throughout the book, we think it is useful to highlight a few of their explanations on how the system works in Singapore. The quotes we have chosen to present here are not meant to comprehensively represent the full range of views. We quote extensively from our interviews with these leaders as well as public comments they have made regarding the civil service so that we can appreciate the different views and perspectives within the public sector.

9.1.1 JY Pillay (Chairman of the Singapore Stock Exchange; Served in the Civil Service from 1961 to 1996; Held Permanent Secretary positions in the Ministries of Defence, Finance, National Development and Monetary Authority of Singapore)

On the achievements of the Civil Service and the importance of good people:

> "The progress of the civil service in the last three-and-a-half decades has been astonishing. The Colonial administration

---

[2] Speech by Prime Minister Lee Hsien Loong in Parliament on 13 November 2006.

undoubtedly bequeathed an excellent infrastructure, as well as a robust framework of a competent bureaucracy, to a self-governing Singapore. What the civil service, under enlightened political leadership, then achieved was to expand the orientation of the nation from preserving civil order to meeting basic aspirations, propelling the country to its goal of developed status, and helping to inculcate a sense of pride in the accomplishments of the nation. In the process civil servants were compelled to formulate policies and programs that recognized the changing demands of an increasingly articulate electorate, that satisfied those demands without upsetting macro-economic stability, that ensured social harmony, that fuelled rapid economic growth in accordance with the dictates of the market, and that reached out to the world... The civil service of Singapore is recognized for its integrity, professionalism and achievements. All that did not just happen. It was the result of the improving quality of the intake of officers, clarity in setting out missions and objectives, and superior personnel management practices."[3]

9.1.2 Lim Siong Guan (Chairman of the Economic Development Board; Served in Civil Service from 1969–2006; Held Permanent Secretary positions in Ministries of Defence, Education, Finance and the Prime Minister's Office, and was Head of the Civil Service from 1999–2005)

On the capacity for original thinking and the courage to be different:

"Many people study Singapore as a model of success. Visitors study the CPF, HDB, EDB, CPIB[4], among others.

---

[3] From his acceptance speech at the National University of Singapore on 27 August 1996 when he was conferred the honorary degree of Doctor of Letters; reproduced in the Civil Service College publication, *Ethos*, in January 1997.

[4] CPF: Central Provident Fund; HDB: Housing Development Board; EDB: Economic Development Board; CPIB: Corruption Practices Investigation Bureau.

The CPF as a social security system is unique in being fully-funded, in encouraging self-reliance, and in offering the breadth of social security in housing, health and education, and not just old age. The HDB manifests our public housing policy which distinguishes us by providing remarkably high levels of home ownership. The EDB demonstrates innovative and imaginative economic development policies which began with Singapore welcoming MNCs in the 1960s at a time when MNCs were an unpopular idea in the world of newly independent countries. The CPIB ferreted out corruption with a vengeance when many societies saw the bribe and grease as a normal way of life and business. What we need to specially recognize about each of these successes is not that we have implemented our policies well, but that they were different from, and even contradictory to, the prevailing wisdom of the time… We have come to where we are today because of a capacity for original thinking; a willingness to try what others say would fail. It is looking at the fundamentals in the issues which confront us and not being distracted by critics and cynics."[5]

On how he led change in the public service:

"I usually don't do very much. When I was in the Ministry of Education, I knew nothing about the theory of education. But I talked to the teachers and principals and listened to them. I just gave expression to their dreams and created the structures to make it happen. They want to do a good job but did not have the authority and resources to make it work. I created a way in which they can get involved. Yes, it is very people-centred — but I am also a very organization man. The question I keep asking is

---

[5] Lim Siong Guan (2000). "The Courage to be Different," *Ethos*, Civil Service College, January.

"What is the purpose of the organization?" For example in MINDEF, it is to create a good SAF. Then we look at people, structures and resources to make it happen. For example, the Music and Drama Company was asked to perform at the Singapore's 150th anniversary ceremony — they wanted to do their normal song and dance performance, but I asked how we could do something that showed up the SAF. Then the director referred to the rifle drill that was performed by the army in Taiwan. I didn't even know it existed. I just asked the questions. He knew about it. That was how precision rifle drill got into the SAF.

When I came to MOF, I looked at e-government and thought the aim should be to make ordinary Singaporeans comfortable with IT so as to give Singapore a strategic competitive advantage. To me the challenge always is how to bring every ordinary action to fit into a greater strategic purpose. Then they can see why they should teach even the older folks to use the ATMs — it is for their own longer-term good. I must give them the moral dimension. Then people can see why we must take tough decisions, for greater strategic objectives. Some people said if we take away the counters, what will the elderly do? We have to serve all the public, they say. But I said that the public is best served if they learn how to use the Internet. If the old lady cannot do it, then we have to think of something. This is why we now have e-clubs and Citizen Connect to help them — this will also define a new role for the community centres (CC). Previously, people used to go to CCs to watch TV. But now everyone has a TV so no one goes to the CCs any more for that. We now want every CC and club to offer these services. CCs become a central point for help with accessing government services.

My way of operating is always to help people discover a higher purpose for their actions. So in MOE, when we build schools, the hoarding proclaims that we are 'moulding the future of the nation.' Not just merely constructing school buildings, or passing exams."[6]

9.1.3 Eddie Teo (Singapore's High Commissioner to Australia; Served in Civil Service from 1970 to 2005; Held Permanent Secretary positions in the Ministry of Defence and the Prime Minister's Office)

On public sector leaders and their working relationship with the political leaders:

> "These were not simply 'yes men' or technocrats. They agreed with the ruling party's basic national goals. But they had their own private views and opinions and would stand up to the political leadership when there was a need to do so. They gave as much as they took and did not behave like eunuchs, cowering before the emperor. Some were more respectful and diplomatic than others, but all were absolutely loyal even when they disagreed. Their high EQ also told them that some politicians should only be challenged in the privacy of their office. In other words, they knew when and how to offer their advice. And once the Cabinet decided, the public servants went about to implement its decisions decisively, swiftly and with conviction."[7]

On the challenges facing the Public Service:

> "Nowadays, if you were to read the Forum page of *The Straits Times*, listen to the debate in Parliament or ride in a taxi, you would think that the Public Service in Singapore is wasteful, inefficient, lazy, inflexible, unthinking, evasive, unresponsive and heartless. The litany of criticism grows by the day. It would seem that in

---

[6] Interview by authors on 22 November 2005.

[7] Eddie Teo (2003). "Can Public Servants be Leaders," *Ethos*, Civil Service College, September.

the eyes of the Singapore public, nothing the civil service does is ever right... In 1976, civil servants were expected to be honorable and incorruptible, but they were forgiven if they lacked courtesy. Today... the government wants, and the public expects, civil servants to be innovative, courteous, open and responsive... The private sector wants government to facilitate, not regulate... The old culture emphasized that government operated on the basis of certain clear principles and a fixed, value framework. People knew their roles and responsibilities and how they should behave. There were rules and regulations to ensure compliance and many civil servants were happy to follow the rules and let the politicians take the responsibility of explaining to the public if mistakes were made or if they wished to overrule the civil servants for being inflexible... But as we move into the new Singapore, the civil service will have to re-examine its ethos and come up with a new value system more befitting of the society we have become or are becoming... to those hard-working, committed and dedicated civil servants who feel despondent in the face of what they regard as unfair criticism and worry about the impact that this may have on the morale and reputation of the Service, I urge them to grow a thicker skin and to look at the benefits of a more transparent and open society."[8]

9.1.4 Peter Ho (Head of the Civil Service and Permanent Secretary for Foreign Affairs; Was previously the Permanent Secretary for Defence)

On the unique elements of the Singapore public service:

"First is the civil service ethos based on meritocracy and incorruptibility, which was set by our founding Prime

---

[8] Speech given to students of the Master in Public Policy Program at the National University of Singapore in August 2002; edited version of speech was published in the Civil Service College publication, *Ethos*.

Minister Lee Kuan Yew. Second is the deep and objective approach to staff work — analysis that is hardheaded, carefully thought-through, and no sentimentality. We inherited it from the British and were reinforced by both Lee Kuan Yew and Goh Keng Swee. They demanded excellence and thorough preparation for discussion. Third is a commitment to looking at the system as a whole, not just the specific instance. Again, it came from Goh Keng Swee and his systems engineering mindset. Fourth are decisions made, not on political orthodoxy but hardnosed pragmatism, of what would best accomplish our objectives. Fifth is the ability to think long-term, not just to solve immediate problems. The confidence of the political leadership helped. They were not trying to do popular things to win the next election. Then there is the ability to recognize talent and to give them the authority to get things done. So we have the likes of Philip Yeo and Lim Siong Guan who were given heavy responsibilities even when they were very young and they accomplished a lot for Singapore. Finally there is the MINDEF factor. Many of the public sector leaders had stints in MINDEF, where they had their ideas experimented on and tested. MINDEF has become a lab for managing government because from the beginning they were given a block budget with autonomy to make its own decisions."[9]

On the traditional decentralized structure of the civil service and the mindset change needed for networked government to work effectively in the future:

"The Public Service has a special role in society. Despite its diversity, the public service has one core mission, which is to work with the elected government to ensure Singapore's continued survival, security and success...

---

[9] Interview by authors on 11 August 2005.

Today the public service is organized into 15 ministries and over 60 statutory boards, each with its own mission and functions. This flat and decentralized arrangement gives individual agencies the autonomy to act fast, and the freedom to innovate. However, more and more of the most strategic challenges that our nation faces require multi-agency responses. But we should recognize that public officers working together in a multi-agency framework is not in the natural order of things. The natural instinct of public officers is to associate their primary duty with their parent ministry or statutory board. Their performance is assessed on what they do inside the ministry, not outside it. Working on inter-ministry issues is often seen as an extra-curricular activity. Going forward, the public service must change if it is to operate effectively multi-agency, network mode. The mindset of our people in the public service must change. They must see work at the whole-of-government level as important as work within their respective agencies."[10]

9.1.5 Teo Chee Hean (Minister of Defence and Minister appointed to oversee the development of the Civil Service; previously Minister of Education and was the Chief of Navy in the Singapore Armed Forces before he left to join PAP to contest the elections)

On what constitutes the Singapore system of governance:[11]

"I see it in terms of our values: meritocracy, incorruptibility, multi-racialisim, self reliance. These are also the values of the PAP. What factors contributed to success? I think it is because these values were developed and accepted by the society at large. It is also about policy

---

[10] Peter Ho (2005), speech by Head of Civil Service at the PS21 EXCEL Convention on 21 November 2005.

[11] All the quotes came from Teo Chee Hean's interview with the authors on 29 December 2006.

execution. In 1999, (as Minister of Education) I briefed the EDB Advisory Board on our plans. We had American, European, Japanese CEOs on the panel. One of them asked: 'These ideas are not new. Everyone has good plans and visions. What makes you think you can succeed?' I thought that was a very astute question. The test is five years down the road, how many of these plans and visions have become reality. It's about execution. Our advisory board members tell us that one of the main elements that gives them satisfaction is that when they come back a few years down the road, they can see that what was discussed has actually come to fruition."

On his role as the minister overseeing the development of the civil service:

"I assist the PM to oversee the Civil Service, to help make sure that we have a civil service that is able to deliver high standards of public service, and ensuring that we maintain the competitiveness and attractiveness of a civil service career. The political leadership has to set benchmarks and standards on issues of civil service pay structure and remuneration. Civil service pay increases and budgets need to have parliamentary support. The civil service has to answer to Parliament for its performance and outcomes."

On the relationship between the political and public sector leadership:

"I would characterize it as one of mutual respect and strong partnership. The political leadership recognizes the role of the civil service and has invested a lot in developing it. And it doesn't just mean resources, but also political capital to ensure that the civil service is well-paid, promoted and rewarded. The political leadership knows that we have a good and capable civil service; and the civil service also knows the courage and vision of the political leadership, that it can take difficult decisions for the long-term good of the country.

There are differences of views, but it's not between civil service and political leaders. It's not set up that way. There are differences of views even among the ministers just as there are between civil servants. That's because the problems are often not simple, and the policy choices are a matter of judgment and not always clear-cut. If there are different views, we discuss and resolve them — we work through them. I talk to my Permanent Secretary all the time, and he discusses with me when there is an issue. We talk about it and discuss the best solution. There is a strong working relationship and lots of discussion. But when there is a decision to be made, the Minister has to make the call. That is the way the system works."

9.1.6 **Lee Hsien Loong** (Prime Minister of Singapore; Was Minister appointed by Prime Minister Goh Chok Tong to oversee the development of the Civil Service when he was Deputy Prime Minister)[12]

On what constituted the Singapore system of governance:

"It is a system with a high degree of national consensus on strategic goals, where the political leadership has a strong mandate to act on behalf of the country and a strong sense of responsibility to look after issues beyond the next election. This is also out of self-interest, because we expect to win the next elections and do not want to create future problems for ourselves. This creates the political context for the Civil Service to make rational policy proposals.

We have very hands-on Ministers who focus on both the policy perspectives and political decisions. They

---

[12] Interview by authors on 17 January 2007. All quotes in this section are from the same interview.

take the lead and present the policies to the public. They are not just involved in politics but also in policies. They know the issues. Between the Ministers and the PSs, the workload is very full. In the ministries, the PSs function as the CEOs with the Ministers as their full-time Chairmen.

Our ministers enable the civil service to make drastic change. The changes in housing, workfare, CPF and the GST — these are all political decisions, not administrative adjustments. You need a good (civil service) team to follow up on the issues, and make sure they work out properly. But at the top you must decide which direction you want to go, and that's the Minister's job. You want rational policies but they are made in a political context. The challenge is how to merge both, and have polices that are a political plus, or at least politically saleable, and at the same time, rational and sustainable over the long-term."

On why the system has worked well so far:

"We continue to find new people of high quality to come into the political leadership and the Civil Service. If we do not get people of that quality, the system will fail. We have good institutions, but only because there is a group of key individuals who hold it together, who understand why we do certain things, who have the organizational memory so that we don't forget and go round in big circles. Sometimes the circumstances have changed, sometime we have different views, but if we forget the rationale, then we go around in big circles. So we need to induct the new administrative officers into this store of organizational values and knowledge — it is very tough, very hard. Even when it is documented, not everybody knows.

The trend is for people to have shorter careers and that has tremendous impact on us. A civil service career is more like the armed forces or the priesthood. Most people come in at the beginning or not at all. How do I have enough people make it to the top to get that institutional memory? In the future, I expect to lose many of the officers who have PS potential, not withstanding competitive salaries. And it has been very difficult to bring in people mid-career or at a senior level. Most governments have not succeeded in doing so."

On what the public service can do to engage the private sector:

"We can never do enough. That is one challenge for the civil service. They must know the economic and commercial perspectives, and how businesses work. In terms of understanding what the urgent issues are, getting private sector inputs on the capabilities we need to build for the economy, we are not doing too badly. We could not have done the Economic Review Committee, or the URA Masterplan reviews without substantial private sector inputs. But in the end somebody must sit down and write the report, it's not just a bottom-up process — somebody must think hard, and integrate all the pieces — the objectives, the overview, the thrusts, the balance, the main themes, etc and present a coherent policy. You can't expect the private sector to give you a ready-made policy.

The private sector also looks at things differently. They tend to be very issue-driven and focused on specific solutions. A policy perspective is different. We have to look longer-term and balance multiple considerations. Yes, the private sector is exposed to the signals of the market everyday and we keep in touch with them, get their inputs, views, and listen carefully to their suggestions. But there needs to be some distilling between market talk and a considered assessment and recommendation. Even the private sector is often caught by surprise by the way the economy goes…"

9.2 Risks and Challenges for the Public Service in Singapore

In this book we study not a perfect governance system but a system that has learnt to adjust, change, adapt, improve and innovate to meet the evolving requirements for effectiveness and relevance. It is a dynamic system, but by no means perfect. Singaporeans know well the potential for further improvement in the public service. A casual read of the forum pages in the daily newspaper will surface letters on lapses in public service, civil servants who behave as rigid bureaucrats, outdated rules, lack of sensitivity in service delivery and wasteful practices.

For all the examples of innovative and thoughtfully adapted policies, there are also many that have attracted criticism. As Ghesquiere states:

> "... IMF staff ha(ve) questioned whether government saving might not be excessive... the subsequent reorientation of the (CPF) scheme to finance widespread home ownership has resulted in insufficient liquid savings and an inadequate prospective income stream for many retirees... the dominant role of public enterprises and government guidance in the economy may have stymied innovative local private entrepreneurship... observers also bemoan the emphasis placed on written examinations in the centuries-old mandarin tradition, which they claim has dulled creativity in education." [13]

Policy-insiders such as retired permanent secretary Ngiam Tong Dow have also publicly acknowledged some policy flaws and weaknesses:[14]

---

[13] Ghesquiere (2007), pp. 2, 3.

[14] Ngiam Tong Dow (2006). *A Mandarin and the Making of Public Policy*. NUS Press, pp. 141–155.

- Failure of population policy to be alert to falling birth rates and remaining on population control auto-pilot too long to the point where Singapore is now unable to replace its population.
- Danger of meritocracy leading to elitism.
- Danger of an inverted pyramid of public finances, "where the most able 10 per cent of the population support the other 90 per cent;" he questioned its sustainability when economic growth inevitably slows.
- Waste of having duopolies to compete for local services such as land transport in a small market like Singapore.
- Loss of competitiveness because of a "perverse land pricing policy" with use of inappropriate opportunity cost concepts leading to substantial increases in rentals and leases for industrial land.

There are many other specific criticisms of policies, some of which have been expressed in articles in the local and international media and there is no need to repeat them here. That is not the purpose of the book. Our focus has been on the system of governance, and the forces that enabled that system to evolve with the times, to become dynamic. Specific policy examples have been used to illustrate the ways in which this dynamism has been manifested. We only wish to make clear that while the policy track record has been good with many positive results, it has clearly not been perfect, and instances of policy failure are conceded by policy-insiders.

Similarly, while the governance system responsible for policy making and policy execution has proved to be remarkably resilient and nimble in adjusting to the changes in its operating context, we also see some potential systemic risks and these risks and challenges are essentially the by-products of this governance system. We will now explore some of the unintended consequences, second-order effects and deep-seated systemic risks of the current system. These risks may not yet be pressing, demanding immediate resolution but they should be considered and pondered. We raise questions for reflection rather than prescribe simplistic solutions. There are no simple or immediate answers. The issues we raise include those relating to blind spots and the intellectual elitism that come with success, the danger of unquestioned cultural assumptions and beliefs, the lack of diversity in the public sector talent pool, and the lack of degrees of freedom between public sector and political leadership.

9.2.1 *Dealing with the Risks of Success: Blind Spots and Intellectual Elitism*

Mention "public consultations" and expressions of skepticism will emanate from many quarters. Many members of the public perceive these consultations to be "consultations" in form rather than substance. Citizens complain that they are being asked to respond when solutions have already been decided, when policy-makers are understandably less open to change because they have already spent so much time and effort deliberating on the issues. "What is the point when they have already made up their minds?" is a common response. Despite much effort by the public sector to improve public consultations, the skepticism remains. What factors have contributed to this state of affairs? Are these valid concerns?

The most cynical will point to what they perceive as signs of intellectual arrogance on the part of the policy elites. They point out that this arrogance is evident when public sector elites speak frequently of the need to "explain and sell government policies." A presumed need to sell the ideas implies that the problem is perceived not in terms of the policies themselves, but in the lack of understanding (or worse, a fundamental inability to understand) from a less discerning group of people. Intellectual arrogance is sometimes manifested in the unspoken attitude that "if only they are as smart as we are, they will understand why we adopt these policies and how these would work out... and since they are not, we, the ones who know better, will have to educate them."

These cynics do not dispute that the public sector elites are smart, have drive and ability, work hard, and achieve results. They recognize that public sector leaders have been charged to be on the lookout for good ideas and they shoulder the responsibility of having to devise policies for the significant challenges facing the nation. But these cynics contend that because public sector elites have done their job so well, their very success may contain the seeds of future failure. The root of the problem, they believe, is that policy elites often do not expect the same quality of thinking and ideas from others who are not like them — these could be the regular graduate officers in their department (the doers vs "us" as thinkers), or the businessmen and entrepreneurs (the self-centered money-makers vs "us" as the guardians of national policies) they are working with. It is then not surprising that policy elites may not expect much from public consultations. Cynics maintain that this attitude predisposes public sector elites to believe that they are more likely to hear complaints about how a particular policy proposal would affect a particular group, rather than real substantive alternatives to the proposed policies. At best they expect feedback that may result in fine tuning and marginal amendments to the implementation process but not fundamental changes to their well-thought through, laid out proposals.

If there is some truth to the above perspective, then the risks to the system are not hard to fathom. The policy leaders who are the core of the system become blind to the fact that the lack of good ideas from others may be simply a self-fulfilling prophecy, the result of their unconscious or subconscious superior mentality: we are the thinkers → "others" are not able to think like us → "others" are put off by the lack of openness to their ideas → "others" slowly stop giving ideas. Meritocracy can easily breed intellectual arrogance and elitism.[15] The potential dangers of this type of intellectual elitism may be greater in the Singapore context because the elitism is subtle and not easy to detect, being embedded in attitudes and mindset and not in displays of wealth.

Are these perceptions grounded in fact? Public sector leaders usually do not respond publicly to these types of comments. But if they did, what would they say?

First of all, they are likely to say that public consultations cannot take place in a vacuum. Consultations must take place with the intent to

---

[15] Chua Mui Hoong (2006). "How Meritocracy can Breed Intellectual Elitism," *The Straits Times*, 10 November 2006.

implement. Ministries and statutory boards must thus know the issues and what some of the possible responses and solutions are, before they are able to frame proposals and questions for public consultation. Otherwise they will be accused of not doing their "homework," not having thought through issues well enough. So agencies will have to have thought through the issues and in so doing, will necessarily have devised some idea of what needs to be done. To ensure that these preliminary proposals are viable, views and inputs from experts and specialists would often be sought. So from the agencies' point of view, by the time the proposals are in good enough shape for the public eye, "people who ought to be consulted (i.e., the experts) have already been consulted." Thus, public sector leaders' reluctance to extend the consultation process to the general public may stem more from efficiency considerations than intellectual arrogance.

That said, public sector leaders will probably acknowledge that in several instances, public feedback did lead to substantive changes and fine tuning, and in one or two cases, resulted in proposals actually being shelved. What policy-makers need to realize is that a more educated and sophisticated citizenry can increasingly understand policy issues, ask tough questions, weigh policy options and assess implications. Thoughtful citizens are increasingly aware of dilemmas involved in policy choices and the inevitable downside of some good policies. An unwillingness to discuss these dilemmas openly and acknowledge the problems and struggles in certain policies only leads to public cynicism. If efficiency is the main factor behind the perceived reluctance to undertake more open public consultation, then public sector leaders need to learn to balance efficiency considerations with the need to engage and connect with an increasingly sophisticated public.

There are those who believe that one reason behind the perceived reluctance to engage more openly is a deep-seated belief that leaders would lose the respect of the people if they appeared weak by admitting mistakes openly. Is this always true? A more mature society does not expect its leaders to be infallible and would not lose respect for them if they appear more human, more willing to acknowledge mistakes and more willing to show a genuine desire for substantively different inputs, perspectives and suggestions.

Greater engagement with citizens and residents, and public sector openness to a diversity of views and perspectives is critical to maintaining the integrity and quality of the Singapore governance system. Intellectual elitism that is closed to alternative views and resistant to expressions of contrary opinion creates systemic blind spots for public sector policy elites — they do not know what they don't know because they do not expect others to know better than they do. The danger is greater when success is often attributed to the policy choices and actions made by the talented elite and there is no intellectual room to accept that success may have come in spite of the policy choices and actions, and in spite of the intelligence of the policy makers. Intellectual elitism and economic success reinforce each other within a closed loop until "sudden" failure occurs — and both insiders and outsiders are caught off-guard since there were no warning signs of impending failure. They do not realize that it may be an inevitable result of a system that has evolved over many years, which for a long time showed that the policy elites were making the right choices and achieving intended results.

It is compounded by the political realities of democratic elections and the need for political leaders to claim credit for success to reinforce its own legitimacy. As a result, policy mistakes are often rationalized, and the downsides of successful policies are not openly acknowledged. The systemic risks can be significant: if public sector leaders subconsciously or unconsciously close themselves off from sources of potential new ideas, views and perspectives, there is a danger that the cycle of openness, learning and adaptation that has been the driver of the dynamism in governance in Singapore may eventually grind to a halt.

9.2.2 Challenging Accepted Assumptions, Beliefs and Principles

Cultural values and beliefs may either facilitate or impede dynamic governance. We have shown how the perceptions of Singapore's vulnerable position shaped its governance purposes and principles which in turn became the foundations for its growth and social progress over 40 years. These deep-seated beliefs consciously and unconsciously exert tremendous influence over how policy issues are perceived, defined, and approached. But are these values, beliefs, principles and assumptions regularly questioned, challenged and refreshed? Is there a process for re-examining these assumptions on a periodic basis? Should there be a process? These are sensitive issues but unless the leaders discuss them openly, the closely-knit and cohesive policy elite can easily degenerate into groupthink.

The Singapore of 2007 is no longer the poor nation born out of forced separation in 1965, struggling to feed a rapidly increasing population without basic education, health care and housing and without much of the needed basic fundamental infrastructure for a modern economy. A completely opposite description is more representative of conditions today. There is no doubt that Singapore is still a small country limited by population and geography. But when does a "siege mentality" become too limiting a mindset? In the new globalized world characterized by information, ideas and innovation, has Singapore missed opportunities to play a bigger role on the global stage because of its preoccupation with its physical limitations and insecurities? Are the assumptions and beliefs that have provided guidance for 40 years still fully valid without some refinement and update? Have they become sacred cows and dogma that cannot be touched and questioned, let alone be slaughtered?

The way that Singapore has managed its relationships with its neighbors has been indisputably business-like, characterized by a tough uncompromising stance based on accepted international laws and standards. This approach may represent the global best practice and may be deemed crucial to maintaining sovereignty and survival but one wonders if the hard-nosed approach may have diminished opportunities for greater economic cooperation and unwittingly contributed to the sluggish development of the region. After independence in 1965, Singapore successfully overcame regional limitations by leapfrogging to seek trade and investments globally. When does leapfrogging become an escape from the effort and commitment needed to build a stronger regional network? We are not suggesting that nothing has been done towards building regional cooperation, and are aware that Singapore has indeed tried very hard to organize the region, whose countries themselves may not be as ready. The question is one of balance between the regional and the global, and whether it has been struck at the appropriate level — this is a strategic issue and should be a subject for further internal dialog.

Domestically, it is widely accepted that economic growth is paramount, perceived almost as an end in itself. There seems to be a deep-seated belief that continuous and strong economic growth is required before other important social values and objectives can be achieved. While there is obvious validity to the belief, will this premise always hold true? While economic and social objectives are not zero-sum outcomes, is it realistic that Singapore will never need to make some trade-offs between the two? As it is, one hears the question "Who is all this growth for?" more and more, particularly as specific segments of the population continue to be displaced even in the face of strong economic growth. Is growth to be pursued for its own sake or is it to facilitate other important national objectives?

Does the principle of pragmatism justify all means in order for the desired ends to be achieved? For more than 40 years, many hardheaded decisions and policies have been explained and defended on the basis that Singapore has to accept reality and take the world as it is, and not the way it wishes it to be. But the ingrained pragmatism is so deep that even the commitment to integrity is sometimes justified, not for its own sake but on the basis of avoiding the corroding effects of corruption on the business and social environment. Can Singapore ever be a great society and an enduring nation without recognizing the need for and having a commitment to strong absolute moral principles and values, not because they are expedient but simply because they are the right things to do and the right ways to be?

Another assumption that may need to be re-examined concerns the role of government in society. In Singapore, the public sector has played a proactive and dominant developmental role, both economically and socially. This was perhaps necessary, especially in the early years when there was virtually no private or social sector to speak of. Government, with the strategic intent, talent and resources took on the roles of proxy private sector, regulator and social reformer, and led Singapore through four decades of successful socio-economic development. The economic and social success of the government-led model in Singapore in the last 40 years is unequivocal. The main consideration today is whether government should continue to play such a dominant role in the future. Can the docility of the private and social sectors be partially attributed the dominance of the public sector? Could the proactive and energetic public sector be contributing to the crippling dependency mentality in the private and social sectors?

Private sector firms face daily the onslaught of changes in the marketplace, customer expectations, global competition and technology developments, and thus have more current market information to assess risk and opportunities. Would a greater involvement of the private sector in policy making lead to better policies and projects? If the public sector pulls back and lets the private sector take the lead, will it step up to fulfill its needed role? Is the private sector adequately organized to play a proactive role in the country's socio-economic development when private sector leaders are more likely to be held accountable for bottom-line financial returns to their shareholders? How can the balance of roles between the public and private sectors be restructured so that a more sustainable process and framework for socio-economic development may emerge?

We are not suggesting that the beliefs and principles that have served Singapore well are no longer able to guide current policy choices and governance decisions. Far from it. In fact, the robustness of these principles and beliefs in guiding decision-making for 40 years has surprised many observers and are being emulated in other countries. The best time to review these assumptions is not when they are obviously obsolete and out-dated but now, when there is time to ponder carefully and resources are available to build capabilities that may be needed for the future. We are suggesting that the public sector uses the same capabilities of thinking ahead, thinking again and thinking across to examine the cultural foundations of governance. That should not be too difficult for an institution that we have found to possess deep and systemic capabilities for re-looking, rethinking and re-examining.

9.2.3 *Lack of Diversity in the Talent Pool*

If the main driver for dynamism in governance is leadership, then increasing the depth and diversity of the talent pool has to be a key strategic priority for the public sector. Political and public sector leaders would agree and have made similar comments. Yet there is remarkable similarity in the education and experience profiles of public sector leaders. Take any Permanent Secretary, and you are likely to find that person majored in either engineering or economics at either Oxford or Cambridge in the UK and or one of the Ivy league universities in the US. He or she would have done a Masters degree in Harvard or Stanford, and have spent most, if not all, of his or her career in the public sector. Many of them would also have served a term as principal private secretary (special assistant) to the current or a previous Prime Minister. It is thus not surprising that there is significant shared vision and values among public sector leaders. However, does such a convergence of education and experience also lead to a lack of diversity in views and perspectives? Uniformity in approach to identifying and resolving issues may reduce conflicts in the short-term but carry significant long-term risks when future issues, threats and opportunities are different from those that arose before and which may require a variety of experiences and perspectives to correctly interpret their meanings and impact, and to adopt the appropriate responses.

Hardly anyone in senior public service positions comes from the private or social sectors. Though statutory boards have been relatively successful in recruiting mid-career professionals to fill specialized jobs, the civil service's record in attracting and retaining mid-career professionals to join the public service has been dismal, despite several attempts at such recruitment. Public service leaders attribute the poor results to the daunting complexity of the public sector and its political context, the multi-dimensionalities of formulating and executing public policies, and the adjustment difficulties of those who come in mid-stream. There is no doubt that specialization, socialization and networking are needed to be successful in the public sector, and these tend to develop only with extended association and experience as is the case in other institutions. The task is complicated because mid-career professionals join in ones and twos, and there is no critical mass or a large enough cohort to make an impact on the establishment. While it may be true that attempts at recruitment of mid-career professionals have not been successful in many other countries, the dangers and implications of not being able to do so are greater for Singapore where the public sector plays a much more critical role and where the country is so much more susceptible to change. An institution that does not have the ability to assimilate different kinds of talent is in danger of ossification. Diversity is needed both in education (institutions, courses of study, countries) and work experience (variety in terms of exposure to public, private and social sectors). The public sector is providing more opportunities for serving officers to have stints in other environments. That is an encouraging development. A more concerted effort will be needed over the long term to diversify the talent pool in the public sector.

It is to the public sector's credit that unconventional leaders such as Philip Yeo can be successful and rise to the highest ranks in the elite administrative service. But it is also true that such "mavericks," while tolerated, are still not incorporated into the public service culture and mainstream models for success. There is still a standard course of progression towards the highest levels of the public sector — get a prestigious government scholarship, graduate with a first-class honors from a top university, focus on analytical policy work and write good staff papers, do not be associated with major blunders, serve quietly, follow the rules, be deferential to your bosses, do not offend senior officials, be rotated to a different job every two to three years, be appointed for a term as special assistant to the Prime Minister, Senior Minister or Minister Mentor, get promoted on schedule, become a deputy secretary in your thirties and a permanent secretary by your early forties. People who deviate from this path and still do well are considered to be "outliers" and do not constitute models to be emulated. Following the straight and narrow path may well be the accepted wisdom but for long-term sustainability, the public service would do better to define alternative paths to success, develop greater tolerance for less conventional modes of operating and encourage greater creativity, experimentation and innovation in how talented people can contribute their best ideas and energies to policy and governance in Singapore.

Perhaps the greatest fundamental challenge is how the public sector can continue to attract and retain the best people in a global environment where talented people have open to them more interesting and challenging opportunities in more sectors and places than their predecessors ever had. Just as talented people move more frequently in private sector jobs and may pursue two or three different careers over the course of their working lives, how attractive and appealing would a lifetime public sector career be? If talented people move more frequently and stay in the public sector only for five to seven years rather than 30, how would the public sector cope? This new public sector would be markedly different from the current. So far, the rotations of administrative officers to different ministries have helped to give them the job variety and challenge to keep them in the public sector. But when the movements are not within the public sector but in and out of the public sector, new approaches to socializing new entrants, learning about the task requirements, creating institutional memory, and assessing performance may be needed. What organizational and human resource changes would be needed to ensure that the public sector remains an effective institution in such an environment? What can or should the public sector start doing today to prepare for such an eventuality?

9.2.4 Lack of Degrees of Separation from Political Leaders

The civil service has served the same ruling political party since independence. It is inevitable that close working relationships would have developed between political and public sector leaders, which have greatly facilitated the successful implementation of policy. The public sector has been able to plan long term in conjunction with the political leaders as it expected the ruling party to win each new election and remain in power. The public sector also has seen several of its leaders being recruited to join the political party to contest elections and subsequently appointed as ministers. Even though political leaders have emphasized the political neutrality of the public sector, that the public sector needs to be politically sensitive but not political, the occasional politicization of public policy strains this espoused separation of the public and the political. In recent elections, the ruling party stipulated that opposition-held constituencies could not expect the same priority in estate upgrading as constituencies under the ruling party, when the upgrading of public housing estates is managed by a public agency (the Housing and Development Board) using public funds. Many, including political analyst Ho Khai Leong, have thus concluded that the civil service has been effectively politicized[16].

Of course much of the lack of real separation is attributable to the public sector's genuine respect for and trust in the political leadership. In our interviews, public sector leaders have routinely, and without prompting, showed their admiration for the political leaders' integrity, long-term perspective, professionalism and rationality. Their mutual respect and commitment made for effective governance but also made true independence difficult to assess. Would the public sector be just as committed to work in partnership with a different ruling party should one win a general election in the future? Ideally the public sector should remain neutral and work with whichever political party is in power, but several public sector leaders admitted in our interviews that they had not thought about this and expressed doubt as to how effective they would be if a different party came to power. They are just being pragmatic of course — they know full well that the probability of that occurring in the foreseeable future is very slim.

Still the risks remain that the relative lack of real separation between public sector and political leaders may make it difficult for the public sector to maintain a strong independent voice if a policy decision is taken that serves only the narrow interests of a political party rather than the broader interests of the nation. Public sector leaders told us that when they saw issues differently, they made their views known to their political leaders in private and appreciated that

---

[16] Ho Khai Leong (2003). *Shared Responsibilities, Unshared Power.* Eastern Universities Press.

their views were always taken seriously. Will the public sector still be able to maintain an effective independent voice in a governance system when a ruling political party with a strong charismatic leader emerges who can persuade the public to accept populist policies that may harm the nation in the long term? Is it realistic to expect public sector leaders who have grown in a system where they genuinely trust and respect their political leaders to suddenly know how to do so? Or must it be a foregone conclusion that they will not have the capacity to do so?

9.3 Key Lessons and Principles from Singapore's Governance System

We have discussed lessons and principles we can learn from different aspects of the Singapore governance experience in the various chapters throughout the book. We will not repeat them here. Instead, we will integrate these lessons and consolidate them into several principles that explain the public sector's capacity to continually adapt, innovate and change in response to changing circumstances and needs, some of which we have already alluded to. We believe the eight key principles we discuss in this section can be generalized beyond Singapore and beyond the public service.

9.3.1 *Good Governance is Dynamic, but Not Without Weaknesses*

This book is not a study of good governance *per se*, but dynamic governance — how a governance system can remain relevant and effective by continually changing, innovating and adapting to new and emerging needs in a changing environment. We do not question the need to adopt a set of good governance principles and practices as a prerequisite to improve standards and achieve desired outcomes. This has been the focus of much of the current debate on governance. But in an era of rapid globalization and technological change, our argument is that this is not sufficient. The capacity and the capabilities to change, in short dynamic governance, are crucial for sustained and sustainable growth and development. We are thus not aiming for just a one-time change, but sustained transformation of public institutions and governance. Yet there is very little understanding of what dynamic governance is, much less how it may be achieved.

The Singapore governance system and experience provided us with a functioning model of how dynamism works in governance and how it evolved over many years. It is by no means without fault and there is no suggestion that it is anywhere close to perfect. The previous section on the challenges faced by the public sector shows the significant risks that exist in the current system and which need to be addressed to prevent the system from becoming dysfunctional. Singapore is fortunate to have political and public service leaders who are aware and recognize the weaknesses and the systemic risks, and who have the drive to work to close the aspiration and performance gaps. Without committed political and public service leaders with vision and high aspirations for Singapore, there can be no effective governance.

The most encouraging lesson from this study of the Singapore system is that a society can enjoy much of the benefits of good governance by adopting a set of basic principles such as rule of law, respect for property rights, non-corruption, meritocracy and effective institutions. Though these principles are universal, their implementation is not. These principles need to be designed into aligned systems and processes and upheld by vision and political will. Effective execution is the key. In addition, continuous learning, innovation, adaptation and improvement in the policies and governance system have greater impact than how perfect the initial policy choices were.

9.3.2 *Effective Political and Public Sector Leadership are Both Needed for Good Governance*

Though the focus of this book is on the public sector, good governance cannot be achieved independent of the political context, system, structure and leadership. It is clear from our study that the political leadership set the direction, exemplified the beliefs and provided the framework for the development of a first-rate civil service. It is the founding political leaders' uncompromising integrity, strategic view of public sector leadership, insistence on intellectual depth and policy design rationality, and relentless drive for results that set the tone for many of the developments in public sector strategies, structure and systems. Prime Minister Lee Hsien Loong described the political context that enabled the civil service to function as it has:

> "We often say that Singapore has done well because it has good leaders at the top, able and committed officers down the ranks, and a system that is clean and efficient. But a superior civil service does not fully explain why we are able to implement good policies. The more basic question is: why is it Singapore can have such a civil service, and what enables it to work properly?
>
> The answer lies in the political realm, and particularly in the unique way politics has evolved in Singapore. Our people are united in purpose, they understand what the Government is trying to do, they have given the Government a strong mandate, and they are working with the Government to implement intelligent and effective solutions to our problems.
>
> Few other countries operate like Singapore. Many governments have to struggle mightily to get the basics right. Not because they do not know what policies they need or lack the talent or capabilities. The difficulty is more fundamental: mustering the political will and consensus to adopt the right policies in the first place. Either vested interests get into the way, or the government of the day cannot afford to pay the political price for an unpopular policy which will only show results beyond the next election."[17]

Minister Teo Chee Hean described the relationships between the public sector and political leadership as one of "mutual respect and

---

[17] Speech by Prime Minister Lee Hsien Loong at the 2005 Administrative Dinner, 24 March 2005.

strong partnership."[18] Both political and public sector leaders have to be credible and visionary for mutual respect. Differences in views among the leaders can then be worked out through exchange, dialog and interaction. Many of the public sector leaders themselves openly acknowledged that they could not have done many of the things with which they were proud to be associated if the political leadership were not as committed, enlightened and forward-looking. They related how their counterparts in other countries could not contemplate trying out some of the practices they had observed and admired in Singapore because they knew that the will to implement politically risky or unpopular policies in their countries was lacking. This is also the limit of application of the governance lessons from Singapore — the political environment has to be supportive and the political leadership must be willing and ready to be engaged on critical policy issues before some of the ideas discussed in this book can be implemented effectively.

9.3.3 *Continual Learning and Effective Execution are the Key Drivers for Dynamism*

Institutions, policies, processes, systems and structures are by themselves not innately dynamic. Citizens or customers who have had to deal with them often find them to be rigid mechanisms rather than malleable organisms. They become dynamic only when the leaders who oversee them and the staff who operate them are motivated to improve and innovate through continually incorporating new ideas and learning new skills. Institutional learning occurs when people are:

(i)   consciously learning and seeking to apply new ideas and explore different ways of doing their work better, or

(ii) observing different systems and their outcomes, and incorporating their new learning and knowledge into the system to improve performance, or

(iii) sensitive to new citizen or customer requirements and learn new knowledge and skills to meet these emerging needs.

---

[18] Interview by authors on 29 December 2006.

Leaders have the added responsibility of creating an environment conducive for their staff to learn, experiment and innovate.

It is not just the amount of knowledge the institution possesses but how much and how quickly the knowledge is being refreshed and renewed, in short, how institutions and their people are learning. Learning refreshes the pool of knowledge and when they are applied to improve institutional performance, they release creative energies that stimulate even more learning. It is this continuous cycle of sensing, learning and applying that is the source of institutional dynamism. The faster the learning cycle and the more cycles there are, the more dynamic an institution becomes. Our framework for dynamic governance with the twin building blocks of culture and capabilities is based on the energizing potential of individual and institutional learning. Dynamic governance is not possible if the individuals and institutions do not aspire to greater heights and are not continuously learning, reflecting on their experiences, observing other practices, discovering new insights, experimenting with new approaches and implementing changes to meet new challenges.

Learning is more than an accumulation of information. We learn more and more effectively through doing, through experience, through execution and through a drive for results. Learning is not just head knowledge, even if the knowledge is new. In Singapore, leaders view implementation and change as evidence of learning. More than just good ideas, this is a place that makes things happen, that turns talk into reality. Though many of the policies are novel and innovative, the real lesson of the Singapore experience is how these are actually executed. Without execution, interesting and novel ideas that come from new exposure and learning will not lead to changes in policy — there would be no dynamic governance. While good ideas may lead to elegant theories, without execution, they will remain just ideas and theories. The Singapore system works because it was made to work. It is a system that faces reality head-on, adjusts to the world as it is, and follows through with discipline. It is a system geared toward execution based on a commitment to making pragmatic policy decisions, rewarding people on merit and performance, building strong institutions with structures and systems to sustain action, evaluating policy options on helicopter qualities, analysis, imagination and realism, and having a strong results orientation and accountability.

The culture and capabilities framework for dynamic governance is all about learning and execution. The culture must support and enable learning, adaptation and change. But there must be capabilities to think and take action, in short, execution. Continual learning and effective execution are the drivers for good and dynamic governance.

9.3.4 Dynamism is not Merely about Speed in Problem-Solving; Even More Important is the Speed in Perceiving and Capturing New Opportunities

Dynamism in the governance system prepared and enabled Singapore public institutions to perceive new developments and respond quickly and decisively to capture its share of global opportunities as they arose. The cultural foundations of position, purpose and principles were established in the early 1960s by the founding political leaders, though the principles were not formally articulated until much later. The organizational capabilities were initially concentrated in pioneer critical public institutions such as the EDB and HDB. The dynamism and tenacity of EDB officers, the institutional culture and organizational capabilities became the face of Singapore's dynamism to large US, European and Japanese multinationals.[19] It was the knowledge, professionalism, can-do spirit and reliability of EDB officers which enabled Singapore to sense and seize the opportunities that opened up in the 1970s as US and European MNCs sought low-cost production bases overseas to counter the competitive threats from Japanese manufacturers.

Similarly, Singapore was able to sense and seize new opportunities to increase its global market share for private banking and wealth management in the aftermath of the 1997 Asian financial crisis. The disruptive and volatile developments and new global threats and imbalances saw investment funds seeking higher returns in alternative safe havens. Singapore was well positioned to capture

---

[19] See Schein (1996) for a discussion of EDB organizational culture.

these new opportunities, which it did, as a result of having liberalized its financial markets and introduced greater competition whilst maintaining a strong prudential regulatory framework. Even though it did not foresee the financial crisis or anticipate the new opportunities that subsequently arose, it was able to take advantage of the new developments and respond quickly and judiciously; its governance system enabled it to sense signals from the global marketplace, assess their impacts, surface options, make decisions and act quickly. The quality difference made by dynamic governance is speed — speed in understanding and solving problems, and more importantly, speed in perceiving and capturing new opportunities, regardless of how and where they may arise.

9.3.5 Dynamism is the Result of Building a Holistic Governance System with a Strong Cultural Foundation of Values and Principles, and an Adaptable Structure of Critical Institutional Capabilities

The main conclusion from our study is that dynamic governance is the result of a system comprising a supportive institutional culture and enabling organizational capabilities that induce continuous change. The sustainability of dynamic governance lies in the way system is designed and implemented. It has to be a holistic system with reinforcing and balancing flows as shown in Figure 9.1, which was first shown and discussed in detail in Chapter 1. It is the on-going process of building systemic links and relationships among the culture, capabilities and change that makes governance dynamic. Leaders seeking to develop dynamism in governance thus have to build the cultural foundations and the critical pillars of organizational capabilities and ensure that their systemic linkages are carefully constructed and constantly reinforced and strengthened.

A society's perception of its position shapes its sense of purpose, which in turn determines the principles that will guide its choices and actions. The systemic links between perceptions of position, articulation of purpose and adoption of guiding principles have to be

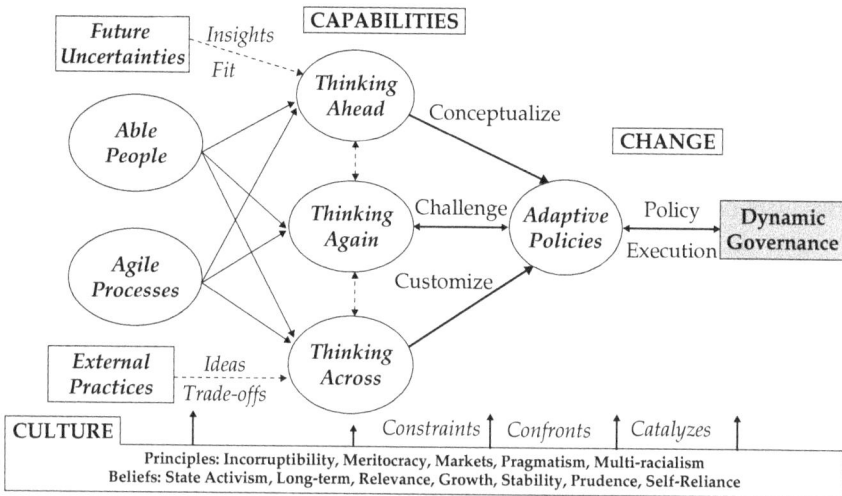

Figure 9.1. Framework for Dynamic Governance System

carefully managed if the culture is to be supportive of constant change and adaptation. While culture can support change, the change levers depend largely on the organizational capabilities to think, learn, make decisions and take action. We have encapsulated these change levers as the capability to think ahead, think again and think across. These capabilities have to be built, strengthened, deepened, diffused and renewed widely within any organization that wants to be proactive and responsive to change. Again, these are not three independent capabilities but are linked and reinforced in a holistic system of relationships that together induce and facilitate change.

9.3.6 Dynamic Governance Capabilities are Created by Able People, Stimulated by Agile Processes and Expressed in Adaptive Policies

The energizing force of the capabilities of thinking ahead, thinking again, and thinking across that creates dynamic governance can only come from able people who are committed to serve the broader good. Governance is about choices. Only people can think, learn and make choices. It takes leaders with drive and commitment to direct limited resources to the most important outcomes. The impact of committed and able leadership on dynamic and effective governance in Singapore is widely recognized. Almost everyone we interviewed attributed Singapore's sustained progress to the quality of its leadership, both in the political realm and in the public sector. Many public sector leaders themselves credited the founding political leaders, especially Lee Kuan Yew, Goh Keng Swee and Hon Sui Sen, for the quality, effectiveness and efficiency of the Singapore governance system. Henri Ghesquiere drew a similar conclusion:[20]

> "Singapore succeeded because its leadership was assiduous, highly intelligent in a practical way, determined to achieve shared prosperity, and committed to act with integrity. Leading with vision and fortitude is possible. Its benefits can be invaluable. That is Singapore's ultimate lesson."

Yet leadership alone is not enough. Leaders achieve results not just by their own intellect, charisma, choices and effort, but by building systems, structures and processes that enable organizations to continue to sustain effort and performance long beyond their tenure. That's the legacy of effective leaders — innovative organizations with the energy to continually pursue worthwhile goals, systems that induce change rather than preserve the status quo, processes that are agile and which encourage improvement and innovation — adaptable institutions that outlast them.

Dynamic governance is not merely an abstract idea — it is expressed in adaptive innovative policies that achieve national goals and serve the people. It requires courage to take institutions inherited from the British such as the CPF and the Corrupt Practices Investigation Bureau, to infuse them with new missions and to expand their scope to meet the different needs of a new nation. It takes confidence and openness to learn the best ideas from others, without the "not invented here" mindset. It then requires creativity to customize them to the

---

[20] Ghesquiere (2007), p. 168.

needs of the local community. Moreover these policies are not static, but are constantly re-evaluated and re-designed in the light of new information, insight and feedback to meet new and emerging needs. Thus dynamism in policies does not come automatically — it has to be designed and built into the policy execution process. That requires able leaders willing to invest in developing agile processes. Able people in leadership, agile processes in organizations, and adaptable public policies are the stuff of dynamic governance.

9.3.7 Public Institutions Played a Crucial Role in Effective Dynamic Governance by Designing and Implementing Policies to Achieve Results

Dynamic governance is more than a set of good ideas and principles. It is ultimately about implementation and policy execution. This is why institutions play such an important role in dynamic governance. Singapore overcame the constraints of a small talent pool but leveraged on the one advantage of its size — it was easier to organize the system to get things done. The lesson here is that a country or organization's size has less influence on its effectiveness than how well it is organized: ultimately it is the organization of effort that determines the quality of outcomes. This is the lesson of Singapore. Singapore's public institutions possess the culture and capabilities to turn good ideas into reality, good policy into enviable results.

Institutions comprise people, systems, the formal rules and informal norms for social and economic interaction. In Singapore, the operating mechanisms for effective governance are also embedded in its public institutions. Many of these public institutions have been discussed in our study, including the EDB, HDB, CPF, MOE, MOF, PSC, MINDEF and NLB. These institutions provided the conceptualization, analyses and organizational mechanisms for identifying and surfacing issues, consulting with stakeholders, gathering feedback, designing policy options, setting rules, recommending solutions, selecting partners, implementing projects, communicating with the public, monitoring progress and adapting programs.

The efficiency and effectiveness of its public institutions played a critical role in Singapore's dynamic governance. Leaders appointed to lead public institutions are carefully selected and given the resources and autonomy to achieve the goals of their agencies. They are accountable for their organization's results, and report on their performance to both their governing boards and their overseeing ministers. Even though public institutions are by nature of their mission and domain natural monopolies, they do not behave as monopolies in Singapore. There is a degree of subtle competition among agencies for recognition and their leaders know that their progression in the public sector hierarchy depends on their performance in leading their assigned agencies. Besides performance in their focused missions, agencies compete for recognition in achieving broad public sector objectives such as the quality and responsiveness of service, financial viability, innovativeness in the design of policies, projects and programs, and commendations in independent studies by external organizations.

Singapore public institutions are also unique in their perspective of global competition. Though they may be technically monopolies domestically, their leaders articulate their contribution to Singapore's competitiveness on a regional and global basis. For example, even though it was the only port in Singapore, the Port of Singapore Authority (PSA) strove and became the largest transshipment port in the world, gaining a global reputation for fast turnaround, connectivity, frequency and reliability by competing for shipping traffic against ports in other countries. Though the port has been privatized and is now a full-fledged commercial entity, it achieved its world-class performance when it was still a statutory board reporting to a parent ministry. Even internal government administrative agencies such as the manpower and internal security agencies see their roles in processing and granting employment permits or visitor passes in a larger context, as helping Singapore attract the global talent needed for continued growth and progress. Given all the above, it is perhaps not surprising that Singapore's public institutions are regularly cited for organizational excellence.[21]

---

[21] For example, for the Singapore Quality Awards which recognize organizational excellence in both public and private sector firms, the majority of winners have been public institutions.

9.3.8 *The Cumulative Effects of Systemic Improvements were Substantial, Even If Individual Policy Changes were only Incremental*

The key issue in fostering change is not whether it is incremental or dramatic, evolutionary or revolutionary. The main principle of sustaining change is whether it is systemic and cumulative. Even if specific policy or program changes are incremental, they will have significant organizational effects if:

(i) they are linked in a systemic manner to other incremental changes in a way that reinforces the values, mental models and behaviors that are required to sustain the momentum of change over the entire organization; and

(ii) they are linked in a cumulative manner to previously approved or implemented changes and future changes to come so that they provide the incentives for people to learn the knowledge, skills and attitudes necessary to sustain the effort over an extended period of time.

The most striking lesson from our study has not been the brilliance of specific individual policies or programs but the sustained pace of improvement and change and the relentless effort to adapt policies to meet new needs as they emerged. Specific policies or programs may only have incremental effects but the cumulative impact of the continued change effort throughout the entire public service yielded truly transformational results. Of course not every public agency performed with the same high level of commitment and enthusiasm all the time — that could not have been expected. But at any point in time, there were always some agencies initiating reviews, improving performance, innovating policies and implementing change. Different agencies provided the stimulus and challenge to the public service at different times. The institutional culture and deep organizational capabilities in the public service encouraged and recognized these path-breaking agencies as success stories and role models, adding to and strengthening both the culture and capabilities as other agencies learnt and sought to be path-breakers themselves. Thus the public service was never static but was always thinking ahead, thinking again, and thinking across — constantly releasing the energies of change which is the heart of dynamic governance.

9.4 Applying the Lessons Beyond the Singapore Public Service

The Singapore governance system can be easily dismissed because of its uniqueness — a small city-state that made the governance tasks easier, a specific charismatic leader in Lee Kuan Yew who cannot be cloned, and particular historical conditions that cannot be replicated. Although the lessons we described throughout the book are drawn from the Singapore public service, we believe that the principles are applicable beyond Singapore and beyond the public sector. But mere cloning or imitation will not work. It is conceptual generalizability that is important — which means that the circumstances need not be the exactly the same before the principles and lessons may be applied. But the principles, perspectives, paths, policies and practices would have to be carefully understood, thought through, adapted and contextualized, and not merely imitated or cloned. Learning and applying the right principles and lessons require conceptual and analytical thinking, open dialog among stakeholders, and careful customization to fit the socio-political context and cultural values of an institution. The institutional transfer of lessons across countries and to private sector organizations is not straightforward and the difficulties should not be under estimated, even if the leaders are enthusiastic about the prospects.

The Straits Times Senior Writer, Andy Ho, made a similar argument in discussing Singapore's water management experience when he said that it is not easy to clone the experience of the Public Utilities Board (PUB):

> "Technology can be bought, pricing and management models can be learnt, but the overall package of governance instruments will be harder to come by. The PUB does not operate in a vacuum. It is able to manage Singapore's water

needs because there is an entire government machinery helping in myriad ways: stressing the need to save water; giving very targeted subsidies to households genuinely unable to pay their utilities bills; allocating land for water catchment; even imposing regulations on when and what kind of water industry can use. So while the PUB can be a poster boy for water management, it is best to remember that it is one among many other institutions all contributing to its success. And institutions are not easily cloned."[22]

The problems that Singapore faced in trying to establish an industrial township in the Chinese city of Suzhou, despite strong mutual interests and endorsements from the highest levels of the Singapore and Chinese central governments, are testimony to the potential pitfalls. Although some knowledge transfer did eventually occur, the initial years after the signing of an agreement in 1994 were a struggle for both sides. Several challenges[23] plagued the project from the outset:[24]

(i)   different objectives of the partners;
(ii) differences in the size of the countries and the organization of their governments;
(iii) differing standards for assessing success;
(iv) differences in the scale between the Suzhou project and previous similar projects;
(v)   difficulties in partner interactions and how knowledge was transferred, especially in the transfer of tacit knowledge;
(vi) local competition, especially from the Suzhou New District that was built and operated by the municipal government;

---

[22] Andy Ho (2007). "Not So Easy to Clone a PUB," *The Straits Times*, 29 January 2007.

[23] John Thomas (2001). "Institutional Innovation and the Prospects for Transference: Transferring Singaporean Institutions to Suzhou, China," John F Kennedy School of Government Research Working Paper RWP02-001, Harvard University.

[24] See also Andrew C Inkpen and Wang Pien (2006). "An Examination of Collaboration and Knowledge Transfer: China-Singapore Suzhou Industrial Park," *Journal of Management Studies*, June, pp. 779–811.

(vii) differences between the perceived and actual difficulty of the project

The situation improved only after January 2001 when the Singapore consortium transferred 30 per cent of its ownership to the Chinese partners, giving the latter the majority ownership of 65 per cent. This realignment of interests resulted in a significantly improved relationship between the partners. The Suzhou Industrial Park is now profitable and plans for expansion have been made.

The task of transferring learning from one context to another should not be taken lightly. Careful study and planning are needed to understand the principles and practices before deciding how they may be adapted and customized. A systematic process of evaluation and reflection should be followed before adaptation and application of the principles and lessons to a specific country (beyond Singapore), company (beyond the public sector) or organization. The process should include these activities:

(i)   understanding the philosophy, perspective and rationale for each principle or practice;

(ii)   understanding the actual experience in implementation in terms of the issues that arose, how they were dealt with, the results achieved and the lessons learnt;

(iii)   considering an organization's unique history, culture, economic conditions and strategic imperatives;

(iv)   analyzing whether the adoption of a similar principle or practice would achieve the intended results, articulating clearly the reasons why it would or would not;

(v)   assessing the likely receptiveness of and impact of the practice on the stakeholders;

(vi)   selecting attributes or features that may be directly applicable and identifying those that may need to be modified;

(vii)   identifying new or additional attributes and features that would make the principle or practice work more effectively in the context of the country or company;

(viii) integrating the selected practices, attributes and features into a coherent system or process and evaluating the likely risks and issues in implementing it in the local context;

(ix) determining how progress would be tracked and how results would be measured;

(x) deciding on the approach, timing and resources needed to make an effective implementation.

We suggest some guidelines as a template for thinking and reflecting on the main principles for designing and implementing dynamic governance in an organization. These guidelines are formulated in terms of questions that may be used individually or in groups to assess the current governance system of an organization and identifying issues for further analysis and potential change. We suggest that organizational leaders ask themselves these questions thoughtfully and engage their teams in reflective dialog at least on an annual basis and craft action plans to start the process of organizational transformation. This ought to be an on-going and dynamic process if the desired outcome is dynamism in governance, leadership, strategy, and management. We propose eleven sets of questions as guidelines. They are not meant to be exhaustive but only representative of the types of dialog needed to create awareness and release the latent energies needed to build dynamic organizations.

1. What is our organizational culture (values, beliefs, assumptions and principles)? How is our culture related to our perception of our position and purpose? How does our culture support and enable organizational change? How does our culture impede change?

2. What parts of our culture do we need to re-examine and revise to support our strategic imperatives? What parts of our culture do we need to reinforce and inculcate more deeply?

3. What dynamic capabilities do we have today? Do we have the organizational capabilities of thinking ahead, thinking again and thinking across? What are the organizational roadblocks in exercising each of these capabilities?

4. How are we thinking ahead to prepare for the future? Does our current process encourage and stimulate real strategic thinking? Or has it degenerated into a bureaucratic process? How can we make thinking ahead a dynamic capability?

5. How are we thinking again the policies, processes, projects and programs we have implemented over the years? Do we have a systemic process for reviewing organizational processes and operational performance for learning and change? What is our organizational process for surfacing and challenging outdated rules and assumptions?

6. How are we thinking across to learn from other organizations, industries, countries and cultures? What are the organizational boundaries that we do not cross and thus do not learn? How can we overcome these boundaries? Do we have a systemic process for assessing and adapting interesting practices outside our domain areas for application and adaptation in our organizations? Do we have people who can span boundaries and network with interesting people and organizations?

7. How can we develop and strengthen these dynamic capabilities through appropriate investments in people, policies and processes? Where in the organization may we inculcate these dynamic capabilities so that they function in a systemic and integrated manner? What results do we expect and how do we measure them?

8. When and how would these capabilities become part of our organizational gene pool? How do we train and develop our people in these capabilities?

9. How do we embed learning and adaptation in our strategies and policies? How can we make our strategic and organizational reviews more reflective and learning-oriented?

10. How do we recruit, renew and retain able people in the organization? How well are these working? Do we have a process for renewing our people management practices?

11. How do we develop agile processes that stimulate and induce change? Do our financial, human resource and IT systems facilitate or inhibit change? What processes do we need to review,

redesign and make more agile? How do we develop the skills to do so?

Creating and sustaining dynamism in governance, whether in the public or corporate sector, is a strategic long-term effort. The potential pay offs are substantial. But there are no short-cuts. Institutional culture and organizational capabilities cannot be built overnight. Able people, agile processes and adaptable policies have to be systematically and cumulatively developed over an extended period of time. Creating a dynamic governance system and an adaptable organization requires deep thinking, open dialog, leadership commitment and effective execution. The guidelines we have proposed in this chapter are only to get you started on the journey. Successful change is not a one-time project, but a continuous process of learning, experimenting, innovating, and improving to remain relevant in a fast changing global environment. Change is always messy and risky. But not changing is far more risky. Dynamism is ultimately about new ideas, fresh perceptions, continual upgrading, quick actions, flexible adaptations and creative innovations. It is an exciting journey. We cannot change the past and we cannot determine the future. We can only hope to be better prepared to face the future by starting the dynamic journey of change today.

Names Index

Subject Index

Agency for Science, Technology and Research (A*STAR)   264–266, 269, 337, 347, 350, 381, 392
Allocate   50, 171, 175, 192, 201, 247
Anticipate   54, 102, 238, 245, 248, 281, 290, 291, 317, 388, 389, 393, 466
Applications of Singapore System   472–475
Area Licensing Scheme   103, 272–275, 283, 284

B

Beliefs   x, 3, 8, 9, 13–15, 18, 20, 21, 23–25, 28, 30, 32, 34, 46, 66, 67, 83, 89, 105, 108, 112, 142, 145–151, 156, 189, 196, 206, 243, 260, 289, 317, 319, 381, 382, 433, 449, 452, 453, 455, 461, 475
Benchmarking   176, 319, 365, 371, 373, 380
  of salaries   176, 365–374, 380
Best Sourcing   405
Biomedical Sciences Development   119, 262–270, 347, 348
  & path dependence   265
  & building domestic capablities   265, 267
Budget, The   3, 108, 130, 131, 174, 179, 180, 190, 210, 231, 232, 254, 260, 294, 299, 347, 385, 392, 394–408, 411, 424, 429, 431, 441
  2006   4
  2007   4
  as a tool for change   395, 396, 401
  annual budget cycle   397–399
  budget allocation principles   399–401
  budget flexibility framework   402, 403
  resource–based accounting   403–405
Bureaucracy   1, 10, 53, 57, 66, 110, 163, 201, 236, 291, 333, 367, 368, 379, 406, 407, 413, 436

C

Cabinet   28, 179, 180, 182, 187, 192, 193, 195, 218, 240, 260, 390, 398, 439
Capabilities   x, 1–6, 9, 12, 14–20, 23, 24, 26, 29, 30, 38, 44–47, 49, 50, 56, 67, 68, 70, 71, 73–83, 112, 132, 135, 138, 145, 146, 164, 189, 191, 196, 201, 211, 214, 229, 232, 236, 240, 242, 243, 249, 252, 263, 265, 284, 317, 318, 326, 376, 377, 379, 381, 383, 384, 386, 391, 399, 403, 407–409, 411, 415, 416, 419, 420, 424, 428, 429, 430, 433, 434, 446, 455, 456, 460, 462, 464–467, 469, 471, 475–477
  see Dynamic Governance Capabilities

Glossary of Acronyms

3G	Third Generation Technology
A*STAR	Agency for Science, Technology and Research
ALS	Area Licensing Scheme
AO	Administrative Officer
ARF	Additional Registration Fee (for cars)
ASEAN	Association of Southeast Asian Nations
ASR	Annual Strategic Review where the Ministry of Finance meet with each ministry at the start of the budget cycle
ATM	Automated Teller Machine
BCCS	Board of Commissioners of Currency of Singapore
BMS	Biomedical Sciences
BMSI	Biomedical Science Initiative
BRM	Budget Review Meeting
BTMICE	Business Travel, Meetings, Incentive Travel, Conventions and Exhibitions
CBD	Central Business District
CC	Community Centers
CDC	Community Development Councils
CEO	Chief Executive Officer
CEP	Currently Estimated Potential — An appraisal system adapted from Shell Petroleum
CIO	Chief Information Officer
COE	Certificate of Entitlement
ComCare	Community Care Fund established in 2004
CPF	Central Provident Fund
CPIB	Corrupt Practices Investigation Bureau

CSC	Civil Service College
CSS	Centre for Shared Services
DBS	Development Bank of Singapore
DEP	Design Evaluation Panel
DNA	Deoxyribonucleic acid
DS	Deputy Secretary
DSO	Defence Science Organisation
EDB	Economic Development Board
EQ	Emotional Quotient
ERC	Economic Review Committee
ERP	Electronic Road Pricing
ERS	Economic Restructuring Shares
FDI	Foreign Direct Investment
FT	Freight tonnes
GATT	General Agreement on Tariffs and Trade
GCE A Level or A Level	Singapore-Cambridge General Certificate of Education (Advance Level) Examination is an annual examination given in Singapore. The examination is set by the University of Cambridge in collaboration with the Singapore's Ministry of Education
GCE O Level or O Level	Singapore-Cambridge General Certificate of Education (Ordinary Level) Examination is an annual examination given in Singapore. The examination is set by the University of Cambridge in collaboration with the Singapore's Ministry of Education
GDFCF	Gross Domestic Fixed Capital Formation
GDP	Gross Domestic Product
GIC	Government of Singapore Investment Corporation
GLC	Government-linked Companies
GNP	Gross National Product
GST	Goods & Services Tax
HAIR	The four criteria in the Shell Petroleum appraisal system (refer to Chapter 5, pages 216–217 and Chapter 7, page 353 for details)

HDB	Housing Development Board
IAC	Industrial Arbitration Court
IBM	International Business Machines
ICT	Information and Communications Technologies
IDA	Infocomm Development Authority
IMF	International Monetary Fund
IQ	Intelligence Quotient
IR	Integrated Resort
IRAS	Inland Revenue Authority of Singapore
IRD	Inland Revenue Department
IT	Information Technologies
ITB	Industrial Training Board (precursor to VITB)
ITE	Institute of Technical Education
IU	In-vehicle Units
JI	Jemaah Islamiyah
JTC	Jurong Town Corporation
KPI	Key Performance Indicator
LAP	Leaders in Administration Program
MA	Management Associates
MAP	Management Associates Program
MAS	Monetary Authority of Singapore
MBA	Master of Business Administration
MCYS	Ministry of Community Development, Youth and Sports
MINDEF	Ministry of Defence
MIT	Massachusetts Institute of Technology
MNC	Multinational Corporations
MOE	Ministry of Education
MOF	Ministry of Finance
MOH	Ministry of Health
MOM	Ministry of Manpower
MP	Members of Parliament

MRT	Mass Rapid Transit
MTI	Ministry of Trade and Industry
NCB	National Computer Board
NCMP	Non-Constituency Member of Parliament
NEV	Net Economic Value
NLB	National Library Board
NMP	Nominated Members Of Parliament
NParks	National Parks Board
NRT	Net registered tons (as defined in Economic Survey of Singapore, 1985)
NSS	New Singapore Shares
NSTB	National Science & Technology Board
NWC	National Wages Council
OA	Ordinary Account (in one's Central Provident Fund Account)
OASIS	Online Application System for Integrated Services
OBLS	Online Business Licensing Services
OBS	Outward Bound School
OECD	Organization for Economic Co-operation and Development
OHQ	Operational Headquarters
OSU	Overseas Singaporean Unit
PAB	Personnel Administration Branch — Part of the Budget Division of the Ministry of Finance
PAP	People's Action Party
PAS	Potential Appraisal System
PERC	Political and Economic Risk Consultancy
PhD	Doctor of Philosophy
PM	Prime Minister
PMO	Prime Minister's Office
POSB	Post Office Savings Bank
PPP	Public-Private-Partnership approach
PR	Permanent Resident

PS	Permanent Secretary
PSL	Public Sector Leadership
PS21	Public Service for the 21st Century
PSA	Port of Singapore Authority
PSC	Public Service Commission
PSD	Public Service Division
PUB	Public Utilities Board
R&D	Research & Development
RPS	Road Pricing Scheme
RSE	Researchers, Scientists and Engineers
RZ	Restricted Zone
SA	Special Account (in one's Central Provident Fund Account)
SAF	Singapore Armed Forces
SARS	Severe Acute Respiratory Syndrome
SBM	Sectoral Budget Meetings where the ministers and permanent secretaries from the economic, social and security/governance meet to generate cross-agency synergies, ideas and programs
SEP	Strategic Economic Plan
SFPPB	Singapore Family Planning and Population Board
SIG	Strategic Issues Group — Part of the Strategic Policy Office in the Prime Minister's Office
SME	Small and Medium Enterprises
SMP	Senior Management Program
SPO	Strategic Policy Office
SQA	Singapore Quality Awards
SSS	Staff Suggestion Scheme
TAA	Tender Approving Authority
TB	Tuberculosis
TEC	Tender Evaluation Committee
URA	Urban Redevelopment Authority
VQS	Vehicle Quota System

W2	Wisconsin Works
WEC	Weekend Car Scheme
WIS	Workfare Income Supplement
WITS	Work Improvement Teams
WTO	World Trade Organization

www.ingramcontent.com/pod-product-compliance
Lightning Source LLC
Chambersburg PA
CBHW070627270326
41926CB00011B/1841